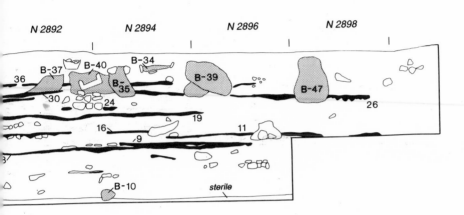

N 2892   N 2894   N 2896   N 2898

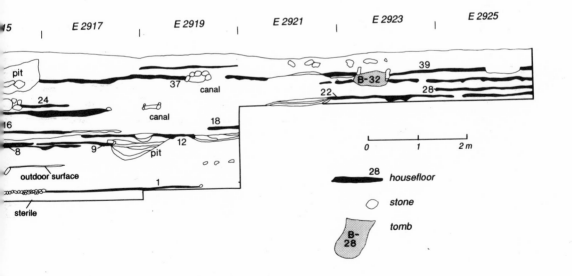

5   E 2917   E 2919   E 2921   E 2923   E 2925

0   1   2 m

28 —— housefloor

○ stone

B-28 tomb

LUKURMATA

**MARC
BERMANN**

Lukurmata

*Household Archaeology in
Prehispanic Bolivia*

PRINCETON UNIVERSITY PRESS
PRINCETON, N.J.

Library of Congress Cataloging-in-Publication Data

Bermann, Marc, 1960–
Lukurmata : household archaeology in prehispanic Bolivia /
Marc Bermann.
    p.   cm.
Includes bibliographical references and index.
ISBN 0-691-03359-5
1. Lukurmata Site (Bolivia)   2. Indians of South America—
Bolivia—Antiquities.   3. Tiwanaku culture.   4. Social change—
Bolivia—Lukurmata Site.   I. Title.
F3319.1.L8B47   1994
984′.101—dc20   93-23366

This book has been composed in Times Roman
Designed by Jan Lilly

Princeton University Press books are printed on
acid-free paper and meet the guidelines for permanence
and durability of the Committee on Production
Guidelines for Book Longevity of the
Council on Library Resources

Printed in the United States of America

10   9   8   7   6   5   4   3   2   1

Dedicated to Wendell Clark Bennett

investigator at Lukurmata,
May to June 1934

Contents

Illustrations and Tables

TABLES

Preface

Judging by the spate of recent works on "household archaeology," we are seeing an explosion of interest in domestic remains. A cynical colleague remarked that this trend may be because all the "really interesting" sites have already been done, leaving nothing but villages composed of houses. I prefer to believe that the boom in household archaeology reflects an ill-defined but growing realization that investigators have long overlooked the potential that domestic remains hold for answering important questions about the past.

Domestic remains can yield insights into more than "household" processes and provide more than a limited worm's-eye view of overarching institutions. Domestic remains hold great promise for refining how archaeologists reconstruct the past, because domestic remains can themselves provide a new point of reference for evaluating change in prehistoric societies. When taken in conjunction with the more traditional archaeological approaches to social change, this household point of reference leads to what I describe as the "local perspective"—an alternative way of viewing and understanding prehistoric political formations.

My approach to domestic remains at the prehispanic site of Lukurmata, Bolivia, differs in several ways from recently published examples of household archaeology. I do not use domestic remains to reconstruct residential organization or social status differences, to analyze household economic patterns, or to learn how the archaeological record forms. Treating Lukurmata domestic remains as an independent unit of analysis in measuring societal change, I contrast the nature and timing of changes at the household, local, and regional levels in prehispanic Bolivia.

Developing the "local perspective" was far from my intent when I began fieldwork at Lukurmata. I had originally planned an entirely conventional analysis of domestic economy at what was then thought to be simply a "provincial center" of the prehispanic Tiwanaku state. However, I quickly discovered that Lukurmata was a settlement of tremendous antiquity, with traditions and history far older than the Tiwanaku state. I also learned that the remains of dwellings, and the objects found with them, may not reveal much about household economy. Given how prehistoric dwellings were used and cleaned, many archaeologists interested in household issues are probably better off excavating outdoor activity areas (where most activities took place) and middens (where the debris of day-to-day life usually ended up).

Finally, Lukurmata residents (Aymara Indians) in describing Lukurmata's past told me, "Tiwanaku was here, then the *señorios* were here, then the Inca were here, then the Spaniards were here, now maybe *gringos* will be here," without acknowledging that Lukurmateños, in a sense, had *always* been there. Their history was a succession of intrusive political systems from elsewhere, the settlement a passive entity definable only in terms of one or another overarching political formation. More than an expression of peasant worldview, the view of Lukurmata residents also expresses a common orientation in Andean archaeology today.

Andean prehistory has been dominated by a concern with the "rise and fall" of large polities. Small sites have often been viewed (and studied) only to learn more about these larger polities. Little attention has been paid to the idea that small sites themselves may be interesting beyond what they reveal about the larger political systems of which they were occasionally part.

In this volume I argue that understanding, even "explaining," societal evolution in the prehispanic Andes, requires us to look at "alternative" histories built on the smallest units and processes of society—on the "structures of everyday life" (to use Braudel's phrase). Hidden below the dramatic geographic spread of eye-catching iconography and the building of monumental architectural centers is an archaeological record—domestic remains—essential for producing prehistories not biased toward the actions and concerns of rulers and elites.

One consequence of pursuing such an "alternative history" may be a reevaluation of the integration of the Tiwanaku state and other great polities of the Andean past. We tend to portray prehispanic political formations as somewhat analogous to modern-day nation-states, tightly integrated politically and economically, pursuing centrally directed "strategies." Such political formations are relatively new in modern European history, dating back perhaps five hundred years. For a long time prior to this, people did not think (or act) as members of "nations," but as members of villages, estates, or feudal domains loosely linked to rulers to form regional polities. Even as late as this century, "empires" could exist more on paper than in the minds of their citizens. The Habsburg Austro-Hungarian empire, for instance, was a notoriously hazy concept for many of its subjects, who tended to see themselves as members of small ethnic or language groups.

Recent political developments in the Balkans and the former Soviet Union demonstrate that important subimperial continuities or cleavage planes may underlie even seemingly well-integrated modern political formations. Might the approaches that archaeologists generally take to prehistoric polities overemphasize the regional integration of such polities? Several scholars (Marcus 1989; Murra et al. 1986) have argued that this is the case, making diachronic studies at the subpolity level of greater importance than ever.

Analyzing the shifts in domestic organization that follow a small settlement's incorporation into a larger political system is one way to begin gauging the nature of the large polities and their cultural evolutionary significance in Andean prehistory. Archaeological studies at the household level, fully recognizing the potential of domestic remains, are an important tool for analyzing the nature and extent of prehistoric social change. Prehistorians will ultimately come to understand the Andean past and prehispanic polities in new ways when they focus on aspects of Andean prehistory that are seldom explored, and integrate differently the lines of information available to them.

Acknowledgments

This book is the product of efforts by many individuals. Foremost among these is Joyce Marcus. I will always be deeply indebted to her for her guidance, incisive criticism, generous sharing of ideas, and critical data on the Wolverines. Also special has been the encouragement of Alan Kolata, who gave me the opportunity to work in Bolivia. Although I often use the first person in this book, it should be understood that my Lukurmata fieldwork was part of Alan's larger *Proyecto Wila-Jawira*. His National Endowment of the Humanities (BNS 8607541) and National Science Foundation (RO21368-86) grants provided me with vehicles, much of my field labor, equipment, field facilities, and radiocarbon dates. My Lukurmata research was also supported by my own grants from the Social Science Research Council and American Council of Learned Societies, the Wenner–Gren Foundation for Anthropological Research, and the Horace H. Rackham School of Graduate Studies, University of Michigan.

A brief acknowledgment cannot express my thanks to three other individuals. No one has done more for Bolivian archaeology than Carlos Ponce Sanginés. His exhaustive knowledge and support made my own research possible. I am proud that my own small project has a place in the research program he envisioned. I am grateful for the support and friendship of Oswaldo Rivera Sundt, co-director of *Proyecto Wila-Jawira*. His energy, dedication to Bolivian archaeology, and enthusiasm in trying conditions remain inspirational. The hospitality of Oswaldo, Norma, and Gabriel is one of the pleasures of working in Bolivia. Last, but hardly least, Lupe Andrade Salmon has long been a wonderful friend of Bolivian archaeology, and has always been selfless in her concern for the visiting American archaeologist. I could not have done the research without her.

I am extremely grateful to Michael Moseley and Charles Stanish, not only for introducing me to Andean archaeology, but also for leading me to think about Andean prehistory in new ways. In a similar vein, I should thank the participants of my Spring 1992 Household Archaeology seminar; although they did not know it, they were a useful sounding board. Many of the themes in this text benefited from their insight, forbearance, and voracious criticism.

Many individuals provided valuable commentary on portions of the manuscript itself or its contents. Among these I particularly wish to thank Joyce Marcus, Alan Kolata, Michael Moseley, Chip Stanish, Henry Wright, Jeffrey Parsons, Richard Ford, Jerry Sabloff, Juan Albarracin-Jordan, Dick Drennan, Sabine McCormack, Jane Buikstra, David Browman, Anne Helsley-Marchbanks, Brian Bauer, Karen Wise, John Hyslop, Christine Hastorf, Heidi Lennstrom, Jeffrey Schwartz, Robert Feldman, Karen Mohr-Chávez, and Kelli Carmean. Despite the input of these individuals, any failings of the text are purely my own.

I owe deep thanks to those who aided me in fieldwork at Lukurmata: Chip Stanish for mapping, Gray Graffam and Paul Goldstein for their excavation of Structure 42, and Sol Bermann for his help in the lab. I also must praise those who helped in preparation of various portions of the manuscript: Nancy Vaida, Alan McPherron, David

Anderson, Karin Mudar, Kay Clahassey, Carl Langebaak, Calogero Santoro, Jerome Crowder, Nicole Couture, and John Janucek. I would like to thank artists Steven Patricia for Figure 12.20, Andrew Redline for Figures 5.3 and 9.3, and Martin Fuess for Figures 8.23 and 12.36. Many of the photographs are courtesy of Alan Kolata and the Proyecto Wila-Jawira archives in Chicago. It has been a wonderful experience to collaborate with the patient William Woodcock, volume editor, who has been tireless in his assistance with this book.

I owe deepest thanks to the current residents of Lukurmata (who did most of the actual digging). In particular, I must single out Pedro Limachi and family who allowed me to excavate their favorite potato field for two consecutive years. The *maestros* of Tiwanaku had the most thankless job, and I will always be in awe of their skill and dedication. *Jefe de la gente* Cesar Callisaya Y., Celio, Pedro, Sixto, Clemente, Mario, Telésforo, and the rest were the best field companions anyone could want.

If academic life were more honest, the name of Catherine DeLoughry would be on the spine of this book as well. Thank you for sharing each concern, participating in every stage of the research, and, above all, for laughing when necessary.

LUKURMATA

1

Interpreting Prehistoric
Social Change

A focus on the capitals of complex societies has characterized Andean archaeology from its inception. Because of this, we know far more about urban sites than we do about villages, far more about temples than about houses, far more about regional administration than about day-to-day life. Families were constituent parts of chiefdoms, states, *ayllus*, *waranqas*, and empires, yet the household has been neglected as an important and revealing unit of study. In no place is this more evident than in traditional approaches to social change and political development in Andean prehistory. The processes of state formation, expansion, and decline have all been well studied at the regional level. But we know virtually nothing about what any of these changes meant at the lowest levels of regional settlement systems, or how these changes affected the lives of the residents of most settlements.

Like any form of history, the prehistory of different parts of the world has been created from those processes or happenings in the past that researchers have considered important and deserving of investigation. Andean prehistory has been shaped by a distinctive and traditional approach to interpreting and reconstructing sociopolitical evolution, particularly when dealing with complex societies (societies characterized by centralized government and formal positions of political power).

This chapter will discuss the strengths and limitations of the traditional archaeological approach to prehistoric social change taken by Andean archaeologists and archaeologists working in other parts of the world. Then, I will present an alternative way of examining—and researching—change in prehistoric complex societies.

REGIONAL APPROACHES TO THE PAST

Nearly forty years ago anthropologist Robert Redfield (1956:28) made a forecast: "I think we shall come to study regional systems. We shall study such systems, not, as we now tend to do, from the viewpoint of some one small community looking outward, but from the viewpoint of an observer who looks down upon the whole larger regional system."

Ironically, this prediction has proved to be more prophetic of archaeology than ethnography. While most ethnographers have remained content with a worm's-eye view of the societies they study, archaeologists have been developing the bird's-eye regional approaches—particularly to complex societies—which Redfield envisioned. The very success of these approaches has led to a situation in which in many parts of the world we now know much more about an ancient civilization's strategies of expansion, bureaucratic organization, and ruling stratum than we do about its ordinary citizens. When humble household remains are investigated, it is often only to learn more about "larger" developments.

Regional approaches to the evolution of prehistoric complex societies have generally focused on two concerns: (1) territorial organization, as seen in settlement patterns, the distribution of population, and regional artifact distributions; and (2) regional patterns of social organization, administrative decision making, craft production, and trade. These two concerns are reflected in the archaeological literature so that someone interested in, for instance, the Uruk or Susa states of fourth-millennium B.C. Mesopotamia, the prehistoric Moundville chiefdom of southeastern North America, or the Wari empire of Middle Horizon period Peru could quickly gather from the archaeological literature an understanding of how that political formation evolved as a regional system (Adams and Nissen 1972; Isbell and Schreiber 1978; Wright and Johnson 1975; Welch 1991).

Typically, a general discussion of the political formation will include information on:

- the polity's boundaries at particular points in time
- the means by which the polity expanded (conquest, indirect hegemony, alliances)
- the geographic spread of artifacts and iconographic elements characteristic of the polity, and the processes by which they spread
- how sites of different sizes and compositions interacted with one another and with the capital, often using locational constructs such as central-place theory, rank-size analysis, and nearest-neighbor analysis
- whether the settlement hierarchy represented an administrative hierarchy of political control, and if so, how many levels of administration were present
- how particular activities, such as agricultural production, trade, and craft production, were divided among the polity's settlements
- where the ruling stratum resided, where craft specialists lived, and where tribute and long-distance trade-goods were collected

What the reader would be less likely to encounter is the prosaic—a detailed treatment of the organization and evolution of domestic life in that polity. The reader would be much more likely to see maps of the polity and illustrations of its public architecture than simple house plans. If mentioned at all, households would probably be discussed in the abstract, and then only in terms of their interaction with the larger system (as providers of tribute or taxes, for instance). Similarly, a reader of the Andean archaeological literature interested in the history of a particular region would probably see the prehistory of the valley organized and presented as a sequence of polities. In Andean archaeology in general, investigation of complex societies has long focused on the origin, functioning, and demise of prehispanic political formations.

This focus on the regional in prehistory reflects more than underlying assumptions about the important elements of prehistory and prehistoric sociopolitical evolution. The paucity of information on household life would seem to reflect a basic lack of investigation: for a surprising number of prehistoric polities (particularly in the Andes), we do not even know what common dwellings may have looked like, because an example has yet to be excavated.

Importance of Regional Approaches in Anthropological Archaeology

Regional approaches to prehistoric societies should not be confused with investigative techniques that are regional in scale such as settlement survey projects. While regional surveys obviously constitute a common and important method in regional approaches, even excavations of individual dwellings can take a regional approach. Regional approaches form a distinct paradigm for investigating societal change, a paradigm with favored types of information, methods of investigation, scope of analysis, and interpretive constructs. Regional approaches share the orientation described by Redfield: an interpretive paradigm in which elements of the archaeological record (artifacts, household remains, sites) are viewed from a regional frame of reference. Communities are treated as components of a settlement system; artifacts are used to learn about intersite interaction and regional exchange networks; domestic remains provide information on social affiliation or societal differentiation.

Regional approaches in archaeology are essential to an understanding of the past. As culture history, they provide basic information on the growth and decline of many important prehistoric polities, as well as an understanding of their overall organization. Regional studies also provide the constructs needed to understand past populations as social wholes; through regional approaches archaeologists have been able to study not just individual settlements or the geographic distribution of decorative motifs on pottery, but societies. In other words, regional approaches have allowed prehistorians to write about the evolution of the Wari state, rather than simply about the spread of Wari-style objects or the development of Wari iconography (as archaeologists commonly did thirty years ago).

Regional studies have also been critical to the study of cultural evolution in general, providing a highly successful basis for cross-cultural comparisons of dynamic processes and regularities in the development of complex societies. As a result, there exists today a solid body of information concerning the characteristic regional processes in settlement, organizational complexity, and intersite interaction that accompany the evolution of ancient states.

Regional approaches allow study of how a political formation develops as an integrated entity, and permit identification of aggregate patterns not recognizable at the subregional level. As Carol Smith (1976:4) observed, "the generalizations that can be made from regional patterns of social organization are clearly of greater comparative relevance than those drawn from community . . . studies alone."

Regional approaches, as a consequence, are more than simply useful for examining cultural evolution. Many of the processes long considered by archaeologists to be important in cultural evolution—such as the growth of decision-making hierarchies and supralocal political orders—can best be examined from a regional perspective (Binford 1964; Flannery 1972). An important distinguishing characteristic of complex societies, for instance, is their regional scale: the political, social, economic, and ideological structures of complex societies extend beyond the single community. Therefore, the "significant" processes in complex societies are precisely those that are regional in scope, linking individual communities (Johnson and Earle 1987).

Complementing Regional Approaches with a Household-Level Approach

Like all investigative paradigms, regional approaches have inherent strengths, limitations, and biases. Even if one believed that significant change *only* takes place at the regional level, regional approaches by themselves could never provide a detailed or complete understanding of social change. As valuable and successful as they have been, regional approaches need to be complemented with investigation at other scales, including that of the household.

There is always a need for differing spatial frameworks in investigating societal change. If we are interested in the sources of change and the levels at which pressures or stimuli for change operate, we need to consider as many levels of society as possible (Whalen 1981). Conversely, we also want to consider where change *does not* take place, which societal institutions are slow or resistant to change.

The most obvious limitation of regional approaches is that they cannot easily yield insights into household- and community-level processes, or provide direct study of processes that originate at the subregional level. Because regional approaches do not provide a "man in the street view" of many processes visible in the aggregate, or at the regional level, it is difficult to determine the segment of society affected by these processes or the extent of that effect. At the other end of the scale, it has been suggested that important processes in both simple and complex societies transcend the regional, requiring transregional or interregional approaches in order to perceive them (Paynter 1982:3–4).

Studies at the household level hold the potential to: (1) document changes not apparent at the regional level to yield a "household view" of regional processes; (2) study those evolutionary processes grounded in the household sphere; (3) provide an alternative unit of analysis to monitor social change and societal evolution; and (4) identify new dimensions of variability in complex societies. In the following pages I will explain in greater detail each of the ways household-level study can contribute to understanding prehistoric societies and social change.

A HOUSEHOLD VIEW OF REGIONAL PROCESSES

Because the household, in one form or another, is a basic social unit in most human societies, studies at the household level provide a valuable worm's-eye view of larger patterns and processes. For instance, a household is the most common unit of production in archaic agrarian societies. Therefore, changes in the larger or regional economy should have implications for domestic productive patterns, and these changes can be studied at the household level. Yet with few exceptions (Costin and Earle 1989; Hastorf 1990a; Stanish 1992), Andean archaeologists have not been concerned with analyzing domestic remains together with associated objects to gain insight into regional economies, or to provide case studies of the relationship between regional economic dynamics and shifts in household economies.

Andean archaeologists have often been content, on the basis of ethnographic and ethnohistoric analogy, to assume that particular household patterns existed in the past. Thus, in many treatments of state evolution in the prehispanic Andes, households enter the discussion only as abstract providers of *mit'a* labor. Yet by providing classes of data not available through regional study, archaeological investigation at the household level may produce information that contradicts generally held assumptions. An excellent example of this is Christine Hastorf's (1990a) study of Sausa domestic contexts. In a brilliant investigation of the effects of Inca conquest on the Sausa population, Hastorf tested a widely accepted assumption that Inca political economy operated outside the domestic sector, leaving the "larder of the peasant . . . untouched" (Murra 1980:79). Using a variety of evidence obtained from Sausa domestic contexts, Hastorf compared Sausa household status, production, consumption, and distribution during the pre-Inca and Inca periods. These comparisons showed that incorporation into the Inca political economy did, in fact, lead to significant changes in Sausa domestic organization, particularly in production and consumption. Her study also suggested a reason for the successful expansion of the Inca state: Inca conquest could result in a "leveling" of local social status differences that improved the life of the nonelite segment of the population.

HOUSEHOLD EVOLUTIONARY PROCESSES

Not all of the processes of social change that can be examined at the regional level are "regional" in origin or operation. We only *choose* to study these processes at the regional level. Significant processes of sociocultural evolution may be fundamentally household or "local" processes, operating or originating at the household level. Certain dynamics of prehistoric societies and political formations may best be understood by focusing on household- or settlement-level processes.

The formation of inegalitarian society, for example, does not consist of the emergence of a settlement hierarchy. This is merely a useful indicator or regional correlate of inegalitarian societies often studied by archaeologists. Inegalitarian organization develops when one household, or set of households, is able to formalize transgenerational inequalities in social status and position.

Similarly, the political economy of complex societies—while frequently studied at the regional level—may be determined by the ambitions and productive activities of households belonging to different social strata. Archaeologists dealing with processes that directly relate to broad issues of sociopolitical evolution, such as the distribution and uses of economic surplus, will be required to investigate patterns at the household level.

Anthropologists are interested in the causes of social change rather than simply describing change. From this perspective, it is important to have insights into the motivations of individuals or sets of individuals, and their frame of action. As William Mitchell (1991:21) has commented, "societies as such never do anything." Significant social changes—even social transformations—are ultimately the result of individual choices. Particular political, ecological, and cultural settings will favor certain responses over others, producing social change (ibid.). Individual actions, in turn, will alter surrounding social and cultural institutions (ibid.:184). Failing to distinguish between "individual" and "social" levels in social evolution, Mitchell (ibid.:21) argues, will "frequently cloud causal issues." From this perspective, anthropologists will ultimately need to treat individuals as actors in order to "explain" many dimensions of cultural evolution, from the shift to food production to the emergence of inegalitarian social order.

Consider, for instance, how individuals aspiring to higher social position in prehistoric societies could improve their social standing. We know from regional studies that prehistoric "big-men" and chiefly societies often displayed a great deal of long-distance trade in exotic objects. Identification of prestige-good exchange systems in the archaeological record is now fairly commonplace, often involving excavation of residential areas. Both ethnographic and archaeological studies have documented how ambitious individuals or households displayed greater participation than others in the regional exchange of status-enhancing, exotic goods. But we know much less about how such individuals used or altered their households, or household production, to increase their ability to participate in this exchange, even though ethnographic studies have described how the aspirations of big-men, for instance, shaped the activities of their household (Sahlins 1972). Nor do we know whether manipulation of household activities was a basis for sociopolitical power or differentiation in cases in which exchange of exotic goods was not important. Even in very complex societies, the household continues to be an important unit of social dynamics, and study of "microlevel" processes is critical to understanding the motivations and actions of different societal segments (Hastorf 1990b).

Finally, sociocultural change needs to be studied at several levels because "institutions that play one role at one level often play a different role at another level in complex societies" (Smith 1976:18). Or, in a variation on "Romer's Rule," change at one level of society may have the effect or purpose of preventing change at another. Changes at the individual household level may have the effect of preserving unchanged some larger institution. Correspondingly, larger institutions may shift to allow household life to continue unchanged.

AN ALTERNATIVE UNIT OF ANALYSIS IN EXAMINING SOCIAL CHANGE

In contrast to some scholars (Binford 1964), I see no reason to assume a priori that "important" societal change is limited to regional-level dynamics (or those seen on the regional scale). In fact, the argument can be made that changes at the lowest levels of society, by altering the base of the social pyramid, are the most "significant." Consider, for example, what may happen when the nobility of several communities form alliances among one another. These alliances (marked by elite exchange of goods or marriage partners) will result in new regional distributions of artifact styles, and thus be highly visible archaeologically. Archaeologists will interpret this development as an important regional transformation, the emergence of political integration, or the "expansion" of a polity. But how can we evaluate the significance of such a development in societal or evolutionary terms? Should we assume this development is significant because *all* elite activities are important? Or because *all* changes visible at the regional level *must* be important?

This issue of what constitutes "significant" history is a basic historiographic question often side-stepped by archaeologists. Behind this problem lies another one: the danger of confusing analytical models with the actual structure and workings of past society. Our models *for* examining change in a past society are usually not models *of* that society (Lévi-Strauss 1953). If we lose sight of this fact, we will arrive at seriously distorted understandings of past societies. As I discuss below, one danger is the tendency to see polities as more integrated and cohesive (i.e., more "regional") than they really were (see Marcus 1989).

IDENTIFYING NEW DIMENSIONS OF VARIATION BETWEEN COMPLEX SOCIETIES

A constant challenge for archaeology is the formulation of alternative constructs of variation and change in the development of complex polities (Earle 1991). All scholars concerned with human society know that communities, and different elements of the community, articulate in various ways and to varying degrees with larger systems. The ruler's control (economic, political, social) of subject peoples is never absolute—subordinate communities are never completely autonomous, nor are they ever completely dominated.

By studying the range of relationships between households and encompassing systems, we should be able to distinguish new forms of variability in ancient political formations. Investigation of how households and local communities articulate with larger systems should provide new axes, or dimensions of variability, along which to study and compare ancient polities.

Instead of distinguishing between different types of prehispanic societies on the basis of organizational complexity, levels of administrative hierarchy, or mode of subsistence, perhaps we could distinguish between polities on the basis of how household units are articulated into larger systems (Renfrew 1974).

SUMMARY

A first step in identifying sources of societal change is identifying the level at which changes originate. If we study processes at different societal levels, we will know, for instance, whether the changes observed at a particular site were exogenic, region-wide, or purely local in origin and scope. The value of multilevel approaches is that they prevent us from assuming that similar sites interact equally with the capital, or that smaller sites are passive, static recipients of change from higher levels. These assumptions tend to be inherent in regional perspectives on societal evolution.

In addition to these theoretical justifications for complementing regional approaches, there are pragmatic reasons for doing so. One reason is simply that much archaeological excavation already takes place in domestic contexts. These investigations have traditionally focused on reconstructing community sociopolitical organization, reconstructing domestic lifeways, or developing middle-range theory. By not using archaeological data from household sources to pose questions about cultural evolution, we have kept ourselves from using the archaeological record to its full potential. Ironically, much useful household-level information for approaching broad questions of cultural evolution already exists, unrecognized in site reports and monographs.

Similarly, a great deal of ethnography has taken the community or village as the unit of study (Redfield 1956; Smith 1976). Archaeologists can and should draw on this rich ethnography to develop models of organization and change at the household and local levels. "Community studies," for instance, provide a source of constructs for interpreting the articulation of households and settlements with larger orders. Several archaeologists interested in change in domestic life, notably Richard Wilk (1991), Carol Kramer (1979, 1982a, 1982b), and Susan Kent (1984, 1987, 1990a, 1990b), have very successfully synthesized archaeological and ethnographic perspectives. Complementing a regional perspective with a local-level approach will open up avenues for re-search in which ethnographic studies can fruitfully be linked to the cultural evolution-ary concerns of archaeologists.

Finally, one of the most pressing reasons to complement regional approaches is to counteract a common bias in them. Regional approaches to prehistoric polities have the tendency to see—and depict—societal change as subsumed by the evolution of centralized administration or government, interaction between settlements, and the activities of elites. I call this view of change the "capital-centric" perspective. Because it characterizes our understanding of the evolution of Andean polities, it needs to be discussed at greater length.

THE "CAPITAL-CENTRIC" VERSUS THE "LOCAL PERSPECTIVE" IN ANDEAN ARCHAEOLOGY

A "capital-centric" or "view-from-the-top down" perspective accompanies the em-phasis on capitals and regional patterns in much of Andean archaeology. Traditional approaches to prehispanic states in the New World, either implicitly or explicitly, have stressed the center, stability, and integration of the state system. Smaller sites in the settlement hierarchy, when considered at all, are viewed from the perspective of the capital. Components of an overarching regional system, such sites are treated in func-tional terms, as sources of goods or services or as passive recipients of political control. Small sites are often characterized as "Tiwanaku" or "Inca" sites, based on interaction with a capital during one or more phases of occupation. The "capital-centric" perspec-tive pays little attention to the small site's degree of autonomy during these phases, or to local history at the site during those times when the site was not interacting with a capital.

Sources of the "Capital-Centric" Perspective

This "capital-centric" perspective is partly rooted in the early history of Andean archaeology when prehistorians worked with archaeological materials for which con-textual information was lacking. In interpreting these materials in a space-time frame-work, early investigators grouped artifacts together on the basis of similarities and organized them into styles (Moseley 1992:18–20). Subsequently, much archaeological study was aimed at delineating the spatial distribution of pottery styles, the temporal relationship between these styles, and the styles' associations with type-sites or large, urban capitals. The implicit equation of pottery with people, ethnic identity, or politi-cal control was an important assumption (Moseley, personal communication).

The resulting "horizon" framework was a construct for chronologically ordering pottery styles as well as a scheme of Andean political evolution. The close equation of art styles with societies led to a reconstruction of Andean prehistory as periods of cultural unity (horizons) separated by periods of heterogeneity and disunity (Moseley 1983; 1992:20). The concern with defining stylistic distributions, determining the ter-ritorial extent of political units, and delineating "boundaries" continues to structure our views of political evolution in the Andes.

A second source of the "capital-centric" perspective was the accounts of the early

Spanish chroniclers. Prevailing sixteenth- and seventeenth-century European notions of state led to the portrayal of the Inca polity as a powerful, centralized empire on the European model. Relying on Inca sources, the chroniclers developed a "Cuzco" view that stressed the stability, regional extent, and integration of the Inca system (D'Altroy 1987a:3; Morris 1988; Murra 1968).

This image of the Inca state has important archaeological implications because the Inca have come to serve as a template for interpreting pre-Inca or "Inca-forerunner" polities such as Wari and Tiwanaku. Studies of pre-Inca state systems, if not explicitly using the Inca state as an analog, often seek to define "early expressions" of principles or statecraft organization such as mit'a labor, *mitmaqkuna*, or state-sponsored "reciprocity" known from the Inca. Recently, our view of the Inca state has begun to change as ethnohistoric and archaeological studies document the great regional diversity and subimperial continuities in the Inca polity (Collier et al. 1982; D'Altroy 1987a, 1987b; Morris 1988). These studies are still largely "capital-centric," however, because they focus on defining and examining regional units from the perspective of the capital, that is, in terms of functions, organizational principles, and modes of incorporation into the larger system.

The "Local Perspective"

Standing in contrast to this "capital-centric" view is what I will call the "local perspective"—a perspective that views the relationship between the capital and a smaller site from the standpoint of the subordinate site. Implicit in the "local perspective" is the idea that the smaller site is an evolving settlement in its own right, with its own traditions, history, and pressures for change. From the "local perspective," incorporation into a larger political system is just a phase in the evolution of the smaller community. The two perspectives—"capital-centric" and "local"—are not mutually exclusive, but tend to entail pursuit of distinct data sets and investigative priorities. "Capital-centric" approaches are inherently regional in scope, focusing on settlement hierarchies, the distribution and nature of administrative architecture, elite provincial residences, and the distribution of elite-serving vessels. Nonelite households are treated as passive producers, and the most important processes are seen as taking place at the regional level. Change at lower-order sites is interpreted in the context of statecraft and administration, and the distribution of ceramic styles is seen as a measure of participation in the overarching political system.

The "local perspective," on the other hand, is inherently diachronic in nature. The concerns of the "local perspective" are local continuities and changes. This involves paying particular attention to the development at the household level of significant processes in cultural evolution, the manner in which larger processes are manifested at the household level, and how the smallest units of society adapt to the sociopolitical setting.

The "local perspective" recognizes that communities have developmental histories prior to contact with expansive polities. As a consequence, life at the site following contact with the state will be shaped by local patterns and trends in addition to processes originating at the supracommunity or state level. This historical and contextual viewpoint is the essence of the "local perspective."

The differences between the two perspectives are readily apparent in archaeological interpretations of regional artifact distributions. A common assumption of the "capital-centric" perspective is that if sites have different assemblages of state-style pottery, for instance, the sites were interacting with the capital or state system in different ways. Put another way, the assemblages of state-style pottery at the smaller site are assumed to reflect *only* the nature of the site's relationship with the state, rather than any historical patterns or traditions at the smaller site. Implicit in this assumption is the idea that various regions and sites themselves were, in fundamental ways, comparable prior to the arrival of the state-style pottery. Any variation between them in terms of state-style pottery must therefore be the result of differential interaction with the state.

In contrast, an archaeologist taking a "local perspective" would recognize that borrowing is a selective process. A peripheral population adapting state-style elements or items would be likely to do so in a way consistent with local traditions. Therefore, an archaeologist adopting a "local perspective" would be more likely to turn to constructs of diffusion (voluntary borrowing of cultural elements) or acculturation (borrowing under pressure from a superordinate society) to explain these regional artifact patterns.

As an illustration of the differences between the two perspectives, I present the case of the prehispanic Tiwanaku state. Centuries before the Inca, the rulers of the Tiwanaku polity dominated the south-central Andes from their capital site of Tiwanaku in present-day Bolivia. Artifacts in the distinctive Tiwanaku style are found at sites spread over a wide area from the edge of the Amazonian forest to the Pacific coasts of Chile and Peru.

Traditional interpretations of the regional distribution of Tiwanaku-style objects have always reflected a "capital-centric" perspective. In this perspective, regional models relating to state strategies of interaction are used to interpret the pattern of Tiwanaku-style artifacts at Chilean, Peruvian, and Bolivian sites. Typically, an archaeologist might decide that the assemblage of Tiwanaku-style artifacts indicates indirect control by Tiwanaku rather than direct conquest, or that the Tiwanaku state exported a limited range of artifacts to this region.

But how much do these artifacts really reveal about the Tiwanaku state? The "capital-centric" archaeologist has already decided. In contrast, the archaeologist taking a "local perspective" would argue that the Tiwanaku-style pottery found at a smaller site may reveal as much (or more) about local traditions and patterns of adoption at the smaller site, than the pottery does about the organization of the Tiwanaku state or "access" to Tiwanaku products.

In short, to truly understand the meaning or significance of the assemblage of Tiwanaku-style artifacts found at a site—even if the pottery is clearly imported from the Tiwanaku capital—will require knowledge of the occupation at that site prior to the appearance of Tiwanaku-style materials. Valid interpretations of regional artifact distributions of this type are dependent on understanding preexisting local traditions and patterns, and then examining the introduction of imported materials in this context. This view has long been "common sense" to generations of cultural anthropologists (and historical archaeologists) concerned with culture contact and acculturation, but it has largely been ignored by Andean archaeologists in their interpretations of regional artifact patterns.

The "Local Perspective" on Community Evolution

The "local perspective" recognizes that smaller settlements are not static or passive, but evolving communities in their own right, with their own developmental trajectories. In Owen Lynch's (1983:14) words, the small community is not an "isolated entity," nor a mechanically linked segment in a larger system, but a stage on which local social and economic orders engage with forces originating at higher levels of the settlement and political system. The challenge is to discern when and how the independent evolution of the settlement articulates with that of larger political units, and how they shape each other. Influence can move both ways; small communities can also affect the capital.

A "local perspective" on community evolution raises important implications for how archaeologists interpret changes at the community level. Anthropological research has shown that peasant populations articulating with overarching systems often develop locally acceptable patterns of interaction with politically dominant centers. Many of the economic, social, and religious institutions and activities of small communities serve as mediating structures through which the inhabitants of the smaller site relate to the larger order (Abercrombie 1986; Redfield 1955; Wolf 1966). Thus, changes in site structure and community organization may represent local reactions to larger orders, not "state reorganization" of the local community.

The archaeological record at a site will reflect local patterns as much as exogenic processes. Because it is shaped by both, the archaeological record will tell us as much about the site's history as it does about the nature of the larger political system. Failing to recognize this will prevent us from fully understanding either the single site or the larger systems of which single sites are part.

In sum, a "local perspective" does not emphasize the community at the expense of supralocal processes, but focuses on how the community's households are integrated into the larger system and how the larger system is "experienced" at the local level. A "local perspective" requires investigation at many levels; it is important to determine the type of settlement under study, the activities of its residents, its relationship to other settlements, and its place within larger social, economic, or political units.

Adopting a "local perspective" is not to argue that a single community alone is adequate to provide a view of the overarching system. We cannot reconstruct the larger society from perceiving its impact on local communities, or make the larger society appear as an extension of its manifestations at the local level. With our fragmentary knowledge of the Tiwanaku polity, for instance, it would be premature to use the Lukurmata data to generalize about the nature of the Tiwanaku polity, or present Lukurmata as a "typical" settlement. No one today would dispute the familiar criticism that a single community is not a microcosm of the larger society. Yet "capital-centric" approaches implicitly treat single communities, if not as microcosms, than as significant only in how they reflect the larger sociopolitical system.

Hence, the differences between the "capital-centric" perspective and the "local perspective" are more than simply differences in the source of information (household versus regional) or the scope of information (detailed versus general). It is a difference in *interpretive* emphasis. Regional approaches interpret local patterns in the context of regional processes; the "local perspective" interprets local patterns in the context of local history and tradition as well as regional processes.

Differing Perspectives, Alternative Histories, and the Texture of the Past

Because it poses different research questions and focuses on different lines of evidence, the "local perspective" can provide a view of the past quite different in "texture," structure, or important constituents than that resulting from regional approaches. Take, for example, the literature dealing with premodern society in India. As Stewart Gordon (1979:61) has suggested, it provides an image of villages as, "the essence of India, stable through good times and bad. Empires washed over them, leaving them unchanged."

The Andean archaeological literature provides the opposite impression: that the essence of the prehispanic Andes lies in the rise and fall of great states and expansionist polities. A reader might even conclude from these divergent impressions that state structures were of more significance in the Andean past than in the Indian, and correspondingly, that villages were a more meaningful social unit in Indian society than in the Andes.

Would such a conclusion be justified? The answer is "no." These images may only reflect differences between traditional historiographic orientations in each area. Our knowledge of premodern India stems largely from ethnographic and ethnohistoric investigations, which use the village as the main unit of study and tend to take the "local perspective." In contrast, our knowledge of Andean prehistory is based on regional archaeological approaches that tend to be "capital-centric."

Gaining a "local perspective" is not simply a matter of learning as much as possible about subregional levels of society, but recognizing that social dynamics must be studied on all levels. Studies employing different units of analysis will provide the "alternative" histories and prehistories that make possible multilevel study. Local patterns can be explored using household and intrasite data to reveal continuities that are often camouflaged by the more striking and archaeologically visible effects of state expansion. Conversely, exploration of local patterns may also reveal changes not visible at the regional level.

Purpose and Structure of this Volume

In this book, I will show how the "rise and fall" of a prehispanic state affected a segment of the nonelite population. Beyond this, I will adopt a "local perspective" in examining the development of a single settlement in the context of its evolving relationship with a prehispanic state in the Andean highlands.

The site of Lukurmata lies under a modern Aymara Indian village on the southern edge of Lake Titicaca in present-day Bolivia (Figure 1.1). My excavations at this site revealed a sequence of superimposed domestic occupations spanning some 1500 years. During this period, the nearby settlement of Tiwanaku grew to be the capital of one of the great native Andean civilizations between A.D. 400 and A.D. 1200 (Figure 1.2). The Tiwanaku polity unified the Lake Titicaca Basin, transformed nearby pampas into agricultural sustaining areas, established a network of temple sites, and extended

Fig. 1.1 Location of Lukurmata, Department of La Paz, Bolivia.

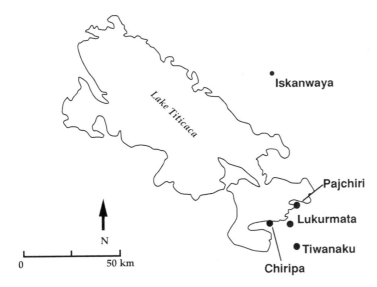

Fig. 1.2 Principal sites discussed in the text.

colonies and ties from the Pacific coast to the tropical forest. Although the public architecture at the capital site of Tiwanaku has been well investigated, little is known about domestic life in the Tiwanaku polity or the ways in which communities outside the capital were integrated into the Tiwanaku system.

As the Tiwanaku polity approached its zenith, Lukurmata was incorporated into the expanding Tiwanaku system, becoming an important subordinate site in the Tiwanaku settlement hierarchy. A much reduced population continued to reside at Lukurmata following the collapse of the Tiwanaku state in the twelfth century A.D.

A sequence of superimposed domestic occupations is the basis for my reconstruction of the evolution of Lukurmata household life over a period of some 1500 years. The Lukurmata sequence of domestic occupations, each consisting of architectural remains and associated features and artifacts, provides a unique opportunity to compare household life at the site before, during, and after Lukurmata's inclusion in the Tiwanaku system (Figure 1.3).

The domestic occupations were separated from one another by layers of fill or midden. The vertical relationship of the occupations is shown schematically in Figure 1.4. Although I was able to distinguish some thirty-five episodes of occupation, each repre-

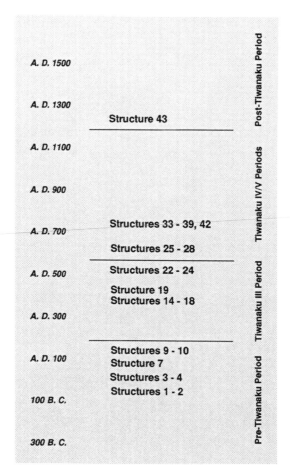

Fig. 1.3 Chronological relationship of the Lukurmata domestic occupations exposed in the main excavation on the ridge.

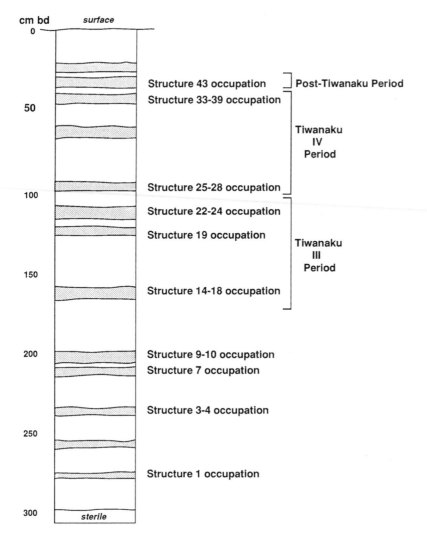

Fig. 1.4 Schematic representation of the vertical relationship of the Lukurmata domestic occupations exposed in the 3 m deep main excavation on the ridge.

sented by features such as house remains, in only seventeen occupations was I able to excavate significant portions of a structure. I have chosen for description in this volume eleven of these seventeen occupations for which I was able to excavate at least one entire structure. For each of these eleven domestic occupations, I will examine developments at the: (1) regional level; (2) site or community level; (3) household unit level; and (4) subhousehold level (in household unit architecture, in household activities, in ceramic style and iconographic preferences).

My household-based "local perspective" on Lukurmata evolution and the Tiwanaku state rests on a two-pronged analysis. One part of analysis is comparing changes over time at the subhousehold, household, settlement, and regional levels to develop a multilevel understanding. Comparing changes at different levels provides a case study of when and how such evolutions articulate, or how changes at different levels of society are related to one another. In addition, I use domestic remains as the primary unit of analysis for reconstructing social change by examining household life in terms of continuity, "tradition," and transformation.

In the following chapter I will present the methods behind this two-pronged approach while reviewing how domestic remains have been used in archaeology in general and in this study. Chapter 3 will introduce the nature of the Lukurmata archaeological remains. Subsequent chapters will outline Lukurmata's evolution as seen through a sequence of housefloors. Chapter 15 returns to larger questions of household archaeology and the interpretation of social change in the Andean past. The discussion in this chapter summarizes the nature of change in Lukurmata household life, and reviews the insights into the prehispanic Andean household and the Tiwanaku polity provided by the Lukurmata domestic remains. I end by outlining the implications the "local perspective" presents for comparative study of Andean political formations and Andean prehistory.

2

Household Archaeology

DOMESTIC REMAINS AND ARCHAEOLOGICAL ANALYSIS

Archaeologists have turned to domestic remains to address a wide range of concerns. Typically, these concerns pertain to archaeological formation processes, prehistoric sociopolitical and economic organization, prehistoric value systems and worldview, and processes of cultural evolution. The popularity of using the domestic remains to address these concerns results from the household status as a universal social form as well as the ubiquity of the domestic archaeological record. Households are often described as "basic units" of human societies, and domestic remains are common at most archaeological sites (Ashmore and Wilk 1988; Sheets 1992; Stanish 1989a; Wilk and Rathje 1982). In addition, households often leave a distinct archaeological "signature," and are thus relatively easy to recognize archaeologically (Ashmore and Wilk 1988; Deetz 1982:724; Sheets 1992; Stanish 1989a; Wilk and Rathje 1982).

Formation Processes

Domestic remains (particularly those left by hunter-gatherer societies) have often been studied to explore how the archaeological record itself forms. In its narrowest version, research of this type centers on the consequences of particular formation processes, or on discovering regularities linking behaviors to archaeological patterns (distinguishing "drop and toss zones," for instance; Binford 1978). Other studies, also often based on ethnoarchaeology or ethnographic analogy, have been concerned with the implications that discard and site abandonment activities have for analyzing household remains and site structure (Arnold 1990; Kent 1987; Lange and Rydberg 1972; Stahl and Zeidler 1990; Stevenson 1982; Yellen 1977).

Sociopolitical and Economic Organization

One of the oldest types of household archaeology is a form of settlement pattern study (Chang 1958). In this approach, domestic remains are treated as basal units of past social and settlement systems. Settlement pattern approaches to domestic remains generally involve reconstructing a site's residential, social, and economic organization through analysis of the spatial distribution and grouping of dwellings, and household-level differentiation in wealth, prestige, social status, access to trade-goods, or domestic activities. Domestic remains are also particularly valuable for exploring issues relating to social variation through comparison of samples drawn from different social strata, economic classes, residential areas, and communities (Santley and Hirth 1993; Smith 1987:234).

The first step of any settlement pattern approach is identifying a "household," or rather the archaeological correlate of this social unit. Doing so is a relatively simple task when a past people lived in discrete, single-family dwellings, but very difficult if the past population did not live in discrete dwellings with good preservational characteristics, if the prehistoric household was not a co-residential group, or if the dwelling was occupied by a group other than the nuclear family.

As household archaeology has become more sophisticated in the past decade, investigators have come to realize that exploring domestic processes does not necessarily need to involve excavating dwelling remains (Hayden and Cannon 1982; Wright et al. 1989). In fact, equating architectural remains with "households" may hinder study of prehistoric domestic life, particularly for those societies in which co-residential groups (represented by dwellings) did not coincide with the groups that performed domestic tasks. Domestic organization and activities in such societies may have little to do with the buildings in which people slept.

A drawback to settlement pattern approaches to domestic remains is that achieving the goals of these studies—reconstructing some aspect of community organization— often requires excavating large numbers of roughly contemporaneous dwellings. Aside from being costly to undertake, such investigations are difficult at smaller sites (hamlets that might only have consisted of a few households) or require special regional survey and sampling (those cases in which settlement consisted of scattered homesteads rather than nucleated villages of houses; Drennan et al. 1991).

A further problem with the settlement pattern approach is the difficulty in identifying relevant material markers of social status at the household level. To measure the relative social status of households, archaeologists have traditionally looked at how individual dwellings vary in terms of:

- associated exotic, highly valued, or long-distance trade items
- associated manufacturing implements or tools
- labor investment and elaboration in construction
- floor area
- storage capacity
- access, or spatial proximity, to critical resources or public architecture
- diet (as reflected in the cooking technology or domestic refuse associated with houses)

A general problem with this approach is that archaeologists do not look at social status directly. Instead, they must use material markers to infer social status. Recently, sophisticated ethnoarchaeological studies have attempted to measure the extent to which such markers vary with household wealth or social standing in existing societies (Hayden and Cannon 1982, 1984; Rathje and McGuire 1982; Smith 1987). These studies suggest that the relationship between wealth (let alone prestige or social ranking) and attributes of the dwelling and its contents is extremely complex at best. For instance, the developmental cycle of households alone means that a household may vary considerably in wealth during its normal lifetime. Furthermore, any such relationship is clouded by a number of preservational, discard, and depositional factors for which an archaeologist will have great difficulty compensating.

Most significant, archaeologists have traditionally used indicators of wealth to infer social status. But we are now beginning to recognize the extent to which status, political power, wealth, and prestige may be unrelated in complex societies (Earle 1991). Put simply, in some societies, wealth and high social ranking do not go hand in hand; the household with the most elaborate dwelling and most possessions may not necessarily have occupied a position of high prestige (Modjeska 1982; White 1985). Linking patterns of archaeological remains to particular societal divisions remains a thorny problem for archaeology (Marcus 1992).

As settlement pattern studies have become more sophisticated in methodology and theoretical orientation, so have studies at the household level, with some going beyond simple concern with variation in house form or contents (Kent 1990). These studies utilize household data, for instance, to examine site structure and mobility in subsistence strategies (Kent 1987, 1990), or community-level demographic shifts associated with the emergence of political complexity (Drennan 1987).

Value Systems and Worldview

Domestic remains have been a favorite line of evidence for scholars interested in reconstructing past worldviews, ideologies, or value systems. Although household studies of this type display a range of theoretical orientations, each focuses on the "meaning" implicit in domestic life and materials. There is a certain innate logic in this approach. As the largest thing that an individual family is likely to build or design, a dwelling is the most likely vehicle of expression for that household's values and concerns (Conrad, personal communication).

For some investigators, the physical structure of the dwelling reflects social relationships, social differentiation, and the nature of domestic roles (Wilk 1990:34). Other investigators view houses as material "grammars" or "texts," expressive of cosmology, ideology, and cognitive structures, as in Henry Glassie's (1975) famous study of historic houses in Middle Virginia (Deetz 1988; Wilk 1990:34). Still another perspective treats domestic space and the built environment in terms of culturally defined notions of privacy, openness, and territory (Glassie 1975).

In reconstructing the "meaning" of domestic remains, archaeologists have generally used (and sometimes combined) two distinct modes of analysis. One mode takes the form of ethnographic analogy, and relies on the large body of ethnographic literature devoted to interpreting indigenous or traditional architecture (Bourdier and Alsayyad 1989; Cunningham 1973; Donley 1987; Douglas 1972; Errington 1979; Hodder 1987; Knapp 1986; Moore 1986; Rodman 1985; Saile 1977a,b).

A second mode of analysis involves application of a general semiotic framework relating to the use of architectural or human space (ekistics, proxemics, structuralism). Studies of this sort, of which Glassie's (1975) is an example, frequently analyze domestic remains in terms of abstract principles (Blake 1991; Deetz 1982; Hodder 1987; Kent 1990b; Lawrence 1989; Sutro and Downing 1988).

If we assume that abstract principles underlie (perhaps unconsciously) choices about household life in all cultures and are "encoded" in domestic architecture, interpretation of archaeological remains does not need to be based on direct ethnographic analogy. Instead, domestic remains can be "deciphered" through application of formal interpretive categories and measures provided by the investigator. Many scholars of this orientation see domestic architecture not as a passive reflection of a worldview, but as an expressive material vehicle for reinforcing value systems and ideology that can be analyzed, for instance, to trace changing attitudes toward women in the past (Rock et al. 1980; Tringham 1991). Unlike the ethnographically based studies, these "decipherment" approaches tend to be "universalizing" rather than culturally specific, and lean toward cross-cultural comparisons (Kent 1990).

With some exceptions (including Glassie 1975), the results of this type of household archaeology have been unimpressive. Conclusions as to what prehistoric domestic remains "meant" or "expressed" for the inhabitants often require questionable ethnographic analogy or use of the direct historical method. On the other hand, interpretations based on abstract canons tend to descend into banal generalizations, and are often loaded with ethnocentric assumptions and typologies.

Regional Patterns and Cultural Evolutionary Processes

Archaeologists have also used household data to answer questions about human organization and change at larger levels. Households can be used as analytical units to examine regional-level institutions or cultural evolutionary processes (Kapches 1990; Rock 1974; Winter 1974). By examining how larger processes were manifested at the household level, these approaches often take a "household perspective" or "view from the bottom" that is essentially "capital-centric" (Costin and Earle 1989; Stanish 1989a, 1992). The previously cited study of the effects at the household level of Inca conquest by Hastorf (1990a) is a good example of the valuable insights such investigations may provide, as are the Mesoamerican studies of Marcus Winter (1974) and Gary Feinman et al. (1984). Other investigators have studied households to examine domestic processes (such as increases in residential density or differential household participation in exchange) that are themselves important to understanding cultural evolution (Bawden 1990; Drennan 1987; Hastorf 1990b; Wilk 1990).

DEFINING THE HOUSEHOLD

Households seem to be readily recognizable in existing societies, but arriving at a theoretical definition of the household has proven more challenging to scholars. The "household" has variously been seen as a family, a co-residential task group (Hammel and Laslett 1974; Laslett 1972:24; Sheets 1992:22), a construct in individuals' minds (Yanagisako 1984), or simply the place where individuals reside (Reyna 1976). Definitions of the household as a social unit typically involve one or more "functions" or attributes—co-residence, domestic activities, familial relations, production, distribution (pooling and sharing resources), reproduction (in the social and biological sense), and transmission (of property and information; Bender 1967; Wilk and Netting 1984:5; Wilk and Rathje 1982:621).

Because functions are organized differently in different societies, the group that shares a living space (co-residence) may not share in the activity of food preparation and consumption, pool resources, or be the unit that rears children (Wilk and Netting 1984:7; Wilk 1991:36). Even within a single community, the boundaries, roles, composition, activities, and developmental cycle of households can vary considerably, both through time and between households of different social status.

Scholars now agree that attempting to arrive at a valid cross-cultural definition of the household is a futile exercise (Netting et al. 1984; Stanish 1989a; Wilk 1984; Wilk and

Rathje 1982). The difficulty in defining the household indicates the extent to which the "household" is contextually constituted. Roles, functions, and membership vary with setting and activity (Wilk and Netting 1984). Other social units, or groups whose membership cross-cuts households, may have roles that complement, replace, or compete with the household (Freeman 1968; Hayden and Cannon 1982; Steponaitis 1981; Wilk and Rathje 1982:621).

A more promising orientation for archaeology is to focus on the way domestic functions are conducted in particular societies, by examining the spatial distribution, timing, and organization of the domestic activities that constitute these functions, and exploring the rules that govern how, where, when, and who conducts these functions. In acknowledgment of the degree to which domestic functions are not isomorphic, Wilk (1991:37) has argued that the household should be defined in terms of "activity groups," with domestic activities or functions viewed as "spheres." Each "activity sphere" consists of the group that carries out that particular activity. Households are defined by the point of maximal overlap of these spheres.

It follows from this activity-based orientation ("a household is as a household does") that household archaeology should explore how particular activities were divided between social units at particular times in the past, what tasks were performed by co-residential groups, and how households were integrated into larger economic and social orders (ibid.). Because this approach can readily be extended through space and time, it has great utility for examining synchronic variation in domestic life, as well as the diachronic relationship between household-level changes and changes in the larger orders of which households are a part (ibid.).

Wilk (ibid.:35) admits that approaching households as activity patterns is "difficult and messy," but his provides a useful archaeological approach to households for several reasons. First, his approach distinguishes between household membership (the size and composition of the household, or morphology) and household activities, placing emphasis on the latter. Archaeology is much better equipped to examine past activities and co-residence than familial composition or socialization of children (Sheets 1992; Stanish 1989a:11). In addition, the remains of past activities may form spatial residues that can aid in delineating "activity spheres" (Sheets 1992:23–24; Wilk 1991:37). This approach to intrasite patterning is not very different from that intuitively used by many archaeologists, and can be readily assimilated to the concept of the archaeological "household unit" discussed below.

THE HOUSEHOLD "SYSTEM"

I suggest that Wilk's definition can be extended further, and that we can view households not simply as "activity groups," but as "open systems" composed of various dimensions (production, transmission, and the rest) as well as activities. These dimensions or attributes are related in complex fashion to one another and to suprahousehold variables (Rapoport 1990). Households are dynamic systems, not simply static patterns, with changes in one dimension having implications for changes in others.

This model of the household is not completely functional. While environmental and economic settings play a critical role in shaping household dimensions and household change, tradition and cultural values are always basic to the principles or "rules" that structure the relationship between different dimensions of the household. This approach to the household recognizes that domestic orders, like other sociocultural forms, are fundamentally "constellations" of beliefs and values that persist through time. Households (and their dimensions) are consciously altered by their members and surrounding circumstances, but are also shaped by beliefs and values, which themselves evolve. For instance, external circumstances may require a household to increase its agricultural production, but traditional domestic values will shape how production is increased and the effects of such a productive change.

A domestic system is a set of "rules" (concerning the organization of sets of activities and household life) that generates domestic patterns in the same way that subsistence strategies generate particular diets or settlement systems generate settlement patterns (Flannery 1976b:162). To borrow Lévi-Strauss' (1960:52) classic illustration, the domestic pattern is analogous to the jigsaw puzzle, while the domestic system is analogous to the mathematical formulas expressing the speed and shape of the cams in the saw that cut the jigsaw pieces. The domestic system, therefore, is something that needs to be *inferred* from the archaeologically observable elements of domestic patterns. We can reconstruct domestic patterns, but "explaining" them requires knowledge of the domestic system that generated the patterns. The domestic system might be recognized in such things as the repeated co-occurrence of particular activities, persistent patterns of spatial organization, and the maintenance of particular activities within the household domain.

The view of the household as a "system" also allows us to distinguish between two types of change: systemic change (changes in existing dimensions of the household system); and transformational change (shifts in the rules or principles that govern domestic organization). In transformational change, the structure of the household system changes. Inclusion or removal of basic functions such as reproduction or distribution from the household domain are transformational changes because they imply changes in the household's role or function in larger systems. An increase in surplus production by a household already involved in surplus production is an example of systemic change, unless the increased production involves the addition or subtraction of particular types of activities from the household. The initial shift by the household from "for-use" production to surplus production is an example of transformational change.

It is important to keep in mind the distinctions between the two types of change, because much of our perceptions of prehistoric cultural change is based, for instance, on changes in the style of objects, rather than changes in underlying organizational principles governing the use of these objects. This distinction can be illustrated with several simple examples. A shift in the decoration on pottery vessels in a household assemblage is one form of cultural change. However, it does not signal a change in household activities or how the pots are actually used. In this same society, burial treatment may always involve arranging particular grave-goods in a certain way around the body. Over time, the types of grave-goods used may change (metal axes substituted for stone ones), but the spatial arrangement of the goods may not vary. These are forms of systemic rather than transformational change. Finally, a hunter-gatherer group pursuing an optimizing resource exploitation strategy can produce very different sites in different areas and under different conditions. But since each site resulted from the same underlying organizational principles, these intersite differences should not interpreted as transformational change.

I am not suggesting by way of these examples that systemic changes are unimportant, unworthy of study, or mere epiphenomena.[1] After all, without settlement patterns archaeologists could not study settlement systems. I am merely pointing out that these empirical patterns are shaped by "hidden rules." It is the persistence of these rules, a type of patterned *continuity* or customary way of doing things, which allows anthropologists to distinguish between different cultures and recognize their persistence through time.

Obviously, the distinction between pattern and underlying system is not a novel proposition in either anthropology or archaeology. I am only arguing that household remains be considered in the same way: that the goal of household archaeology should involve study of the organizational principles underlying patterns of household remains (Bawden 1990). And a diachronic perspective is necessary to reveal those cases in which styles, objects, and even specific activities change, but underlying organizational principles do not.

In adopting a "local perspective," I am interested in how changes in material patterns relate to changes in the underlying domestic *system*. The degree of continuity in the latter provides a measure of the stability of the Andean household as an adaptive unit. As a marker of the "depth" of change, shifts in the household system indicate a deeper—perhaps more significant, but at least different—form of change than change in household patterns.

HOUSEHOLD CHANGE

Dimensions of Household Change

What causes change (other than the household developmental cycle) in household organization? Most anthropologists have focused on the effects of urbanization or participation in the world market on traditional households (Maclachlan 1987). These studies link household-level change (particularly household size and composition) to economic or ecological conditions (Pasternak et al. 1976; Reyna 1976; Wilk 1990). This approach also finds expression in archaeological research as in Richard Wilk and William Rathje's (1982) discussion of how differences in economy and ecological setting may have resulted in the various forms of residential organization of lowland Maya populations.

These adaptive or functionalist approaches, as Wilk (1991:38) points out, contain an order of causation in which external economic factors lead to shifts in household productive activities and relationships, household composition, and, ultimately, the rules and values that govern the household as a cultural entity. Wilk (1991:38) goes on to say:

> There are good arguments for alternative models of change. Linares (1984) presents a good case of an initial change in religious beliefs and gender roles that later led to reorganization of activities and morphology. Guyer (1981) finds cases of the value of labor and goods changing first, followed by the household decision-making system, and the distribution of power, and only then by activities and

---

[1] See Rogers (1990) for an excellent discussion of the archaeological perception of prehistoric cultural change.

morphology. Imported ideals of household organization and role behavior have well-documented effects on Caribbean households (Brown 1971 Rubenstein 1975).

Political ambition may also lead to changes in individual household organization, with household production forming a basis for political power or social standing (Arnold 1992; Blake 1991; Hastorf 1990b).

Evaluating the Significance of Household Change

What is the significance of changes in household organization? The answer to this question depends partly on the nature of the "household." From one perspective, households (and, by extension, the domestic domain and household units) are fundamentally *adaptive* units. They are dynamic, highly flexible, and sensitive to demographic, economic, sociopolitical, and environmental conditions (Wilk and Rathje 1982:619). As such, household structure and activities change in response to localized, short-term fluctuations in the economy or environment, or the opportunities and constraints confronting the individual family. Therefore, changes in household organization are not necessarily reflective of or responses to shifts in overarching institutions, regional-level processes, or suprahousehold pressures (Netting 1979; Wilk and Rathje 1982). From this adaptive perspective, variation over time in the domestic domain is to be *expected*, even if the larger economic, ecological, or sociopolitical setting of the household does not change.

A contrasting perspective views households as less flexible or dynamic in the face of economic opportunities and constraints. This second perspective emphasizes the role of tradition in determining household organization and activities (Wilk 1991:37; Yanagisako 1979, 1984). Like any other form of social organization, households are structured primarily by history, cultural values, and ideals. Because they are manifestations of social values or cultural identity, households and domestic patterns are essentially stable and conservative, even rather static, and subject to change only under extreme pressures. This viewpoint recognizes that particular household forms seem to characterize particular societies over long periods of time regardless of changing settings (Bourdier and Alsayyad 1989; Netting et al. 1984:xxx; Wilk 1991:37; Wolf 1984).

From this second perspective, diachronic shifts in household form are likely to follow transformations in larger sociopolitical orders, or very basic productive relations, rather than short-term adaptations to "local" pressures or the ambitions of individual families. The latter will be met within the existing framework of household organization, or at the suprahousehold level. As a result, we would expect great continuity and stability in household form through time. Causes of major household change will be the result of shifts in suprahousehold systems, or in the household's articulation with such systems.

It follows from emphasis on the stability of the household that changes at the household level are highly significant for discerning social change or evolution. Household changes will represent shifts at the "lowest," and presumably, most conservative level of the social pyramid, and are indicators of major change in the larger frameworks of which households are components. To many social historians, a gross measure of the significance of societal change is the degree to which it affects life at the household or "grass roots" level.

Disarticulating the Household Unit

Conclusions drawn from anthropological studies of household change cannot easily be applied to archaeology. However, as a whole, they provide valuable testimony to the difficulty of predicting cross-culturally how households will change under given pressures or conditions. More important, ethnographic studies illustrate the extent to which household change can be understood as changes in particular *elements* or *dimensions* of the household, rather than the household as a whole.

Wilk (1988, 1991) has cited a number of ethnographic case studies that support this argument. For instance, major changes in the construction materials, outside plan, and appearance of Vanuatu and Kekchi houses were not accompanied by shifts in the use of interior space (Rodman 1985; Wilk 1988, 1990). Margaret Rodman (1985) documents how significant changes in the use or interior activities of Vanuatu men's houses (*na gamal*) were not accompanied by changes in the structure's plan or appearance. Her interpretation is that houses, as the containers of women and wealth (both inherently malleable in Vanuatu thought), are subject to change, while communal men's houses are expressive containers of tradition (ibid.:277–78).

In a comparative study of societal and architectural change in three native communities of central Brazil, Christiana Barreto (n.d.) shows that shifts in subsistence, residential mobility, domestic architectural style, and daily tasks were not accompanied by changes in the spatial organization of activities within houses. Xinguano groups adopting nontraditional houses continued to spatially organize patterns of storage, sleeping, preparation of food, and social activities in traditional ways. Therefore, the observed changes in architectural form reflected societal processes of acculturation, rather than major changes in domestic organization.

These types of studies, Wilk (1991:38–39) notes, demonstrate the complex way in which the various dimensions of the household may be related. Changes in one dimension may or may not cause, or indicate, changes in other dimensions. Different dimensions may change at different rates, and household change may be characterized by minor and gradual change in many dimensions, or major and rapid change in a single dimension. Because of this, it is difficult (maybe even impossible) to capture household change with general predictive models or causal sequences (ibid.:38).

Given the above, it is analytically useful to disarticulate the household into component attributes or dimensions. As the studies I have cited suggest, the process of household change can be broken down, examined, and understood in terms of changes in particular dimensions of the household. This approach is a promising one for studying household change in prehistory as well, particularly since much household change is reflected in dimensions that can be monitored archaeologically: household size, use of space, domestic architecture, activities, marking of status, and wealth.

General domestic functions (production, consumption, etc.) can be treated as household dimensions in studying change, as can principles of use of domestic space. So can material lines of evidence such as architectural elaboration, domestic activities, and house size. Comparing changes through time in specific elements of the household, by opening up the "black box" of the archaeological household, will always provide a more detailed understanding of domestic change.

Disarticulating the household also remedies one of the limitations of the settlement pattern approach described earlier. The (often implicit) aim of many household settlement pattern studies is simply *classifying* household remains as "elite," "wealthy," or "craft specialist." This can become a sterile typological exercise that obscures the very processes of interest to most archaeologists. After all, we are interested in understanding the role of domestic activities in elite social status, not simply in distinguishing elite and commoner houses. In other words, instead of simply identifying households as "elite," we should want to distinguish "elite activities" (or the " elite" characteristics of universal activities) in household contexts. This approach shifts the focus of investigation from the percentage of elaborate serving vessels found in elite versus commoner households to considering *why* elite households might have more serving vessels, and *why* serving activities might play an important role in emergent social inequality.

A number of recent archaeological studies have examined changes in separate elements of the household. Hastorf (1990a) analyzed prehispanic Sausa households in terms of production, distribution, and consumption. This revealed that "commoner" and "elite" households did not uniformly differ in each of these elements. Although "elite" households had greater access to maize, there were no significant differences in "commoner" and "elite" maize consumption (ibid.:284). Instead, "elite" households valued maize for exchange (distribution), an important insight into the nature and activities of Sausa nobility.

Summary: Understanding Household Change

Although archaeology is uniquely suited to addressing issues of long-term change, there has been little systematic investigation of household change. Archaeological study of household change has often lacked analytical frameworks of regional approaches relating shifts in archaeological patterns to larger theoretical issues.

Wilk (1988, 1991) is one of the few scholars to develop both a suitable analytical framework and a relevant body of accompanying theory. The analytical framework, drawing on ethnographic studies of domestic change, focuses on perceiving "household change" as changes in different household dimensions. Which dimensions of the household change, and how, are determined by a complex interplay of tradition and external pressures. This approach allows a focus on processural concerns and relating specific dimensions of household life to one another and to larger social, economic, and political processes.

Wilk's (1991:38–39) treatment of households as adaptive units is the basis for his general model of "adaptive strategy" that links household patterns to the political economy and the natural environment. It would be ideal to examine Lukurmata households from a similar perspective. Unfortunately, the regional and contextual data that would allow this are lacking. Therefore, in the following section I present a more limited construct addressing somewhat different issues. This framework simply serves as a guide for examining household change at Lukurmata in terms of (1) the role of tradition in domestic organization; and (2) interaction with supralocal systems, particularly the Tiwanaku political economy.

ANALYZING HOUSEHOLD CHANGE AT LUKURMATA

My "local perspective" on change in household life at Lukurmata revolves around two lines of analysis. The first focuses on the sequential development of household organization at Lukurmata. "Disarticulating" Lukurmata domestic remains to examine diachronic changes in the analytical units of the household provides information on changes in various household dimensions. These changes in dimensions, in turn, tell us something about the nature of the Lukurmata household as a system and the persistence of traditional patterns of domestic organization. In other words, this line of analysis will explore continuity and change in the "rules" or principles of household life at Lukurmata. I will describe the methodology of this investigation below.

The second line of analysis involves linking levels of analysis, that is, comparing the household sequence at Lukurmata to processes at the community and regional levels. Since previous investigation of regional processes in Bolivia have centered on Tiwanaku, this line of analysis will focus on interaction between individual Lukurmata households and Tiwanaku. A general framework for examining interaction between the capital and households of subsidiary sites in regional settlement hierarchies is also presented below.

ANALYTICAL COMPONENTS OF HOUSEHOLD UNITS AT LUKURMATA

> *Conceptually we have accustomed ourselves*
> *to a vision of the past that is evocative of a*
> *series of palimpsest portraits (or over-lapping*
> *structures), the pigments and compositions of*
> *which, have been painted with taphonomic*
> *brushes. (Gnivecki 1987:176)*

Archaeologists do not excavate households. They excavate the material remains of dwellings and a small portion of the items once associated with dwellings. Kent Flannery (1983:45) has provided an analytically useful unit: the "household unit." This refers to the "complex of structures and features resulting from a typical . . . household" (ibid.).

We cannot directly examine change in Lukurmata household life. What we can examine are changes in a "household unit" that does not represent all the dimensions of past household life. Aspects of household life must be inferred from the household unit, a process made problematic by the complex relationship between household life and archaeological remains of domestic activities. Not all household changes are physically manifested in the household unit, and certain attributes or "functions" of the household, such as co-residence and domestic activities, are easier to approach than others (labor allocation or familial organization). Furthermore, different types of household change may result in the same shift in the household unit. An increase in house size, for instance, could represent either a shift in household membership or a change in the time devoted to a particular indoor activity.

An additional obstacle to generalizing about change in the household unit through time is the natural household developmental cycle. At different points in its life, the same dwelling may house small nuclear families or large three-generational (stem) families. If there was a close degree of fit between the size of the household and the size of the dwelling, two very different household units could simply represent households at different stages in the developmental cycle, rather than differences in household organization (David 1971; Oswald 1987; Sheehy 1991; Tourtellot 1988). Conversely, if the fit between the household and the physical dwelling is loose, many changes in household organization or activities will not be reflected in shifts in the household unit. Unfortunately, my sample size of houses is far too small to resolve this problem.

The difficulty of exposing an entire household unit further complicates matters. Prehispanic Lukurmata residential architecture was composed of free-standing, spatially separated structures (rather than agglutinated architecture or residential compounds). This made it relatively easy to identify the principal architectural component of household units. However, the dwelling is only a portion of the household unit, and not necessarily the center of it. By way of comparison, modern Aymara household units cover more than 500 m^2, when one takes into account the house compound (with three or four buildings) and the associated activity areas and house buildings. Most activities take place in the courtyard.

Thus, we probably exposed at Lukurmata a *part* of each household unit, resulting in a bias toward those activities that took place in and adjacent to the house. We have little information on the domestic activities that took place at outlying activity areas or in agricultural fields. Many studies in household archaeology are systematically biased in this manner (Kent 1987; Seymour and Schiffer 1987). True investigations of domestic processes should involve excavation away from residential architecture, and information gathered from what are usually considered "nondomestic" contexts.

Archaeologists investigating domestic remains have many sources of information. Household archaeology generally focuses on the nature and spatial patterning of domestic architecture and associated features and artifacts. Prehistorians have also intensively analyzed particular materials from domestic contexts to gain greater insights into household organization and processes, including pottery (Hally 1983, 1984; Hill 1970; Longacre 1970), stone-tool remains (Parry 1987), paleobotanical remains (Hastorf 1990a), even human skeletal remains (Storey 1992). Finally, innovative studies have highlighted the great potential that residue and chemical analysis of occupational surfaces holds for reconstructing the nature and distribution of household activities (Barba 1986; Manzanilla and Barba 1990; Smyth 1991).

In analyzing Lukurmata domestic remains, I have elected to focus on information pertaining to three things—domestic architecture, domestic activities, and style of domestic pottery—traditionally recorded as part of all archaeological investigations. As will be seen, *comparison* of the timing and nature of change for each of these lines of evidence (architecture, artifacts, pottery styles) reveals a Lukurmata history different from that which would be provided by a "capital-centric" approach.

Architecture

Domestic architecture has been viewed in various ways by anthropologists, paralleling the diversity of thought concerning households in general. Domestic architecture has been viewed as cultural convention (Rapoport 1976); manifestation of social relations or worldview (Errington 1979); or roofed "space" defined in response to the intersecting requirements of building materials, activities, residential composition, and environment (Kent 1984; McGuire and Schiffer 1983).

If the house is the product of tradition, the material construction of a worldview, or the material marker of social position, shifts in household architecture may be indicative of changes in "ethnic" identity, political affiliation, and social status (Stanish 1989a; Wilk 1990). Or, as holders of the "roofed space" view argue, the house is an adaptive tool, reflective of the social organization of domestic work (McGuire and Schiffer 1983; Wilk 1983). Therefore, changes in household membership, activities, or the organization of tasks should result in architectural changes.

Archaeologists have tended to treat domestic architecture as conservative, either because the dwelling is seen as an optimal "adaptation" to an unchanging physical or economic environment, or because it is a culturally determined marker of ethnic or social identity. Given this perspective, significant change in domestic architecture (particularly in the layout or form of structures) is often viewed as indicative of major societal change ranging from population replacement to sweeping economic shifts (Stanish 1989a).

Household Activities

My second line of evidence consists of the range, spatial patterning, and frequency of household activities. We learn about household activities largely from the types and distribution of features and artifacts associated with houses. Of particular interest are the range and organization of *universal household activities*, or those activities conducted by each household, and variation between household units indicative of *household specialization* (Flannery and Winter 1976:36–38). Unfortunately, lacking detailed functional or residue analysis of objects, I was sometimes unable to identify their uses. In other cases ethnographic analogy was sufficient to provide clues to the function of items and the activities they represented.

Manning Nash (1967) has suggested that household technology in prestate societies and peasant societies is relatively simple, and the number of different tasks involved in any productive activity are few. Division of labor is determined by sex and age, and persons learn their productive tasks in the course of growing up. Given these considerations, it might be expected that at whatever stage of its life-cycle, a household would perform a similar range of activities. Therefore, it is less likely that the differences we observed in Lukurmata household units reflect households at different stages in the developmental cycle.

Domestic Pottery

I use domestic pottery as the third line of evidence, both to gauge the persistence of tradition at Lukurmata and as a measure of interaction with other sites. I will focus on continuity over time in the range of vessel types used by households, and the pattern of acceptance of nonlocal (including Tiwanaku) pottery. Questions I will consider include: Did imported pottery replace a preexisting form or expand the household inventory? Were familiar shapes accepted before unfamiliar shapes?

Traditionally, ceramic styles have been used in Andean archaeology to identify ethnic groups and the boundaries of political formations (Moseley 1992). Changes in
ceramic-style preferences are often treated by Andean archaeologists as measures of
change in past societies; many treatments of Andean prehistory are little more than
elaborate pottery sequences. This is particularly true in "capital-centric" approaches
preoccupied with relating sites to larger systems defined on the basis of the distribution
of decorated pottery.

Despite this orientation, there has been little testing of the ideas that ceramic complexes mark ethnic affiliation or political association, and that shifts in pottery-style
preferences really reflect significant social or political change (Marcus and Silva
1988). These assumptions are directly challenged when a "local perspective" is taken.
One method of examining the meaning of ceramic-style preferences (and their value
for discerning social change in the past) is to compare changes in household pottery
assemblages with changes in architecture and domestic activities.

Linking Levels of Analysis

All households are members of larger systems organized at the suprahousehold,
community, regional, and pan-regional levels. Households may be parts of residential
barrios, kinship units, chiefdoms or states, exchange networks, or marketing regions.
Interaction with these larger frameworks should, as ethnographic studies indicate, be
important in stimulating and guiding household change. Therefore, interpretation of
household change at Lukurmata requires examining household evolution in a wider or
regional context. I do this by comparing changes through time at the subhousehold and
household levels to changes at the site and regional levels.

Comparing the timing of changes at different societal levels holds two dangers. The
first danger is creating trivial linkages or spurious associations between variables at
different levels. If we arbitrarily choose to compare particular features at the household
and regional levels simply because it is *possible* to do so, we run the risk of creating
chance "linkages" that are, in reality, only a product of the analytical method.

The second danger is producing an ad hoc, "just-so story" interpretation that con-
fuses association and causation. If we use characteristics of the larger system to "explain" household characteristics, we can supply *apparent* causal relationships where
none may exist.

How, then, can linkages between changes at particular societal levels be evaluated?
How is it possible to convincingly argue that an aspect of the larger system, say a
state's need for surplus production, resulted in intensified production at the household
level?

One test of proposed linkages is the strength of the construct logically connecting
the variables involved. We might claim, for instance, that cash cropping leads to larger
households, but without any bridging arguments or reasonable suggestions as to *why*
such processes may be related, the argument by itself would not be very convincing.
To fulfill this need in the Lukurmata–Tiwanaku case, I will outline a general model of
household-state interaction based on comparative studies of other complex societies.
The purpose of this model is to suggest why, and in what ways, we might reasonably
expect the Tiwanaku political economy to affect Lukurmata households.

A second test of any proposed linkages involves taking a long-term diachronic perspective, and looking at the timing of changes at each level. If significant shifts at the household level coincide in time with particular shifts at the communal or regional level, we can at least suggest that the two changes are associated, although the nature of their linkage remains to be explained. For instance, if patterns in the household division of labor have changed very little over centuries but shift rapidly when cash cropping is introduced, the hypothesis that the two events are related is at least a reasonable one.

A third general test of the strength or probability of particular linkages is through cross-cultural comparison. If a shift to larger households *always* seems to follow a shift to cash cropping, the argument that the two are related in any single case is strengthened, even through the nature of the linkage may not be clear. For instance, it has been forcefully argued on the basis of cross-cultural study that mobile peoples (in the present and the past) construct circular dwellings (McGuire and Schiffer 1983). However, such an association does not rule out the possibility that both mobility and round houses are the result of yet a third factor. We must also keep in mind that such associations are often one-way (while mobile groups may build circular dwellings, not all circular dwellings are constructed by mobile groups, so we cannot use the presence of round structures to infer mobility).

The participation of households in larger systems can vary widely, depending on the status of the individual household; the number and complexity of institutions intermediate between provincial households and rulers; and the nature of interaction between the household and suprahousehold systems.

The Role of Household Status

Household involvement with larger systems will vary depending on the status and ambitions of the individual household. Not all households in a community will interact equally with the capital or supracommunity systems. Households of greater wealth or higher social status (or those desiring to be so) may have more supralocal interaction as local elites, clients of rulers, or simply ambitious intermediaries between local populations and overarching institutions.

Hastorf's (1990a) study of the Sausa incorporation into the Inca state presents an example of this phenomenon. Inca policies affected Sausa elite and commoner households in different ways. These policies resulted in an effective "leveling" of wealth differences, with a decline in the standard of living for elite Sausa households and an increase in the standard of living for commoner Sausa households.

The Effect of Intermediate Institutions

Directly relating household change to regional processes is also complicated by the variety of intermediate institutions that may exist between individual households and the state. For instance, it may be impossible to determine if changes in household production resulted from demands by a state system or from local elites with their own motives for acquiring surplus. Showing that such a change followed incorporation of the community into a state system may *suggest* state-level effects on household production, but other explanations cannot be ruled out.

As a general rule, the greater the number of intermediaries between household and state institutions, the more difficult it is to relate household-level changes to state strategies. The situation is further complicated by the ability of states, with their specialized, decentralized decision-making apparatus, to bypass intermediate bodies and implement decisions at the household level (Spencer 1982).

Interaction with state systems may even *cause* the growth of intermediate institutions. As the agents of interaction with supralocal systems, intermediate institutions can shield households from outside pressures; often they are intended to do so. Therefore, one result of interaction with centralized polities may be the emergence of suprahousehold organizations, rather than changes in individual households themselves. For example, if residential patterns at a site change following state conquest, such changes could be interpreted by an archaeologist as a "state reorganization" of residential order. But the change could also signal the emergence of "buffer" institutions, even local elites, intended to meet state demands at a suprahousehold level, thus preserving the traditional household unit. From the "capital-centric" perspective, such shifts are usually interpreted as evidence of state administration and control. From the "local perspective," they might be interpreted as a form of resistance, conservatism, or adaptation.

The existence of intermediary institutions has other implications for the interpretation of change in household organization. The prior existence of complex governing institutions allowed the Inca, following some of their conquests, to incorporate populations into the imperial system with virtually no changes at the household level (D'Altroy 1987a, 1987b).

Intermediaries may also cause changes in household organization to occur in a "punctuated" rather than a gradual manner. Long periods of little change in household organization might be followed by sudden and marked shifts as the intermediate institutions promoting continuity are overcome.

Household-State Interaction

An important means of establishing the role of households in larger systems is to explore how they interacted with larger systems. Such exploration provides insights into the nature of both institutions.

Interaction between households and an overarching polity may take a variety of forms. It may be relatively direct and frequent, with village households tightly integrated into centrally directed political and economic systems. Subordinate sites may be administered by representatives of the rulers. Household activity and economy may be structured by state economic demands, with their material well-being depending on institutions of the central government. Religion, systems of social ranking, and marking of social identity at the smaller site may be part of larger regional or pan-regional frameworks.

At the other end of the spectrum, interaction between subordinate sites and the institutions of the capital can also be extremely limited. The state may rule indirectly through local elites, and there may be little or no involvement by the capital in local decision making. In this case, subordinate communities may be relatively autonomous in economic terms, contributing little to larger economic systems and remaining little affected by them. The only ties between individual households and the capital may be shared religious or social identity. Households in these settlements may not even consider themselves members of a larger political system (just as medieval peasants would not have considered themselves members of the Holy Roman Empire).

To determine how a subordinate site and the capital may have interacted, it is useful to answer two questions: What was the *nature* of interaction? What was the *degree* of integration?

THE NATURE OF INTERACTION

The complete range of interaction between households and larger institutions is often difficult to recognize and characterize in ethnographic cases, let alone in archaeological settings. Different forms of interaction may coexist at different times; individual households in the community may have different relationships with larger institutions; and interaction is often a complex web of economic, ideological, political, and social relations.

In general, archaeologists consider larger sites with public architecture as centers for goods and services for residents of smaller sites. In such settlement systems, interaction may be religious, social, or economic in nature, with residents of smaller sites traveling to the larger one for ceremonies, ritual activities, or markets.

Interaction may take the form of various types of exchange relationships. Residents of the smaller community may obtain craft-goods or long-distance trade items from the capital directly, or from middlemen in a capital-dominated exchange system.

Interaction may be politically structured, with households incorporated into the capital's administrative system or subject to political control by the rulers in the capital. Political control can range from indirect hegemony by local elites to direct control by officials transplanted from the capital. Such connections may result in extensive economic ties between households and the dominant political formation, with households at the smaller sites having tribute or labor obligations. The well-known Inca decimal tribute system is the best documented example of such obligations (Julien 1982). Archaeological evidence suggests that other prehispanic Andean states, including the Moche polity (A.D. 200–A.D. 600) of the north coast of Peru and the highland Wari state (A.D. 600–A.D. 1000), levied similar obligations on subject peoples (D'Altroy 1987a; Moseley 1992; Schreiber 1987a, 1992).

THE DEGREE OF INTEGRATION

The nature of interaction between a smaller site and the rulers should be considered part of the overall integration of the polity. "Integration" refers to the extent to which subsystems and variables in the system are articulated. Some complex societies may be considered hypercoherent: the various subsystems making up these polities are tightly linked so that changes in one variable or subsystem invariably have consequences (not always foreseen) for other variables or subsystems (Adams 1979; D'Altroy 1987a; Flannery 1972; Spencer 1990). State systems tend to be highly integrated, with extensive vertical linkages in subsystems and specialized decision-making subsystems, allowing higher-order managers to effectively make decisions at the household level.

The Inca state, with its impressive administrative, storage, and productive systems, is often cited as an example of a highly integrated polity although it is now acknowledged that the Inca did not impose a uniform homogeneous rule on subject populations. As Terence D'Altroy (1987a:3) has noted, the old, "prevailing view that the Inca ran a tight ship, controlling the organization and behavior of the subject populace through an efficient bureaucracy centered at the imperial capital of Cuzco," has been replaced by a recognition that the Inca were not the monolithic, centrally directed polity that scholars once thought (Marcus 1987b; Morris 1988).

Little is known about the manner in which the Tiwanaku political formation was integrated. However, Tiwanaku lacks many features of the administrative infrastructure that are present in many other prehispanic Andean states, suggesting that the Tiwanaku polity was either quite small (limited perhaps to the area around the capital itself), not tightly integrated in terms of decision making or administrative control, or integrated in very different ways than other prehispanic Andean states.

ARCHAEOLOGICAL ASSESSMENT OF INTERACTION AT THE HOUSEHOLD LEVEL

We can use a number of lines of evidence to understand the interaction between provincial households and an overarching political system. At the regional level, the presence of an administrative settlement hierarchy, or central place system, provides clues about general patterns of interaction between small sites and large sites (Smith 1976).

At the household level, we can discern the nature of interaction by examining:

1. how particular types of items from the capital or system were incorporated into household activities
2. the manner in which capital-associated styles of iconography, architecture, or social display were incorporated into the household domain
3. changes in local patterns of domestic organization resulting from interaction with the capital

For analytical convenience, I divide these forms of interaction into the familiar categories of religious interaction, exchange, and political control. Such a division requires justification.

I have selected these three categories only because they correspond to how Andean archaeologists have traditionally characterized interaction between a political capital and outlying populations. In addition, distinguishing among these three categories archaeologically is fairly straightforward, at least superficially. In fact, interaction between households and states is always more complex than a simple typology can capture, and these categories probably would have had little meaning in the prehispanic Andes, particularly for states, including the Inca, in which religion, politics, and economic relations were inextricably interwoven. Nonetheless, we must be prepared to recognize cases in which shared religion did not involve political domination, or in which trade relations were independent of religious relationships. The relationship between Lukurmata households and the Tiwanaku polity at any point in time may have involved one or more of these types of interaction.

Religious Interaction

Smaller sites may be incorporated into a regional religious system centered at a particular site without being politically dominated by that site. Such "religious interaction spheres" are known to have existed in Andean prehistory. The first-millennium B.C. Chavín-style horizon and the Mito tradition of the Peruvian Andes probably represent this phenomenon, but the best-studied example is the Inca-contemporary Pachacamac cult (Moseley 1992).

In contrast, nonsyncretic state religions were important components of prehispanic Andean statecraft. State rulers were divine or semidivine, and stood at the head of a religious hierarchy closely associated with state administration and the ruling elite (ibid.). The Inca church was an extensive landholding body and had great power and wealth. Subjugated populations were incorporated into the Inca church, although they were often allowed to continue pre-Inca religious activities as well. State religions were generally marked by highly distinctive iconographic and architectural styles closely linked to, or filling the role of, state corporate iconographic styles (ibid.).

The strong religious aspect of the Tiwanaku polity has long been recognized, both for the massive amounts of "ceremonial" architecture at the capital and the widespread distribution in the south-central Andes of Tiwanaku-style items of ritual use. David Browman (1981), for instance, has suggested that Tiwanaku represented a cult or theocratic federation, rather than a polity integrated by political domination or economic power such as the Wari or Inca state.

Given this, we would expect one aspect of interaction between Lukurmata and the Tiwanaku capital to have been religious in nature. This hypothesis is strongly suggested by the Tiwanaku-style semi-subterranean temple at Lukurmata. However, we want to know if involvement in the Tiwanaku religious sphere took place at the individual household level, and if this preceded other forms of interaction, as Browman (ibid.) has suggested.

Exchange

Most small sites are incorporated into regional exchange systems of one size or another. The goods moving in these systems may range from " prestige-goods" (exotic long-distance trade items) to utilitarian craft-goods (pottery, food, or stone tools). Andean archaeology has long had the problem of distinguishing regional exchange (particularly of pottery) from other processes such as political control, missionary activity, or population movement. Archaeological approaches to exchange often focus on the form of exchange, movement of prestige-goods between elites, down-the-line trade, redistribution, and so on. Other approaches center on the implications of differential household involvement at the community level in regional exchange systems.

Attempts to understand the nature of the Tiwanaku polity, particularly its interaction with distant areas such as coastal Chile, have traditionally been object-oriented. The archaeologist focuses on the types of Tiwanaku-style goods found (whether "prestige" or "utilitarian" items), and the context in which they are found (tomb or dwelling) to infer the degree of interaction between the local population and Tiwanaku, and by extension, the nature of interaction (colony, client, or trade-partner). These object-oriented approaches that have characterized Tiwanaku archaeology fatally confuse archaeological context with cultural context (Stanish 1992).

In contrast to studies that focus on objects alone, any study adapting the "local perspective" must involve looking at the acceptance of objects in local historical context. Therefore, I am more interested in exploring how Tiwanaku-style items were incorporated into pre-Tiwanaku domestic patterns and activities at Lukurmata. Did Tiwanaku-style items replace other items in the domestic assemblage? Were Tiwanaku-style items used in "traditional" household activities, or did they represent new activities for Lukurmata households?

I will treat the presence of nonlocal objects in Lukurmata households as a general measure of the household's interaction (directly or indirectly) with other populations, including that of Tiwanaku. Analysis of the quantity and range of nonlocal items, the circumstances in which they appeared, and the way they were incorporated into household activities reveals the role of traditional domestic patterns in Lukurmata households and how households articulated with the Tiwanaku system.

A difficulty in studying intersite exchange is distinguishing between direct exchange with the capital and participation in a regional exchange system that the capital dominates. As of yet it is virtually impossible to determine whether Lukurmata residents acquired goods directly from Tiwanaku or participated in a Tiwanaku-dominated regional exchange system. Future research in the region will be necessary before archaeologists can understand the position Tiwanaku assumed in preexisting southern Andean exchange networks.

Political Incorporation and Surplus Production

Political economy refers to the means by which a polity supports the costs of regulation (Spencer 1982:7). The acquisition of revenue to meet such costs is usually treated as a typical, even necessary, feature of complex societies (Peebles and Black 1987; Spencer 1982, 1987; Steponaitis 1978; Tainter 1988).

In chiefdoms, the political establishment that derives support from commoner tribute may include the chief, retainers, and religious and craft specialists. Surplus is also needed to subsidize activities that aid in legitimating the chief's rule—construction of monumental architecture, acquisition of sumptuary goods, and displays of largesse (Lightfoot 1984; 1987:48; Steponaitis 1978:430). The amount of surplus needed may vary with, among other things, the degree of political complexity or amount of nonprimary producers that need to be supported. However, surplus production may be much less important in those societies in which differences in social rank are not accompanied by coercive economic power or marked differences in wealth.

States, with their larger and more complex political structure, should have correspondingly greater per-capita regulation costs or "administrative overhead" (Spencer 1982; Tainter 1988). Surplus is needed to support rulers, full-time craft specialists, officials, religious institutions, and often a military establishment (Tainter 1988). Again, however, states vary in their need to generate revenue and in the ways they do so.

A polity can pursue a variety of means to meet its costs of regulation. Goods can be exacted from conquered territories, and taxes can be levied on transactions or the movement of goods. However, the most common method is for the ruling stratum to acquire resources (as comestibles, craft-goods, or labor) from primary producing units (Sahlins 1972; Steponaitis 1978, 1981; Tainter 1988). "Surplus" can be generated from producing units in a number of ways. These vary in terms of their effect at the household level: *intrahousehold* strategies involve a transformation of household-level production, while *extrahousehold* strategies involve little or no change in previous household production patterns (Bermann n.d.).

Intrahousehold strategies operate within the sphere of domestic production and thus involve change in household-level productive patterns. Such strategies may involve intensifying household production (labor intensification), reorganizing household production to emphasize particular activities, or extracting the normal household stored "surplus" or replacement fund (Wolf 1966).

Extrahousehold strategies are typically organized at the suprahousehold level, and may only involve drawing periodically on the labor of household members. These strategies generally leave traditional patterns of domestic production unchanged (Hastorf 1990a:263).

The strategies outlined above may be enacted regularly or intermittently, and in various contexts (including ceremonial obligations, fictive-kin relationships, mortuary rites). The ruling stratum may choose to directly intercede in the household domain only in times of economic crisis. As Marshall Sahlins (1972:147) has noted, household economies have a "moral limit" beyond which it is dangerous for rulers to push. An intrahousehold strategy does not preclude extrahousehold strategies, and rulers may pursue a set of interrelated strategies to extract surplus from the same household.

In the works of Cathy Costin and Timothy Earle (1989) and Hastorf (1990a) we see examples of how the Inca state political economy affected household patterns. Hastorf (1990a) shows that Inca political economy, widely considered to consist of extrahousehold strategies of mobilization that left "the larder of the peasant . . . untouched" (Murra 1980:79), actually involved intrahousehold strategies that greatly affected Sausa domestic productive patterns, including increases in textile and maize production.

The Inca archaeological record indicates that this pattern was not limited to the Sausa population of the Mantaro Valley. In many regions, Inca conquest led to significant shifts in domestic patterns, intensified production, imposition of a mit'a labor system, introduction of new crops or agricultural techniques, a leveling of social statuses, even, as in the Sausa case, relocation of local populations to maximize agricultural output (Murra 1980). Archaeological surveys have suggested that incorporation into earlier prehispanic states such as the Moche and Wari entailed similar population and production shifts (Schreiber 1987).

However, in other cases incorporation into the Inca polity involved only the creation of ties and obligations at the highest level of decision making—between regional elites and Inca institutions. In these cases, Inca political economy had little effect on household-level patterns.

We lack comparable studies providing insight into the nature of the Tiwanaku political economy, or the strategies used by Tiwanaku rulers to acquire surplus production. The first steps in this direction are being taken by Alan Kolata and his students who have documented the existence of a highly integrated, centralized, regional system of intensified agricultural production in the Tiwanaku heartland to the south of Lake Titicaca (Albarracin-Jordan and Mathews 1990; Kolata 1991).

The Lukurmata household sequence is intended to investigate the effects at the household level of participation in the Tiwanaku system, and thus complement the formidable regional contributions made by Kolata et al. (Albarracin-Jordan and Mathews 1990; Kolata 1991).

If the Tiwanaku polity was the type of extractive system that other prehispanic Andean states seem to have been, we can predict that shifts in household production would have been likely to occur at four points in Lukurmata's history:

1. The moment when Lukurmata was incorporated politically into the Tiwanaku polity. Shifts in household productive patterns might provide a better measure of when Lukurmata's interaction with Tiwanaku came to involve political domination than changes in pottery-style preferences. I will treat the range and quantity of productive implements and facilities as the principal correlates of household production.

2. The fourth–fifth centuries A.D. (start of the Tiwanaku IV period), when the Tiwanaku polity seems to have undergone a great expansion, accompanied by an increase in the complexity of regional settlement. The evidence supporting such an evolution is presented in later chapters. Given the nature and scale of state-level societies, we would expect this increase in political complexity to be accompanied by a greater need for surplus by the Tiwanaku political structure, and the introduction of new forms of surplus production or mobilization.

3. In the ninth or tenth century A.D. (beginning of the Tiwanaku V period). Regional-level shifts in settlement and pottery-style distributions at this time suggest a "reorganization" of the Tiwanaku polity, perhaps one associated with further expansion.

4. In the twelfth or thirteenth century A.D., after the collapse of the Tiwanaku polity. Assuming that Lukurmata was not immediately incorporated into a similar overarching polity, the disappearance of the Tiwanaku political economy should have released Lukurmata households from surplus production obligations, leading to decreased household production.

It should be emphasized that changes in domestic productive patterns cannot always be attributed to the extraction of surplus by elites or centralized institutions. Whether primitive households will maintain "subsistence" or "for-use" production unless moved by exogenous factors has been the subject of considerable debate. Mechanisms do exist in many primitive and peasant societies to discourage "surplus" production. On the other hand, households may have their own reasons, including political ambitions, for altering productive patterns (Sahlins 1972). The *co-ocurrence* of changes in domestic production and the needs of a regional political formation should suggest some causal relationship between the household changes and regional-level processes.

Summary and Research Questions for Lukurmata

The approach to household remains taken in this volume differs from previous approaches not so much in the type of information utilized, but in how this information is interpreted. I provide a "view from the provincial household" of Tiwanaku state formation, expansion, and collapse, but I also, following from the "local perspective," use household data to understand incorporation into the Tiwanaku system as a phase in the evolution of the Lukurmata community. In short, the focus of this book is Lukurmata rather than the Tiwanaku state. In contrast to conventional "view from the household" approaches, the emphasis of my study is on the effects of Tiwanaku evolution on the Lukurmata household, not on using household data to examine the evolution of Tiwanaku.

In order to treat Lukurmata as a settlement with its own local evolution, history, and traditions, I collect information at the household level by "disarticulating" the Lukurmata archaeological household unit. The "local perspective" entails using household data to address a number of questions:

1. In what ways did household life at Lukurmata change?
2. Were any changes at the household level concurrent with changes at the community or regional level?
3. Do such changes indicate increases in household production?
4. What were the initial forms of interaction between Lukurmata and Tiwanaku, and how did the Lukurmata–Tiwanaku relationship change through time?
5. What does Lukurmata household evolution and Lukurmata–Tiwanaku interaction suggest about: (a) the stability and independence of Lukurmata households, and (b) the nature of the Tiwanaku polity as a political formation?

3

Lukurmata: Setting, Methodology, and Previous Research

The *altiplano* of the Lake Titicaca Basin is delimited by the Cordillera Occidental and Cordillera Real. It is a cold, windswept plateau ranging from 3500 m to over 4000 m above sea level in elevation and is subject to marked wet and dry seasons. The wet season (November–March) is characterized by daily rainfall and violent storms, as well as by occasional light snow, frost, and hailstorms. The dry season (April–October) is dusty and virtually without precipitation.

Visitors to the Bolivian altiplano, particularly during the dry season, are inevitably impressed by its bleakness and sparse vegetation. Its apparent desolation has long affected how its modern inhabitants, the Aymara Indians, are perceived. Aymara settlements seem to huddle defensively in the overwhelming, oppressive monotony of the landscape; the "notorious sullenness" and "emotional lability" of their inhabitants have been viewed as an outgrowth of their "precarious existence" in a "marginal landscape."[1] The "lot of the Aymara," noted Harry Tschopik (1951:172), "is a hard one," and the "hostile, inclement, physical environment of the *altiplano*" has made the Aymara a "tough (tension-productive)" culture.

This reaction to the altiplano has also shaped investigators' perceptions of the prehistory of the region. Nothing was more striking to early researchers than the location of the massive stone ruins of Tiwanaku in the center of this "marginal" environment, one seemingly incapable of supporting a major population center. This paradox structured early interpretations of the Tiwanaku site, and helped to produce theories ranging from cataclysmic prehistoric environmental and geological changes to explain Tiwanaku's "desert" setting, to the more recent view that Tiwanaku was a vacant ceremonial center.

Despite the supposed marginality of the environment, the Titicaca Basin actually has a vast biotic potential and has always supported a large indigenous population (Kolata 1982:13). The extensive altiplano political formations (from the early Pucara and Tiwanaku polities to the Lupaca and Colla kingdoms) reflect the altiplano's important place in prehispanic Andean cultural geography. The altiplano, particularly the northern area around Lake Titicaca, remains the center of population and agricultural production in Bolivia today (Kolata 1986:749).

LUKURMATA'S SETTING

Lukurmata is located on the northern edge of the Taraco Peninsula, a 30 km landform extending into the Lago Menor, the smaller portion of Lake Titicaca (Figure 3.1).

---

[1] The first two quotations are from La Barre 1948:51; the second two quotations are from Tschopik 1951:154.

Fig. 3.1 View north from the ridge excavation at Lukurmata, showing the edge of Lake Titicaca and a modern Aymara Indian house compound. Prehispanic dwellings at Lukurmata were nearly identical in construction materials and techniques.

Lukurmata is situated in the environmental zone that characterizes much of the Bolivian altiplano (bh-MST: bosque húmedo-Montaña sub-Trópical), but its climate is ameliorated by the nearby lake.[2] The natural vegetation of the zone is sparse and xerophytic; the most common plants are *ichu* grass (*Stipa ichu*) and small shrubs such as *kiswara* (*Polylepis racemosa*). The temperature in this zone typically ranges from 7° C (June–August) to 12° C (November–January), with an annual average of 9° C. As is typical of tropical systems, diurnal temperature variation, sometimes as much as 15° C, is greater than seasonal variation. During the dry season, the nocturnal temperature often drops below freezing. Lukurmata, benefiting from the lake warming effect, tends to stay slightly warmer and to exhibit less temperature variation. Annual rainfall, chiefly during the wet season, averages 697 ± 138 mm. Lukurmata, again because of the lake setting, receives slightly more. Agriculture is practiced today throughout the zone, but the semiarid soils near the lake are the most productive. In the annual cultivation cycle, planting begins with the arrival of the wet season in September and harvests take place from March to May.

To the northeast of Lukurmata is the Pampa Koani (Figure 3.2). This is a broad,

[2] This environmental zone (Biozone-bosque húmedo; Altitudinal floor-Montano; Latitudinal region-Subtropical) is described as among the most favorable in Bolivia for agriculture and raising livestock (Unzueta 1975:177).

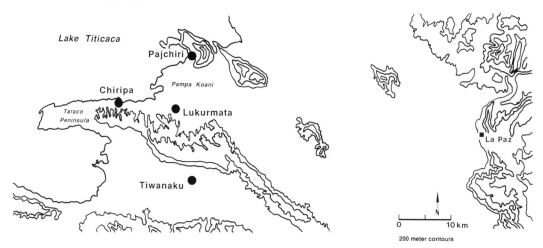

Fig. 3.2 The location of Lukurmata, nearby major archaeological sites, the Pampa Koani, and the Taraco Peninsula (adapted from Kolata 1986: Figure 2).

low-lying plain roughly 10 km wide, cut by the Río Catari. Excessive salinity and poor drainage (causing "water logging" of plant roots) have prevented modern agriculture in the Pampa, but fossil raised fields are clearly visible under the grass and scrub.[3] The low hills and rocky outcroppings of the Cumana Peninsula define the northern edge of the Pampa. To the south of Lukurmata are the Taraco Hills, a low mountain range of Tertiary origin that runs down the center of the Taraco Peninsula (Kolata and Ortloff 1989). Natural springs and seepages, modern houses, and agricultural fields dot the low northern face of this hill range. A ribbon of gently sloping grassland that gradually changes to marsh separates the Taraco Hills from the edge of the lake along the Taraco Peninsula. To the north and west of Lukurmata is Lake Titicaca.[4] In 1986 and 1987 the Lukurmata hill (known locally as *Wila Kollu*) was a peninsula-like form jutting into the reedy shallows of the lake. Several hundred meters from the shore the deeper water of the lake was relatively free of vegetation.

At the time of my fieldwork at Lukurmata, Lake Titicaca covered much of the Pampa Koani. The lake has receded considerably since 1987, and the Lukurmata hill now overlooks lowlying pampa. As of 1992 the edge of the lake was roughly 1 km to the west of Lukurmata.

The disastrous inundation of September 1985–April 1986 saw the lake rise nearly 3 m above its usual elevation of 3809 msl, destroying an estimated 11,000 ha of agricultural fields in the circum-lake area (Kolata 1989:235). Although Lukurmata itself was not flooded, neighboring settlements on the pampas to the north and east of Lukurmata

[3] "Local *campesino* informants explain that the pampas zone is 'only good for forage for cattle, pigs, sheep, and goats.' These informants (residents of the villages of Lakaya, Chokara, Quiripujo and Korila on the southern site of the Catari sub-basin near the archaeological site of Lukurmata) uniformly state that potatoes would 'never grow' in the pampas because the swampy conditions of this zone would cause plants to rot and to develop fungus" (Ortloff and Kolata 1989:3).

[4] As Ponce (1989:13) points out, the "official" maps produced by the IGM in 1965 from 1955 air photos mistakenly show the edge of Lake Titicaca 4 km west of Lukurmata. They also omit the Wila Kollu hill entirely—as Ponce says, an "*omisión en verdad censurable .*"

were submerged. The inundation drastically limited the availablity of fodder and pasturage for animals, and modern Lukurmata residents lost a considerable quantity of cattle and sheep.

The periodicity and magnitude of fluctuations in the level of Lake Titicaca remain poorly understood (Wirrmann 1987; Lennon 1982; Binford and Brenner 1989). Sedimentological studies suggest fluctuations ranging from +11 m to −50 m over the past 12,000 years. Recorded lake levels over the past century have ranged from a low of 3805 msl to a high of 3811.5 msl (Ponce 1989:284). During the time period of most concern to us (roughly 100 B.C.–A.D. 1400) the lake is thought to have been near the modern 3809 msl level. At this level, the lake does not extend much east of Lukurmata, and is separated from Lukurmata by seasonally wet marsh.

We do not yet know the extent of these fluctuations, or what role they may have played in Lukurmata prehistory. Clearly, however, fluctuations in the level of Lake Titicaca would have had dramatic effects on prehispanic settlement and agricultural production in the Pampa Koani.

Lukurmata is at the interface of several distinct resource zones to which the Lukurmata inhabitants would have had daily access: the altiplano plain and hills, the Pampa Koani, Lake Titicaca, and the marshy lake margin. Although we do not yet have the kind of detailed ecological data we need for each zone, the following sections will outline the known resources of each area.

Altiplano Plain and Hills

All of the land around Lukurmata, except for a small amount of steep terrain near the southern edge of the site, is suitable for cultivation. Prehispanic crops of the altiplano included: (a) tubers—potato (*Solanum tuberosum, S. andigenum*), *oca* (*Oxalis tuberosa*), *ullucu* (*Ullucus tuberosus*), *mashwa* (*Tropaeolum tuberosum*); (b) unique high-altitude grains—*quinoa* (*Chenopodium quinoa*), *cañiwa* (*C. pallidicaule*), *achita* (*Amaranthus caudatus*); and (c) beans—*frejol* (*Phaseolus vulgaris*), *jícama* (*Pachyrrhizus ahipa*), and *tarwi* (*Lupinus mutabilis*). Any of these could have been dry farmed at Lukurmata and in the hills south of the site. Although today some of this land is planted with crops introduced since the Spanish Conquest, the potato remains the most important agricultural product of the area.

In addition to the *ichu* grass, the vegetation around Lukurmata includes members of the Gramineae, Scropulariaceae, and Compositae families, "greasebush" (*Baccharis incarum* or *Lepidoplyllum quadrangulare*), various lichens, and *yareta*—a semi-subterranean woody plant sometimes used as fuel (La Barre 1948:18). The prehispanic distribution of trees in the area is not known, and most of today's trees were introduced.

Unfortunately, little is known about the prehispanic use of wild plants in the area, but there is no evidence that any of them constituted a large part of the diet. Browman (1981:412) cites *Opuntia* spp. as one of various cacti whose fruits were collected and eaten, although I did not see any in the Lukurmata environs. The natural vegetation of the area would have provided basketry material and thatch for roofs (*Stipa ichu*) and good pasturage for the domestic camelids, the llama (*Lama glama glama*) and alpaca (*Lama glama pacos*).

Fauna in the area around Lukurmata may have included guanaco (*Lama glama guanicoe*), Andean deer (*Hippocamelus antisiensis*), Andean fox (*Dusicyon culpaeus andinus*), vizcacha (*Lagidium peruvianum*), rabbit, small rodents (rats and mice), snakes (*Tachymenis peruviana*), and amphibians. The prehispanic distribution of these animals is not well known. Vizcacha are most commonly found today in the rocky outcroppings of the Taraco foothills south of the site, and this may have been the favored habitat of the deer and fox as well. Most of the avifauna around Lukurmata would have been lake, marsh, or shorebirds, but a number of other birds would have been found in the hills south of Lukurmata. The largest of these, and most likely to be used as food, were the ornate tinamou (*Nothoprocta ornata*), Darwin's nothura (*N. darwinii*), puna tinamou (*Tinamotis pentlandii*), and perhaps the lesser rhea (*Pterocnemia pennata*). The latter is thought to have been found near the lake prehispanically, but has since disappeared from the area. The current Lukurmata inhabitants capture birds with simple snares and projectiles (launched from rubber sling-shots), but used slings and *boleadores* in the past.

The Lake, Lake Margins, and Marsh

Most of the Lago Menor of Lake Titicaca is between 2 m and 8 m deep. The shallowest areas, including the shore margins, are covered with large fields of *totora* (an endemic *Scripus* sp.), reeds (*Juncus* sp.), thick growths of algae, and other submerged vascular plants. These lake shallows and marshy areas constituted an important concentration of potential resources (Horn 1984). In addition to providing plants that could be used for building, craft-goods, food, and fodder, they provided an important habitat for aquatic avifauna (ibid.).

The totora is best known as the material used for constructing the famous Lake Titicaca native reed boats or *balsas*. Like other reeds, it would also have been valuable for roofing houses and basketry. The totora and several of the other lakeside and marsh plants may also have been major food sources. The tender pith and roots of the totora are edible and eaten today as a delicacy (Browman 1981:412). An important edible aquatic vascular plant is the versatile green "*lima*," usually identified as *Lemnaceae* sp. This plant can also be used to roof houses or make clothing, and is excellent animal fodder (Gundermann K. 1984). It is treated as a "starvation food" by today's Lukurmata residents, who normally collect it in large quantities to feed cattle (Figure 3.3). Other edible vascular water "weeds" include the protein rich *Azolla* sp., *Elodea* sp., and *Potamogeton* sp. Browman (1981:412) has identified various algae (*Chara, Nostoc, Cladophora*) as food resources, noting that dried bricks of these water plants are still collected and traded inland.

Large numbers of birds are attracted to the aquatic insects and other fauna along the lake margin; the reedy marshes provide nesting sites for many species. These include ducks, geese, gulls, coots, grebes, herons, ibises, and flamingos. Various North American gulls and small shorebirds winter in the wet areas, such as Franklin's gull (*Larus pipixcan*). Two South American shorebirds common in the fields near the lake are the Andean lapwing (*Vanellus resplendens*) and the tawny-throated dotterel (*Eureopholus rufficollis*).

At the time of the Spanish Conquest, Lake Titicaca contained only two types of fish—a small killifish of the genus *Orestias* and the siluoid genus *Trichomycterus*

Fig. 3.3 Modern fishing boats at Lukurmata. To the left of the first boat is a load of *lima*. Vascular plants from the lake margin were probably an important resource for prehispanic populations as well.

(Villwock 1986). However, in an impressive display of adaptive radiation, the former speciated into more than forty species (Parenti 1984). One of the largest of the genus was the now-extinct *O. cuvieri*, which reached lengths of 23 cm. Most of the *Orestias* are much smaller, ranging from 3 cm to 12 cm in length as adults. Limited field surveys and gut content analysis of specimens have provided a small quantity of information on the distribution, ecology, and feeding habits of particular classes of *Orestias*. The largest of the *Orestias* (including *O. pentlandii* and *O. cuvieri*) are "swarm fish," forming small shoals that are found pelagically in the open water, feeding at the surface on mosquito larvae and zooplankton (Villwock 1986:393). These species are often caught with drag nets or fixed submerged nets, but at certain times during the day and night they can be netted from the surface with cast or dip nets. A second "species flock" (some fifteen species) includes small plant feeders most common in the submerged vegetation of the shallows, and larger specimens (such as *O. agasii*) that live just beyond the totora belt in slightly deeper water. The species of this flock are preferred by modern Lukurmata inhabitants. Today, a score or so can easily be caught within an hour by standing on shore using a dip net, which, in older times was made from llama wool. An Aymara technique described by Tschopik (1946) and still used in places today is "fence" fishing. This entails building a 20 m long screen of totora reeds extending from the totora beds into deeper water. Fish are channeled to the open-water end of the screen where the fisherman waits with a dip net. Hooks are not used today by the Aymara, and have not been reported from lake-side archaeological sites.

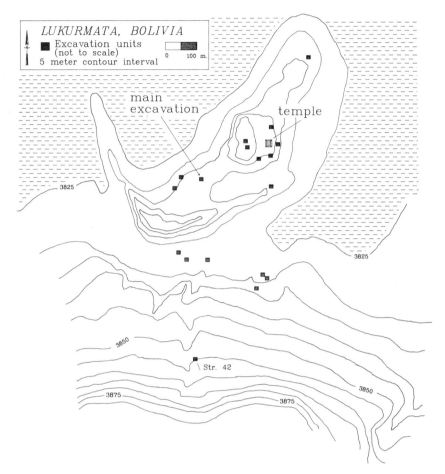

Fig. 3.4 Topographic map of Lukurmata showing position of 1986–87 excavation units and the location of the main excavation on the ridge west of the temple hill. Dashed area to the north marks low-lying pampa subject to periodic inundation. This area was underwater during 1986–87 (adapted from Ponce 1989: Figures 16 and 17).

TOPOGRAPHY OF THE LUKURMATA SITE

The site of Lukurmata lies under the modern community of Lukurmata, on the northern edge of the Taraco Peninsula. The site can be divided on a topographic basis into three parts: northern, central, and southern (Figure 3.4). The northern part of the site is an elevated area or "acropolis escarpment." This consists of the temple hill (Wila Kollu) and associated ridges. The top of the flat temple hill is at 3838 m above sea level, a modest 28 m above the level of the lake (Ponce 1989:12). The hill measures roughly 830 m × 600 m, with steep western and southern sides and gentle eastern and northern faces (ibid.). A low ridge extending west from the hilltop overlooks the lake. Most of the structures I will discuss were excavated in the "main excavation" on this

Fig. 3.5 The ridge west of the temple hill as seen from the hilltop. The arrow marks the location of the main excavation in a modern agricultural field.

ridge (Figure 3.5). South of this ridge is a swale, and beyond that is a second, crescent-shaped ridge with rocky outcroppings. This second ridge completely encloses the elevated area of the site, and extends as a spur into Lake Titicaca to the west of the temple hilltop.

The second part of the site—the central section—is a 200–400 m wide expanse of low-lying grassland south of the crescent ridge and the elevated areas described above. The modern La Paz–Taraco road runs through this gently sloping area. The third, or southern, part of the site is a hillslope that rises to over 3900 m above sea level. This slope is the northern flank of the Taraco Hills that run the length of the Taraco Peninsula.

HOUSEHOLD ARCHAEOLOGY IN HIGHLAND BOLIVIA AND PREVIOUS RESEARCH AT LUKURMATA

Until very recently, there has been little investigation of prehispanic domestic life in the altiplano, particularly in the Tiwanaku region. The early archaeologists working in the area (including Adolph Bandelier and Wendell Bennett) occasionally uncovered domestic remains. However, they did not do so by design, and they devoted less attention to domestic remains than to monumental architecture or pottery decoration.

Chiripa

Some of the first structures to be described as "dwellings" were excavated by Bennett at the Formative site of Chiripa, on the Taraco Peninsula, roughly 12.5 km to the west of Lukurmata (Figure 3.2). The site of Chiripa consists of a mound enclosed on three sides by a retaining wall erected around 850 B.C. The earliest structures at the site, which are semi-subterranean in nature, date to the Llusco phase (850 B.C.–600 B.C.).

More is known of the sixteen Classic phase (600 B.C.–100 B.C.) "houses" found ranged around the sunken temple in the center of the mound (Bennett 1936; Kidder 1956; Ponce 1970). These structures, measuring 6 m × 5 m, are distinctive for their sliding door entrance and double wall construction creating an interior storage space reached through internal niches (Bennett 1936; Kidder 1956; Ponce 1970). The walls and floors of these structures may have been covered with plaster and decorated with yellow paint (Ponce 1970). Although described as "single-family" dwellings, or "residences," these were probably specialized structures associated with temple activities. Their prominent location, storage capabilities, and lack of internal features, including hearths, all suggest a nondomestic function. The initial, Structure 1, occupation at Lukurmata may have been contemporaneous with the Mamani (Classic or Chiripa II) phase of Chiripa development thought to have ended around 100 B.C. (Browman 1980; Chávez 1988). The "houses" at Chiripa bear little resemblance, in layout or construction techniques, to Lukurmata's prehispanic structures.

Wankarani

The "Wankarani Culture" is the term used to characterize Formative period (2000 B.C.–A.D. 500) sites found to the south near Lake Poopó, in what is now the southern portion of the Department of La Paz and the Department of Oruro (Ponce 1970; Wasson 1967). Wankarani sites commonly appear as mounds, each formed of the remains of fifteen to five hundred houses and a thick accumulation of occupational refuse. Wankarani communities consisted of a cluster of circular stone and adobe houses, 3–5 m in diameter, with interior hearths and thatched roofs (Walter 1966; Wasson 1967). Wankarani structures bear little similarity to any of the pre-Tiwanaku period dwellings I found at Lukurmata.

Previous Investigation at Lukurmata

Until recently, investigation at Tiwanaku sites was limited exclusively to public architecture and mortuary contexts. Prior to the work of the *Proyecto Wila-Jawira* in the mid-1980s, domestic remains at sites affiliated with Tiwanaku were only accidentally exposed by archaeologists. Such was the case at Lukurmata.

The presence of a sunken temple caused Lukurmata to be recognized as an archaeological site before the turn of the century by Max Uhle (Ponce 1989:32; Uhle 1912). The first digging at the site was done by amateur archaeologist Ambrose Viganó Morante, who excavated a series of pits in and around the temple (Bennett 1936:469; Ponce 1989:81–83).

The first systematic archaeological work at Lukurmata was conducted in 1934 by Wendell Bennett of the American Museum of Natural History. Bennett's approach was the antithesis of the "local perspective." During the era of regional study and chronology building in which he worked, residential areas were of interest chiefly for their potential to provide the specimens needed to construct ceramic sequences. This orientation explains why Bennett's excavation strategy focused on Lukurmata's public architecture. In addition to the temple at Lukurmata, Bennett placed several excavation pits areas north of the temple, in the low-lying area near the burial platform and in the swale immediately south of the temple (his Section K).

Domestic remains were exposed in one of the three pits made in Section K, and Bennett offered a brief account of a two-room structure, with wall foundations of "rough and dressed stone" and a large quantity of ash and ceramics on the floor (1936:491).[5] The use of cut stones, probably robbed from the temple complex, may date this house to the Tiwanaku V or post-Tiwanaku period. Bennett (ibid.:492) went on to conclude that two chronological periods—Classic and Decadent Tiwanaku— were represented at Lukurmata, although there was no "indication of good stratigraphy which might show different periods of occupation."

The next archaeologist to work at Lukurmata (in the late 1960s and early 1970s) was the Bolivian *Instituto Nacional de Arqueología* archaeologist Gregorio Cordero Miranda, who also excavated several test pits. These test pits are believed to have been located on the ridge west of the temple hill, the site of my main excavation. I was informed by the *maestros* who worked with Cordero that they discovered house remains in these excavations, but Cordero's notes have yet to be published.

As a result, Bennett's description of the house remains at Lukurmata (see note 5) constituted all that was known of "Tiwanaku" household life until 1986! At that time, Kolata's *Proyecto Wila-Jawira* began systematic investigation of domestic contexts at Tiwanaku and Tiwanaku-affiliated sites.

[5] Bennett excavated three pits totaling over 10 m² in Section K, the depression or "saddle dip" south of the ruins I describe as a "swale." It is not known exactly where Bennett's excavations were located, but his discovery of house remains in Section K led me to place my N 2859 E 3110 excavation (see Chapter 13) in the same area in 1986. Bennett's (1936:491) description of "Pit Ka" is (in its entirety):

> At the eastern end of the dip, southeast of the ruins, a pit 5.00 meters square revealed a house floor at 1.40 meters depth with stone side wall. The walls are of rough and dressed stone and are about 30 centimeters wide and high. They probably represent the base of adobe walls. One room about 3.00 by 1.90 meters is indicated, with a small side room, 1.45 by 1.20 meters (all inside measurements). Ash and pottery in considerable quantity were found on the floor. The cut stones were probably taken from the ruins, as they are not well enough placed to suggest special cutting.

Bennett's (n.d.) field notes show that he originally excavated this pit as "Section L." His notes for that section state: "Foundation walls of house 30 cm high and 20 wide. See drawing. Much pottery." The drawing is now missing from the American Museum of Natural History archives. A short breakdown of the undecorated pottery is preserved in his notes, showing that he was attempting to classify vessel types based on handle, rim, and base characteristics. The use of cut stones probably robbed from the temple complex may date the house to the Tiwanaku V or post-Tiwanaku period.

Bennett also made several pits in an area of "lake flats still used for agriculture" in "the vicinity of the plantation house" (Section L). This was in the grassy low-lying area of the site that separates the acropolis escarpment from the Taraco Hills. His pits were probably very near to the modern school compound, "just north of the automobile road from Lacaya to Taraco" (1936:492). He reported that these two pits (one measuring 4 m × 2 m, the other 3 m × 1.5 m) reached "yellow clay" at 1.5 m depth and yielded a "tremendous quantity" of pottery fragments, many from "good quality Tiahuanaco" vessels. Although he wrote (ibid.) that "no remains of houses or temple sites were revealed," he may have unknowingly exposed part of the burial platform I describe in Chapter 12 (Janusek and Earnest 1988). Three additional pits were made south of the road, with "no results."

METHODOLOGY

My research at Lukurmata had the broad aim of providing household-level data to complement the information gathered by *Proyecto Wila-Jawira* excavations at other sites (including Tiwanaku) and regional survey of the Pampa Koani and Tiwanaku Valley. In order to achieve this, I set two goals. The first goal was to trace the evolution of domestic life over the longest period of time possible. This required excavation of a sequence of houses from a single sector of the site. I felt that comparison of houses from the same part of the site would minimize those differences in household organization that might reflect contemporaneous differences in status or household specialization, providing a clearer picture of household change through time.

My second goal was to place the household sequence at Lukurmata in a larger context by obtaining some knowledge of the evolution of the site as a whole. Ideally, I would have made comparable excavations in as many portions of the site as possible, but time and financial constraints ruled this out. Instead, a systematic surface collection was conducted, and smaller excavations were made at various places in the site to test the type and extent of cultural deposits.

Surface Collection

To collect information on intrasite variation and determine the extent of the settlement, a systematic, aligned surface collection was done during the 1986 season . The collection was also designed to provide information on the density and types of artifacts on the surface. The first step was imposing a grid oriented to the cardinal directions on the site. The 2 m × 2 m collection units were aligned along the grid and separated by 50 m intervals. All artifacts (or suspected artifacts) in each unit were collected. This was a relatively simple sampling design, but because of erosion and modern occupation (particularly plowing), more sophisticated surface programs would not have been more effective. The systematic surface collection was supplemented during the 1987 season by judgmentally placed 2 m × 2 m collection units. These grew out of specific concerns about intrasite variation and discard/taphonomic issues.

Overall, the surface collection strategy fulfilled its limited goals. The 2 m × 2 m collection units generally proved to be representative of the larger 50 m × 50 m areas, providing a useful measure of surface artifact density (Stanish 1989b:48). At a different level—as a "predictor" of subsurface remains—the surface collection was less valuable. Some of the areas where the artifact density was highest were shown by excavation to have had intensive residential occupations. Other areas of high density simply marked rainy season run-off catchments. The surface collection material alone, whether considering gross artifact density or the types and range of surface artifacts, was not predictive of buried house remains.

Not unexpectedly, the surface collection at Lukurmata revealed very little about the early occupation at the site. We prematurely identified as "Chiripa" pottery those fragments of fiber tempered pottery found on the surface. Only after excavation and analysis did we learn that a great deal of the Tiwanaku period plainware pottery used at Lukurmata was fiber tempered. After excavation, a reexamination of the surface collection sherds revealed that what had originally been called "Chiripa" pottery were sherds from later Tiwanaku period utilitarian vessels. In fact, high densities of fiber tempered ceramics were a fairly good indicator of a buried Tiwanaku residential occupation, telling us more about intrasite variation than site chronology. Ironically, an early occupation (perhaps even as old as Chiripa) was found nearly 3 m below ground level, but none of the materials from this occupation appeared on the surface.

Excavation Strategy

The excavations were designed to furnish information on changes over time in household activities, the spatial organization of residential units, and intrasite variation in domestic artifacts and features. To achieve these ends, emphasis was placed on careful stratigraphic techniques to maintain context, to allow assessment of types of deposition, and to discover the diachronic relationships between remains.

Excavations were done in 2 m × 2 m units using natural and arbitrary levels. When thicker than 10 cm, a natural level was divided into arbitrary levels, each no thicker than 10 cm. Most fill was dry screened through one-quarter-inch screen, but deposits likely to contain organic remains were put through a fine-screening procedure, and appropriate samples were taken. Plan views and cross-sections were made of all features, and soil samples were taken from each feature for later dry screening or flotation. When features displayed stratigraphy, a soil sample was taken from each stratum. The volume of most features was calculated by measuring the fill removed. To recover fish bones and other very small items soil samples were systematically taken from general fill levels. Because fish bone and chipped stone debitage were almost impossible to recover from the clayey soil without fine screening, we should assume that they are consistently underrepresented in nonfeature contexts.

A three-dimensional coordinate system allowed the precise recording of artifact locations and associations. Elevations were taken with line-levels from datum points scattered around the edge of the excavation. Using a theodolite, the elevation of each datum point was tied into one of the site's master data, set in cement. However, the elevations I will use here have been adjusted to the datum point on the ridge that I used most during excavation.

Excavation unit designations were based on the site grid. Each unit designation was taken from the southwest corner of the unit, and consisted of a four-digit "north" number followed by a four-digit "east" number (e.g., N2892 E2925). The 2 m × 2 m excavation units were usually excavated as individual operations with their own feature and level numbering systems. However, when I encountered obvious natural or cultural features (such as distinct deposits or housefloors) that continued into other units, I made an attempt to standardize the number of that level across the entire excavation.

DOMESTIC ARCHITECTURE AT LUKURMATA

Domestic structures at Lukurmata displayed similar construction materials and techniques over a period of 1500 years. The initial stage of construction of most houses was the pouring of a 5–10 cm thick layer of clean, orange clay on a flat area. Once this prepared surface had hardened, walls were built on top of it. The resultant floor "apron," and subsequent erosion, resulted in the characteristic irregular shape of Lukurmata housefloors.

Walls consisted of mud brick or cut sod set on a footing of unmodified fieldstones.

Fig. 3.6 A modern mud brick house decaying roughly fifteen years after abandonment. Prehispanic houses at Lukurmata would have decayed in a similar way, covering the housefloor with "wall melt."

Often sections of the footing were all that were left of the walls. But in many cases, it was possible to determine the shape of the house by examining linear deposits along the edge of the floor or the "shadow walls" left in the fill and wall melt by unpreserved walls. The roofs of Lukurmata structures were probably very similar to those of the modern Aymara structures shown in Figure 3.1. House roofs at Lukurmata today are composed of bundles of thatch or reed supported on a framework of light poles, and have a gable or hip form.

Structures of these type are capable of lasting fifty years or more. My study of vacant modern structures at Lukurmata showed that, once abandoned, adobe houses collapse into a heap of wall melt within ten years, and within fifty years exist only as a low mound 20 cm to 30 cm high (Figure 3.6).

HOUSEFLOOR CONTEXTS

It is difficult to distinguish primary refuse dropped during the occupation of a house from materials deposited during abandonment or postabandonment activities. One approach to this dilemma is to carefully examine floor associations. Accordingly, "floor provenience" has been defined in various way by archaeologists (Kent 1987; Parry 1987).[6] I treat as floor artifacts *only* those objects found resting directly on (not simply touching) or impressed into the floor.

[6] Some excavators of sand or earth housefloors have treated as floor artifacts only those found lying within the floor, below the final occupational surface. However, the hard clay floors of the prehispanic Lukurmata dwellings prevented many items from becoming incorporated into the floor material. Other researchers have treated as floor artifacts those items lying directly on the floor, or within a certain distance of the floor, or between the floor and roof or wall collapse (Parry 1987; Spencer 1981).

Not all of the artifacts found lying directly on housefloors were the result of household activities. Items on the floor may have been the result of abandonment activities (the smashing of unwanted pottery vessels, for instance) or may have been dumped as refuse on the floor before aeolian deposits could form. Thus, carefully distinguishing floor associations alone is insufficient to determine which items accumulated during the occupation of a house. A number of investigators have attempted to differentiate occupational and nonoccupational deposition by examining the characteristics of the artifacts themselves and their spatial arrangement. Primary refuse should exhibit discrete activity areas or spatial distributions constrained by architectural features or activity areas. This is less likely in redeposited materials where spatial distributions result from the "vagaries of dumping" (Parry 1987:7). Second, primary refuse should consist of smaller items since cleaning is more likely to remove the larger ones. Correspondingly, artifacts should be larger in refuse or midden contexts (ibid.). Third, if artifacts are part of household activities and are primary deposits, then conjoining should be common. Conjoining should be less common in midden or refuse contexts because artifacts become broken and separated (ibid.).

It cannot be assumed that artifacts lying on floors are always associated with the primary occupation or use of the structure. This is particularly true in public architecture or elite residences where postabandonment occupations by squatters could leave floor debris. However, it is unlikely that this immediate reoccupation represented a problem with the nonelite, and not particularly long-lived Lukurmata residences I excavated. In fact, we found no evidence of squatters or secondary occupations of this sort.

We should also remember that if not all floor artifacts represent household activities, not all activities carried out in a house will be represented by floor artifacts (preservation aside). Some house contents may have been removed at abandonment. Such items at Lukurmata may have included large grinding stones (*metates*) as well as wooden poles or posts (given the paucity of wood on the altiplano).

By and large, the types of artifacts found on Lukurmata housefloors were those likely to be overlooked during cleaning. They were kicked into corners, or discarded and left when the house was abandoned. These materials do not provide equal representation of the activities that produced them, which is why I have refrained from certain quantified approaches when comparing house occupations or contents. Some artifacts by their nature are more likely to be missed in cleaning or trampled into housefloors. Many generalizations that cover these situations can be proposed: sharp objects are more likely to be moved from the floor than dull-edged objects; difficult to replace items are less likely to be thrown away than easily replaceable ones; the discard rate of an object is in inverse relation to its manufacture time. These concerns are most useful as cautionary tales to the household archaeologist who investigates contexts in which formation processes are highly complex.[7]

I have also largely refrained from analyzing the spatial patterning of artifacts on the

[7] During excavation and analysis I attempted carefully to distinguish primary from redeposition contexts. Additionally, when discussing in the text the relative quantity of a particular item (e.g., "more projectile points"), this represents a relative quantity based on the number of the item divided by 100 sherds or the total diagnostics. I also experimented with looking at the relative weights instead of counts, of classes of artifacts, size of artifacts, etc. Where relevant, these methods are discussed in the text.

Lukurmata housefloors. Archaeologists once enthusiastically plotted the position of artifacts on living floors in order to reconstruct toolkits, activity areas, and the use of the living floors. This technique has yielded significant insights in some cases (Flannery 1986), but a host of recent studies has raised significant questions about the general utility of such approaches to floor artifacts. These studies have demonstrated the extent to which the spatial distribution of debris on living floors may reflect modes of artifact discard, differential artifact weight, and a range of noncultural factors (Binford 1978, 1983; Kent 1987; Thomas 1983).

THE CERAMIC SEQUENCE AND TIWANAKU PERIODS

The Tiwanaku-style pottery in the Lukurmata excavations allowed us to correlate our levels with the broad, regional Tiwanaku chronological framework. Contemporaneity among deposits was established through stratigraphic associations (between adjoining excavation units), and less frequently through seriation or ceramic associations (separated excavation areas).

One of the necessary aims of the excavation was refining the Tiwanaku ceramic sequence. Bennett (1934), who completed the first systematic excavations at Tiwanaku, divided Tiwanaku prehistory into three periods: Early, Classic, and Decadent. Unlike previous investigators, Bennett had the advantage of stratigraphy in formulating his rough sequence. Nonetheless, as his period designations imply, he had difficulty distinguishing between Tiwanaku ceramics of different times, and ultimately resorted to assumptions about the degradation of art styles to differentiate later Tiwanaku pottery (Goldstein 1985:6).

Bennett's sequence has formed the basis for all subsequent chronologies (Ponce 1947; Rydén 1947), although his original periods have been renamed. The current

Table 3.1 Tiwanaku Chronological Periods

Period Designation Used in This Study	Alternative Designations
Post-Tiwanaku	
A.D. 1200 - - - - - - - -	
Tiwanaku V	Decadent, Expansive, *Estadio Imperial*
A.D. 800 - - - - - - - -	
Tiwanaku IV	Classic, *Estadio Urbano Maduro*
A.D. 400 - - - - - - - -	
Tiwanaku III	Qeya, Early, *Estadio Urbano Temprano*
200 B.C. - - - - - - - -	
Tiwanaku I	Kalasasaya, *Estadio Aldeano*

Tiwanaku sequence of five numbered periods (Tiwanaku I–V) is shown in Table 3.1. This sequence was proposed by Carlos Ponce in 1961 (Disselhoff 1968), and is based on both stylistic seriation and stratigraphic excavations at Tiwanaku in the 1950s. The "Tiwanaku II period" has yet to be well defined, and will not be used here. The absolute dating of each period is based on a series of radiocarbon dates presented by Ponce (1981a). Table 3.1 gives generally accepted dates for each period, as well as alternative designations.

The 1986 field season revealed that it would not be necessary to start from scratch in constructing a local sequence for Lukurmata pottery. The Bennett–Ponce sequence was stratigraphically accurate (i.e., Tiwanaku III-style materials were found below Tiwanaku IV-style materials) and suitable for cross-dating Lukurmata's cultural deposits. But excavation of domestic contexts promised to provide a great deal of undecorated, utilitarian pottery, and unfortunately, virtually no work has been done on Tiwanaku plainwares. The traditional Tiwanaku ceramic chronology was formulated with *decorated* pottery. Reluctantly—for I do not want to imply that Lukurmata pottery styles were restricted to Lukurmata—I have gone ahead and named characteristic ceramic forms. These should someday be renamed when their regional distributions are better understood.

In this study I will treat the designated Tiwanaku periods simply as chronological units. That is, a Tiwanaku IV period house is a house dating to the A.D. 400–A.D. 800 period. When I refer specifically to decorative style, I show this by appending the word "style" (e.g., "Tiwanaku IV-style jars"). Some of the pottery recovered from Tiwanaku IV period occupations at Lukurmata would be classified as "Tiwanaku V-style" in the Bennett–Ponce scheme. To keep things simple, I have chosen to refer to these ceramics as "Tiwanaku IV-style" pottery, but note in the text that they might be considered otherwise in the Bennett–Ponce classification.

DATING THE LUKURMATA OCCUPATIONS

A handful of radiocarbon dates and the Tiwanaku decorated ceramic chronology provide information for roughly dating the housefloors in the Lukurmata sequence. Material from the main ridgetop excavation provided five radiocarbon dates (Appendix III). Of these, one date (SMU 2164) can be discounted. The four remaining dates are reasonable in the context of their ceramic associations.

The Lukurmata occupations were also roughly "dated" by cross-reference to the Tiwanaku ceramic sequence, but this proved problematic. For instance, we might consider the appearance of Tiwanaku III-style materials at Lukurmata to coincide with the beginning of the general Tiwanaku IV period (200 B.C.–A.D. 400), defined by the emergence of Tiwanaku III-style iconography at Tiwanaku. But one of the earliest occupations in the Lukurmata sequence to have Tiwanaku III-style ceramics is the Structure 16 occupation, and a radiocarbon sample from this occupation gives a calibrated date of A.D. 430 ± 80. And four distinct occupations above this one also display Tiwanaku III-style pottery, suggesting that occupants used Tiwanaku III-style pottery well into the fifth century A.D., if not later. While it would be a mistake to revise the Bennett–Ponce sequence on the basis of a handful of radiocarbon dates, the Lukurmata evidence suggests that the stylistic divisions in the sequence may not be as diachronic as is often assumed.[8]

Because of the problems outlined above, I have refrained from giving all but the most general (e.g., ninth century A.D.) dates to the various housefloors. To arrive at these, I weighed the radiocarbon dates, the pottery styles represented, and the general amount of fill separating the occupation from occupations above and below it. All dates should be considered highly tentative. The Lukurmata housefloor sequence will have to stand as a self-contained "time-line" only loosely tied to regional chronologies until the Bennett–Ponce sequence can be refined or more absolute dates from Lukurmata are available.

---

[8] The chronological position of the occupations relative to one another was self-evident because the housefloors were superimposed. But while the occupations are arranged in a temporal sequence, it is much more difficult to determine the number of years separating the successive occupations. The radiocarbon dates are not particularly helpful in this regard. The earliest, with a calibrated date of 20 ± 80 B.C., is associated with the earliest occupation in the sequence. The latest, with a calibrated date of A.D. 840 ± 115, is associated with the Structure 33–39 occupation. Some 2.4 m of fill separate these two occupations, so if we assumed uniform deposition, we might expect that each century saw roughly 0.3 m of fill accumulate. However, we cannot assume a uniform rate of deposition, and the additional radiocarbon dates and ceramic associations strongly suggest that deposition was far from uniform. The entire Tiwanaku IV period occupation, for instance, presumably spanning four hundred years (A.D. 400–A.D. 800), is limited to less than 0.5 m of fill.

4

Lukurmata's Earliest Occupation

The earliest occupation at Lukurmata was found just above sterile soil, at a depth of 275 cm below datum. We excavated 48 contiguous m^2 at this level, exposing the remains of a single structure and an associated outdoor activity area with several features (Figure 4.1). Basing our estimate on stratigraphy and ceramic cross-references, a date of 200 B.C.–A.D. 50 can be suggested for the occupation. A single sample of charcoal from one of the features gave a corrected age of 2000 ± 60 B.P. (calibrated date: 20 ± 80 B.C.).

SITE COMPOSITION

Test pits were extended to sterile soil in nineteen locations at Lukurmata during the 1986 and 1987 seasons. Deposits with pre-Tiwanaku materials were found *only* in the main excavation on the ridge, suggesting that the ridge is the oldest residential area of the site. The Lukurmata population at this time was probably very small, consisting of scattered homesteads.

DOMESTIC ARCHITECTURE

The floor of Structure 1 consisted of a thin layer of stained, compacted soil, measuring roughly 4 m × 3.5 m. A section of the western portion of the floor had been paved with smooth cobbles. The southeast edge of the floor surface had been destroyed by intrusive burials. A double row of rough fieldstones along the northern and eastern edges of the floor may represent a wall foundation for mud brick or cut sod walls. However, because no wall melt was found on or above the floor, we do not know the composition of the walls; the structure could have been made of cane or brush. There were no internal features (hearths, storage pits, or even postholes). A short line of stones extending northeast from the floor may have been the foundation for a wall outside the structure.

It did not appear that the structure had been used very intensively or occupied for a long period of time. There was virtually no refuse on the floor, nor signs that the floor had been resurfaced.

DOMESTIC ACTIVITIES

North of Structure 1 was a hard-packed, sandy, outdoor surface measuring roughly 20 m^2. Four outdoor features were found in the surface: (1) a hearth, consisting of a shallow, conical pit filled with ash, fragments of burned bone, burned llama dung, and

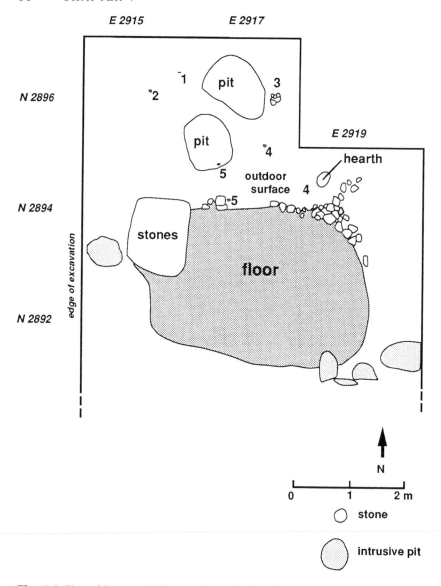

Fig. 4.1 Plan of Structure 1 floor and associated outdoor surface with selected artifacts plotted. *Key:* (1) worked camelid bone, (2) cone, (3) pottery fragment, (4) Thin Redware bowl fragment, (5) polished bone tube.

chunks of charcoal; (2) two large, shallow refuse pits containing charcoal and ash, bone fragments, ceramics, fire-cracked rock, and stone flakes; and (3) a small pit, located to the northwest, filled with charcoal. A sample of this was used for the radio-carbon date. Based on ethnographic analogy, it is probable that the residents conducted most activities outdoors; the house itself may have simply been a place in which to sleep (Horn 1984).

Items of worked bone were found both inside and outside the structure. We recovered several tubular beads made from small fragments of camelid bone. A large llama

Fig. 4.2 Stone cones of unknown function were associated with most of the Lukurmata domestic occupations. The specimens shown here are from the fill context above Structure 1.

rib smoothed along the edge had been used as a scraper. A section of antler tine probably served as a pressure flaker in chipped stone tool manufacture.

Flakes of chipped stone were scattered across the outdoor surface, together with a small stone scraper, several smoothed river cobbles with signs of pecking, and small pieces of debitage (chips and angular fragments).

A large stone "cone" (7.4 cm high and 5.85 cm wide at the base) was found lying on the outdoor surface northwest of the refuse pits (Figure 4.2). A large number of these enigmatic objects were found at Lukurmata, and identical specimens have been reported from both Tiwanaku and Tiwanaku regional sites such as Khonko Wankani, Pajchiri, and Omo. The function of these cones is unknown.

The faunal remains indicate a generalized meat diet of camelid/deer, lake fauna, and guinea pig or rabbit.[1] Excluding fish remains, roughly 86 percent of the animal bones of this occupation were from camelids, and roughly 13 percent from birds.

Nearly all the fish bones are from the genus *Orestias*, although we did find a single large vertebra, possibly representing the *Silurian* lake fish. Fish consumption is difficult to quantify. Even though some fish bones were found in nearly all deposits at Lukurmata, ethnoarchaeological research suggests that fish consumption will be grossly underrepresented in altiplano archaeological contexts (Horn 1984). Time con-

---

[1] In analyzing the faunal remains I did not distinguish between camelid and deer. However, for the sake of convenience I refer to all camelid/deer remains as "camelid," because llama/alpaca bones clearly constitute the majority of the faunal remains.

straints ruled out the type of extensive fine screening that systematic recovery of fish bones requires, and screening small soil samples did not provide a useful measure of fish exploitation. Ethnographic analogy, the general ubiquity of fish remains, and Lukurmata's proximity to Lake Titicaca, all strongly suggest that fish were an important part of the diet during the Structure 1 occupation.

No agricultural or grinding implements were found with this occupation, but the occupants would have had access to a variety of altiplano tubers and grains, as well as wild resources including cactus fruits, rhizomes, and reeds from the lake (Browman 1981). Soil samples from several deposits associated with the Structure 1 occupation were floated to recover macrobotanical remains. The identified remains reflect plants common to lakeshore vegetative communities: wild grasses, chenopods, and members of the sedge, mallow, and mustard families. No remains from domesticated plants were found in these samples (Hastorf, personal communication).

A clay figurine (Figure 4.3) was found on an isolated patch of occupational surface roughly 5 m south of the structure. This occupational surface cannot be directly associated with the Structure 1 occupation, although it appears to be stratigraphically contemporaneous. Small clay figurines are frequent components of early Bolivian sites in the region southeast of the lake, and appear to have been a widespread feature of pre-Tiwanaku period ritual at the household level (Bermann 1990). However, no figurines have been reported from Tiwanaku or Bolivian lakeside sites.

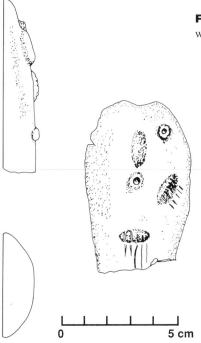

Fig. 4.3 Clay figurine associated with Structure 1.

0   5 cm

Fig. 4.4 Local Tradition pottery. Vessels of this type made up the bulk of the Lukurmata domestic pottery assemblage for centuries. The two most common Local Tradition forms: (a) Lorokea Fiber olla, (b) Lorokea Fiber annular-base bowl.

Household Pottery: The Local Tradition

The ceramic assemblage associated with Structure 1 was very limited and utilitarian, consisting of perhaps seven different vessel forms and sizes. Over 95 percent of the sherds associated with this occupation represented Lorokea Fiber and Lorokea Non-Fiber unslipped plainware with roughly smoothed surfaces. The most common Lorokea forms were jars with handles, wide-mouth ollas, and bowls of various sizes (Figures 4.4, 4.5, 4.6). Remains of very large storage jars (capacity greater than 20 l) were not found with this occupation. Fragments of wide-mouth ollas—the most common form—were often fire-blackened and were probably used for most cooking duties. Carbonized fish remains (scales, fins, cranial bones) were found adhering to the interior of several fragments. This might indicate that the early site inhabitants, like modern Lukurmata residents, consumed a fish stew in which the *Orestias* sp. was cooked whole. My examination of modern pots used for fish stew showed a similar pattern of burned fish remains sticking to the interior of the vessel.

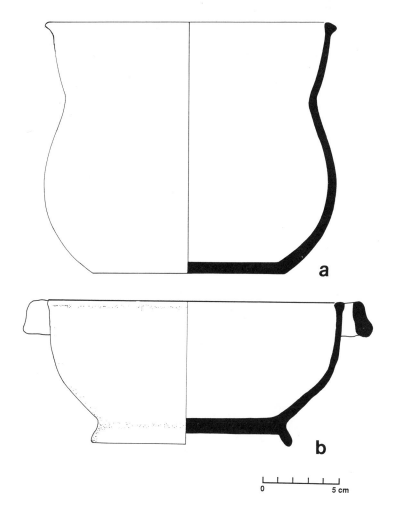

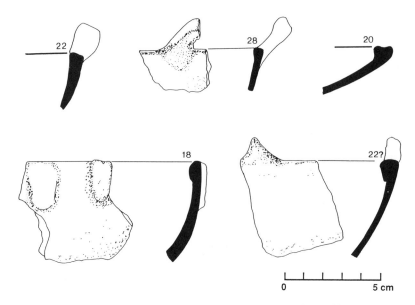

Fig. 4.5 Fragments of Lorokea Fiber annular-base bowl rims with rim diameters in cm.

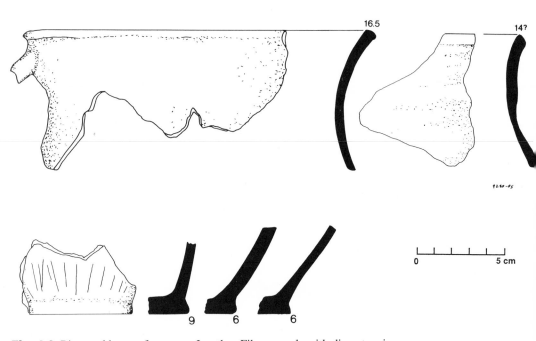

Fig. 4.6 Rims and bases of common Lorokea Fiber vessels with diameters in cm.

While fragments of jars and ollas were scattered fairly evenly around the outdoor surface on each side of Structure 1, fragments of Thin Redware bowls (Figure 4.7b) were concentrated around the hearth and in the refuse pit nearest the hearth. None of the Thin Redware bowls were fire-blackened; they were probably serving vessels rather than cooking vessels.

Taken together, the vessels seen in this occupation, with the exception of the Thin Redware bowls, form what can be called the "Local Tradition." Examples of the most common components of the Local Tradition (the Lorokea vessels) are shown in Figures 4.4–4.7a. Although we do not know that they were indeed made locally, these vessel types—in terms of form, size, paste, and temper—continued, with only slight modifications, to be part of the basic household pottery assemblage at the site for over one thousand years.

Domestic Activities: Summary

The artifacts associated with Structure 1 are indicative of simple household tasks: fishing; preparation and consumption of camelid, deer, lake fish, guinea pig, and bird; scraping tasks (hide working or food preparation); limited stone working (expedient flake production); eating/serving activities at an outdoor hearth; and possible ritual activities involving figurines.

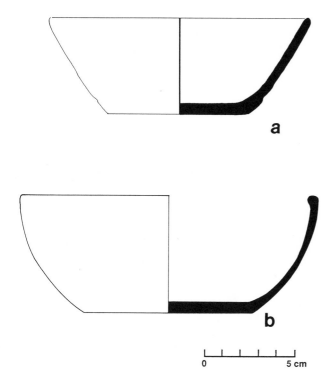

Fig. 4.7 Other Local Tradition vessels common in the early occupations at Lukurmata: (a) straight-sided bowl, (b) Thin Redware bowl.

Lukurmata in Regional Perspective

The settlement pattern for the area south of Lake Titicaca during this time has been described as small, autonomous villages, with communities seldom exceeding fifty households (Ponce 1980). This characterization has been reinforced by the results of the recent survey of the Tiwanaku Valley (Albarracin-Jordan and Mathews 1990). Formative period (1500 B.C.–A.D. 100) archaeological sites in the valley consisted of small, dispersed sherd scatters (1 scatter per 5 km^2) left by single homesteads or small hamlets (ibid.:58).

Subsistence throughout the region was based on farming of altiplano tubers and grains, camelid herding, and, at lakeside sites, lacustrine resources (Albarracin-Jordan and Mathews 1990; Browman 1981).

We believe that during this time, Pucara, in the northern Lake Titicaca Basin, was emerging as a major political center. Closer to Lukurmata, the ruins at Chiripa probably represent a small chiefly center. No other site south of Lake Titicaca presents any evidence of social hierarchy during this period, and there is no evidence of regional political unity.

Chiripa

Ceramics constitute our principal line of information for evaluating Lukurmata's interaction with the sites of Chiripa and Tiwanaku. Chiripa-style materials are found at sites widely distributed along the southeast edge of the lake (Arellano 1985; Bennett 1936; Browman 1981; Chávez 1988; Kolata 1983; Mujica 1978; Ponce 1970, 1981a; Tapia 1984c).

The Structure 1 occupation at Lukurmata may have occurred near the end of the Mamani phase at Chiripa (600–100 B.C.), or may have followed Chiripa abandonment at the end of the Mamani phase (Browman 1980; Chávez 1988). Despite the proximity of Lukurmata and Chiripa, no Chiripa-style ceramics were found in the Structure 1 occupation.[2]

The lack of Chiripa-style pottery at Lukurmata may indicate that occupation at the two sites was not contemporaneous, but other explanations are possible. If Lukurmata was only a marginal, rural hamlet, it simply may not have participated in the decorated pottery tradition and in the long-distance exchange network centered at Chiripa.

Tiwanaku

At the time of the Structure 1 occupation, Tiwanaku was probably a small settlement not much different from Lukurmata (Ponce 1969a). Occupation is thought to have begun at Tiwanaku around 300 B.C.

[2] Pottery from the two sites differs greatly in vessel form, size, and decoration. No examples of the distinctive Chiripa-style red-on-yellow painted wares, incised, modeled ceramics, vertical-sided bowls, or ceramic tubes were found at Lukurmata. Nor were any of the typical Chiripa-style utilitarian forms found at Lukurmata. Conversely, the Local Tradition forms and types at Lukurmata have no parallels at Chiripa. Although the early Lukurmata pottery generally exhibited fiber temper, sometimes regarded as a "diagnostic" or spatial marker of the Chiripa culture (Tapia 1984a), the use of vegetable fiber for temper seems to have been common in the area southeast of Lake Titicaca (Browman 1981).

We do not know if the pottery styles from the Structure 1 occupation at Lukurmata are also found at Tiwanaku. No specimens resembling the published Tiwanaku I-style pottery were found with the Structure 1 occupation.

Tiwanaku I period utilitarian wares have not been fully described. My own examination of the earliest undecorated ceramics from Tiwanaku shows marked similarities to the Local Tradition pottery in both paste and temper. There is a strong resemblance in form between one component of the Local Tradition, the Lorokea Fiber annular-base bowl, and certain Tiwanaku I period vessels from Tiwanaku.[3] Overall, the pottery from the earliest occupation at Lukurmata resembles in several respects the earliest Tiwanaku materials. However, the Lukurmata assemblage is sufficiently distinct to suggest that the similarities represent pottery styles common to the region, rather than a relationship or interaction between the Lukurmata and Tiwanaku populations.

Regional Perspective: Summary

The artifacts from the Structure 1 occupation do not suggest strong ties to early centers of the region, such as Pucara and Chiripa, or to sites such as Tiwanaku. There is no evidence of participation in regional exchange networks. None of the long-distance trade items seen in subsequent occupations (marine shell, basalt, sodalite, obsidian) were found with the Structure 1 occupation.

SUMMARY

Lukurmata appears to have begun as a small site, probably a hamlet of scattered homesteads. The earliest occupation exposed in my excavations consisted of a single structure and a small number of associated features. We do not know if this structure represents a seasonal or year-round occupation. Indications that the house was not intensively used, and the lack of an internal hearth, might suggest only seasonal use. However, a deep layer of occupational refuse above the structure indicates that even if this were only a seasonal encampment, the area was returned to regularly for a long period of time.

Although lake resources were important, subsistence during this initial occupation was not focused entirely on the lake. The diet was a generalized one, including significant amounts of camelid.

There is no evidence that Lukurmata began as a "colony" of Chiripa or Tiwanaku. The pottery used by the first Lukurmata inhabitants does not resemble that known from any other site, and there are no indications of regional political unity during this time. Given the lack of clear ties to a larger center, it is probable that Lukurmata was politically, as well as economically, autonomous.

[3] This Lukurmata form (Figure 4.4b) is an open, hemispherical walled bowl with a hollow base and horizontal strap-handles at the rim. The Tiwanaku specimens differ in several ways, although the overall form is the same. In contrast to the Lorokea bowl, Tiwanaku specimens are: burnished, often decorated (with a band of red paint around the rim), lack fiber temper, and lack the lipping around the inside of the rim (Ponce 1971: Figure 2—#2, #5, #21, #23). However, all of the Tiwanaku I pottery that has been published is from burial or offering contexts. We know virtually nothing about Tiwanaku I period domestic pottery.

5

Ties with Tiwanaku

People continued to live on the ridge after Structure 1 was abandoned. During this time, the area excavated served as a burial ground, outdoor activity area (possibly an agricultural field), and midden.

The poorly preserved remains of Structure 2 were 255 cm below datum, or 20 cm above Structure 1. This house measured 4 m × 3 m. Two postholes and a possible hearth were associated with the floor, but we could not define an associated outdoor occupational surface. The artifacts found in the fill around Structure 2 were identical in type and style to those of Structure 1, indicating continuity in household activities and in the Local Tradition household pottery assemblage. Structure 2 was abandoned after what appears to have been a short occupation.

The remains of later dwellings were found at 235 cm below datum. By excavating 48 contiguous m² at this depth, we were able to expose the remains of two contemporaneous houses (Structures 3 and 4), a large area of associated outdoor surface, three hearths, and two middens (Figure 5.1). No absolute dates are available for the Structure 3–4 occupation, but ceramic associations suggest a first-century A.D. occupation.

SITE COMPOSITION

There is no evidence that the residential population at Lukurmata had increased since the Structure 1 occupation; the eighteen other test pits excavated to sterile soil at Lukurmata revealed no contemporaneous cultural remains. There were almost certainly more structures at Lukurmata dating to the first century A.D. than those I excavated (it is unlikely that I happened to find the *only* structures) but occupation at the site probably continued to be either widely dispersed or limited to the ridge.

DOMESTIC ARCHITECTURE

Stone wall foundations and two patches of floor were the only architectural remains of Structure 3. The structure was slightly trapezoidal in plan, measuring roughly 3.3 m × 3.4 m (Figure 5.2). The packed earth floor sections were organically stained and covered by a thin layer of sand and silt. A double row of fieldstones, faced on both sides and preserved three courses high in places, formed the wall foundations. The walls probably had been made of mud bricks or cut sod. Several fragments of burned adobe bricks were recovered from near Structure 3. One of these bricks displayed a "sun-like" circle with radiating lines painted in faint red pigment. If this brick came from the Structure 3 wall, it would suggest that Structure 3, like Tiwanaku I period houses at Tiwanaku, was decorated on the exterior (Ponce 1980).

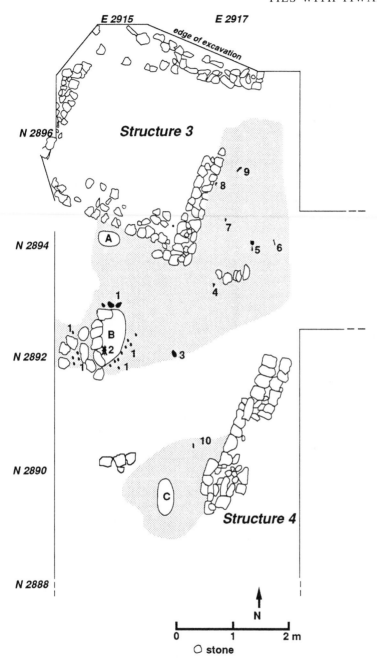

Fig. 5.1 Structure 3–4 occupation with selected artifacts plotted and intrusive features omitted. Shading indicates preserved outdoor surfaces. Hearths are designated as A, B, and C. *Key*: (1) Tiwanaku I-style bowl fragments, (2) fish bone concentration, (3) chipped stone chopper/scraper, (4) pecked cobble, (5) fire-cracked rock, (6) bone needle, (7) lithic flakes, (8) burned bone needle and worked bone fragment, (9) incised pottery fragment shown in Figure 5.5b, (10) bone awl or punch fragment.

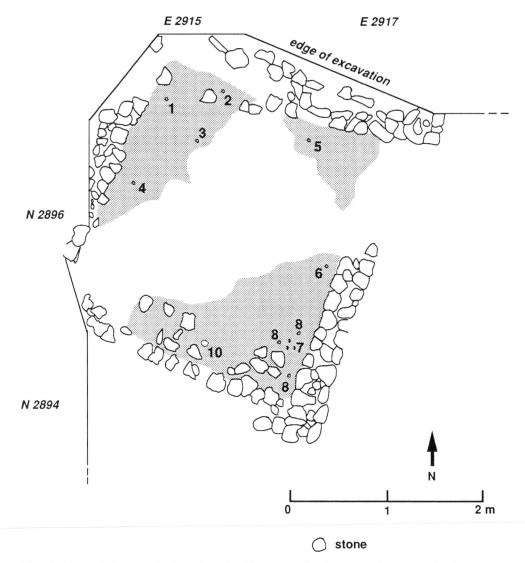

Fig. 5.2 Plan of Structure 3 with selected artifacts plotted and intrusive features omitted. Shading indicates preserved floor. *Key*: (1) pottery fragments, (2) spindle whorl, (3) carved bone fragment illustrated in Figure 5.4, (4) ceramic "button," (5) sharpened rodent mandibles, (6) pecked cobble, (7) lithic debitage, (8) flakes, (10) intact small pottery vessel.

Although there were no postholes or other clues to the nature of the roof, the structure was small enough that the roof could have been supported by the walls. The house
entrance could not be located.

Only the northwestern wall of Structure 4 was excavated, enough to suggest that
Structure 4 could have been similar in size and plan to Structure 3.

DOMESTIC ACTIVITIES

Structure 3 did not appear to have been a dump after abandonment, and many of the
artifacts found on preserved floor sections were the type that would have accumulated
during the occupation of the house. The northwestern section of floor yielded sherds
from various utilitarian vessels, fragments of camelid bone, a round ceramic spindle
whorl, and a small carved bone. The latter, which appeared to have broken off from an
ornament or utensil, may depict a hand (Figure 5.3). The southeastern corner had artifacts reflecting preparation of simple flake tools, in addition to undecorated sherds and
fragments of camelid bone.

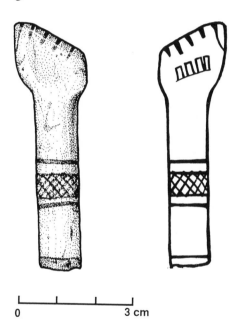

0   3 cm

Fig. 5.3 Fragment of bone carved in
the shape of a hand from the floor of
Structure 3.

Outdoor Features

A principal locus for household activities was the area south of Structure 3. Intensive use of this space had created a stained, sandy, hard-packed surface with features
and artifact scatters. Two sections of this had preserved, one of roughly 9.4 m², the
other 3.2 m². Two other areas had been used as refuse dumps. The thin layers of midden deposit in these areas contained large quantities of ash and faunal remains. The
marks on several of the bones from these deposits suggest that they were favored
scavenging places for dogs.

Three outdoor hearths were found—two smaller ones near the houses and a large one west of Structure 4. Hearths A and C were simple, partially stone-lined pits. They contained fragments of fire-cracked rock, cooking vessels, and camelid bone. As shown in Figure 5.1, artifacts were scattered on the surface around Hearth C including a cone, a concentration of burned camelid bone, and fragments from a single Queruni Orange utilitarian vessel.

Hearth B, the largest and most elaborate of the three hearths, was stone-lined, circular, and measured roughly 64 cm in diameter and 15 cm deep. The fill contained large quantities of fish bone, pottery fragments, and fire-cracked rock. The quantity and size of the stones found around this feature suggest that originally Hearth 3 may have had an architectural superstructure.

Differences in associated artifacts also suggest that the larger hearth was used differently from the two smaller ones. Fish bone, bird bone, and camelid remains were found with the larger hearth. In contrast, only faunal remains were associated with the two smaller hearths.

Reconstructable specimens of Tiwanaku I-style, red-on-chestnut bowls (Figure 5.4) were recovered from the large hearth and the associated refuse pit. The distribution of bowl fragments suggests that these bowls were used only for activities taking place at the large hearth. Fragments of this type of bowl were not found anywhere else in the occupation.

0   5 cm

Fig. 5.4 Tiwanaku I-style red-on-chestnut bowl from Hearth C of the Structure 3–4 occupation. These imported bowls were probably used in serving activities.

Other Household Activities

Two large, chopper-like bifaces were found on the occupational surface between the structures. Traditionally called "hoes," these may have been used in agriculture. Evidence for small-scale stoneworking found outside of the structures included pecking stones, flakes, and debitage. Several bone needles were found discarded in a refuse pit, along with rodent mandibles and a fragment of a bone awl. The latter may have been used in making clothing or baskets.

An interesting pottery fragment found east of Structure 3 was the incised fragment of a ceramic tube or "trumpet" (Figure 5.5c). Similar ceramic pieces are characteristic of the early Titicaca Basin cultures, including Chiripa, Tiwanaku, and Pucara (Mohr 1966; Chávez 1988; Ponce 1970, 1971). Intact specimens from these cultures typically display polychrome zoomorphic designs, such as felines. The ceramic tubes have usually been considered objects of ritual use, musical instruments, or bellows for blowing on fires (Ponce 1970).

Other artifacts associated with the occupation included the mysterious cones (from midden and refuse contexts) and the equally mysterious "miniature bowls" (Figure 5.5b). The latter are small, fired clay bowls, with small holes drilled through each side. Usually described as "buttons," they may have had ornamental uses, either sewn on clothing or strung as bracelets or necklaces. These artifacts are only known only from "Tiwanaku" sites, and generally only from the earliest levels of these sites (levels dating to earlier than A.D. 400). Identical specimens have been found at Tiwanaku and Khonko Wankani (Bennett 1934:451; Rydén 1947:109, Figures 41 V and 41 W).

One of the refuse pits also contained some fragments of a small white "cup" made of an unknown plaster-like material (Figure 5.6). Although their use is not known, one suggestion has been that they were molds or crucibles used in metallurgy (Kolata, personal communication). Similar artifacts apparently associated with slag from metal working have been found at Tiwanaku and sites in the Pampa Koani (Kolata, personal communication). An alternative possibility is that the white "cups" are hardened lime or *llipta* used by coca-chewers, with a shape corresponding to the perishable vessel that once contained the lime (Mohr Chávez, personal communication).

Faunal remains were found scattered across the occupational surface, with concentrations near hearths and in refuse areas. Camelid remains made up most of the large bone assemblage, with a significant proportion of birds (16.9%) and the ubiquitous *Orestias* fish bones. There were few bones from dog, guinea pig, and rabbit or vizcacha. The Tiwanaku 3 and 4 faunal assemblage is roughly comparable to that of Structure 1, so it appears that the meat portion of the Lukurmata residents' diet had not changed (Appendix II).

Shifts in Domestic Pottery

The most striking change in household artifacts was the appearance in significant quantity of two new styles of pottery: decorated Tiwanaku I-style vessels and Queruni Orangeware utilitarian vessels. Two Tiwanaku I-style pottery forms appeared at Lukurmata: shallow bowls (Figure 5.3) and globular-bodied pots (Figure 5.8).[1] These

---

[1] Like the Tiwanaku specimens, the Lukurmata bowls are convex in shape, with a deep yellow or (chestnut) burnished slip and a painted red band around the rim (several of the Lukurmata bowls have a smaller black band under the red one). Also, like the Tiwanaku specimens, some of the Lukurmata Tiwanaku I-style bowls have a very slight annular base and are painted red on the bottom. Finally, like the Tiwanaku examples, the Lukurmata bowls are characterized by either horizontal strap-handles at the rim, or handles extending up above the rim at an oblique angle (some bowls at both sites have a single handle, others have two). Microscopic comparisons of paste and temper revealed no differences

specimens are nearly identical in every respect to the pottery at Tiwanaku and may have come from the same source (Ponce 1971:Figure 1—#4, #12, and #13).

The distribution of Tiwanaku I-style ceramics at Lukurmata indicates their special status. The bowls were only found near the large hearth, and globular-bodied pots were found in mortuary contexts. The Tiwanaku I-style bowls appear to have replaced Thin Redware bowls in Lukurmata household activities. Fragments of them occur in the same context (associated with an outdoor hearth) and no Thin Redware bowl fragments were found in the Structure 3–4 occupation.

The "special" status of Tiwanaku I-style bowls is further indicated by their local imitation, using the paste and temper that characterized Lukurmata utilitarian wares. "Imitation" bowls took the same form (including handles) and were decorated in a similar fashion (with a red band). Fragments from these imitation bowls were found in the same contexts as fragments of the Tiwanaku-style red-on-chestnut bowls.

Even more striking than the appearance of Tiwanaku I-style decorated vessels was the change in undecorated pottery, as Queruni Orange vessels replaced several of the Local Tradition pottery forms. The morphological characteristics of Queruni Orange pottery, its presence in domestic contexts, and the fire blackening indicate that the Queruni pottery represents a utilitarian cookingware. Queruni Orange pottery differs from Local Tradition pottery in paste, temper, and shape (Bermann 1990). Because we recovered few vessels that could be reconstructed, we cannot determine the forms of all Queruni vessels. The four most common forms were:

1. a small (maximum diameter = 14 cm) concave-sided bowl with a flat rim
2. a larger, shouldered bowl or olla with a long neck and thickened rim
3. a simple high-walled bowl
4. a globular pot or olla ranging from 12 cm to 18 cm in rim diameter, one version with a vertical rim and one with a flaring rim

The evidence suggests that the Queruni Orangewares came to Lukurmata as a whole complex not long after Structure 2 was abandoned. All four basic forms originally appeared together, quickly coming to constitute 60 percent to 70 percent of the undecorated sherds in the ceramic assemblages. This percentage declined rapidly and steadily over time, so that by the Structure 3 occupation, Queruni Orange sherds constituted roughly 25 percent of the total. Queruni Orange pottery disappeared completely after Structure 3 was abandoned.

Interestingly, the Queruni vessels do not replicate Local Tradition forms. There are no Orangeware equivalents of the Lorokea annular bowl, large jar, or olla. Conversely,

---

between the red-banded bowls from either site. Although the Tiwanaku specimens appear to be more highly burnished and have a brighter yellow slip, this may be the result of the curation methods applied to the Tiwanaku finds. The Tiwanaku I-style bowls found at Lukurmata fell into three size classes: 14 cm, 17 cm, and 20 cm in rim diameter, suggesting that they may have been "nestable," a common phenomenon for bowls. Standard, nested sizes allow easy storage and transportation, and less breakage during transportation. The bowls from Tiwanaku were on the average slightly smaller (Ponce [1971:15] gives the rim diameters as 17.5, 13.5, 11.7, 15.3, 16.8). Fragments of red-on-chestnut jars were found with the Structure 2 occupation. These too have counterparts at Tiwanaku, and most resemble flaring rim pots (Ponce 1971:21, Figures 27–30) and globular body vessels (ibid.:19, Figure 22). In addition, we found fragments at Lukurmata that may have come from the flaring rim bowl forms illustrated by Ponce (ibid.: Figure 18).

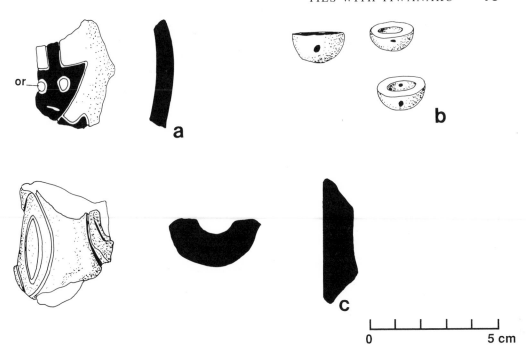

Fig. 5.5 Ceramic artifacts from early Lukurmata occupations: (a) incised sherd from the Structure 1 occupation, (b) ceramic "buttons" of unknown function (found in nearly all of the early occupations at Lukurmata), (c) fragment of an incised ceramic tube or "trumpet" associated with the Structure 3–4 occupation.

Fig. 5.6 "Cups" made of an unknown lime/plaster-like material and of unknown function were associated with many Lukurmata domestic occupations. This specimen was associated with the Structure 3–4 occupation.

the Local Tradition had no equivalent to the Queruni concave, flat rim bowls or long-necked vessels. Therefore, even when the percentage of Queruni Orangeware was at its highest, nearly the full range of Local Tradition forms continued to be used in Lukurmata households. In other words, the Queruni Orange pottery added to the range of pottery *shapes* used by the Lukurmata household, without replacing any traditional *forms*.

Given the contemporaneous appearance of the Tiwanaku I-style decorated pottery, the most logical source of the Queruni Orange pottery is Tiwanaku. However, until Tiwanaku I period domestic contexts at Tiwanaku are excavated, we cannot know if the orange pottery is the utilitarian component of the Tiwanaku I household assemblage.[2]

Domestic Pottery: Summary

In summary, the Structure 3–4 occupation possessed a greater variety of vessel styles and shapes than that associated with Structure 1 or Structure 2. There was also a great deal of continuity in household pottery, as the Local Tradition (Lorokea Fiber) wares continued to make up a large part of the domestic assemblage.

The parallel distribution around outdoor hearths of the Thin Redware and Tiwanaku I-style bowl fragments suggests that changes in bowl preferences were not accompanied by changes in the household tasks in which they were used. The Tiwanaku I forms may simply have replaced the Thin Redware in offering/prestation activities.

CONTEXT AND THE "LOCAL PERSPECTIVE"

The Tiwanaku I-style pottery of the Structure 3–4 occupation provides a useful point of departure from which to contrast the "capital-centric" and "local" perspectives. From the "capital-centric" perspective, the bowls are seen as a measure of interaction between Lukurmata and Tiwanaku, and evidence for Lukurmata participation in a Tiwanaku exchange or even political "sphere." However, if we take a "local perspective," we see that the presence and distribution of bowls at Lukurmata might also be explicable in terms of diffusion and the persistence of Lukurmata traditions.

---

[2] The Lukurmata Local Tradition pottery also has not been reported from Tiwanaku. Unlike the published descriptions of Tiwanaku I-style ceramics, most of the the Local Tradition vessels (the Lorokea Fiberware) are fiber tempered, and they have distinctive characteristics (rim forms and exterior finish) not present in Ponce's Tiwanaku I collection. However, the annular-base bowls in Ponce's Tiwanaku I collection (Ponce 1971: 20, Figures 2, 5, 21, 23) are very similar in form to the Lorokea Fiber annular bowls. Like the Lorokea bowls, the bowls illustrated by Ponce have direct or slightly incurving sides, are hollow- or pedestal-based, and have horizontal strap-handles at the rim. They are also comparable to the Lukurmata examples in rim diameter and height. They have a different paste and temper than Lorokea bowls, however.

Although fiber tempered ceramics have not yet been reported from Tiwanaku, I was able to examine several collections of sherds recently excavated from Tiwanaku I period strata at Tiwanaku. A large percentage (perhaps 25%) of the plainware fragments did, in fact, have some fiber temper, and were similar in form and surface finish to Lukurmata Lorokea Fiber pottery.

Cultural Selection in Borrowing and Imitation

Only a small subset of the known Tiwanaku I-style pottery appeared at Lukurmata: the red-on-chestnut shallow bowl and the globular-bodied bowl. The more elaborately decorated Tiwanaku I-style pottery, bearing zoomorphic and anthropomorphic images, is not represented in the Structure 3–4 occupation.

The shallow bowl and the globular-bodied bowl were also the only two forms chosen for local imitation. This imitation involved duplicating both the form *and* decoration of the Tiwanaku bowls. We did not find, for instance, Local Tradition shapes adorned with red bands. In contrast, imitative pottery from later Lukurmata occupations involved the addition of Tiwanaku decorative motifs to familiar vessel forms. As with the choice of imported ware, the vessels chosen for imitation at Lukurmata were not the elaborate Tiwanaku I-style pottery with iconographic motifs.

This pattern can be interpreted three ways. Lukurmata households (1) were outside the distribution network of the most elaborate Tiwanaku I-style pottery; (2) did not accept the underlying ideas expressed in the more elaborate iconography of Tiwanaku pottery; or (3) were more accepting of familiar shapes than of different styles.

The first interpretation would be typical of a "capital-centric" perspective. From this perspective, for example, we might suggest that the more elaborate Tiwanaku I pottery represented a "prestige-good" that circulated among chiefly families who used their acquisition as a means to create, signal, and reinforce their elite status. Such items would not "trickle down" to commoner households in small hamlets; Lukurmata residents would not have access to these goods circulating in an elite interaction sphere. The restricted use of Southern Cult symbols in the Mississippian populations of the southeastern United States is an archaeological example of this pattern (Brown 1976; Peebles and Kus 1977).

Adopting a "local perspective" leads to an alternative explanation. Instead of interpreting the Tiwanaku I-style artifact assemblage solely in terms of models of interaction with Tiwanaku, we must interpret the assemblage in the context of local values and "selective borrowing."

No human population randomly or uniformly accepts introduced objects (Linton 1940; Rogers 1990; Spicer 1961). As anthropologists have long pointed out, the process of adoption or borrowing of external traits is culturally selective; peoples voluntarily accept only traits or objects that can be integrated with local values and practices. Passed from one generation to another as "tradition," these values and practices form the historical framework that underlies the concept of culture (Sahlins 1976; Stocking 1974:6).

This historical framework of tradition, together with the nature of the external contact, structure the acceptance of particular traits and objects (Linton 1940; Rogers 1990; Spicer 1961). That the diffusion of objects from one human group to another is a selective process, conditioned by the traditions of the recipient group, has been staple fare in introductory textbooks for decades. Nevertheless, this historical-contextual approach is often overlooked or ignored in archaeological discussions of regional artifact distributions.

From the "local perspective," Lukurmata would not have passively received iconography or pottery from Tiwanaku (as is the usual archaeological portrayal of smaller or subsidiary sites). Instead, Lukurmata traditions would have shaped the residents' material culture and stylistic preferences. Perhaps the more elaborate Tiwanaku I period pottery could not be integrated with Lukurmata traditions as easily as the simple Tiwanaku I bowls. Perhaps the red-on-chestnut vessels were used because they harmonized best with local traditions and activities, not because the nature of the Lukurmata–Tiwanaku relationship allowed access only to them.

From the "local perspective," the lack of the more elaborate Tiwanaku iconography at Lukurmata could be the result of local nonacceptance of what the iconography represented, or it could signal that the Tiwanaku I-style bowls were more important to Lukurmata for their form and "nonlocal" qualities than as iconographic vehicles associated with Tiwanaku. The spatial distribution of the Tiwanaku I-style bowls supports the latter interpretation.

Multiple Interpretations: Persistence of Local Traditions and a New Relationship with Tiwanaku

Prior to the Structure 3–4 occupation, the Thin Redware bowls (probably also imported) already played a special serving role in Lukurmata household activities. These were replaced by the Tiwanaku I-style bowls. Of the range of Tiwanaku I-style pottery available to use in activities around the outdoor hearth, the Lukurmata residents chose one that most resembled the vessels they had been using previously.

The Tiwanaku I-style bowls may have been valued by Lukurmata residents because of their ability to fulfill local needs and traditions. Ethnologists have suggested that often it is the *form* of a trait, not the object's original meaning or function, that shapes how that trait is adopted (Ember and Ember 1985:449; Foster 1962; Linton 1940). The familiar and useful shape of the Tiwanaku I-style bowls, together with their generally valued status as "imports," may have made them suitable replacements for the Thin Redware vessels in traditional household activities. The fact that the bowls were from the site of Tiwanaku may have been secondary or entirely incidental.

From the "local perspective," the use of the Tiwanaku bowls may be an example of what Edward Spicer (1961:530) defined as "incorporative integration." In incorporative integration, elements from one culture system are integrated into another culture system "in such a way that they conform to meaningful and functional relations within the latter." In a useful classification of material culture change, J. Daniel Rogers (1990:106) has referred to changes of this type, in which the "overall composition of the material assemblage remains unchanged," as "replacement." No traditional artifact categories are abandoned, but the style or source of artifacts in that category are altered. As a result, what may superficially appear to be a dramatic change can actually be a reinforcement of traditional values or organizational patterns (Spicer 1961:530).

In sum, the presence of Tiwanaku I bowls at Lukurmata may tell us a great deal about traditional, local patterns and relatively little about Lukurmata's relationship with Tiwanaku. In this sense, the Tiwanaku I-style bowls' value or meaning for Lukurmata inhabitants was locally and contextually constructed, rather than intrinsic. This interpretation is part of a much larger debate. In contrast to what cultural anthropologists have discovered in a century of study of diffusion and acculturation, Andean archaeologists usually assume in regional studies that the same type of vessel (or design element, building, or deity) has comparable uses and meanings at each site in which it is found. These items are used to determine the relationship of the smaller site with the capital or larger center, or as evidence of inclusion in a political system or "cult." Andean archaeologists thus generally implicitly assume the spread of such items to represent what Spicer (1961) described as "assimilative integration." In assimilative integration, the receiving cultural system accepts both the items and their meaning from the donor cultural system. Such items thus represent the adoption of new cultural behavior or values by the receiving population.

To review, in adopting a "capital-centric" view, I would be interested in using the pattern of Tiwanaku pottery remains in the Structure 3–4 occupation to "reconstruct" the interaction between Tiwanaku and Lukurmata. The presence of bowls alone could be interpreted as indicating a particular form of interaction between Tiwanaku and neighboring sites, a type of interaction that precluded Lukurmata's access to more elaborate pottery. I would treat the presence of Tiwanaku bowls as diagnostic of a particular type of regional interaction, perhaps a "bowl-exchange sphere."

Yet the Tiwanaku I bowls may appear in the Structure 3–4 occupation because they alone were acceptable for use in traditional household activities. Rather than not having access to more elaborate pottery, Lukurmata residents may not have desired it. The pattern of Tiwanaku I-style pottery at Lukurmata may have been structured more by local values and tradition than restricted Tiwanaku distribution networks. If a traditional serving activity around outdoor hearths using shallow bowls had not *already* existed, the Tiwanaku I-style bowls might not have appeared at Lukurmata. With the historical perspective afforded by the Structure 1 occupation, this alternative interpretation could not have presented itself. This is why archaeologists studying cultural change, like anthropologists, must take a historical or diachronic perspective.

The differing interpretations of the Tiwanaku I bowls at Lukurmata serve to illuminate one of the key differences between the "capital-centric" and "local perspective" approaches to small sites: the supposition of external and regional rather than local and historical explanations for artifact patterns. Naturally, the two constructs are *not* mutually exclusive. Newly adopted objects may function within a preexisting cultural context, yet still be distinct for their source of origin or exotic attributes (Rogers 1990:107). That the red-on-chestnut bowls were from Tiwanaku may have enhanced their importance for Lukurmata residents, and made them preferable to Thin Redware bowls. That the bowls were from Tiwanaku also provides some insight, if only very limited, to the nature of Lukurmata–Tiwanaku interaction. My purpose in taking a "local perspective" is not to substitute one explanation for another, but to raise alternative interpretations.

MORTUARY ACTIVITIES

The outlines of the burial pits were not preserved, making it impossible to determine precisely when the nine burials described below occurred. All were intrusive to the Structure 1 occupation level, and at least three appear to date to the Structure 3–4 occupation.

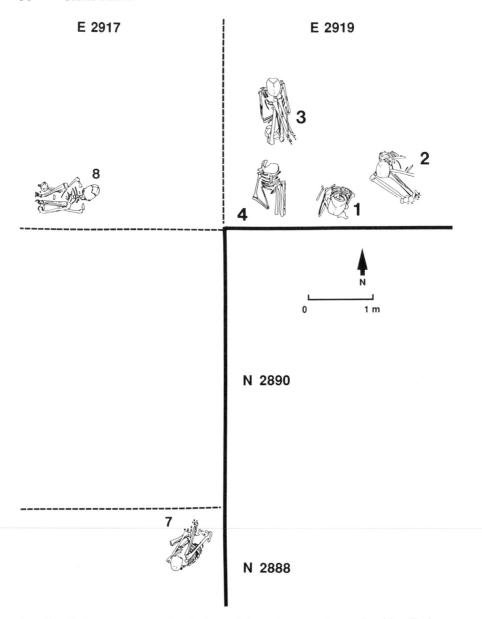

Fig. 5.7 Early graves exposed at the base of the main excavation on the ridge. Each penetrated into sterile soil and probably dates to the Tiwanaku I period.

A Small Cemetery: Burials 1–5

Five burials formed a small cluster to the east of Structure 1 (Figure 5.7). These date to sometime between the Structure 1 occupation and the Structure 9 occupation. Each consisted of a single individual in a simple, unmodified pit. We found three adults (an older male, a female, and an individual of undetermined gender), a juvenile (14–18 years of age), and an infant (9–24 months old). Body position and orientation were consistent; with the exception of the infant, each had been placed in a flexed, seated/reclining position, with the arms resting in the lap. Four individuals faced south, and one faced southeast.

Each individual, but the infant, exhibited artificial cranial deformation. Two distinct forms of deformation were represented. One involved flattening the frontal bone and creating a sagittal saddle that "elongated" the parietals. The other, displayed by the adult female, was more "cone-like," with the lambda, rather than the apex, forming the most elevated point on the skull (Figure 5.8).

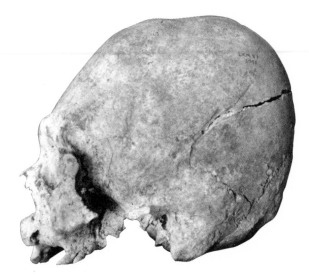

Fig. 5.8 One style of artificial cranial deformation, at Lukurmata: Burial 1.

Only the tomb of the old adult male contained grave-goods. An alignment of four sodalite disk beads behind the cranium suggested that the individual had been buried wearing a necklace. The beads are our first evidence for long-distance trade-goods arriving at Lukurmata; the nearest source of sodalite is Cerro Sapo in Cochabamba, some 165 km away (Browman 1981:416). Just north of the body were two large sandstone cones (8.9 cm × 6 cm in size and weighing 450 g). A camelid scapula and the broken base of a plainware pot were also found with the burial, suggesting that the individual had been accompanied by an offering of meat.

Burials 6–9

Three of the four other burials may date to the Structure 3–4 occupation at the site. These three present a different burial pattern. They lacked the shared cardinal orientation of the earlier cemetery group; in fact, none faced south. And, in contrast to Burials 1–5, each of the three was accompanied by a single, nonutilitarian pot vessel of "Tiwanaku-style."

Burial 6 was an old adult male placed in a seated and flexed position facing east. The sole grave-good was a small vessel found lying on its side east of the skeleton, near the feet. The form and deep-red slip of this vessel resemble Tiwanaku I-style pottery, but the fiber temper of the pot suggests that it may have been a "local" imitation of the Tiwanaku I style.

Burial 7 was a less well preserved old adult buried in a seated and flexed position, facing northeast. The sole associated artifact was an upright Tiwanaku I-style pot (Figure 5.9) just northwest of the pelvis. The lack of fiber temper in this vessel suggests that it was a Tiwanaku import rather than a local copy.

Burial 8 was a young adult male in a reclining, flexed position, facing due west (Figure 5.10). This individual was accompanied by a single pot standing upright on the right side of the skeleton, near the ankles (Figure 5.11). This vessel resembles the distinctive double-spouted "duck" or "llama" pots found at both Tiwanaku and Chiripa, but largely resembles the Tiwanaku specimens.

Burial 9 was a child (7–10 years old) with an artificially deformed cranium. It had been buried without grave-goods in a seated, flexed position, facing northeast.

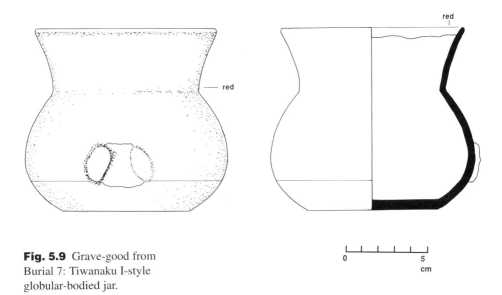

Fig. 5.9 Grave-good from Burial 7: Tiwanaku I-style globular-bodied jar.

0   5
                 cm

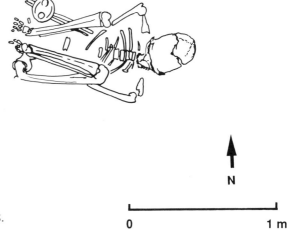

Fig. 5.10 Burial 8.

N

0   1 m

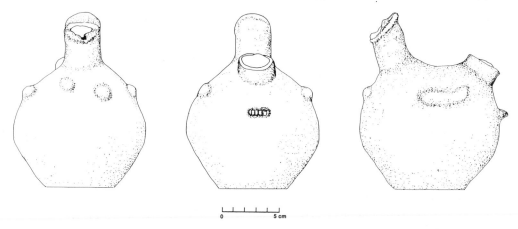

Fig. 5.11 Grave-good from Burial 8: "duck" vessel, possibly Tiwanaku-style.

LUKURMATA IN REGIONAL PERSPECTIVE

The recent settlement survey of the Tiwanaku Valley by Juan Albarracin-Jordan and James Mathews has provided solid regional information on nearby settlement during the Tiwanaku I period. Albarracin-Jordan and Mathews found approximately eighty sites roughly dated by ceramic associations to the Formative period (Tiwanaku I period or earlier) in their intensive survey of the Tiwanaku Valley (1990). Widely dispersed, the sites appear to have loosely grouped into eleven clusters, each separated by 3–4 km. The majority of the sites with Tiwanaku-style artifacts were located on elevations overlooking the valley floor. Lukurmata's setting is similar to these sites, at roughly 3850 m.

One of the larger Tiwanaku I period sites in the valley (covering 1.4 ha) is TMV-189. Architectural remains visible on the surface include a stone rectilinear structure measuring 6 m on a side, several adjacent mounds forming a small patio (30 m × 30 m), and possible terraces (Albarracin-Jordan and Mathews 1990:62). Although post-Tiwanaku ceramics are also associated with these structures, the architecture appears to belong to the earlier period (Albarracin-Jordan, personal communication).

Little is known about Tiwanaku's size or residential occupation during this period. Ponce (1980) has suggested that it was itself a small village, in an "estadio de desarrollo aldeano." The Tiwanaku I period is generally accepted as preceding the construction of any of the monumental architecture at Tiwanaku (Ponce 1970, 1980, 1981a), so Tiwanaku was probably not yet an influential center. Aside from TMV-189, there is no evidence for a settlement hierarchy in the Tiwanaku Valley, let alone political unification.

Knowledge of Tiwanaku I period houses is equally sketchy.[3] A Tiwanaku I period

---

[3] Our knowledge of residential architecture at Tiwanaku during the Tiwanaku I period is quite limited. Although the "typical" Tiwanaku I house has been sketched by Ponce (1980), details have not been published. Ponce (ibid.:11) describes Tiwanaku I residences as rectangular, adobe-walled structures, with steep gable roofs. Some houses had attached circular rooms used as kitchens.

A ceramic "whistle" recovered from the Kalasasaya monument at Tiwanaku portrays such a structure, with distinctive molded "T-shaped" recesses—one surrounding and one slightly above the door. A series of niches is shown on the front of the structure just below the thatched roof. Ponce further adds that such houses may have displayed painted walls (Ponce, personal communication).

structure recently excavated at Tiwanaku displayed many similarities to Structure 3 in size, form, materials, and construction technique (Portugal O. 1987).[4] The contents of this structure have yet to be analyzed.

The artifacts associated with the Structure 3–4 occupation indicate changes for the Lukurmata population involving greater participation in long-distance and regional exchange networks; direct, or more intensive, interaction with Tiwanaku; or the appearance of colonists from Tiwanaku.

The latter possibility is suggested by the appearance at Lukurmata of Tiwanaku I-style pottery and domestic architecture. Archaeologists in the Andes have traditionally treated shifts in utilitarian, as opposed to decorated, household pottery as evidence for population replacement or political domination. If this was the case, the continuity in activities and forms represented in the domestic pottery assemblage could be because such activities and the pottery assemblage would have been typical of any altiplano household of the time.

Overall, we do not know if the similarities between the Lukurmata and Tiwanaku pottery represent intensive interaction between the two sites, or Lukurmata's participation in a Tiwanaku-dominated regional ceramic distribution network. Similarly, it is difficult to know if the differences between the Lukurmata and Tiwanaku assemblages reflect real differences, or our limited knowledge of Tiwanaku I period domestic life at Tiwanaku.

SUMMARY

Lukurmata appears to have continued as a small, economically self-sufficient hamlet during the first centuries A.D., subsisting on agriculture, herding, and exploitation of lacustrine resources.

Aside from pottery, the styles and types of household artifacts found with Structures 3 and 4 were the same as those found with earlier Lukurmata occupations. Therefore, despite the changes in architectural style and use of Tiwanaku-style pottery, household activities appear to have remained very much the same. These activities would have included food preparation and consumption, spinning, weaving, hide working or basketry, production of cutting and scraping tools, and serving or offering activities involving nonlocal bowls. Mortuary behavior involved burial near domestic structures. The lack of infants and young children suggests that an age-based achieved status was necessary for this treatment. We do not yet know where children and infants were buried.

---

[4] Only the eastern section of this structure was excavated, but it displayed architecture similar to Structure 3 at Lukurmata. The Tiwanaku house was not quite rectangular in plan (like Structure 3), having a trapezoidal shape, and may have been slightly smaller, measuring roughly 2.5 m on a side (Portugal O. 1987:Figure 3). Linear wall foundations of rough fieldstones probably provided a base for adobe walls. These foundations averaged 30 cm thick, were faced on both sides (at least in places), and were preserved to a height of roughly 11 cm (ibid.). The floor consisted of packed, dark-gray earth rather than a prepared or poured clay surface (ibid.). A roughly circular hearth (45–50 cm in diameter), ringed with small stones, was set against the north wall of the structure. The hearth was filled with ash and burned organic material (Portugal O., personal communication). There was also evidence that the Tiwanaku structure may have been decorated. Flat pieces of plaster recovered from near the structure displayed traces of yellow, green, and blue paint. These may represent wall material (Portugal O., personal communication).

Tiwanaku-style materials may have been limited to burial contexts prior to this occupation, but the Structure 3–4 occupation was the first in which such materials were recovered from domestic contexts. Tiwanaku-style bowls seems to have completely replaced the Thin Redware bowls, and the Local Tradition plainwares were partially supplanted by distinctive Queruni Orangeware vessels. These pottery changes are amenable to a range of interpretations or explanations. As I have suggested, the presence of Tiwanaku I vessels in Lukurmata might stem from their ability to fulfill a role in traditional Lukurmata activities, rather than any early political or ideological linkages to Tiwanaku. The bowls may have resulted from Lukurmata's participation in a loose regional ceramic exchange network rather than direct contact. Exchange with nearby communities was probably simple and organized on an individual household basis.

The artifactual and stylistic ties with Tiwanaku are what most clearly differentiate the Structure 3–4 occupation from the Structure 1 occupation. As will be seen in the next chapter, these ties with Tiwanaku either disappeared or took very different forms in subsequent occupations.

6

Continuity and Change

Occupation continued on the ridge after Structures 3 and 4 were abandoned. Structures 5 and 6, represented only by poorly preserved patches of clay floor, were found 15 cm above the Structure 3–4 occupation, at 225 cm below datum. Because these house remains were so fragmentary, I will describe the subsequent Structure 7–8 and 9–10 occupations. Structures 5 and 6 appear to have been small (4 m × 3 m) dwellings similar in size and shape to Structure 7.

Excavation of a contiguous 52 m^2 at 210 cm below datum exposed the remains of Structures 7 and 8. Structures 9 and 10 were encountered at 200 cm below datum. Ceramic and stratigraphic associations suggest that these occupations date to the third century A.D.

SITE COMPOSITION

Lukurmata during this period probably remained a hamlet or small village. As before, materials dating to this period were found only in the main excavation on the ridge, suggesting that the residential population continued to be very small, or at least dispersed.

DOMESTIC ARCHITECTURE: STRUCTURE 7

The remains of Structure 7 consisted of a housefloor, a short section of foundation, and several interior features (Figure 6.1). We could not define an associated outdoor surface. The floor, a layer of prepared orange clay, was roughly oblong, measuring 4.5 m × 3.2 m. The dimensions of the house itself may have been somewhat smaller, probably 4 m × 2.9 m. Although the actual shape of the structure could not be determined, patterns in the soil ("shadow walls") indicated that the house had straight walls. The structure was sufficiently small that the roof could have rested on the walls. The only major interior feature was a shallow, not heavily used, firepit. It consisted of a simple, unlined pit dug through the floor. A thin ash deposit on the bottom contained fish bone and several small, fire-blackened undecorated sherds.

DOMESTIC ACTIVITIES: STRUCTURE 7

Structure 7 cannot truly be treated as a "household unit" because we could not locate an exterior activity area or associated outdoor features. The few artifacts found on the floor of Structure 7 included fragments of Local Tradition pottery, a cylindrical metal bead, and two fragments of incised polychrome pottery.

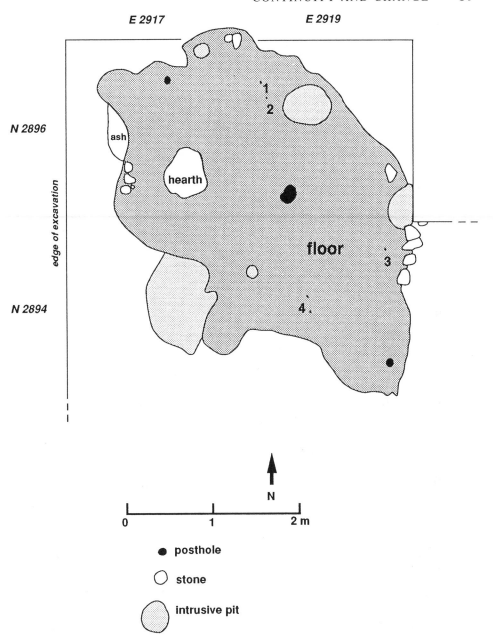

Fig. 6.1 Plan of Structure 7 floor with selected artifacts plotted. *Key*: (1) lithic flake, (2) metal bead, (3) worked camelid bone, (4) undecorated pottery fragments.

Fortunately, portions of other surfaces and isolated outdoor features from roughly contemporaneous levels allow us to determine the *range* of "household" activities during this phase. The artifacts from these contexts indicate strong continuity with Structures 3 and 4 in the types and quantities of household artifacts. Tasks such as food preparation, spinning and weaving, preparation of stone tools for cutting and scraping, serving/offering activities, and perhaps hide working and basketry continued as household activities. Items of unknown function such as white plaster "molds," ceramic "buttons," and stone cones continued to appear in household contexts.

The faunal remains included camelid, fish, bird, and dog or fox bones. Because these animals were represented in roughly the same proportions as in earlier occupations at the site, it appears that the meat component of the diet had not changed.

In place of the Queruni Orangeware, the household ceramic assemblage was once again dominated by the Local Tradition pottery. The ceramics associated with Structure 7 were identical in form, paste, temper, and finish to earlier Local Tradition ceramics, suggesting interaction with the same pottery source, or participation in the same exchange network. The Local Tradition forms of the Structure 7 occupation were represented in roughly the same proportions as in the Structure 1 and Structure 2 occupations, indicating that household architecture and pottery assemblages quickly reverted to pre-Structure 3 and 4 patterns.

The only difference between these domestic pottery assemblages was the greater representation of large (capacity greater than 20 l) water/grain storage vessels in the Structure 7 occupation. Several fragments of nonlocal bowls, including Thin Redware, were also found. The latter may indicate that the offering/prestation activities continued, with the nonlocal bowls replacing the Tiwanaku I-style vessels.

While the style of much of the pottery used in domestic contexts differed from that of the Structure 3–4 occupation, there seems to have been less change in the underlying range of household activities.

One probable change in activities was a shift in mortuary behavior. No burials were found that could be dated stratigraphically to the Structure 5–6, 7, or 9–10 occupations, suggesting that the dead were not placed below floors or near residences. As I discussed in the previous chapter, several of the graves found in or near sterile soil were accompanied by Tiwanaku I-style vessels, and probably associated with the Structure 3–4 occupation. The lack of burials from subsequent occupations, therefore, may indicate a shift from a burial pattern in which the dead were placed near or below houses.

From the functional or activity perspective, the Structure 7 occupation does not really represent a "return" to local patterns, since the Structure 3–4 occupation had not really been a complete departure from local patterns of domestic organization. The same range of artifacts and domestic tasks characterized household activities. The activity "dimension" of the household unit changed much less than stylistic preferences in pottery, or the external form of houses. It is largely the abrupt appearance and disappearance of Tiwanaku I and Queruni Orangeware pottery that cause the Structure 3–4 occupation to form such a strikingly visible archaeological horizon. Perhaps the Structure 7 occupation could best be characterized as a return to local styles.

The value of the "local perspective" is that its focus on comparison through time forces us to recognize local patterns. These may endure and be quite resilient. At times they appear to surface (as a "return") because they never really disappeared; they were only hidden by what are to the archaeologist more striking traits or patterns (Marcus 1989).

DOMESTIC ARCHITECTURE: STRUCTURES 9 AND 10

Structure 9 was a fairly large house (5 m diameter), roughly circular in plan (Figure 6.2). Preserved sections of stone wall footings and "shadow wall" deposits suggest curved rather than straight walls. A tongue of floor, probably the remains of an entrance, extended to the southeast. The house had been completely refloored with a 6–10 cm thick layer of orange clay and slightly expanded during the course of occupa-

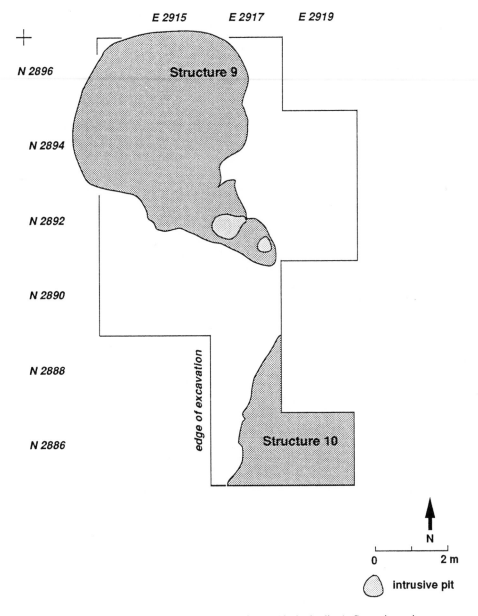

Fig. 6.2 Structure 9–10 occupation showing floors (dark shading). Some intrusive features omitted.

tion, but had not been significantly remodeled in other ways. It retained the same general shape, entrance, and posthole pattern.

Features in Structure 9 included a hearth and several minor refuse pits (Figure 6.3). The presence of an interior partition extending toward the center of the house from the southwestern edge of the floor was indicated by an alignment of small postholes along with a linear charcoal/ash deposit.

Only 7.5 m^2 of the western edge of Structure 10 was exposed (Figure 6.4). This structure was probably architecturally similar to Structure 9 with a circular plan, poured clay floor, and features such as postholes and small refuse pits.

DOMESTIC ACTIVITIES: STRUCTURES 9 AND 10

The types of objects found on the floor of Structures 9 and 10 and the associated outdoor surfaces suggest that the inhabitants' household tasks were similar to those of earlier occupations: cooking and eating, spinning and weaving, possibly hide working or basketry, scraping tasks, and preparation of flake tools. In addition, there was a suggestion of spatial patterning in the floor artifacts of Structure 9, as if certain tasks were "grouped," perhaps based on a gender division of labor.

Artifacts found on the floor in the northeast section of the house included bone splinters, stone flakes, bone needle fragments and burins, a spindle whorl fragment, a stone bead, a sharpened llama tooth, a clay "button," a polished celt or smoothing stone, and fragments of bone scrapers. The hearth was also located in this area. Around it were fragments of a plainware jar base, a small amount of lithic debitage, and bird and fish bone. On the floor in the southeast section of the house, east of the partition, and in front of the entrance were different types of items—stone flakes, an antler fragment, two pecking stones of different sizes, and lithic debitage.

The artifacts from the northeast section of the house seem largely concerned with food preparation and clothing (weaving and hide working). In contrast, the artifacts near the southeastern section of the house are more likely to have been used in small-scale tool preparation and flaking activities.

If weaving, preparation of clothing, and cooking were tasks carried out by women—and the strong ethnographic association makes this a reasonable assumption—then the northeastern group of artifacts may denote a woman's work area. In contrast, the southeastern cluster of artifacts, which represent stone chipping and/or woodworking, may indicate a man's work area, perhaps situated so as to take advantage of light from the house entrance.

Two areas of outdoor surface, totaling roughly 6.5 m^2, were preserved near Structure 9. These sandy surfaces were littered with sherds and bone fragments. Also found on them were two projectile points, a chipped stone scraper, a bone needle fragment, and a stone core. Three pits and a small hearth were found in the surfaces. The largest refuse pit was filled with ash, pottery fragments, and faunal remains including camelid fish, bird, and guinea pig. Comparison of the faunal remains with those from earlier occupations showed roughly the same proportion of camelid, fish, and bird in the diet.

The pottery from Structures 9 and 10 was very similar to that of both Structures 1 and 7. The Local Tradition vessels continued to dominate the domestic pottery assemblage. This strong continuity was seen both in the style of vessels and in the rough proportions of vessel forms or types making up the occupation's ceramic assemblage.

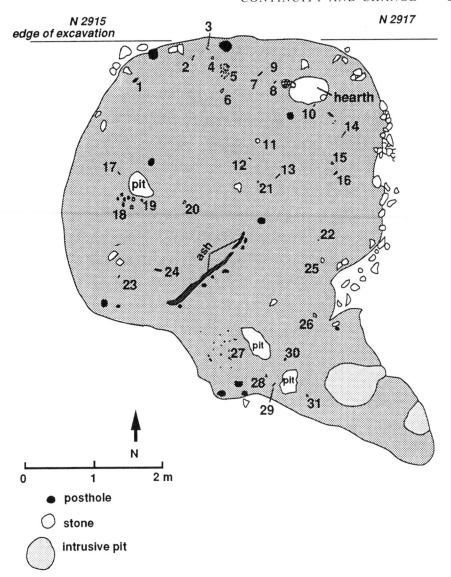

Fig. 6.3 Plan of Structure 9 floor with selected artifacts plotted. *Key*: (1) smoothed bone, (2) bone needle, (3) stone perforator, (4) retouched flake, (5) camelid bone splinters, (6) ground stone celt, (7) bone scraper made from camelid rib, (8) bone needle fragment, (9) base of fire-blackened pot, (10) stone disk bead, (11) bone scraper fragment made from camelid scapula, (12) stone disk bead, (13) stone perforator, (14) bone needle fragment, (15) sharpened llama tooth, (16) stone spindle whorl fragment, (17) unretouched flake, (18) bowl fragments, (19) unretouched flake, (20) stone scraper, (21) ceramic "button," (22) ceramic "button," (23) projectile point, (24) worked camelid bone, (25) pecked cobble, (26) pottery fragment, (27) lithic debitage (small flakes and fragments), (28) antler fragment, (29) unretouched flakes, (30) pecked cobble, (31) pecked cobble.

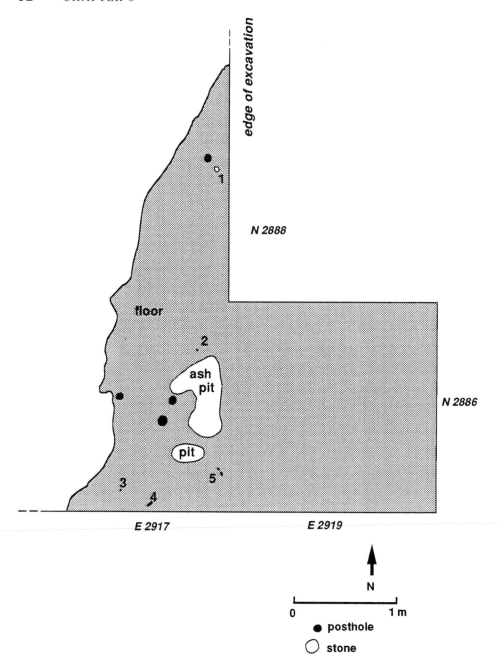

Fig. 6.4 Plan of Structure 10 floor with selected artifacts plotted. *Key*: (1) hammerstone, (2) ceramic "button," (3) ceramic "button," (4) unretouched flakes, (5) smoothed bone.

The hearth, a simple pit in the ground, contained charcoal, ash, fish and camelid bones, and four fragments from Thin Redware bowls. An additional Thin Redware bowl fragment was found in one of the pits.

LUKURMATA IN REGIONAL PERSPECTIVE

During the Structure 7 and Structure 9–10 occupations at Lukurmata, Tiwanaku was evolving and growing, emerging as a major ceremonial and demographic center in the Tiwanaku III period. Virtually nothing is known of the processes that accompanied this transformation. Further excavation at Tiwanaku may demonstrate that the growth of Tiwanaku was not really as abrupt as it seems, but for the moment, the apparent contrast between the *estadio aldeano* of the Tiwanaku I period and the *estadio urbano* of the Tiwanaku III period is striking (Ponce 1980).

It is clear that with the abandonment of Structures 3 and 4, the relationship between Lukurmata and Tiwanaku changed. It is difficult to be more specific about the nature of this change, however. The Tiwanaku I-style ceramics vanished with little legacy. Domestic life at Lukurmata did not seem to have been permanently altered by the strong Tiwanaku influences. The "copies" of Tiwanaku I-style vessels found at Lukurmata disappeared at the same time. However, we cannot equate an absence of Tiwanaku I-style ceramics at Lukurmata with a cessation of ties between the two sites. A carved feline-serpent hairpin (Figure 6.5) found in a midden deposit between the Structure 5–6 and Structure 7 occupations reminds us that exchange between the two sites may have been in items that did not preserve. This item is notable as the first appearance of the feline motif in any form at Lukurmata. Felines, particularly pumas, are common elements of southern Andean iconography during this period, and were a corporate symbol of both the Pucara and Tiwanaku polities (Cook 1985a).

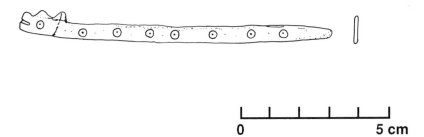

```
0                    5 cm
```

Fig. 6.5 Carved bone pin found in a layer of fill at 213 cm bd, just below the Structure 7–8 occupation.

Excavation of Tiwanaku III and IV period burials in Chile, where preservation is excellent, often reveals that Tiwanaku motifs are only found in textiles or other perishable items, such as wooden spoons and snuff trays.

As Tiwanaku grew, Pucara had begun to decline. This site north of Lake Titicaca may have been the first urban settlement on the altiplano, with a public architectural complex as elaborate as that of Tiwanaku. It lasted as an influential center from

500 B.C. to roughly A.D. 200 (Chávez 1988; Mujica 1978). No evidence was found at Lukurmata to suggest contact with Pucara, which may have been abandoned in the third century A.D. (Carlevato 1988).

There is no evidence for Tiwanaku control or domination over Lukurmata during these occupations, and interaction may have been limited to simple household exchange of items such as the hairpin described above.

The presence of nonlocal, non-Tiwanaku pottery such as the Thin Redware bowls indicates that the Lukurmata population maintained ties to communities other than Tiwanaku. There is no evidence that Lukurmata was involved in regional exchange during this time.

CHANGES IN THE HOUSEHOLD SYSTEM

One of the contributions of a "local perspective" is the insight it provides into understanding change at the household level. In Chapter 2, I outlined the ways that household life can change and how this change can be analyzed and interpreted archaeologically. I suggested that household organization can be treated as a "system" of underlying relationships, or domestic domains, which generate the household unit archaeologists recover. Viewing households systemically provides a criterion for distinguishing between different types of household change.

In the Structure 1 occupation Thin Redware bowls were associated only with the outdoor hearth. In the Structure 3–4 occupation, they were replaced by Tiwanaku I-style bowls. The Structure 9–10 occupation saw the Thin Redware bowls return to the outdoor hearth context. The shift in the style of bowls in the occupations is one form of household change, but it does not represent transformational change. In other words, the underlying household activity—serving or offering activities around outdoor hearths using special vessels—did not change. From the "capital-centric" view, with its focus on the distribution of corporate styles, the shift might appear to represent a significant change in household life at Lukurmata. But if we take the systemic household unit as the unit of analysis to measure change at Lukurmata, the significance of the shift is overshadowed by the continuity in household activities.

Similarly, the shift in house form—from rectangular to round—does not appear to have been accompanied by a change in the range of household activities. The change in house layout, too, may not represent a shift in the underlying principles of domestic organization.

In contrast, the shift in house size may represent a shift in the underlying principles of domestic organization, perhaps the first in the Lukurmata housefloor sequence. The interior space of Structure 3 was approximately the same as that of Structure 7 (9 m²), but Structure 9 was significantly larger (16 m²).

This increase in house size has several interpretations. It may mark a shift in where domestic activities were performed, resulting in a greater need for additional interior space. Alternatively, the increase in house size could have resulted from changes in the time commitments given to particular tasks, the composition of groups that carried out tasks, or the size of households themselves. These changes could be considered "transformational" to the extent that they involved changes in the household's domain or role in society.

SUMMARY

After the abandonment of Structures 3 and 4, domestic architecture seemed to have initially reverted to previous styles. This was accompanied by a shift in household pottery as the Tiwanaku I pottery and the Queruni Orangewares abruptly disappeared. But domestic organization was not static, and by the end of the period, perhaps the third century A.D., a new form of dwelling had emerged.

The single-family dwellings of the Structure 7 and Structure 9–10 occupations display no evidence of specialization, but contain a uniform set of implements and items for daily household activities. Domestic artifact assemblages continued to be limited and strikingly uniform from house to house, with little or no variation in the appearance or variety of artifacts in each house, and even between noncontemporary houses. The household pottery assemblage during this period was an equally limited and well defined collection of Local Tradition cooking vessels, together with a very small number of distinctive bowls, perhaps used in prestation/offering activities or other special contexts.

Comparing Structures 3 and 4, 7, and 9 and 10 reveals some clear changes in house plan. Yet at the same time, comparison of associated artifacts also demonstrates clear continuity in the range of household activities. In addition, despite the changes in architectural style, the interior floor space of Structures 3 and 7 is comparable.

The "disjunction" between the Structure 3–4 occupation and ensuing occupations was made very clear during excavation by the disappearance of Tiwanaku I-style materials. But comparison of artifact types and house contents shows that the "break" was more apparent than real. Household activities remained much the same, despite changes in pottery preferences.

The changes displayed by the Structure 9–10 occupation may represent changes of great significance for two reasons: first, because the differences may represent changes in the household system or the underlying principles of household organization; and second, because they may represent autonomous change, not linked to outside influence or interaction with Tiwanaku. This reminds us that Lukurmata, like all small sites, was a dynamic community in its own right.

SUMMARY OF THE PRE-TIWANAKU PERIOD (100 B.C.–A.D. 300) AT LUKURMATA

The sequence of household remains suggests that the Lukurmata household unit during this period included a small, single-family dwelling of mud brick and stone with hearths. The dimensions of the household that changed least through time were structure size (until Structure 9) and the range of household activities. A remarkably uniform artifact assemblage was associated with each structure, indicating that the same activities continued to be performed in or near Lukurmata dwellings. The greatest change was seen in the shape of dwellings and in pottery-style preferences. If the household is viewed as a system, the sequence suggests little "transformational" change, or change in the underlying principles of household organization (at least until the Structure 9–10 occupation). Instead, most of the changes appear to have been in the style (not the type) of artifacts such as pottery. This change is striking to the archaeologist accustomed to treating changes in pottery style as the equivalent of social change. However, if one looks at activities, or the range of vessel shapes in the domestic assemblage, the argument for "significant" change is weakened.

Whether shifts in pottery styles are significant depends on the meaning placed on pottery decoration. If such styles are viewed as markers of social or ethnic identity, than such shifts are highly significant social changes. If, however, pottery style communicates a range of contextual information or messages, then shifts in stylistic preferences may not be related to changes in "identity" or the "strength" of interaction with outside populations. To support this interpretation, I have shown that the Tiwanaku I-style bowls incorporated into Lukurmata households replaced a similar form of bowl in particular domestic activities, probably serving activities. Therefore, the appearance of the Tiwanaku bowls may have been structured by local patterns rather than by shifts in ethnic identity or an external, Tiwanaku-dominated exchange system. In short, from the "local perspective," the use of the Tiwanaku bowls may reveal more about Lukurmata domestic patterns than interaction with Tiwanaku or the sociopolitical affiliation of Lukurmata households.

The latter half of the early period at Lukurmata (from the first century B.C. to the third century A.D.) was a pivotal period in the circum-lake area—one that saw the rise of a city that would come to dominate the southern altiplano and eclipse rival centers, such as Pucara. At Tiwanaku, construction of monumental architecture was beginning and regional ties were stretching into the area that is now Peru.

Throughout this period, Lukurmata was a small hamlet or village of socially undifferentiated households. It would have been economically self-sufficient, with a mixed economy of fishing, herding, and agriculture. Lukurmata was probably politically independent as well. There is no evidence for Tiwanaku control or domination over Lukurmata. Interaction between Lukurmata households and Tiwanaku probably took the form of simple exchange on an individual household basis, or participation in the same exchange networks. With the possible exception of the Structure 3–4 occupation, there is no evidence for extensive ties to any of the larger centers of the region. There is no evidence that Lukurmata was unique at this time; it was probably one of many similar communities along the lake.

7

The Rise of the Tiwanaku
Polity

*The distribution of Tiahuanaco culture and
influence throughout the Andean Area is a
complex problem, restricted on all sides
by lack of definite information.*
(Bennett 1934: 483)

TIWANAKU DURING THE TIWANAKU III PERIOD
(200 B.C.–A.D. 400)

The site of Tiwanaku is located in the Tiwanaku Valley, a flat and windswept drain-age broken by low hills and ravines (see Figure 3.2). The valley is well defined, bounded by the hill ranges of Kimsa Cjata projecting 200 m above the valley floor to the south, and the Taraco and Achuta hill ranges to the north (Browman 1981, 1984; Girault 1977b; Ponce 1981a). Lukurmata lies on the other side of the Taraco–Achuta Hills.

The transformation of Tiwanaku from a small village to an urban center during the first four centuries of our era remains poorly understood. As research continues at Tiwanaku, we can only identify some general processes of this singular transforma-tion: (1) a concentration of population at Tiwanaku; (2) the construction of large quan-tities of public architecture at the site; and (3) the emergence and spread of a distinctive corporate art style and iconography from the Tiwanaku center.

The most striking change in the region was the growth of Tiwanaku into a huge ceremonial center, with vast monumental complexes laid out in a grid pattern oriented to the cardinal directions. These complexes—including terrace platforms, elaborate high-walled enclosures, and sunken courts—form a 16 ha public/ceremonial core of the site (Browman 1981; Tapia 1984c).

The quantity and distribution of Tiwanaku III-style pottery on the surface at Lukur-mata suggest that a substantial residential population surrounded the public architec-ture during the Tiwanaku III period, but the size of this population cannot be estimated in any meaningful way. What is clear, however, is that by end of the Tiwanaku III period, Tiwanaku would have been the largest demographic center in the southern Andes (Moseley 1992). The two stone-faced pyramids or platform mounds of Akapana and Pumapunku dominate the site (Kolata 1983; Ponce 1969a, 1980, 1981a). The Akapana monument, 200 m on a side and 15 m high, was formed by terracing and facing a natural hill. Excavations along the eastern edge of the Akapana suggest that the monument had three stepped terraces, with retaining walls of large stone blocks (Ponce 1969c; Tapia 1984c). Pumapunku is a smaller terraced mound, measuring 150 m on a side and 5 m high. It also may have had three tiers, as well as a large interior patio or "sunken court" lined with smaller structures (Ponce 1969c; Tapia 1984c). Access to this complex was provided by two large stone staircases on the east face.

The Kalasasaya enclosure is a multilevel platform to the north of the Akapana. Bounded by a 3 m high masonry wall, it measures roughly 145 m × 125 m and contains a sunken patio. Elaborate entrance gates and stairways are on the east face (Kolata 1983; Ponce 1961).

The semi-subterranean temple at Tiwanaku is a nearly square construction measuring between 25 m and 30 m on a side, lined by masonry retaining walls (Kotala 1992; Ponce 1969a). Dozens of tenoned carved stone human heads were set in these walls. Some of the larger sandstone pillars in the retaining walls show traces of bas-relief carving of anthropomorphic figures (Kolata 1992; Ponce 1969a). Entrance is provided by a wide stone staircase in the eastern wall.

Two construction periods can be distinguished on the basis of building material: an early one (Tiwanaku III period 200 B.C.–A.D. 400) in which red sandstone was the primary construction material, and a later one (Tiwanaku IV period, A.D. 400–A.D. 1200) in which andesite was more widely used. All of the larger monumental architecture is believed to have been constructed during the Tiwanaku III period, with additions made during the following period (Ponce et al. 1971; Ponce 1980; Tapia 1984c). The sandstone was brought from quarries located roughly 10 km south of Tiwanaku. The dressing/cutting and transport of the tremendous quantity of sandstone blocks suggest that Tiwanaku was already able to mobilize a large labor force in the first centuries B.C. The andesite, on the other hand, was brought from quarries on the Copacabana Peninsula, probably first by boat to the Tiwanaku "port" of Iwawe, and then overland to Tiwanaku itself, a journey of some 70 km. The largest andesite block at Tiwanaku reportedly weighs 41 tons (Browman 1981).

Three features of the monumental architecture at Tiwanaku are noteworthy because they also occur at smaller public architecture sites in the Tiwanaku settlement hierarchy. These features are the (1) central, rectangular sunken court, (2) large-walled enclosure, and (3) distinctive construction technique used for the largest monuments in which tall sandstone pillars were set into the ground at intervals and the intervening spaces were filled with smaller, carefully fitted rectangular blocks. This "pillar and sillar" style of construction is considered diagnostic of Tiwanaku public architecture (Tapia 1984c).

Tiwanaku Valley Settlement

Settlement in the Valley of Tiwanaku appears to have shifted dramatically during the Tiwanaku III period. Only three sites found by Albarracin-Jordan and Mathews could be securely assigned to the Tiwanaku III period: LV-24, LV-50, and LV-487. Together, these constitute a settlement area of less than 3.79 ha. Albarracin-Jordan and Mathews (1990:82) suggest that the depopulation in the valley reflects the large-scale movement of people to the capital site. Population aggregation at the capital was a common demographic process in the development of complex societies, resulting in the highly primate rank-size distributions characteristic of prehistoric states, in which the state capital is more than twice the size of the next largest settlement in the settlement hierarchy (Isbell 1988; Isbell and Schreiber 1978; Johnson 1977; Wright 1986). From this comparative perspective, the Tiwanaku III period settlement shifts in the Tiwanaku Valley seem consistent with the emergence of a highly centralized polity. However, there still remain major problems with the poorly defined Tiwanaku III period ceramic sequence, and more work is needed before we can fully reconstruct the processes taking place in and around Tiwanaku during this time.

Many of the Tiwanaku Valley "Formative" sites may be Tiwanaku III period sites lacking Tiwanaku III-style materials (Albarracin-Jordan, personal communication). Therefore, the apparent demographic shift could actually reflect a change in the *distribution* of Tiwanaku-style materials.

The Tiwanaku Corporate Art Style

The emergence of Tiwanaku as a major center was accompanied by the development of a highly recognizable corporate art style, presumably reflecting a powerful ideology. This art style can be seen in the impressive carved stelae and panels that adorn the monumental architecture of the capital, and on textiles, basketry, wooded and bone objects, and pottery. Tiwanaku III period iconography incorporates elements of earlier iconographic styles (particularly that of Qaluyu or Pucara) and contains elaborations of many pan-Andean motifs. The most common components of the iconographic inventory are a standing anthropomorphic figure (known variously as the "Staff God," "Front Face Deity," or "Gateway Figure") and zoomorphic representations, particularly the "zig-zag" serpent and the feline. More or less coeval with the emergence of this iconographic style was the development of a Tiwanaku pottery assemblage distinctive in both decoration and vessel shape. This pottery bore little resemblance to Tiwanaku I pottery.

The most common forms of the new pottery assemblage were ceremonial burners, often modeled in the form of a feline (Figure 7.1b, d), bottles (Figure 7.1a), and spittoons (Figure 7.1c). Tiwanaku III-style pottery was typically unslipped so that most examples display the buff or light brown color of the clay. Decoration usually consisted of polychrome painting in red, black, orange, and yellow, or pigment-filled incising. The most common designs were step designs, interlocking triangles, and zoomorphic figures. The most common zoomorphic design was a multicolored animal usually described as a stylized condor or puma.[1]

---

[1] I am following Bolivian archaeological convention in describing the felines in Tiwanaku artwork and pottery as "pumas." As Karen Mohr Chávez has pointed out (personal communication), we do not really know in most cases whether a piece really depicts a puma (*Felis concolor*) or one of nine other large native cats, including the ocelot (*F. pardalis*) or the jaguar (*Leo onca*).

The same objection can be raised to the use of the label "condor" (*Condor andino*) in describing Tiwanaku large bird representations. Paul Goldstein (1985) and Dwight Wallace (1957) present valuable discussions on the identification of particular species in Tiwanaku artwork.

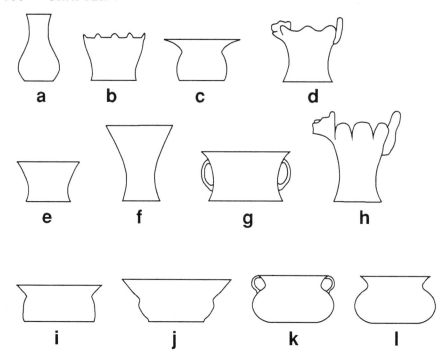

Fig. 7.1 Common Tiwanaku III, IV, and V period pottery forms: (a) Tiwanaku III-style bottle or flask, (b) Tiwanaku III-style incensario or ceremonial burner, (c) Tiwanaku III-style spittoon, (d) Tiwanaku III-style modeled puma incensario, (e) flaring-sided bowl or tazon, (f) kero, (g) hollow-base libation bowl; (h) Tiwanaku IV/V-style modeled puma incensario, (i) flat-bottom, open-rim bowl, (j) open wide-rim bowl, (k and l) round-base open bowls (adapted from Bennett 1934; Ibarra Grasso and Lewis 1986:207; Wallace 1957).

EXPANSIONIST POLITY OR WIDESPREAD RELIGION?

During the Tiwanaku III period, Tiwanaku may have been the capital of a prestate or chiefly society, perhaps the paramount center in a complex chiefdom, or—*primus inter pares*—one of several influential centers in the southern Andes (Bermann 1990; Browman 1981; Goldstein, personal communication).

As part of a "capital-centric" perspective, the regional distributions of different types of Tiwanaku III-style materials have traditionally been used to reconstruct the relationship between Tiwanaku and smaller sites. But, as I argued in a previous chapter, the distribution of Tiwanaku materials may tell more about the sites interacting with Tiwanaku than they do about Tiwanaku as a capital. The regional distribution of Tiwanaku III-style materials may relate more to the internal organization and local traditions of sites where Tiwanaku-style materials are found, than to the structure of the Tiwanaku polity.

Most of the sites at which Tiwanaku III-style materials have been found are located near the southeastern edge of Lake Titicaca. Exceptions are the Peruvian Puno and

Taraco sites at the northwest end of the lake, and Wankani (also called Khonko Wankani or San Jesús de Machaca), which is roughly 20 km south of Tiwanaku.

Ponce (1969a:80) argues from the distribution of these sites that the Tiwanaku III period polity extended over a large territory around Lake Titicaca. He estimates the area extent of the Tiwanaku III culture as 4500 km^2 (Ponce 1981a:217). However, the same types of Tiwanaku III-style items are not found at every site. At many of these sites the only criteria for assignment to the Tiwanaku culture are one or two examples of stone carving, and the Tiwanaku III affiliation for these pieces has been questioned (Chávez and Chávez 1975).

Tiwanaku III-style ceramics, other than ceremonial burners or *incensarios*, have been recovered from only three locales outside the Tiwanaku Valley: Lukurmata, Qeya Qolla Chico (on an island in Lake Titicaca), and several sites near Juli, Peru (Stanish, personal communication). To date, the only site at which Tiwanaku III-style ceramics have been found in clear domestic contexts is Lukurmata, probably because residential areas at few other circum-lake sites have been explored. Thus, Bennett's observation, quoted at the beginning of this chapter, remains an apt one.

The Tiwanaku III-style vessel whose regional distribution has been best documented is the incised, hollow-based, modeled feline incensario or ceremonial burner (Chávez 1985). This had a wider distribution than other Tiwanaku III-style vessels, and is found at sites throughout the southern Andes, as well as sites in Cuzco and Puno, Peru (ibid.). Chávez (ibid.:148) writes:

> That these ceremonial burners served a religious function as sacred ritual objects is supported by the following evidence: 1) Their ritual context, as at Pucara in the temple area, or at Qeya Qolla Chico in burials. The fact that some of the vessels are whole generally suggests they came from a ritual deposit of some kind, even burial, rather than from habitation refuse. 2) Their associated mythological feline depictions. 3) Their apparent scarcity reflecting a special purpose. 4) The labor intensive elaboration of decoration that goes beyond an ordinary or utilitarian function such as for braziers.

Chávez (ibid.:152) notes that the Cuzco and Puno examples are sufficiently unlike the Tiwanaku specimens to "suggest they are regionally distinctive and not direct imports from the Tiwanaku area." A second form of the Tiwanaku III period modeled puma incensario was one with painted, not incised, decoration. This type was more common at Tiwanaku than the incised varieties, but did not achieve widespread distribution or imitation. Only a few fragments from painted puma vessels were recovered at Lukurmata.

Tiwanaku has long been considered the source of powerful religious doctrines, perhaps even the center of a powerful religious movement (Browman 1985). Accordingly, the means of diffusion of Tiwanaku-style materials is often suggested to have been missionaries, religious pilgrims, or roving medicine men (Browman 1978a; Cook 1985b; Isbell 1983, Chávez 1985). Several investigators have taken the distribution of Tiwanaku III-style materials as evidence for such a mode of dispersal. Chávez (1985:153) cautiously suggests that "the stamped pottery . . . provides . . . a case of the spread of some aspects of Early Tiahuanaco religion."

Browman (1978a:336) suggests that during the Tiwanaku III period, Tiwanaku influence in other regions may have taken the form of a "drug culture" represented by ceremonial burners, snuff trays and tubes, fur pouches, textiles (?), wooden mortars, and various hallucinogenic plants. He (1985:61) suggests that the initial penetration of "Tiwanaku influences" into other areas may have been carried out by Callawaya-like medicine men.

This construct involving the spread of a Tiwanaku religion at least affords us a testable hypothesis. If initial interaction with Tiwanaku involved incorporation into the outer "religious" sphere, we would expect ritual items to appear in Lukurmata households before other Tiwanaku III-style objects.

From this perspective, we can view the regional distribution of these ritual items as marking an "outer sphere" of the Tiwanaku III system. As Chávez (1985) notes, the Tiwanaku III-style vessels in this outer sphere resemble pottery from centers other than Tiwanaku (such as Pucara), as well as pre-Tiwanaku period vessels. The "generic" nature of these artifacts may indicate that they were linked to widespread and long-standing traditions, or to beliefs and cosmologies not yet associated with a particular demographic center.

If the feline ceremonial burners and drug-related items mark the "outer sphere" of the Tiwanaku III system, the regional distribution of other Tiwanaku III-style pottery types delimits an "inner sphere," including sites in the Tiwanaku Valley or close to Tiwanaku (such as Lukurmata, the Pampa Koani sites, and Qeya Qolla Chico). In contrast to the pan-Andean feline incensarios of the outer sphere, *distinctly Tiwanaku* materials and symbols circulated in the inner sphere: the Tiwanaku III-style stylized puma, and the decorated spittoon and bottle pottery vessels. These items were probably produced at Tiwanaku itself, and do not resemble materials from other centers or regions.

Very little is known about the widespread religious traditions, ceremonial activities, and underlying cosmology shared by so many people over the southern Andes between five hundred and one thousand years ago. It is interesting that no examples of the iconography (Front Face God or Staff Deity, serpents, raptorial birds, and felines/ pumas) associated with these religious traditions were found in the pre-Tiwanaku period occupations at Lukurmata.[2] Among the explanations for the lack of these items is that they were made of perishable materials (textiles or basketry), were not discarded near habitations (Chávez 1985), or were simply not used in household rituals at Lukurmata.

[2] The single exception is the carved bone hairpin described in Chapter 6.

8

Lukurmata during the
Tiwanaku III Period

The Tiwanaku III period at Lukurmata began with the appearance of small quantities of Tiwanaku III-style ceramics in midden deposits at 170–175 cm below datum in the main excavation on the ridge. These pottery fragments were from small, decorated bowls and cups rather than the elaborate incensarios described in the previous chapter.

The first occupation clearly associated with Tiwanaku III-style materials was at 160 cm below datum, and could date from 50 to 150 years after the initial appearance of Tiwanaku III-style materials. Clearing 84 contiguous m² at this depth exposed the remains of five contemporary structures—Structures 14–18—and associated outdoor artifacts and features (see Figure 8.4). Material from the floor of Structure 16 provided a single calibrated radiocarbon date of A.D. 430 ± 80, although the styles of associated ceramics suggest the occupation could be somewhat older.

Another occupation with Tiwanaku III-style ceramics was exposed in a nearby excavation along the face of the terrace, some 50 m to the northwest of the central excavation (Figure 8.1). Structure 13, exposed in this excavation, represents the earliest occupation on this part of the ridge. Charcoal from this occupation yielded a radiocarbon date calibrated to A.D. 270 ± 280.

SITE COMPOSITION

The appearance of Tiwanaku III-style materials in a second part of the ridge could indicate that the density of occupation at Lukurmata was increasing. However, habitation may still have been limited to the ridge, and Lukurmata probably remained a small settlement of less than three hundred inhabitants.[1]

The Structure 14–18 occupation did suggest a shift in intrasite patterning, with the ridge residents living in household units consisting of two or more small, adjacent structures, one of which was used for nonresidential activities. The Structure 14–18 occupation also showed signs of a different, perhaps more formal, organization of the residential area, with architectural partitioning of outdoor space and drains that may have separated social groups.

[1] If we assume that each residential structure housed an arbitrary five people the Structure 14–16 occupation would give us 10 people for 185 m². The area of the ridge available for occupation (excluding possible terraces) is roughly 6000 m², so if settlement on the rest of the ridge was identical to what we uncovered, we can suggest a figure of 300 people as the upper limit for ridge population during this occupation. Quite possibly the actual population was far below this, and the total for the site itself may not have been this high.

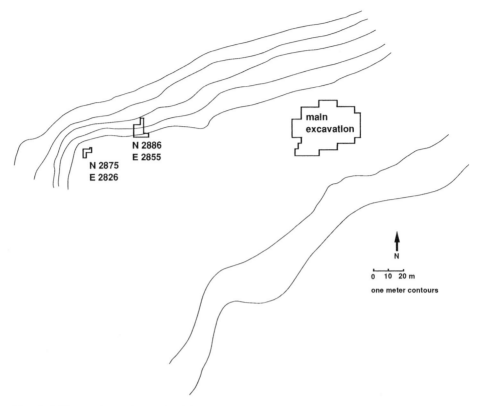

Fig. 8.1 Excavation units on the ridge west of the temple hill. House remains dating to the Tiwanaku III period were found in the main excavation and N2886 E2885.

DOMESTIC ARCHITECTURE: STRUCTURE 13

Roughly 7 m² of the Structure 13 occupation was exposed at 200 cm below datum in excavation N2886 E2855 (Figure 8.2). This occupation consisted of the remains of a structure and an activity surface with a hearth and several ash pits. The structure was represented by a wall foundation—a double alignment of rough fieldstones faced on both sides. South of this wall was a 10 cm thick layer of gray-white clay.

A slightly gravelly, sandy surface north of the wall foundation was clearly an occupational surface. This could have been the living surface of Structure 13 rather than the white clay. Major features in this surface included a circular hearth; a small pit containing charcoal, ash, a pecked cobble, and plainware sherds; a large, shallow refuse pit; and an alignment of stones.

Surface items consisted of domestic debris: fragments of mammal bone, projectile points, a stone cone, several small flakes, a large stone scraper, a small amount of debitage, and a set of deer antlers, one end of which showed a considerable amount of wear around the point. Ethnographic accounts (Venero 1987) portray identical tools serving as hoes in harvesting tubers (Figure 8.3). Another set of antlers with the same

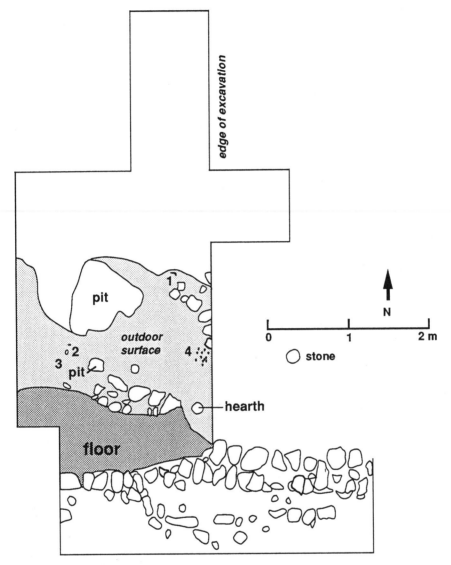

Fig. 8.2 Plan of Structure 13 floor (dark shading) and associated outdoor surface (light shading) exposed in N2886 E2855. Selected artifacts plotted. *Key:* (1) deer antler illustrated in Figure 8.3, (2) projectile point, (3) stone scraper, (4) lithic debitage.

type of wear was found just below the sandy surface in the western side of the unit. Similar artifacts have been recovered from other prehispanic sites in Bolivia (Liendo 1956: Figure 38). Pottery remains found on the Structure 13 floor and associated out-door surface included fragments of a black plainware vessel coated on the interior with a burned white (mineral?) material, parts of a single Lorokea Fiber globular-bodied jar, and two decorated Tiwanaku III-style sherds.

0   5 cm

a

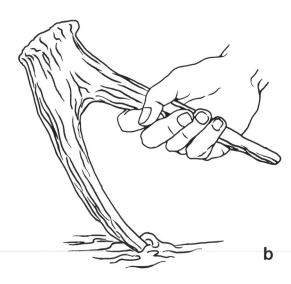

b

Fig. 8.3 (a) Deer antler from the outdoor surface outside Structure 13. (b) Identical tools, known as *chinchas*, are still used in tuber cultivation in the Andes (after Venero 1987).

DOMESTIC ARCHITECTURE AND ACTIVITIES: STRUCTURES 14–18

The floors of this occupation display amorphous shapes, but the structures themselves would have been rectangular in plan, with straight walls (Figure 8.4). They averaged roughly 5 m × 3 m in size. The floors were made of a 10 cm thick layer of orange clay, and the largest postholes were located near the corners of the floor. The shape of the dwellings and posthole patterns suggest that the structures probably had gable or hip thatch roofs, as shown in the artist's reconstruction (Figure 8.23). Not all house entrances could be determined, but that of Structure 14 was in the southeast wall.

Structures 14, 16, and 17 were completely excavated. Portions of the Structure 15 floor (6.5 m²) and the Structure 18 floor (2 m²) were also exposed.

Although all of the structures of this occupation were architecturally similar, they varied in associated features and artifacts. The structures can be divided into two groups: those with hearths (Structures 14, 15, and 16) and those without hearths (Structure 17).

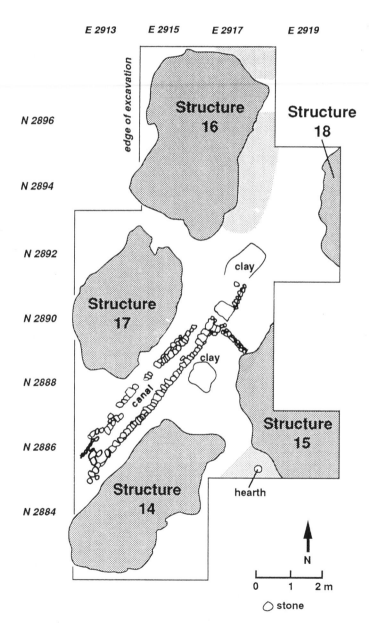

Fig. 8.4 Structure 14–18 occupation showing floors (dark shading), preserved outdoor surfaces (light shading), and clay-lined drain. Intrusive features not shown.

Structures with Hearths (14–16)

Structures 14, 15, and 16 each possessed a hearth at one end of the structure and a small storage pit at the opposite end. The Structure 14 hearth consisted of an unmodified pit (55 cm × 42 cm, and 7 cm deep) scraped into the floor (Figure 8.5). A shallow pit in the center of the structure held refuse from the hearth. The roughly circular storage pit at the other end of the house (55 cm in diameter, and 30 cm deep) had smooth, vertical, unlined walls and a flat, sandy bottom. It held fragments of fire-cracked rock, chunks of charcoal, a flat stone disk, a *mano* or grinding stone fragment, and the base of a large plainware vessel.

Structure 16 contained similar features (Figure 8.6). The hearth at one time may have consisted of two adjacent pits scraped into the floor. Fish bones and Lorokea Fiber sherds were found in each pit. The storage pit was 34 cm × 30 cm wide, slightly bell-shaped, and between 20 cm and 25 cm deep. It was not clear whether the pit contents were associated with the occupation of the house. The fill contained camelid bone, sherds, fragments of fire-cracked rock, and a ceramic "button." The partially exposed floor of Structure 15 held a number of postholes and a large firepit (Figure 8.7). The latter feature was only partly excavated.

The similar range of items recovered from the floors of Structures 14, 15, and 16 represents the typical debris of household tasks and personal adornment. These items included small grinding stones (manos), bone needles and awls (*wichuñas*), spindle whorls, and flakes and lithic debitage. Structure 16 also contained a flat bead fragment made from polished white shell (*Conus* sp., a marine genus). Camelids, fish, guinea pig, and bird were represented in the faunal assemblage of each structure.

Structures 14, 15, and 16 shared a similar pottery assemblage as well. Most of the fragments were from Local Tradition Lorokea Fiber utilitarian vessels. Also associated with the structures was a new style of utilitarian pottery not found with previous occupations: Cutini Creamware. The decorated sherds from these structures included fragments of Tiwanaku III-style vessels (tripod bowls and "antler" cups), as well as fragments of several different non-Tiwanaku bowls of styles not seen earlier at Lukurmata.

Structures without Hearths

Although Structure 17 was similar to Structures 14 and 16 architecturally, it differed sharply in contents and interior features, lacking the features and artifacts we would expect of a structure used as a dwelling (Figure 8.8). The only interior features were a shallow depression in the north end of the floor, a small pit, and postholes.

There were few pottery fragments on the floor of Structure 17, virtually no bone fragments, a single bone tool, and no recognizable stone tools or debitage. The few sherds present came from the largest Local Tradition vessels (the Lorokea Fiber vertical rim ollas) or large Cutini Creamware pots. No decorated ceramics or fragments of cooking vessels were found on the floor.

Structure 18 was only partly excavated (Figure 8.9). Even though it is a small sample, the artifact assemblage recovered from 2 m² of the Structure 18 floor resembled that of Structure 17, rather than Structures 14–16. On this basis, I would predict that if fully excavated, Structure 18 would not have displayed a hearth.

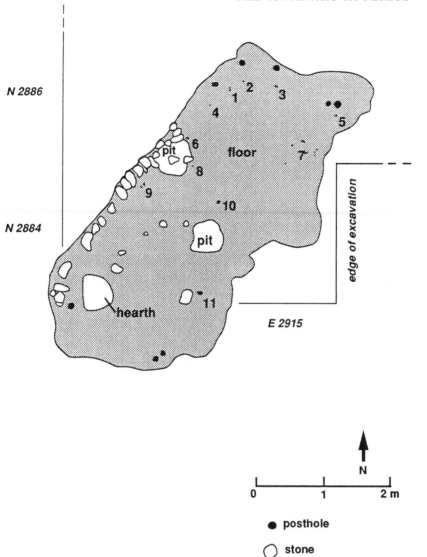

Fig. 8.5 Plan of Structure 14 floor with selected artifacts plotted. *Key*: (1) flakes, (2) bone needle fragment, (3) wichuña, (4) ceramic spindle whorl, (5) pecked cobble, (6) hammerstone, (7) lithic debitage, (8) retouched flake, (9) mano, (10) pecked (?) cobble, (11) intact bird leg bones.

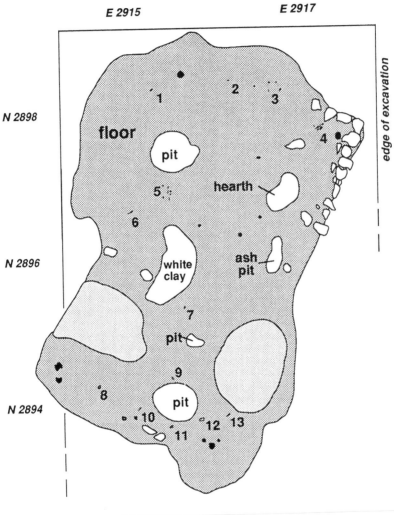

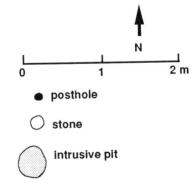

Fig. 8.6 Plan of Structure 16 floor with selected artifacts plotted. *Key*: (1) retouched flake, (2) bone bead, (3) lithic debitage, (4) bird bones, (5) lithic debitage, (6) bone needle, (7) wichuña fragment, (8) stone scraper, (9) stone perforator, (10) bone needle, (11) wichuña fragment, (12) pecked cobble, (13) two bone awls.

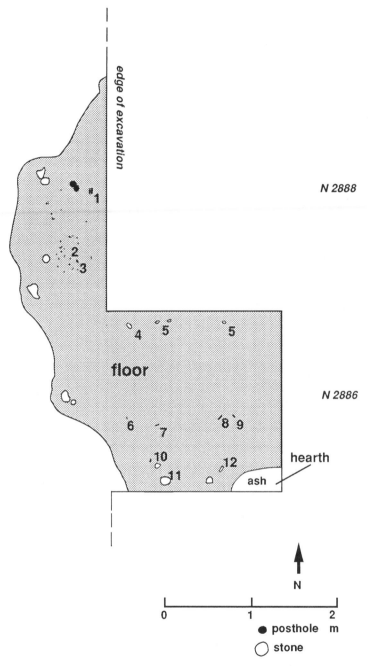

Fig. 8.7 Plan of Structure 15 floor with selected artifacts plotted. *Key*:
(1) worked camelid phalanges, (2) lithic debitage, (3) decortication flake,
(4) worked bone tablet, (5) polished camelid bone fragment, (6) bead
fragment, (7) bone tube fragment, (8) bone needle, (9) bone needle fragment,
(10) stone chopper/scraper, (11) grinding stone, (12) worked camelid
tibia (punch?).

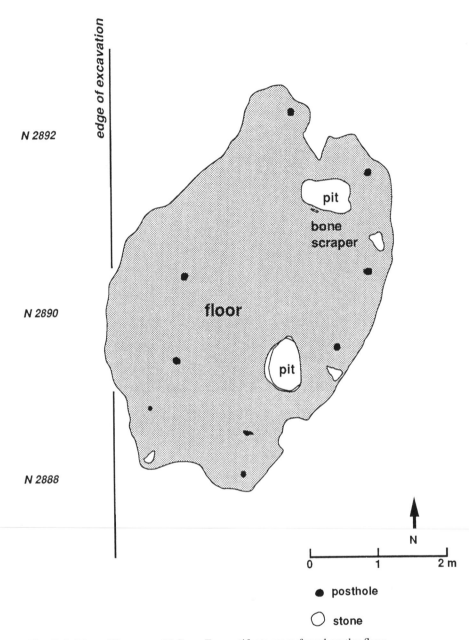

Fig. 8.8 Plan of Structure 17 floor. Few artifacts were found on the floor.

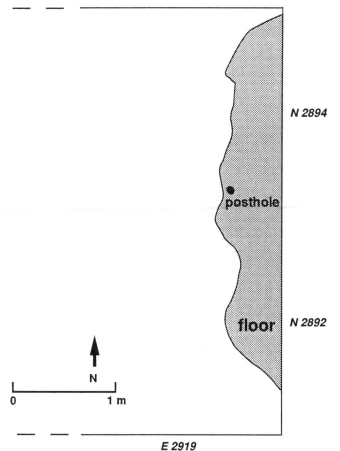

Fig. 8.9 Plan of Structure 18 floor.

Outdoor Activity Areas

Reconstructing outdoor activities for this occupation is difficult because the density of houses and intrusive pits made it possible to locate only 8.4 m² of associated outdoor surfaces. The locations of these surfaces are shown in Figure 8.4. The artifacts from the outdoor surfaces suggest that interstructure areas were used for broadly the same range of activities as indoor spaces.

An area of particularly high artifact density (130 sherds/m²) between Structures 14 and 15 marked the top of a shallow midden deposit. Artifacts in this midden included fragments of various types of pottery and of camelid, bird, fish, rodent, and dog bone. Stone artifacts from the surface included large hammerstones, ground stones, scrapers, axes or knives, two bifaces, many small flakes, and debitage. A large deposit of gray ash containing fish bone and fine bone fragments just west of Structure 15 probably consisted of material cleaned out from hearths.

The spaces between the houses and the drain were probably used for refuse disposal. The area between Structure 16 and the drain yielded small bits of bone, some lithic debris, remains of cooking ollas and Lorokea Fiber bowls, and fragments of Tiwanaku III-style vessels (from "antler" cups and spittoons). The artifact assemblage here closely paralleled the floor assemblage of Structure 16, and quite probably came from that house.

In contrast, the artifacts on the outdoor surface south of Structure 17—a more spacious and accessible area probably used for outdoor activities rather than simply refuse disposal—were fragments from large ceramic vessels (Cutini Creamware) that may have been used for outdoor storage. This surface also yielded cortex fragments of river cobbles, and pieces of the white plaster "cups." Traces of a small firepit were found just east of Structure 14. Scattered in and around it were small flakes and debris from the preparation of flake tools.

Summary of Domestic Activities

The contents of structures with hearths—the debris of daily domestic tasks and discarded items of personal adornment—indicate that these buildings were used as habitations. Faunal remains indicate the cooking and consumption of camelids, fish, guinea pig, and fowl. Grinding stones (Figure 8.10) suggest the processing of plant foods. Each household also probably made or repaired many of their own bone and stone tools for scraping, cutting, and sewing tasks. Artifacts used in spinning and weaving were found in each house, together with items that might have been used in wood working, basket making, and hide working.

The bulk of each household's pottery consisted of the same type of Local Tradition

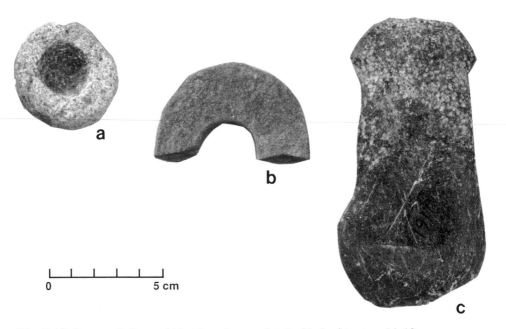

a

b

0   5 cm

c

Fig. 8.10 Stone tools from midden deposits associated with the Structure 14–18 occupation: (a) stone mortar, (b) ring fragment, and (c) basalt ax or hoe.

utilitarian vessels described for earlier occupations. Lorokea Fiber open-mouth ollas and Lorokea annular bowls were widely used for cooking. Each household also possessed a number of larger ollas, and different sizes of pitchers or jars for storage or carrying water. The small collection of decorated pottery (both Tiwanaku III-style ceramics and imported bowls) maintained by each household may have been used in serving activities. Although there were very strong continuities in the amount and variety of domestic pottery, the Structure 14–18 occupation displayed some marked changes in the domestic pottery assemblage.

One obvious change from previous occupations was the use of Tiwanaku III-style pottery in Lukurmata households. A second change was an increase in the range of pottery shapes in the household assemblage. The social or functional significance of this is unclear, but previous occupations at Lukurmata had been distinguished by a remarkably limited range of pottery shapes. The Structure 14–18 households simply used a greater variety of pottery than had previous occupations. Part of this increase resulted from the addition of a range of decorated Tiwanaku III-style pottery to the household assemblage, giving individual households a greater collection of decorated, "social display" vessels than ever before.

Just as Tiwanaku I-style pottery had entered Lukurmata households accompanied by a distinctive utilitarian ware, the Tiwanaku III-style pottery was accompanied by Cutini Creamware (Figures 8.11, 8.12). However, unlike Queruni Orangeware, Cutini Creamware vessels did not *replace* traditional vessel types. Instead, Cutini Creamware represents the addition of a new pottery shape to the household assemblage—that of a large storage-type jar.

The presence of interior storage pits, an increase in the representation of large storage vessels, and the presence of the special-purpose structures such as Structure 17 are good evidence that household storage activities at Lukurmata had become more important.

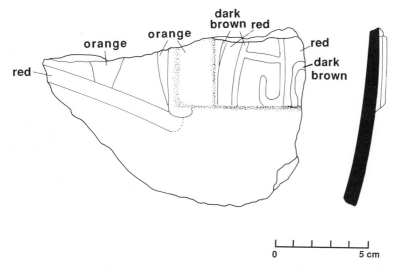

Fig. 8.11 Cutini Creamware used in Tiwanaku III period Lukurmata dwellings. Part of large Cutini Creamware storage vessel.

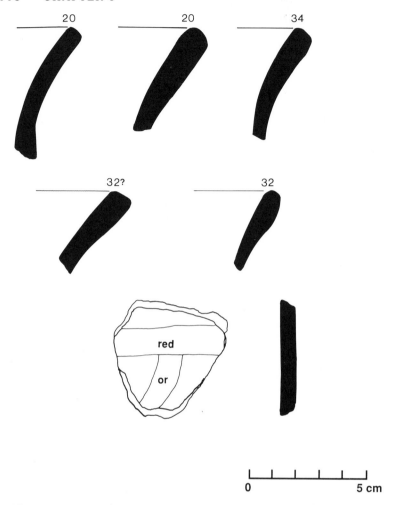

Fig. 8.12 Common Cutini Creamware rim forms with rim diameters in cm.

CONTINUITY AND CHANGE IN HOUSEHOLD LIFE

This occupation was similar to earlier occupations in many ways, but different in several others. Structures 14–18 were built with the same materials and techniques used in earlier domestic architecture at Lukurmata. The types of artifacts recovered from these structures also suggest that the same range of activities continued as universal domestic tasks. Thus, in some respects, domestic life probably continued in much the same manner as it had for centuries.

On the other hand, some dimensions of the household appear to have changed markedly with the Structure 14–18 occupation. While the range of activities did not change, the organization or spatial structure of particular activities may have. The Structure 14–18 occupation was the first at Lukurmata to display major differences in the content and features of buildings, particularly the addition of buildings used for special purposes by the household unit. We do not know if the special-purpose structures were necessitated by a change in a traditional domestic activity (such as increased storage), the introduction of new activities to the household domain, or shifts in household structure, membership, or residence patterns.

Formerly, the interior area used by a household was under one roof; with the Structure 14–18 occupation, the household's interior floor space was divided up between buildings. This is an important shift in the distribution of floor space and presumably the spatial organization of tasks.

Dietary Change

The Structure 14–18 occupation also provided evidence of a change in the meat portion of the diet of ridge residents. Lake and shore fowl (represented by bones and egg shell) had been a significant part of the diet when Structures 9 and 10 were occupied, but as shown in Table 8.1 and Appendix II, the bird bone representation dropped significantly with the Structure 14–18 occupation. Our impressions while excavating were that there was also less fish bone in the Structure 14–18 deposits, but we do not have the quantitative data to test this hypothesis. Overall, however, it appears that lake faunal resources became less important around the time of the Structure 14–18 occupation. This change represents the first major dietary shift seen in the occupational sequence at Lukurmata.

Table 8.1 Decline in Bird Consumption

Occupation	%[a]	N
Structure 9–10	13.7 ± 1.5	5
Structure 14–18	4.4 ± 1.2	8

Mean percentages of bird bones in randomly selected excavation lots from the Structure 9–10 and 14–18 occupations. Mann-Whitney $U = 39$, $p < .01$.

[a] Plus or minus terms represent one standard error.

The drop in lake faunal resources may have been related to developments on the Pampa Koani. The Tiwanaku-directed construction of raised fields, begun during the Tiwanaku III period (Kolata 1986), may have disrupted avian habitats and at the same time increased reliance on agricultural products. Or the expanded population in the Pampa Koani could have begun to compete with Lukurmata residents for lacustrine and littoral resources, while restricting the harvesting range of Lukurmata inhabitants. Finally, we cannot rule out the possibility that changes in lake level moved the shoreline—the richest avian area—away from Lukurmata. The shoreline may have been some distance away, with several communities lying between the water and Lukurmata.

A New Form of Household Unit

The buildings from this occupation provide the first evidence in the Lukurmata occupation of buildings put to different uses, or, to look at it another way, that household activities were carried out in more than one structure. Each household unit included a central building where day-to-day activities were performed as well as a special-purpose structure. Alternatively, access to a special-purpose structure was shared by nearby households.

THE DRAIN

The residences exposed in the main ridgetop excavation were separated by a drain running diagonally across the excavation. The drain had mud and stone walls and was lined with clay (Figure 8.13). The bottom of the drain channel gently sloped to the southeast (about 1 cm per m), suggesting that between November and March the drain carried water from the temple hilltop. Water management was a long-standing concern of the prehispanic inhabitants at Lukurmata, and nearly every subsequent occupation included drains. Some drainage systems elsewhere at the site were fairly elaborate (Kolata and Ortloff 1989; Ortloff and Kolata 1989). We also discovered a construction or maintenance feature associated with the drain. This was a large pit (90 cm × 80 cm × 15 cm) to the east of the drain filled with the same clay that was used to line the drain (Figure 8.4).

Extending southeast from the drain to the west side of Structure 15 was the field-stone base for a short wall. This wall is significant as the first evidence of formal partitioning of the outdoor domestic areas at Lukurmata. In fact, as I discuss below, the drain itself may have demarcated a social boundary or division between two residential units.

Fig. 8.13 Detail of drain construction.

HOUSEHOLD DIFFERENCES IN STYLISTIC PREFERENCES?

Although fragments of most pottery types were found throughout the occupation, certain vessel types and decoration motifs were found in deposits east of the drain, while different types and styles were limited to the area west of the drain.

Structures 14, 15, and 16 all contained fragments of Tiwanaku III-style vessels. Fragments of "antler" cups (Figures 8.14–8.17b) were associated with all of these structures. But tripod bowls (Figures 8.17a, 8.18) were limited to the floors of Structures 14 and 15 and to deposits east of the drain. In contrast, fragments of bottles and spittoons (Figures 8.19, 8.20) were limited to Structure 16 and deposits west of the drain. This east-west division extended to the spatial patterning of fragments from non-Tiwanaku bowls as well (Figure 8.21), with non-Tiwanaku bowl fragments found east of the drain differing in style from those to the west.

In summary, while each household possessed a small quantity of decorated ceramics (both Tiwanaku III-style materials and "imported" bowls), the distribution of Tiwanaku III-style pottery suggests that the drain separated two household units (one composed in part of Structures 16 and 17, and the other of Structures 14, 15, and 18), each possessing a slightly different assemblage of prestige or serving vessels.

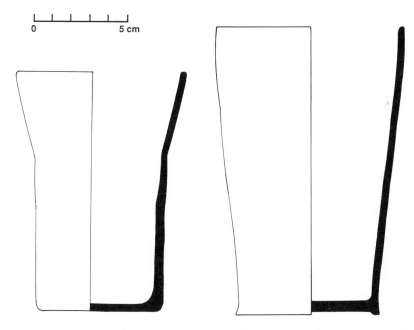

0   5 cm

Fig. 8.14 A previously unknown Tiwanaku III-style pottery form, these kero-like cups were common in Lukurmata domestic contexts.

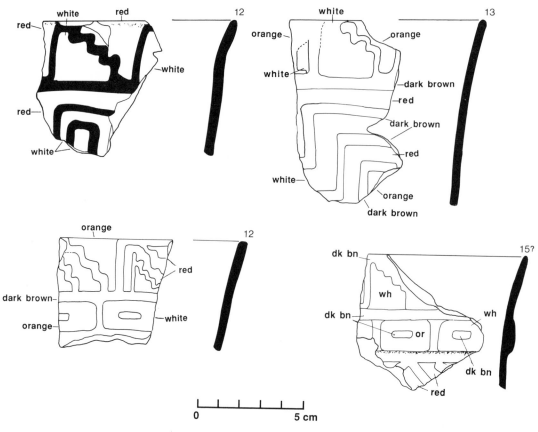

Fig. 8.15 Tiwanaku III-style cups from the Structure 14–18 occupation. Polychrome decoration over an unslipped light brown surface. Rim diameters in cm.

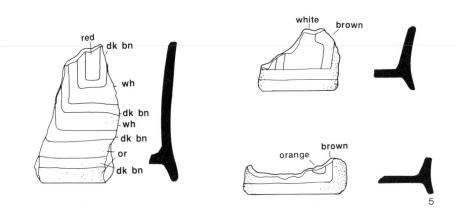

Fig. 8.16
Tiwanaku III-style
cup bases.

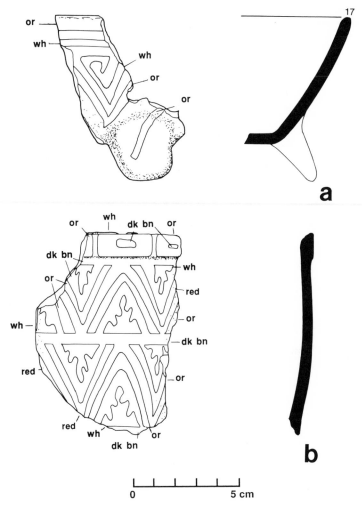

Fig. 8.17 Tiwanaku III-style ceramics from Structure 14 floor:
(a) bowl fragment, (b) cup fragment displaying "antler" decoration.

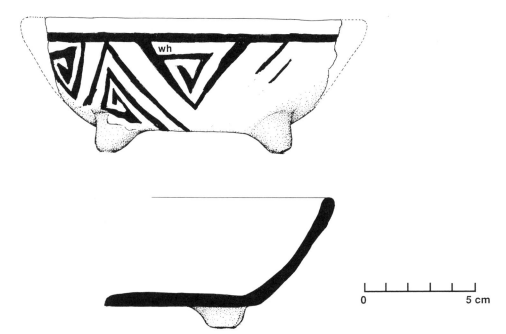

wh

0   5 cm

Fig. 8.18 Typical Tiwanaku III-style tripod bowl. This specimen was found on the floor of Structure 22.

Fig. 8.19 Tiwanaku III-style spittoon fragments from floors and deposits to the west of the drain.

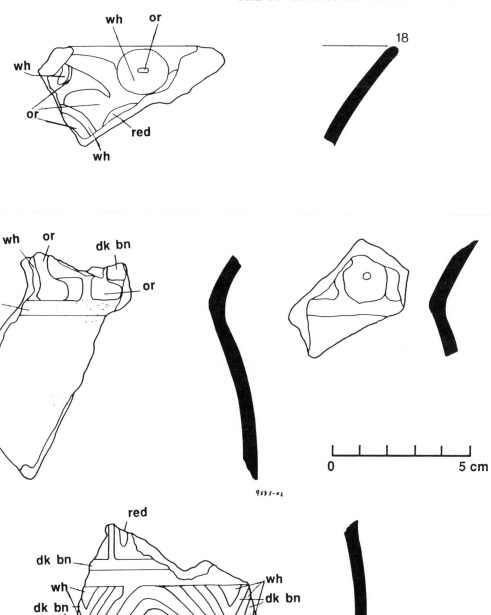

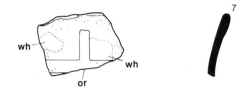

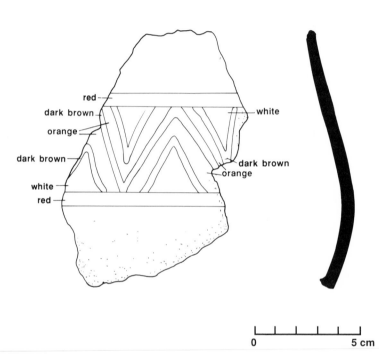

Fig. 8.20 Tiwanaku III-style bottle fragments from floors and deposits to the west of the drain.

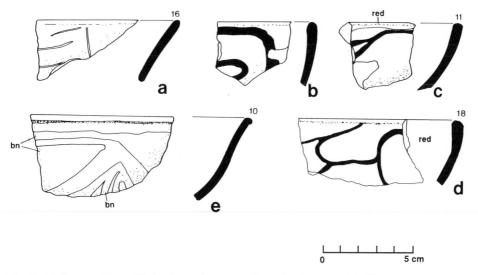

Fig. 8.21 Imported, non-Tiwanaku-style pottery from the Structure 14–18 occupation.

Mortuary Activities

Only one tomb found at Lukurmata could be securely dated (by pottery associations) to the Tiwanaku III period, suggesting that burials were not placed below floors or near houses. Burial 10 lay below the intact floor in the southwest corner of Structure 16, indicating that interment predated the Structure 14–18 occupation.

The tomb was over a meter deep. Although not stone-lined, the pit had been capped with several large fieldstones that had subsequently fallen into the pit. The individual—an old adult—had been placed in a seated and flexed position, facing northeast. The cranium exhibited a type of artificial deformation similar to the majority of the burials described in Chapter 5. The only grave goods with Burial 10 were the body of a decorated Tiwanaku III-style bottle broken at the neck and a cut section of a camelid rib.

Lukurmata in Regional Perspective

The Structure 14–18 occupation clearly displayed increased interaction with other populations at the regional and interregional levels. One change was greater participation in long-distance exchange networks (Table 8.2). Items of marine shell (from the Pacific coast), sodalite (Cochabamba), obsidian (Puno or Arequipa), and basalt (Lake Poopó area) were all found in the Structure 14–18 occupation. These appear to have entered Lukurmata as finished products rather than as raw materials.

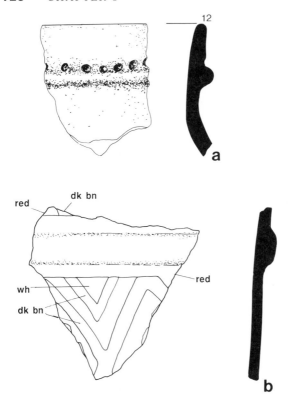

0   5 cm

Fig. 8.22 Tiwanaku III-style pottery fragments displaying vegetable fiber temper.

Table 8.2 Imported Materials in Tiwanaku III/IV Period Domestic Occupations at Lukurmata

Material	Location of Source	Reference
Mizque pottery	southern Cochabamba, northern Chuquisaca	Rydén 1956
Mojocoya pottery	southern Cochabamba, northern Chuquisaca	Branisa 1957
Juruquilla pottery	western Potosí	Ibarra Grasso 1965
Yampara pottery	Cochabamba, Potosí Chuquisaca	Rydén 1956
basalt	Querimita, Oruro	Ponce 1981a:194
andesite	Copacabana Peninsula	Browman 1978a:332
sodalite	Cerro Sapo, Cochabamba	Browman 1981:416
obsidian	Arequipa (?), Peru	Burger and Asaro 1977:315
marine shell	Pacific Ocean	

Articulation with the Tiwanaku Polity

What was the relationship between Lukurmata and Tiwanaku during the Structure 14–18 occupation? We can tentatively suggest that by the time of the Structure 14–18 occupation, Lukurmata had been incorporated into the Tiwanaku political economy.

The ceramic evidence at Lukurmata suggests that the Lukurmata population did not have the same religious or ceremonial involvement with the Tiwanaku system as the sites in Puno and Cuzco cited by Chávez (1985). As I discussed in the previous chapter, the regional distribution of Tiwanaku III-style pottery presents a concentric pattern of inner and outer spheres, with the feline incensario or ceremonial burner spread over a much wider area than the bulk of Tiwanaku III-style pottery (Chávez 1985). Fragments of ceremonial burners are extremely rare at Lukurmata (only a handful were found in all of the excavations), and the highly decorated vessels were not the initial Tiwanaku III-style pottery to appear at Lukurmata. This would suggest that the initial interaction of Lukurmata with the Tiwanaku system was not mediated through ritual or ceremonial ties, but took other forms.

In this context it may be revealing that the first Tiwanaku III-style vessels to appear at Lukurmata were vessels decorated with geometric designs, not the most elaborate decorated Tiwanaku pottery (bearing representations of zoomorphic or anthropomorphic deities). Tiwanaku III-style pottery with zoomorphic representations only began to appear in very small quantities with the Structure 14–18 occupation, and the most elaborate Tiwanaku III vessels, the ceremonial burners, did not really appear at all in Lukurmata houses.

Another form of interaction between Lukurmata and Tiwanaku could have been simple exchange (outside of political control). The presence of large quantities of Tiwanaku pottery indicates that some Lukurmata households were importing a significant amount of household pottery from Tiwanaku, or acquiring it through the regional exchange system. The Tiwanaku III-style items found at Lukurmata were largely simple bowls and cups that may have had a traditional place in the Lukurmata household and a traditional role as serving/prestation vessels in household activities.

Other evidence (discussed below) suggests that interaction between Lukurmata households and Tiwanaku involved more than simple exchange.

The third possible form of interaction was political control. To determine if Lukurmata was now a subordinate site to Tiwanaku, we can look at both regional lines of evidence (settlement patterns) and household patterns.

Developments on the Pampa Koani provide information of great value in assessing Lukurmata–Tiwanaku interaction at this time. Kolata (1986) argues that the twin pyramids PK-5 and PK-6 and the raised field systems of the Pampa were built during the Tiwanaku III period. If so, the Pampa area (and Lukurmata) may already have been politically and economically incorporated into the Tiwanaku system. Lukurmata was not directly adjacent to the main body of raised fields, and may have remained the small village it had always been; its inhabitants acquiring Tiwanaku III-style goods "second-hand" from an elite stratum residing at the sites on the Pampa Koani.

Household Consequences of Tiwanaku Political Economy

In Chapter 2 I reviewed the measures that archaeologists have used to detect shifts in household production. In order to detect changes in household production represented by the Structure 14–18 occupation, I chose to look at changes through time in the relative representation of tools and storage facilities. These measures have been successfully used by other archaeologists (Lightfoot 1984; Stanish 1985).

Using the relative representation of tools to monitor levels of production entails a number of methodological difficulties. First, we have to identify the specific tools associated with each type of production (such as spindle whorls or wichuñas and textile production). We also need to assume that intensified use of these tools will result in increased discard. This type of analysis requires devising a proportional measure, such as number of tools per unit of floor area, volume of fill, or animal bone or body sherd fragments. Finally, we have to assume that changes in tool representation represent changes in productive activities, rather than shifts in cleaning or discard patterns.

I compared the Structure 14–18 occupation to previous occupations by calculating the number of various types of tools per square meter of floor and per one thousand animal bone fragments for each occupation. This was done for weaving and spinning implements (wichuñas and spindle whorls), other bone tools (scrapers, awls, and needles), grinding stones, other agricultural implements (stone and antler hoes), and total number of tools of all types.

The results of this analysis were inconclusive. In most cases sample sizes were too small to allow meaningful comparisons. The variety and quantity of bone tools (other than weaving/spinning implements) from the Structure 14–18 occupation samples were larger than that of previous occupations, but not beyond what we might expect from chance variation. Similarly, the representation of grinding stones and hoes (items linked to agriculture) was greater in the Structure 14–18 occupation, but again, this could represent chance variation.

We can also study changes in production by turning to the "infrastructure" of agricultural output, that is, the facilities and buildings associated with an increase in productivity, such as storage structures. In this case, the appearance of the special-purpose Structure 17 is clear evidence for an increase in storage directly associated with residential units. Although our sample size of buildings is very small, I suggest that the increase in storage can be interpreted as reflecting an increase in household production.

The other indication that Lukurmata production shifts resulted from Tiwanaku surplus demands lies in the *concurrence* of change. That major changes in the Lukurmata household unit closely followed the appearance of Tiwanaku-style materials in significant quantities at the household level suggests that interaction with the Tiwanaku polity affected household production. This in turn implies that Lukurmata was now part of the Tiwanaku political economic system, and that at least one of the strategies for surplus mobilization used by the Tiwanaku polity was of the "intrahousehold" type, involving significant shifts in household economic patterns.

Incorporation into the Tiwanaku Polity: Process or Event?

The growth of Tiwanaku during this period may have consisted of the expansion of loose, but not completely indistinguishable, "spheres of influence," a combination of shared ritual activities, economic and exchange ties, and kinship-based alliances. These gradually spread Tiwanaku materials from the center, and increasingly pulled outlying communities into the Tiwanaku system. For this reason, we might be advised to talk of the general level of "participation" in the Tiwanaku system, rather than seek to define a particular point in time when Lukurmata came under Tiwanaku "control." Incorporation may not be very noticeable (or important) at the household level if it is very gradual, or only involves ties created at the highest level of society. However, I think the Lukurmata interaction with the expanding Tiwanaku chiefdom took a different form.

Incorporation into the Tiwanaku polity was not gradual; major changes in the household unit took place shortly after Tiwanaku III-style materials began to appear. The changes displayed in many dimensions of the Structure 14–18 household units are sufficient to suggest that interaction with the Tiwanaku polity *did cause* significant changes in how Lukurmata residents lived. Unlike the Structure 3–4 and Structure 9–10 cases, with this occupation the regional and household lines of evidence are in agreement, both indicating that this was a time of change for Lukurmata residents.

Summary of the Structure 14–18 Occupation

The Tiwanaku III period at Lukurmata saw major changes in household organization, although the composition of the community does not appear to have been altered greatly. Not unexpectedly, several of the differences between the earliest Tiwanaku III period occupations and the previous occupations reflect increasing participation in the Tiwanaku system. Nevertheless, it is difficult to specify *when* Lukurmata actually came under the control of the Tiwanaku polity. Many aspects of household life at Lukurmata did not change even though it was included in larger political units.

Household units of this occupation exhibited no signs of specialization or status differentiation. Household units were of comparable size and appearance, and associated with comparable quantities of faunal remains. Each household appears to have had access to comparable imported goods, including pottery from Tiwanaku and elsewhere, and small long-distance trade items such as shell and sodalite. Although there

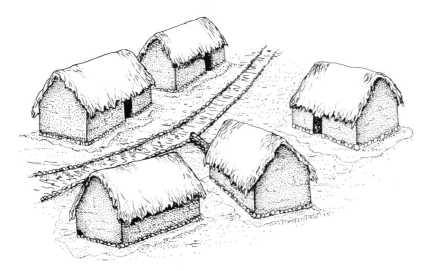

Fig. 8.23 Artist's reconstruction of the Structure 14–18 occupation.

were stylistic differences in household assemblage, each household had the same range of pottery forms and the same tools, and presumably, carried out the same daily domestic activities.

The Structure 14–18 occupation (Figure 8.23) represents a greater amount of change in the Lukurmata household unit than seen previously. These changes in the household unit suggest changes in the household's role and function. These changes in the household system reflect transformational change, whereas previous changes in Lukurmata household units are more indicative of systemic change. Lacking evidence for purely local evolutionary pressures, I believe that the Structure 14–18 occupation changes stemmed from Lukurmata households serving new roles within a larger system—as surplus producing units in the Tiwanaku polity economy.

9

Late Tiwanaku III Period Structures

A sequence of midden deposits indicates that occupation continued on the ridge after the abandonment of Structures 14–18. A total of 96 contiguous m² excavated at 125 cm below datum exposed the remains of three later structures, Structures 19–21, and an associated outdoor surface (Figure 9.1). No absolute dates for this occupation are available, but its stratigraphic relationship to other occupations with radiocarbon dates suggests an early to mid-sixth-century A.D. date.

There is no evidence that the residential population at Lukurmata was any larger than during the previous occupation, or had spread beyond the ridge. Lukurmata probably continued as a small village. Tiwanaku III-style pottery was only found in the excavations located on the ridge.

DOMESTIC ARCHITECTURE

The single completely excavated structure of this occupation was Structure 19 (Figure 9.2). A 4 m² section of the northwest edge of Structure 20 was excavated as well. Structure 21 consisted only of some patches of clay floor to the southeast of Structure 19.

Structure 19 exhibited a misshapen floor measuring 6.5 m × 6 m. It is possible that the structure had two alcoves or smaller rooms, one extending to the north, the other to the south. The structure had seen heavy use. The floor had been patched in places, and the entire building had been refloored at least once. The entrance could not be located. A line of small postholes near the northern edge of the floor marked an interior partition.

Near the east wall of the building were two circular depressions in the floor, each roughly 20 cm in diameter and 2 cm deep. These appear to have been formed by the bases of large jars. Unlike many of the Lukurmata structures, Structure 19 did not have an interior hearth, although we found a burned patch of floor and a small ash pit. The ash pit fill was a very fine, homogeneous white ash that was very different from the usual hearth contents at Lukurmata. A small mound of identical ash had been dumped on the floor just east of the ash pit.

A unique feature associated with Structure 19 was the complete fetal/infant camelid skeleton found in a below-floor pit. Although burial of a fetal or infant camelid as a dedicatory offering was a widespread custom throughout the altiplano during and after the Tiwanaku period, this was the only instance recorded at Lukurmata (Goldstein 1989:191–92).

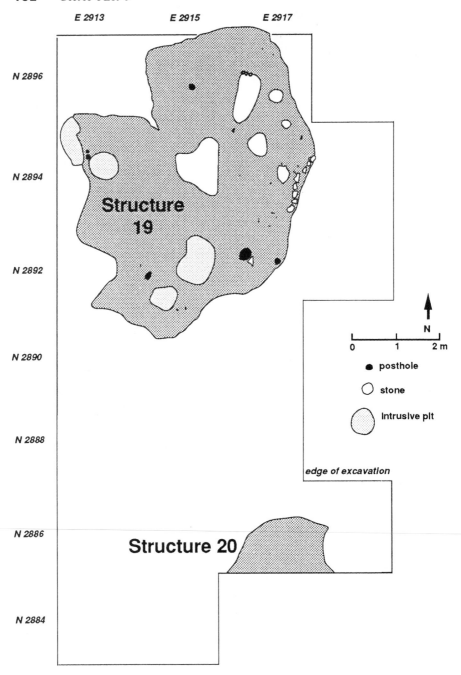

Fig. 9.1 Structure 19–21 occupation showing floors (dark shading). Some intrusive features omitted.

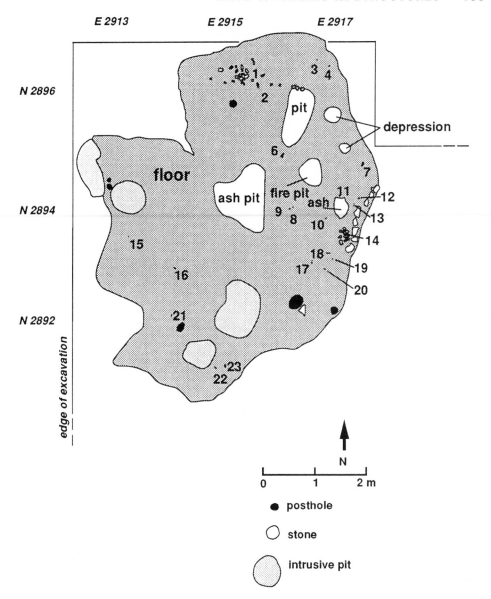

Fig. 9.2 Plan of Structure 19 floor with selected artifacts plotted. *Key*: (1) bowl fragments with white residue on interior, (2) biface, (3) shell bead, (4) shell fragment, (5) shell disk, (6) bone needle fragments (2 needles), (7) bone fragment decorated with birds illustrated in Figure 9.3, (8) spoon fragment with red pigment (Figure 9.4b), (9) worked camelid third phalange, (10) bone tool with red pigment (Figure 9.4a), (11) bone spoon fragment, (12) bone needle, (13) perforator, (14) spittoon fragments, (15) stone pendant, (16) bone needle, (17) lithic debitage, (18) wichuña fragment, (19) bone needle, (20) retouched flake, (21) stone scraper, (22) bone spoon fragment, (23) bone disk fragment.

DOMESTIC ACTIVITIES

Most of the contents of Structure 19 were typical of buildings used as habitations: fragments of Local Tradition Lorokea Fiber pottery, camelid bone, and fish bone. What made the artifact assemblage of the Structure 19 floor different from that of other Lukurmata floors was the quantity and variety of worked bone items and bone tools.

Worked bone items included a 7 cm long fragment of an elaborate pyro-engraved bone made from a camelid long bone and decorated with stylized condor heads (Figure 9.3). Although the ceramics associated with Structure 19 are Tiwanaku III-style, this fragment of carving is much closer to the Tiwanaku IV-style, suggesting that the representation of Tiwanaku iconography on various media may have been "evolving" at different rates. Other bone artifacts found on the floor represent items used for adornment: disk beads (made from bird long bones), a disk showing traces of carving around the edge, a highly polished finger ring, and a fragment of a carved pendant.

Complete specimens or fragments of five bone needles (with eyes) were recovered from the floor, together with a bone awl or punch. These may have been a toolkit used in sewing or hide working. The functions of other bone items were less obvious, such as the small (3 cm long) bullet-shaped object. Also of unknown function was a flat and slightly bowed piece of bone, with a notch carved in one end (Figure 9.4a). This was decorated with fine incisions containing red pigment. Red pigment was also found adhering to the broken-off end of a flat bone spoon (Figure 9.4b).

Items of adornment were not limited to bone. Fragments of polished shell (part of a bead, a disk, a fragment of inlay) and stone disk beads were found as well. The shell inlay was made of shell of marine origin, and one of the beads was made of sodalite, both long-distance trade materials.

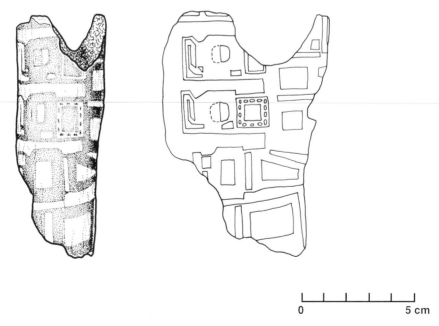

0   5 cm

Fig. 9.3 Pyro-engraved camelid bone from the floor of Structure 19.

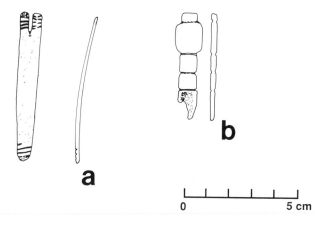

Fig. 9.4 Two of the many bone items found on the floor of Structure 19: (a) tool of unknown function, (b) spoon fragment.

On the floor toward the north end of Structure 19 were fragments of a type of vessel not seen before at Lukurmata—a moderately large, annular-base bowl with a 21 cm rim diameter. Although undecorated, this partially reconstructable vessel had the paste and temper characteristic of Tiwanaku III-style decorated pottery. The interior of the vessel was completely covered with a white material resembling calcium carbonate or plaster.[1]

Outdoor Features and Artifacts

A poorly preserved outdoor surface covering approximately 6 m^2 was exposed between Structures 19 and 20. This consisted of a hard-packed, stained, sandy surface. Among the artifacts found on it were fragments of grinding stones, and a small concentration of lithic debitage and flakes including two very small pieces of black obsidian—the first obsidian seen in the occupational sequence.

To the east of Structure 19 was a substantial deposit of stratified midden probably associated with the occupation of the structures. In addition to great quantities of plainware pottery fragments, fire-cracked rock, and camelid bone, it contained fragments of a wichuña (a weaving implement), lithic debitage, a piece of a thin polished bone tube, and the end of a bone spoon.

Domestic Pottery

The utilitarian pottery assemblage of this occupation consisted of the same range of of Lorokea Fiber vessels and large Cutini Creamware jars as found with the Structure 14–18 occupation. But the percentage of Tiwanaku III-style pottery in Lukurmata households had increased. Roughly 8 percent of the 369 total sherds of this occupation were from Tiwanaku III-style decorated pottery, as opposed to 3 percent of the 643 sherds associated with the Structure 14–18 occupation. The pottery assemblage also contained fragments of nonlocal, non-Tiwanaku bowls similar in style to those of the Structure 14–18 occupation. The origin of these bowls has not been determined. The Structure 19–20 ceramic assemblage included a handful of fragments from the type of

[1] This white material may be dried lime, the "*llipta*" chewed with coca, but has not been analyzed.

incised ceremonial burner described in Chapter 7 (Figure 9.5). This type of vessel was rarely represented in Lukurmata domestic contexts.

Household Activities: Summary

The artifacts of this occupation were similar in range and style to those of the previous occupation, indicating continuity in the range of household activities. Food preparation and consumption, spinning and weaving, basketry or hide working, and limited flake production remained household activities.

A new household activity may be represented by the two spoons and bone tube fragment: ingestion of hallucinogenic drugs. As noted previously, items related to drug use such as snuff tubes, *rapé* trays, and spoons are frequently found at Tiwanaku sites (Browman 1981).

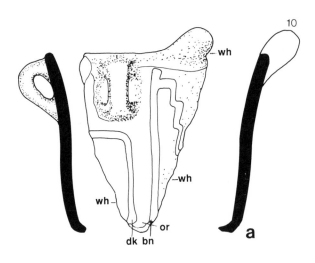

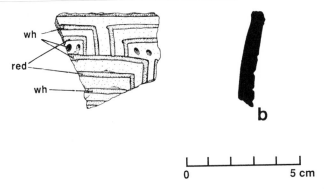

Fig. 9.5 Fragments of Tiwanaku III-style incensarios (ceremonial burners) from Lukurmata Tiwanaku III period domestic contexts.

LUKURMATA IN REGIONAL PERSPECTIVE

The increase in Tiwanaku III-style materials suggests greater interaction between Lukurmata and Tiwanaku, or greater participation in the Tiwanaku-dominated regional exchange system. Long-distance trade items from the Structure 19–21 occupation included marine shell, obsidian (probably from a source in Puno or Arequipa),[2] and sodalite (from Cerro Sapo in Cochabamba). These goods probably passed through Tiwanaku before arriving in very small quantities, and arrived as finished products in Lukurmata households. The few bits of obsidian debitage associated with the Structure 19–21 occupation suggest resharpening of a blade rather than production of a tool.

Although Lukurmata residents were probably interacting more with Tiwanaku than any other site, the non–local, non-Tiwanaku bowls of the Structure 19–21 occupation indicate that Lukurmata residents continued to maintain old ties to other communities.

SUMMARY

It is not clear how Structure 19 was used. A portion of the contents (fragments of bone and undecorated vessels, small flake tools and debitage, bone needles, items of adornment) are comparable to the contents of other Lukurmata households. The absence of particular types of household items in the Structure 19 occupation should not be considered overly significant. We would not expect *every* dwelling to have comparable contents (although the Lukurmata structures were, by and large, remarkably uniform in this respect). Overall, the Structure 19–21 occupation reflects continuity in many household activities and ties in to other settlements.

[2] The Lukurmata obsidian has not been analyzed but is thought by Instituto Nacional de Arqueología investigators to be of the Hoya del Titicaca type, common in the Lake Titicaca area and at the site of Tiwanaku (Burger and Asaro 1977:313–15). The source has not been located, but is thought to be in the Departments of Puno or Arequipa, Peru (Browman 1981).

Terminal Tiwanaku III Period
Occupation: Specialized Architecture

A short time after Structures 19 and 20 were abandoned, a new set of structures was built over their remains. Ceramic affiliations and the stratigraphic relationship to occupations with absolute dates suggest a late sixth-century A.D. date for the Structure 22–24 occupation. The occupation consisted of the remains of three structures, together with associated outdoor surfaces and features, at roughly 110 cm below datum (Figure 10.1). A total of 184 contiguous m^2 was exposed at this level.

Lukurmata probably remained a small village, no larger than it had been earlier in the Tiwanaku III period. Occupation may still have been restricted to the ridge.

ARCHITECTURE

Structures 22 (Figure 10.2) and 23 (Figure 10.3) were similar in size and construction to Structure 19. Although the preserved floors are very irregular in shape, the "shadow walls" seen in the soil indicate that both structures were rectangular. Structure 22 would have measured roughly 7 m × 4 m, while Structure 23 would have been slightly smaller at 6.5 m × 3 m. The floor of each consisted of a 6–10 cm thick layer of discolored orange clay. Because of the many intrusive pits, we had great difficulty finding internal features in either structure. Both possessed circular, sand-lined hearths. The location of entrances could not be determined.

Structure 24 was unique. It was a small, two-room building, each room measuring roughly 2 m on a side (Figure 10.4). In places where the walls were not preserved, the edge of the prepared clay floor marked the limit of the rooms. Structure 24 differed architecturally from Structures 22 and 23 in several ways. First, the wall foundations consisted of two rows of fieldstones rather than one. Second, in contrast to most buildings at Lukurmata (including Structures 22 and 23), the walls of Structure 24 had been built before the floor. The floor was the same type of clay as in Structures 22 and 23, but exhibited no features, organic staining, or occupational refuse.

DOMESTIC ACTIVITIES

Floor artifacts from Structures 22 and 23 included fragments of cooking vessels; animal bone; tools such as needles, scrapers, wichuñas, and spindle whorls; small grinding stones; stone flakes, cores, and debitage; and stone cones. A similar range of materials was recovered from outdoor surfaces, a midden area, and four small refuse pits along the edges of the housefloors.

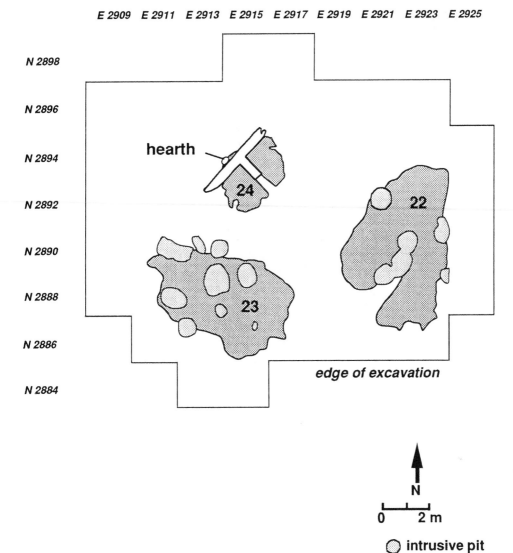

Fig. 10.1 Structure 22–24 occupation showing floors (dark shading). Some intrusive features omitted.

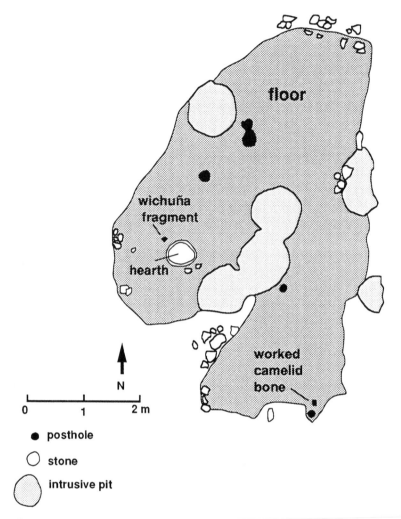

Fig. 10.2 Plan of Structure 22 floor with selected artifacts plotted.

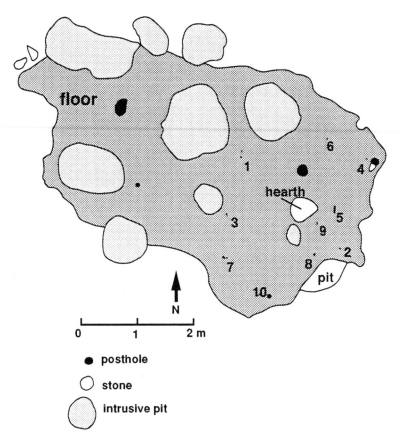

Fig. 10.3 Plan of Structure 23 floor with selected artifacts plotted. *Key:*
(1) smoothed camelid bone fragments, (2) bone tube fragments, (3) bone needle,
(4) bone needle, (5) bone scraper made from camelid rib, (6) wichuña fragment,
(7) exhausted lithic cores, (8) grinding stone, (9) spindle whorl and spindle whorl
fragment, (10) lithic flakes.

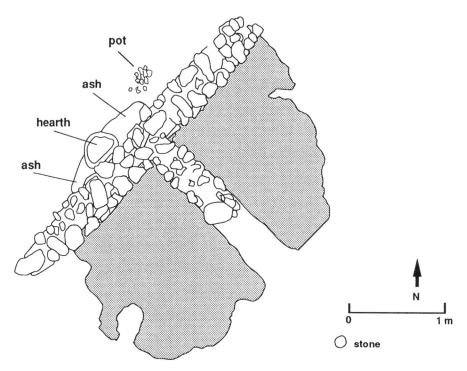

Fig. 10.4 Plan of Structure 24, a specialized storage structure. Shading indicates extent of preserved floor.

Other items found in outdoor contexts included fragments of antler tine, items of adornment (fragments of bone hair pins and metal clothing pins), projectile points, and pieces of the white plaster "molds." Fragments of worked bone bearing traces of red pigment (one of them a smoothed camelid rib) were found outside of both houses.

A large outdoor hearth and associated ash pits were found just west of Structure 24. This hearth appeared to have been used more intensively than either of the interior hearths. It was surrounded by fragments of camelid bone (some crushed and others with stone tool cut marks) and pieces of large cooking vessels. No bowl fragments were found around the hearth, suggesting that the earlier tradition involving imported bowls in serving/offering activities had disappeared. Thin Redware disappeared from Lukurmata households with the Structure 14–18 occupation.

There is no evidence for dietary change from previous Tiwanaku III period occupations. The representation of agricultural implements did not increase, and the proportion of camelid, bird, and fish bone remained the same as in earlier Tiwanaku III period occupations (Appendix II).

A New Household Activity: Drug Use

Fragments of smoothed bone tubes and small bone spoons or spatulas were found in refuse contexts outside of both structures, and a snuff tube (Figure 10.5) was found on the Structure 22 floor. As I noted in the previous chapter, tubes and spoons are common at Tiwanaku sites, and were probably used to ingest hallucinogenic drugs. Although the tube and spoon fragments of the Structure 19 occupation may well have been related to drug use, the complete snuff tube clearly associated with a typical residence (Structure 22) is stronger evidence for drug use in household rituals at Lukurmata.

Identical bone tubes have been found in association with wooden rapé trays, and with the remains of hallucinogenic plants at sites with better preservation in Moquegua and the Chilean desert. Browman (1978a:336–37) has identified a "hallucinogenic complex" consisting of stone mortars, pestles and bowls, snuff tablets, incensarios, snuff tubes, and snuff spoons as "the most frequently identified mark of Tiahuanaco influence in an area." This "drug culture" he states, "becomes one of the most frequently recognized attributes of Tiahuanaco influence" (ibid.:336). Since many of these items were made of wood, they would not have preserved at Lukurmata. The Lukurmata residents may have had access to the same psychoactive lowland plants found with the famous "medicine man" at Niño Korin, *Banisteriopsis*, *Ilex*, and *Datura* (Wassén 1972, 1973).

Domestic Pottery and Iconographic Preferences

This was last occupation at Lukurmata during which residents used Tiwanaku III-style pottery. In many respects, the domestic pottery assemblage of this occupation was similar to that of previous Tiwanaku III period occupations. As with earlier occupations, the pottery used by each household included a range of undecorated, utilitarian vessels; non-Tiwanaku, nonlocal, or "imported" vessels; and Tiwanaku-style vessels. A small number of fragments from Tiwanaku IV-style vessels were found with this occupation.

Most of the ceramics associated with Structures 22 and 23 represented utilitarian vessels in the Local Tradition used for cooking and serving (including Lorokea Fiber annular bowls and open-mouth ollas), and larger vessels probably used for storage of food and water (including Cutini Creamware).

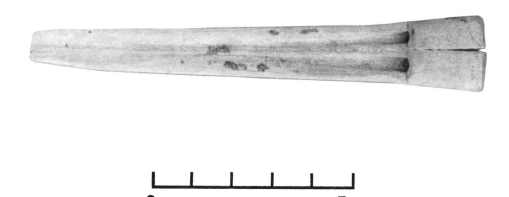

0   5 cm

Fig. 10.5 Snuff tray made from camelid bone from the floor of Structure 22.

One difference between the Structure 22–24 occupation and the Structure 19 occupation was the greater variety of Tiwanaku III-style pottery in the Structure 22–24 occupation. Not only is every form of Tiwanaku III-style pottery known from Tiwanaku represented in the Structure 22–24 occupation and the fill around it, but the range of Tiwanaku III-style pottery at Lukurmata is actually larger than that known from the capital. Either Lukurmata households now had full "access" to the entire range of Tiwanaku III-style pottery, or Lukurmata residents had now been able to adopt this pottery completely into local traditions and activities. Most of the Tiwanaku III-style decorated pottery consists of serving vessels such as cups, bowls, and platters, suggesting that serving activities, perhaps displays of ritual hospitality, had become more important to Lukurmata households.

Other changes from earlier Tiwanaku III period occupations were an increase in pottery with zoomorphic decoration (particularly puma and condor representations), and the appearance of the modeled puma or ceremonial burner pottery form (Figure 10.6). Pottery with zoomorphic representations was rare or absent in earlier occupations. Spittoon fragments, with the puma motif around the rim, were represented in

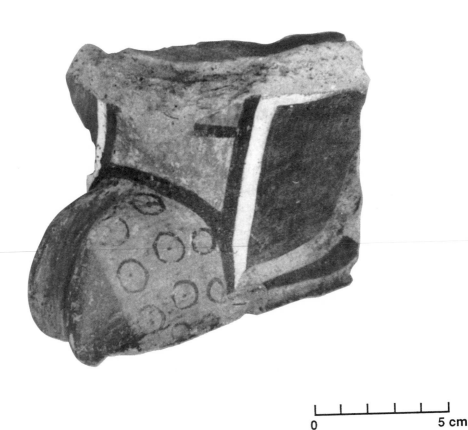

0   5 cm

Fig. 10.6 A Tiwanaku ceramic llama foot found in a fill deposit to the east of Structure 23.

earlier occupations, but in very small quantities. We do not know if this change reflects a shift in iconographic preferences by Lukurmata residents, or a general temporal shift in the Tiwanaku III iconographic styles.

Coupled with the potential change in ritual household activity represented by snuff spoons and tubes, the greater number of spittoons and puma incensarios (with their zoomorphic iconography) may show an increased acceptance of Tiwanaku iconography. This could have involved closer ceremonial ties to Tiwanaku (with new rituals appearing at the household level), or adoption of that iconography for their own purposes.

LUKURMATA IN REGIONAL PERSPECTIVE

In addition to the plainware vessels, Structures 22 and 23 also contained fragments of vessels imported from somewhere other than Tiwanaku. Each Lukurmata household, going back to the earliest occupation at the site, possessed a small number of such "nonlocal, non-Tiwanaku" vessels that may have been used for special serving or presentation activities. Although Structures 22 and 23 contained fragments of such imported vessels, the relative proportion had declined from the previous occupations. The decline in the appearance of these types of pottery suggests that while Lukurmata households still had access to the products of sites other than Tiwanaku, such access may have been declining, or that Tiwanaku-style vessels were increasingly preferred. Some of the non-Tiwanaku ceramics resemble pottery of the Juruquilla culture of southern Bolivia (western Potosí). Pottery fragments in the Juruquilla style were found in later occupations at Lukurmata as well.

The most probable explanation for the increase in Tiwanaku-style ceramics at Lukurmata is intensified interaction with the capital. However, other explanations are possible. For instance, Tiwanaku may have came to dominate the regional exchange system at the end of the Tiwanaku III period, and the Structure 22–24 occupation pottery reflects changes in a regional pottery exchange network rather than changes in political ties.

SUMMARY

Lukurmata at this time was probably still a small, economically self-sufficient settlement. While there may not have been much change at the site level, household organization continued to evolve.

Although our sample size of structure is far smaller than I would like, the Structure 22–24 occupation provides evidence for continuing transformational change in household organization at Lukurmata: increasing functional differentiation between domestic structures. Structure 24 constituted the first example of *specialized* architecture and architectural variation between contemporaneous structures. The earlier occupations included structures that differed in contents and features, but there were no architectural differences between buildings until this occupation. In contrast, Structure 24 was not "all purpose" architecture, but a building clearly constructed for a particular function. The intentional building of a structure dedicated to storage reflects the increasing importance of storage in the household organization.

Many aspects of domestic life continued to be similar to earlier occupations. Cooking and eating, spinning, weaving, basketry or hide working, manufacture of cutting and scraping tools, and grinding activities continued to be universal household tasks. If the spoon and tube fragments associated with Structures 22 and 23 do represent drug-related items, it would suggest that rituals involving hallucinogenic plants were added to the range of domestic activities at the end of the Tiwanaku III period.

This occupation also displays a greater range of Tiwanaku-style vessels in Lukurmata household use than seen previously. This could be the result of a shift from using or disposing of Tiwanaku III-style vessels in ceremonial/mortuary contexts to domestic contexts; new patterns of ceramic distribution within Lukurmata; increased acceptance of Tiwanaku-style iconography; or an increase in the degree of social differentiation within the community accompanied by a rise in the amount and variety of material markers of social difference. The drop in non-Tiwanaku imported pottery suggests changes in Lukurmata's ties to other sites, or in participation in exchange networks.

Tiwanaku III Period Summary

The Tiwanaku III period at Lukurmata began with the appearance of Tiwanaku III-style pottery shortly before the Structure 8–12 occupation, and ended with the disappearance of Tiwanaku III-style pottery after the abandonment of Structures 22–24. Important regional developments during this several centuries-long period included the rise of Tiwanaku as a major center, eclipsing Chiripa and Pucara, and the construction of raised field agricultural systems in the Pampa Koani, probably under Tiwanaku direction.

We could find no evidence that the Lukurmata residential population significantly grew during this period, or that Lukurmata was anything other than a simple, small settlement of homesteads. In contrast to this continuity at the site level, there were major changes at the regional and household levels. Ties between Lukurmata and other sites, particularly Tiwanaku, seem to have increased dramatically, if we use the percentages of imported pottery and materials as a measure of these relationships. By the end of the period, Lukurmata may have been assuming a different role in the larger Tiwanaku system.

At the level of the individual household, the Tiwanaku III period saw significant continuity and change in the Lukurmata household "system." Many aspects of domestic life continued to be similar to pre-Tiwanaku period patterns. Techniques of house construction, for instance, did not change, nor did the general range of household productive activities. However, the development of functional differences between structures and specialized architecture indicate that significant shifts in the importance, complexity, or organization of particular household activities led to changes in how domestic space was organized.

Part of this change was a shift in the distribution of floor space. Formerly, the interior area used by a household was under one roof; but in the two most complete Tiwanaku III period occupations exposed, a household's interior floor space was divided between buildings. The Tiwanaku III period occupations also revealed that the size and plan of domestic residences continued to vary.

Another change was an overall increase in the amount of Tiwanaku-style pottery and other nonlocal materials (including marine shell, obsidian, and sodalite) reaching the household level. The beginning of the Tiwanaku III period saw the amount of nonlocal pottery used by Lukurmata households rise sharply. This pottery came from a variety of sites, although Tiwanaku III-style pottery was the most common. By the end of the Tiwanaku III period, Lukurmata households had more nonlocal pottery than ever. Virtually all of it was coming from Tiwanaku, suggesting ties with Tiwanaku were supplanting ties with other populations. The appearance in household contexts of drug paraphernalia and vessels bearing the distinctive Tiwanaku zoomorphic iconography (some of them nonutilitarian, incensario vessels) may indicate that Tiwanaku-influenced rituals had been added to household activities.

One interpretation of these changes is that as Lukurmata's interaction with Tiwanaku intensified (represented by the steady increase in Tiwanaku-style pottery), households at Lukurmata may have come to more closely resemble Tiwanaku households in terms of range of domestic activities and styles of domestic items. From this perspective, the changes in activities and decorated pottery during the Tiwanaku III period may signal the gradual but full integration of Lukurmata households into a Tiwanaku social order.

THE TIWANAKU III–IV PERIOD TRANSITION

After the abandonment of Structures 22–24, all forms of Tiwanaku III-style pottery concurrently disappeared from Lukurmata. In contrast to the en bloc disappearance of Tiwanaku III-style pottery, certain types of Tiwanaku IV-style pottery appeared before others in Lukurmata residences. Fragments of these in the Structure 22–24 occupation represent modeled animal incensarios (Figure 10.6) and open-mouth bowls decorated with elaborate zoomorphic designs, rather than the ubiquitous Tiwanaku IV-style red-slipped *keros* and flaring-sided bowls that would dominate the later decorated assemblages. The presence of vessels featuring zoomorphic iconography rather than geometric designs is further evidence for the addition of new rituals to household activities. The modeled animal incensarios were clearly intended for ceremonial purposes (specimens from later occupations were filled with burned vegetable matter), while the open-mouth bowls with their striking puma, condor, and serpent designs around the inner rim may have been special serving vessels.

Previous Tiwanaku ceramic chronologies (constructed largely on stylistic criteria using specimens from poor contexts) have portrayed the Tiwanaku III–IV stylistic shift as one of abrupt replacement. They do not include transitional III–IV-style ceramics, nor do they allow for the simultaneous use of Tiwanaku III- and IV-style vessels.

This portrayal of the pottery shift is only partially supported by the Lukurmata household sequence. The disappearance of Tiwanaku III-style pottery *was* fairly abrupt in the Lukurmata sequence, and virtually no examples of pottery "transitional" in artistic style were recovered. But the Structure 22–24 occupation also shows that

Tiwanaku III- and IV-style vessels were in use at the same time, at least for a short period.[1]

After the abandonment of Structures 22–24, the site of Lukurmata began to change dramatically. Household life continued to change as well. The direction of this development was already becoming clear in the Tiwanaku III period occupations. The trend toward greater complexity and variation in domestic life, increased participation in the Tiwanaku system, and the disappearance of distinctly "local" traditions (and materials) all continued during the subsequent Tiwanaku IV period.

[1] Therefore the III/IV distinction may not be as diachronic as has been portrayed in previous Tiwanaku ceramic chronologies. Coexisting ceramic styles would also account for the apparent "late" dates (dates within the fifth and sixth centuries A.D.) for the Lukurmata occupations with Tiwanaku III-style materials.

11

Lukurmata and the Tiwanaku State

The Tiwanaku IV period (A.D. 400–A.D. 800) was characterized by dramatic change at Lukurmata and throughout the region. Concurrent with the emergence of a new Tiwanaku iconographic style (the Tiwanaku IV style) was a transformation in the regional scale and complexity of the Tiwanaku polity, including the expansion of the Tiwanaku system beyond the Lake Titicaca Basin, the development of a regional settlement hierarchy in the Tiwanaku heartland, and the creation of a vast sustaining hinterland for the huge population at the capital. Connected to the latter two developments was the rapid growth of Lukurmata from simple hamlet to demographic and ceremonial center.

THE TIWANAKU IV CORPORATE ART STYLE

The Tiwanaku IV period began at Lukurmata and elsewhere in the Andes with the appearance of a new corporate art style and new Tiwanaku pottery forms. Dominating the Tiwanaku IV corporate style were a handful of anthropomorphic and zoomorphic representations of which the Staff God (also called the Front Face Deity or Gateway Figure) and the puma were the most important. Although depictions of these conventionalized figures varied in detail, as a whole their expression was remarkably consistent and standardized throughout the Tiwanaku IV period.

The Staff God representation depicts an erect, masked (?) figure seen from the front (Figure 11.1). Each hand of the figure's raised arms grasps a vertical staff. His elaborate costume (a belted tunic, often with a breastplate) and headdress are decorated with zoomorphic kennings such as feathers and puma and condor heads. On Tiwanaku pottery the Staff God is often simply reduced to a disembodied head as in Figures 11.2 and 11.3 (Demarest 1981; Isbell 1983). Depiction of the Staff God long predates the rise of Tiwanaku, but the Staff God was a very minor element of Tiwanaku iconography prior to the Tiwanaku IV period. [1]

Often shown flanking the Staff God are Attendant or "angel" figures (Figure 11.4). Always depicted in profile, these figures have one leg forward as through kneeling or running. In Tiwanaku iconography, Attendant figures are often depicted with "wings," elaborate headdresses, and masks. A common variant of the Attendant figure

---

[1] One of the oldest and most widespread figures in Andean prehistory, the Front Face Deity appears as early as 900–800 B.C. in the Chavín artwork of the central Andes (the famous Raimondi Stele, for example). The figure was also a major component of Pucara iconography and Wari artwork (Cook 1985a; Demarest 1981). Because the figure was not an element of Tiwanaku III-style iconography, it has been argued that it represents an example of "archaism" on the part of Tiwanaku that was adopted from Pucara iconography (Cook 1983).

in Tiwanaku IV period iconography is the "Sacrificer." Instead of holding a staff, the "Sacrificer" is shown holding an axe and/or a severed "trophy" head (Figure 11.5).

Zoomorphic elements of Tiwanaku IV iconography include stylized representations of the puma, condor, serpent, and llama. The puma was the most common decorative motif on Tiwanaku IV period pottery. Its standardized profile depiction during the Tiwanaku IV period was sometimes elaborated by wings, giving it a "griffin"-like appearance (Figure 11.6).

Fig. 11.1 Front Face Deity or Staff God as depicted on the Gateway of the Sun, Tiwanaku (after Fiedel 1987).

Fig. 11.3 Tiwanaku IV-style pottery from Lukurmata domestic contexts: (a) base of polished blackware kero, (b) modeled representation of the Staff God from a kero.

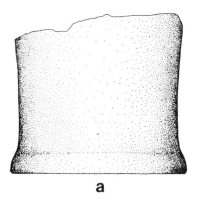

a

0   5
cm

Fig. 11.2 Head of the Staff God on a kero from a Tiwanaku V period Lukurmata tomb.

b

Fig. 11.4 Attendant Figure from the Gateway of the Sun, Tiwanaku.

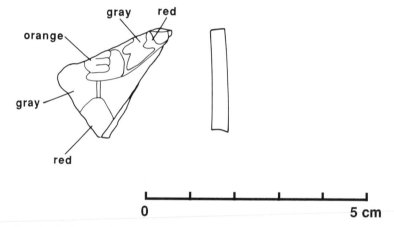

Fig. 11.5 Pottery fragment from midden associated with the Structure 33–39 occupation showing the hand and severed trophy head of the "Sacrificer" Attendant figure.

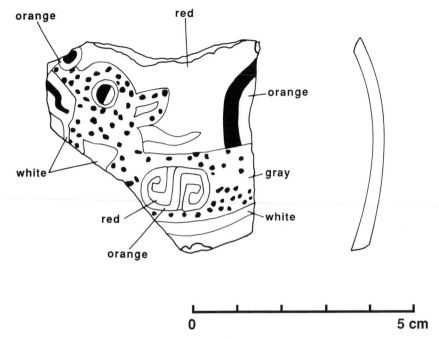

Fig. 11.6 Pottery fragment showing a typical Tiwanaku IV-style spotted puma (found on the surface at Lukurmata).

The Tiwanaku IV period corporate art style displays only a moderate degree of continuity from the Tiwanaku III period. The Tiwanaku IV period saw the introduction of many new thematic elements and a new style of presentation. In general, Tiwanaku IV period iconography resembles Pucara iconography more closely than it does Tiwanaku III period iconography. The similarity in thematic content and presentation style between Tiwanaku IV iconography and Pucara iconography suggests that as Tiwanaku expanded in size, supplanting Pucara as the dominant center of the Titicaca Basin, it adopted a Pucara iconography that was already well known in the southern Andes and perhaps symbolic of political domination (Kolata 1992).

William Isbell (1983) has suggested that use of the Staff God and Attendant figures was generally associated with expansionist polities (such as the Wari and Pucara states), or at least with periods of increased social unification and political integration. The centrality of the Staff God in the new iconographic style may have signaled an ideological transformation at Tiwanaku at the beginning of the Tiwanaku IV period, with adoption of the Staff God as the "state-patron" deity of the imperialistic Tiwanaku polity (Cook 1985a). If so, this development may have been analogous to that described for the Aztec, in which ideological reforms (leading to the emergence of Huitzilopochtli as the patron deity of a powerful cult) played a crucial role in Aztec imperial expansion (Conrad and Demarest 1984).

Both the Staff God and the puma are common on two Tiwanaku IV period pottery forms: the kero (Figure 7.1f) and the *tazón* or flaring-sided bowl (Figure 7.1c). These vessel shapes remained characteristic Tiwanaku products for many centuries, and serve as diagnostic markers of Tiwanaku influence throughout the southern Andes. The workshops producing these and other items in the Tiwanaku corporate style have recently been located at Tiwanaku and other sites in the Tiwanaku Valley (Kolata, personal communication).

TIWANAKU SETTLEMENT HIERARCHY

The settlement patterns of complex societies are characterized by settlement hierarchy: a pattern in which sites differ in size, function, amount, and variety of public architecture. Settlement hierarchies reflect underlying systems of economic, political, or religious interaction, or a combination of the three. Because political power, wealth, and religious importance were often closely connected in prehistoric societies, the settlement hierarchies of archaic states often reflect an administrative hierarchy, a pyramidal pattern in which the settlement system is dominated (politically and economically) by a single site, with various levels of subordinate sites below (Wright 1986).

Typically, the site at the apex of a prehistoric settlement hierarchy is at once the residential site of the ruling stratum, the political capital, and the primary locus of economic and ceremonial activity. Such sites are the largest in the settlement system, display the greatest amount and variety of public architecture, and have functions that other sites do not.

Second- and third-order settlement hierarchies are smaller and possess less public architecture. These sites often exhibit specialized administrative facilities, or smaller versions of public architecture found at the capital. Second- and third-order settlements represent the residential sites of minor nobility or state officials, and function as provincial administrative centers, providing special goods or services to surrounding communities.

At the base of the regional settlement pyramid, often grouped around regional centers, are villages and hamlets lacking public architecture. All of the inhabitants of these settlements typically engage in primary production.

By the sixth century A.D., Tiwanaku had become the urban capital of a powerful polity that would dominate the south-central Andes for the next five centuries. Excavations and studies of surface artifact patterns at Tiwanaku indicate that the ceremonial core of the site was surrounded by large residential areas during the Tiwanaku IV period (A.D. 400–A.D. 800). Tiwanaku covered some 6 km^2, with an estimated residential population of forty thousand to eighty thousand, making it the largest demographic center in the Andes (Albarracin-Jordan and Mathews 1990; Kolata 1983).

Tiwanaku stood at the apex of a settlement hierarchy extending over an estimated 7000 km^2 area in the Lake Titicaca Basin (Figure 11.7). This "core area" of the Tiwanaku polity was delimited by a set of sizable subsidiary centers (each covering 1–2 km^2) and large amounts of Tiwanaku-style public architecture (Bermann 1990; Ponce 1981a). Kolata (1986) has persuasively argued that Lukurmata, Pajchiri, and Khonko

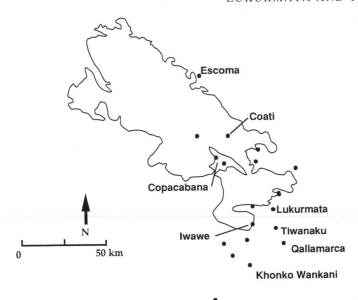

Fig. 11.7 Location of major Tiwanaku IV/V period sites around Lake Titicaca (adapted from Kolata 1985: Figure 1).

Wankani represent second-order or regional centers in a Tiwanaku IV/V period administrative hierarchy. Two public architecture forms from the capital—sunken temples and Kalasasaya-like enclosures—are replicated at these sites. The public architecture at each site resembles the public architecture of the capital (large dressed andesite blocks in the "pillar and sillar" construction), and each was founded, or grew dramatically, during the Tiwanaku IV period.

A handful of smaller sites (under 1 km²) possessing only a small quantity of public architecture (for instance, a single Tiwanaku-style sunken temple) represent third-order sites in the Tiwanaku settlement hierarchy, perhaps functioning as local centers. These include the Bolivian sites of Chiripa, LV-55, TMV-561, Iwawe, Escoma, Qallamarca, PK-5, PK-6 (in the Pampa Koani), and the Peruvian sites of Sillumocco and Palermo (Albarracin-Jordan and Mathews 1990; Bennett 1934; Goldstein 1993; Kolata 1986, 1991; Stanish, personal communication).

The lower-order sites in the Tiwanaku IV period settlement hierarchy consisted of scattered villages, hamlets, and homesteads. In the Tiwanaku Valley, the only core area of the Tiwanaku state yet surveyed, nearly one hundred such sites were recorded, most less than 1 ha in size (Albarracin-Jordan and Mathews 1990:217–42). Albarracin-Jordan and Mathews (ibid.:89–90, Figure 11) note that most of these lower-order sites were associated with agricultural fields, with large villages (5–10 ha) exhibiting a regular spacing from one another of 3 to 6 km. Hamlets (generally less than 1 ha in size) seem to have clustered around the large villages, and may represent daughter communities.

REGIONAL DISTRIBUTION OF TIWANAKU ARTIFACTS IN THE SOUTHERN ANDES

During the Tiwanaku IV period, the Tiwanaku sphere expanded dramatically from its earlier Lake Titicaca Basin setting. Tiwanaku IV-style materials have been found at sites on the Pacific coasts of Chile and Peru, the southern Bolivia pampa, and the eastern slopes of the Andes (Figure 11.8). The distribution of Tiwanaku IV-style materials outside the "core" area presents a highly heterogeneous pattern, with different quantities and types of remains found in each region (Berenguer et al. 1980; Browman 1980, 1981; Goldstein 1989, 1993; Kolata 1983; Mujica 1978, 1985; Ponce 1981a; Stanish 1992).

There is little agreement among archaeologists as to what this transregional artifact pattern represents, or the processes behind the movement of Tiwanaku-style objects. Processes of colonization, conquest, missionary activities, and trade have each been proposed for various regions. To some investigators, the distribution of Tiwanaku IV/V-style materials reflects a powerful political empire; to others, a loose federation of population centers headed by the religious-trade center of Tiwanaku and linked by an extensive network of llama caravans (Browman 1980, 1981; Goldstein 1989).

Fig. 11.8 Regions in which significant quantities of Tiwanaku IV/V-style materials are found include the Moquequa, Azapa, and Mizque valleys, and the San Pedro de Atacama region.

At the heart of the debate is how to interpret the variation between the assemblages of Tiwanaku-style artifacts found at "peripheral" sites in Bolivia, Peru, and Chile. With few exceptions, archaeologists have treated intersite differences between Tiwanaku-style artifact assemblages as evidence of different modes of interaction with Tiwanaku. Goldstein (1989), for instance, argues that while the Chilean Tiwanaku materials reflect llama caravan trade, Peruvian Moquegua sites were part of an "administered archipelago" of transplanted Tiwanaku colonists.

Similarly, other investigators have pointed to the contrast between the "bulky," utilitarian materials of the Azapa region, and the exotic, "social display" items of the San Pedro de Atacama sites as evidence for two different types of interaction between Tiwanaku and the coastal-sierra Chilean populations (Berenguer et al. 1980; Browman 1985). They see a greater Tiwanaku socioeconomic "presence" in the Azapa region, involving the movement of foodstuffs, and a religious "presence" in the San Pedro region, as evidenced by the emphasis on easily transportable "hallucinogenic complex" items and Tiwanaku Staff God iconography.

The Chilean Azapa sites have been variously interpreted. One interpretation—the "archipelago" perspective—is that by the end of the Tiwanaku IV period these sites were colonies directly linked to Tiwanaku by state-managed caravans. They may even have been mitmaqkuna established to provide non-altiplano products: marine resources, maize, coca, fruits, cotton, legumes (Berenguer et al. 1980; Browman 1985; Kolata 1983:278).

Other scholars see the Azapa sites simply as Tiwanaku trade partners, indirectly interacting with Tiwanaku through Tiwanaku's participation in previously established highland-lowland exchange networks (Browman 1980, 1985; Foccaci 1983). From this perspective, the Tiwanaku-style materials found in northern Chile reflect not an expanding empire, but that Tiwanaku was one of many centers linked through the regional exchange of status-related goods.

The Tiwanaku-style materials found in the San Pedro de Atacama region have brought about equally diverse interpretations. While some scholars have interpreted the Tiwanaku-style remains in the Atacama as evidence of Tiwanaku control or colonists (Kolata 1983:278–79; Oakland 1993), others have argued that the Tiwanaku-style materials suggest participation by local elites in a prestige-good "interaction sphere" of exotic and magico-religious artifacts (Berenguer et al. 1980; Muñoz 1983; Stanish 1992:83).

The debate over the nature and regional extent of the Tiwanaku polity reflects more than a preoccupation with the vague concept of "influence" still holding sway in too many areas of Andean archaeology. Instead, the debate is a result of the "capital-centric" approaches that have characterized southern Andean archaeology to date. It also illustrates the limitations of regional approaches. We will never be able to "explain" the distribution of Tiwanaku-style materials simply by turning to increasingly refined theoretical models of political interaction or imperial expansion. Ultimately, we will have to learn something about the history of sites where Tiwanaku materials appear.

Archaeological interpretations have been informed by an object-oriented focus on the Tiwanaku-style artifacts themselves at these peripheral sites (Stanish 1992). The presence of these artifacts has not been interpreted in the context of the community's own evolution and traditions. Until the Lukurmata research, no investigators had attempted to examine how local traditions and activities may have shaped the adoption of Tiwanaku-style materials, or how Tiwanaku items were integrated into local orders. Valuable information was lost by not studying the appearance of Tiwanaku materials in context.

This orientation is both a cause and result of the little importance accorded the archaeological context of Tiwanaku-style materials at sites in Chile and Peru. Many Tiwanaku-style items at these regions are from unknown, unrecorded, or questionable contexts, and excavation has focused on mortuary contexts rather than residential settings. As a result, we have very poor general knowledge of the societies that buried individuals with Tiwanaku-style items. Little is known of domestic organization at the pre-Tiwanaku Alto Ramírez and Cabuza phase sites. Furthermore, materials from tombs are clearly weak evidence from which to assess interregional relationships, particularly ethnic or political affiliation in the southern Andes in general (Stanish 1989a).

Equally implicit in traditional studies of the distribution of Tiwanaku-style materials in the southern Andes is an assumption that the various regions and sites were, in fundamental ways, comparable prior to the arrival of Tiwanaku material. Therefore, any variation in the Tiwanaku-style artifact assemblages between regions must be the result of differing relationships with Tiwanaku. Yet it seems more likely that the differences between these areas *before* contact with Tiwanaku led to differing forms of interaction with Tiwanaku.

Browman (1981, 1984) has come closest to the "local perspective" in interpreting the diversity of Tiwanaku-style artifact assemblages. He (1981:417) suggests that, in contrast to the Wari sites of Peru, "each separate center in Bolivia, Chile, and Argentina exhibits a unique assemblage of Tiwanaku materials." This variation, he argues, may be due to each community having selected from Tiwanaku traders an assemblage of trade-goods appropriate to its needs and traditions.

Overall, we do not know what changes may have accompanied the appearance of Tiwanaku-style materials at the Chilean sites. There is a long history of interaction between northern Chilean communities and the altiplano prior to the rise of Tiwanaku (Browman 1980; Mujica 1978; Nuñez and Dillehay 1978). These earlier patterns of interaction have not been compared with the Tiwanaku period relationship to determine if the later pattern is truly different (indicative of colonies or political control, for instance) or if the "Tiwanaku presence" is only more visible archaeologically because of the highly recognizable Tiwanaku iconographic style.

For instance, José Berenguer et al. (1980) argue that a number of distinct altiplano ethnic populations or polities maintained long-standing ties to Chilean communities during the Tiwanaku period. Exchange took place in the context of the traditional relationships these groups maintained with Chilean settlements, not through imperial Tiwanaku caravans. Tiwanaku-style artifacts naturally became items in this pre-existing long-distance trade. As a result, the variation seen in the Tiwanaku-style artifact assemblages of Chilean sites reflects the relationship between the highland groups and Tiwanaku, *and* the relationship between these highland groups and lowland communities.

In summary, the Tiwanaku artifact distributions in Chile and Peru have usually been interpreted from a "capital-centric" viewpoint in which the Tiwanaku-style materials are used to gauge interaction with Tiwanaku rather than the traditions and history of the local community. Lacking knowledge of previous life at these sites, we have not yet been able to evaluate contextually what the appearance of Tiwanaku-style materials represented, how Tiwanaku-style materials were incorporated into local patterns, or how the relationship with the Tiwanaku polity differed from earlier forms of local interaction with highland groups.

THE EARLY TIWANAKU IV PERIOD AT LUKURMATA

Information on household life during the early Tiwanaku IV period at Lukurmata comes from the Structure 26–28 occupation. Excavation of 244 contiguous m² revealed the remains of four buildings 95 cm below datum. Two of these buildings, Structures 26 and 27, were completely excavated. Virtually no associated outdoor activity surfaces could be traced, but two associated middens were found. We do not have any absolute dates for the Structure 26–28 occupation, but ceramic and stratigraphic evidence suggests an early seventh-century A.D. date.

SITE COMPOSITION

The major changes at Lukurmata during the Tiwanaku IV period can be summarized as: (1) growth of the residential population; (2) construction of public architecture; and (3) increased intrasite complexity, with the settlement divided into discrete ceremonial, mortuary, and residential areas (Figure 11.9). We cannot determine precisely when during the Tiwanaku IV period these changes took place, but they appear to date to early in the Tiwanaku IV period, around A.D. 550–650.

Increase in Residential Population

During the early part of the Tiwanaku IV period, Lukurmata grew to cover roughly 120 ha, rapidly expanding from a handful of households to a settlement of thousands of inhabitants. Tiwanaku IV-style surface artifact remains and test excavations suggest that domestic occupation during the Tiwanaku IV period expanded to the east of the ridge, on the sides and surface of the temple hilltop, and in the central and southern sections of the site. Charles Stanish (1989b:51) has estimated that the residential area during the Tiwanaku IV period covered 70 ha. But excavations have shown that the density of settlement revealed on the ridge cannot be extended to the site as a whole. Given this, a Tiwanaku IV period population of five thousand to ten thousand at Lukurmata seems reasonable.

Public Architecture: A Tiwanaku Microcosm

The first public architecture at Lukurmata appeared during the Tiwanaku IV period. This consisted of a hilltop temple complex imitating at smaller scale the public architecture at Tiwanaku, and a solitary, large terraced platform in the center of the site.

The temple complex consisted of a Tiwanaku-style semi-subterranean temple and several low, terraced platforms. The temple, shown in Figures 11.10 and 11.11, measured 9.5 m on a side, and like most of the Tiwanaku IV period buildings at Tiwanaku, it was built with large, dressed blocks of gray andesite (Bennett 1936; Ponce 1989;

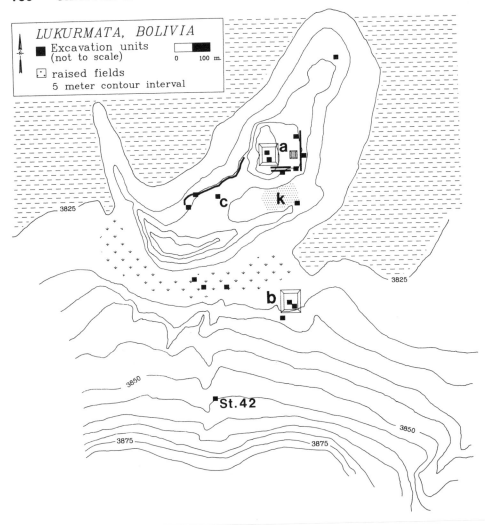

Fig. 11.9 Lukurmata during the Tiwanaku IV/V period showing public architecture, major walls, raised fields, and Bennett's Section K south of the temple hill. *Key*: (a) temple and enclosure complex, (b) raised burial platform, (c) main excavation, (k) Bennett's Section K. Dark lines show the location of major outdoor walls exposed in excavation.

Fig. 11.10 Interior of Tiwanaku-style sunken temple at Lukurmata during excavation.

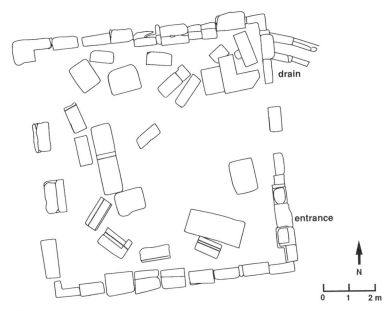

Fig. 11.11 Plan of andesite blocks of the sunken temple in situ.

Rivera 1989).[2] The Lukurmata temple is a smaller version of the semi-subterranean temple at Tiwanaku.

We do not know what activities took place in the Lukurmata temple. No artifacts were found on the floor, and no associated trash deposits have been discovered. Two offerings were found buried just outside the temple in a surface dating to the time of the structure. Each consisted of a jar and a Tiwanaku IV-style modeled puma incense burner filled with burned organic material. All four vessels had been buried upright and intact (Rivera 1989). Similar buried puma offerings were found in other Tiwanaku IV period contexts at Lukurmata, and are reported from other Tiwanaku temple sites (ibid.:69).

The temple was set into a low, stone-faced platform. Immediately to the east of this platform was a second, larger terraced platform (approximately 75 m × 75 m in size, 0.5 m to 2.0 m high) with clean clay fill (Graffam 1989; Rivera 1989). The eastern side of this platform was surmounted by a wall built in the characteristic Tiwanaku "pillar and sillar" manner.[3] This large platform at Lukurmata probably was similar in appearance to the Kalasasaya, albeit on a much smaller scale.[4]

The presence on the Lukurmata temple hilltop of two stairways, each carved from a single block of stone, suggests that the Lukurmata platform had stairways similar to those on the east face of the Kalasasaya. The spatial relationship of the two structures at Lukurmata resembles that at Tiwanaku, with the sunken temple directly east of the "pillar and sillar" platform enclosure.

In contrast to the fairly well-preserved public architecture on the southern half of the temple hilltop, the northern part of the hill presents few overt indications of large-scale architecture. However, a test trench excavated 50 m south of the sunken temple in 1986 revealed a deeply buried, fractured pisé terrace retaining wall, running roughly north-south. This wall (not shown in Figure 11.9) may have been the eastern side of a low earthen platform, oriented in the same cardinal directions as the temple.[5]

The Tiwanaku IV period also saw large-scale modification of the hill topography. The southern section of the hilltop was artificially leveled (Bennett 1936). In addition, the discovery during the 1986 and 1987 seasons of buried stone retaining walls and

[2] Bennett (1936:481) has persuasively argued that the blocks of the Lukurmata temple were once part of an earlier, more elaborate, structure, either at Lukurmata or elsewhere. He notes the disparity between the high quality of finishing of individual stones and the poor wall construction methods, and that many fitting joints on stones have no function in their present position in the temple (ibid.). Our assignment of the Lukurmata temple to the Tiwanaku IV period is based principally on the style of pottery recovered from a "construction" floor exposed outside the temple walls by the *Proyecto Wila-Jawira* (Rivera 1989).

[3] This building style consists of a row of massive, vertical pillars, with the gaps filled with much smaller blocks. Eighteen of the "pillars" still stand in situ at Lukurmata. Few of the dressed "sillar" blocks have been recovered from the temple area at Lukurmata, but these may have been the targets of stone robbing. Dressed "sillar"-type andesite blocks were frequently used to construct Tiwanaku V period and post-Tiwanaku tombs at Lukurmata.

[4] The Kalasasaya measures 145 m × 125 m in size and has a 3 m high wall.

[5] The ceramics from the trench indicate that the wall was built during the Tiwanaku IV period. The artifacts and features from this trench are not indicative of a domestic occupation. East (or "outside") of the wall was a group of burials. These consisted of the incomplete but articulated remains of several individuals, and may represent reburial. There were no grave-goods to provide a date for these burials, but recent excavations at Tiwanaku have uncovered similar partial, articulated burials associated with a Tiwanaku IV period dedicatory ceremony at the Akapana platform (Manzanilla, personal communication.

sloping terrace faces to the east and south of the sunken temple suggests that the entire southern and eastern faces of the hill had been converted into huge terraplaned surfaces. The southern face of the hilltop would have had at least three terraces extending down from the hill crest a distance of 25–30 m (Bermann 1989b; Graffam 1989; Rivera 1989, personal communication).

The remaining Tiwanaku IV period public architecture at Lukurmata consisted of a single platform located roughly 400 m to the south of the temple hilltop (Janusek and Earnest 1988). The dimensions of the platform are not yet known, but can be estimated as 50 m × 75 m, and 1.5–2 m high. The platform was composed of poured clay or adobe and was paved with round cobbles. During the early Tiwanaku IV period, the platform supported smaller structures of unknown function. The platform was also used for high-status burials sometime during the Tiwanaku IV period (ibid.).[6]

Increased Intrasite Complexity

The Tiwanaku IV period at Lukurmata also saw the division of the site into spatially separate mortuary, ceremonial, and domestic areas, as well as an increase in features such as terraces, walls, and canals to delineate or divide areas of the site.

A segregated burial area , an "elite" cemetery, was located in the paved platform at the center of the site, and the entire temple hilltop was transformed into a distinct civic-ceremonial precinct.

As part of this transformation, a terrace was built along the northern face of the ridge west of the temple hill. Excavation along the northern edge of this ridge revealed the large fieldstone foundation for a wall that would have run the length of the ridge (Figures 11.12, 11.13). This feature would have been a free-standing wall, rather than part of the terrace retaining wall. The wall, the foundations of which can be dimly followed on the surface, extended several hundred meters, from the western flank of the temple hill itself along the northern face of the ridge, before curling around a *quebrada* at the western edge of the ridge.

No signs of residential occupation were encountered on the hilltop proper, nor on the terraces built into the southern face of the hill or the northern face of the ridge extending west from the hill. Instead, as I discuss below, the terrace halfway up the north face of the ridge may have been used for ceremonial activities.

A crescent-shaped strip of low land lies between the site's "acropolis escarpment" and the broad hillslope that forms the southern sector of the site. This strip of land contains a row of raised field segments initially constructed during the Tiwanaku IV period (Kolata and Graffam 1989; Kolata and Ortloff 1989). A long canal, roughly 3 m wide, ran through these fields, heading out into the pampa at either end. The fields and moat-like canal would effectively have separated the elevated hilltop section of Lukurmata from the rest of the settlement.

A horizontal alignment of roughly a dozen large slabs of dressed stone visible on the surface halfway up the steep southwestern face of the escarpment may mark another wall or "pillar and sillar" terrace face—additional evidence that the elevated area of

---

[6] Subsequently, the platform was covered by a substantial layer of ashy midden containing ceramics dating to the early Tiwanaku V period. The nature of this deposit suggests that this was not the natural accumulation from a domestic occupation on the platform, but rather that the platform was eventually used as a dump.

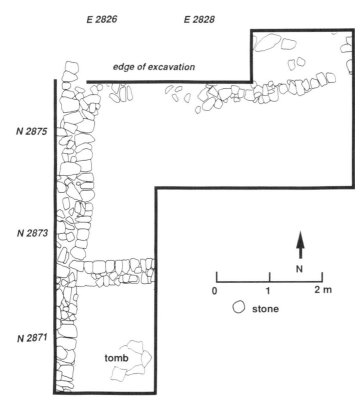

Fig. 11.12 Plan of N2875 E2826 excavation on the west end of the ridge showing the base of the Tiwanaku IV period ridge wall.

Fig. 11.13 This Tiwanaku IV period wall ran approximately 200 m along the north face ridge and the east side of the temple hill.

Lukurmata was separated from the rest of the site (Bennett 1936:468–69). The canal, walls, and terraces would have served to restrict access to both the civic-ceremonial architecture on the hill and the adjoining ridge.

Domestic Architecture: Structures 25–28

The buildings of this occupation (Figure 11.14) displayed construction materials and techniques similar to those of earlier occupations, with prepared clay floors and mud brick walls. Burned fragments of rectangular mud bricks were found scattered in and around the structures. Wall bases and linear soot deposits (marking the inside edge of walls) suggest that the structures were probably rectangular with straight walls. The houses of this occupation were somewhat larger than those of the previous occupation, with an interior floor area in the range of 30–35 m².

Structures 26 (Figure 11.15) and 27 (Figure 11.16) would have measured approximately 8 m × 5 m. The southeastern edge of the Structure 26 floor ended at the standing wall segment of Structure 24. The standing wall of this older building may have been incorporated into Structure 26. In fact, Structure 24 may still have been in use. The

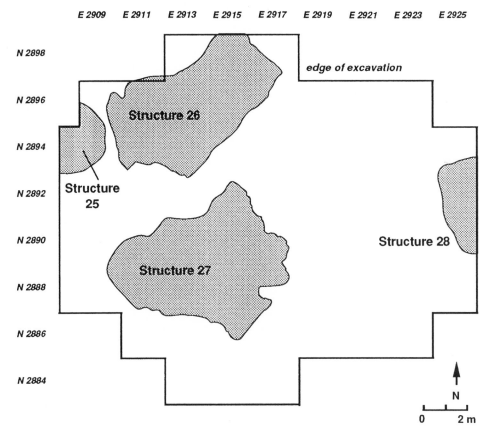

Fig. 11.14 Plan of Structure 25–28 occupation showing housefloors (shading). Intrusive features omitted.

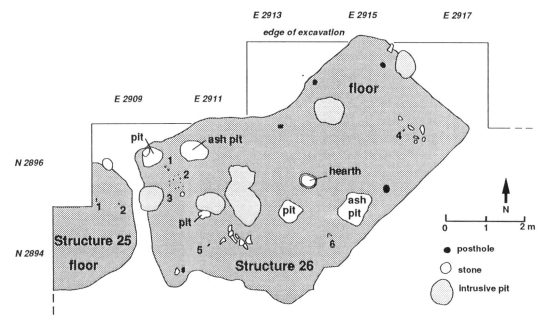

Fig. 11.15 Plan of Structure 25 and 26 floors with selected artifacts plotted. *Key, Structure 25*: (1) exhausted lithic core, (2) stone scraper; *Key, Structure 26*: (1) scrapers made from smoothed sherds, (2) lithic debitage, (3) flakes, (4) ground stone, (5) bone needle fragments, (6) bone needle fragments.

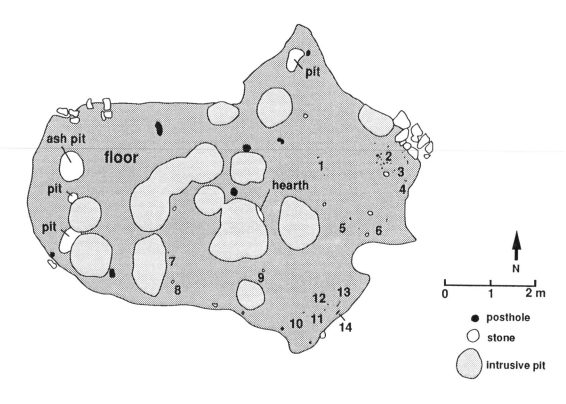

position of Structure 27, directly above Structure 22, suggests that it could represent the rebuilding and enlargement of the earlier structure.

An alignment of stones (1.5 m long) on the Structure 26 floor represents the remains of an internal partition or feature. Postholes were found near the edges and corners of each floor, but we do not know what shape the roofs took. We could not define the entrances to either structure.

Each structure contained a hearth (a shallow, sand-lined pit) and refuse and ash pits. Intrusive pits made it difficult to determine if the houses had contained other internal features. Only portions of the floors of Structures 25 and 28 were exposed (Figure 11.17).

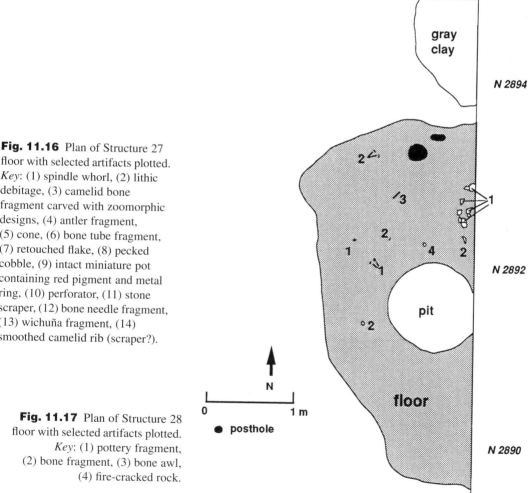

Fig. 11.16 Plan of Structure 27 floor with selected artifacts plotted. *Key*: (1) spindle whorl, (2) lithic debitage, (3) camelid bone fragment carved with zoomorphic designs, (4) antler fragment, (5) cone, (6) bone tube fragment, (7) retouched flake, (8) pecked cobble, (9) intact miniature pot containing red pigment and metal ring, (10) perforator, (11) stone scraper, (12) bone needle fragment, (13) wichuña fragment, (14) smoothed camelid rib (scraper?).

Fig. 11.17 Plan of Structure 28 floor with selected artifacts plotted. *Key*: (1) pottery fragment, (2) bone fragment, (3) bone awl, (4) fire-cracked rock.

DOMESTIC ACTIVITIES

A similar variety of artifacts was found on the floors of Structures 26 and 27. These included fragments of decorated Tiwanaku IV-style pottery, cooking vessels and animal bone; bone needles; spindle whorls; small grinding stones; pecked cobbles; chert flakes and debitage; and fire-cracked rock. Artifacts of the same type were found on the excavated floor sections of Structures 25 and 28, suggesting that these were used as dwellings as well. The midden deposits contained a slightly broader range of artifacts, including a metal *tupu*-style pin, projectile points, and two fragments of the small, white plaster "molds" of unknown function. A small vessel containing powdery, red mineral pigment and a copper finger ring was found on the Structure 27 floor (Figure 11.18).

The faunal assemblage was composed of camelid, fish, bird, rodent, and deer bones. These remains were present in roughly the same proportion as in the Structure 22–24 occupation.

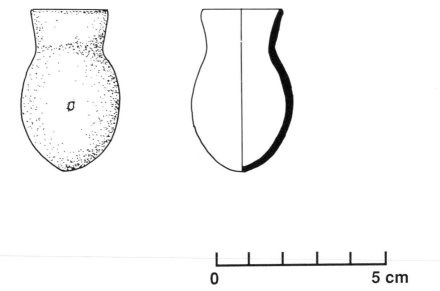

Fig. 11.18 This small pot found on the floor of Structure 27 contained red mineral pigment and a metal ring.

Domestic Pottery

The ceramic assemblage from the housefloors and midden deposits indicate that households possessed a range of utilitarian plainware vessels as well as various types of imported Tiwanaku decorated pottery. Most cooking was done with undecorated pottery. The Tiwanaku vessels were seldom fire-blackened and probably played a serving role.

A change from previous domestic pottery assemblages was the sharp decline in the use of both Lorokea Fiber vessels and the Local Tradition forms. These utilitarian

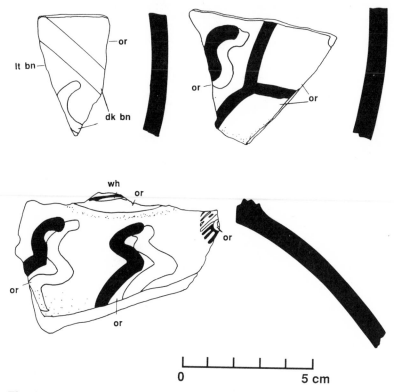

0   5 cm

Fig. 11.19 Fragments of Lillimani-style storage vessels. Large
Lillimani jars were commonly used by Lukurmata households during the
Tiwanaku IV period.

vessels were replaced by a range of Tiwanaku-style plainware vessels, including Lillimani Creamware (Figure 11.19).

The decorated Tiwanaku-style pottery found with the Structure 25–28 occupation falls
into three categories: red-slipped ware; polished blackware; and tanware. The first
two categories are common and distinctive Tiwanaku ceramics, and are well known
from Tiwanaku and other sites (Bennett 1934, 1936; Rydén 1947; Wallace 1957).
Although "tanware" has not been reported from sites other than Lukurmata, the
decoration and forms of tanware vessels resemble particular red-slipped Tiwanaku
vessels, and the paste and temper are similar to ceramics from Tiwanaku (Figures
11.20, 11.21).

The most common decorated Tiwanaku pottery forms in the Structure 25–28 occupation were the kero and flaring-sided bowl, also the most common forms at Tiwanaku
itself. Undoubtedly, each household possessed a number of these vessels. Other decorated Tiwanaku pottery forms possessed by Tiwanaku IV period Lukurmata households included (using Bennett's 1934 terminology): (a) wide open, flaring rim bowls;
(b) narrow rim, wide open bowls; (c) hollow-base libation bowls; (d) modeled puma
incensarios; (e) narrow neck, globular pitchers; (f) convex bowls; (g) *cuencas*; and

—orange

0   5 cm

Fig. 11.20 Tanware flaring-sided bowl from a midden deposit associated with the Structure 25–28 occupation. Tanware has not been found at Tiwanaku, and may be restricted to lakeshore sites (Janusek, personal communication).

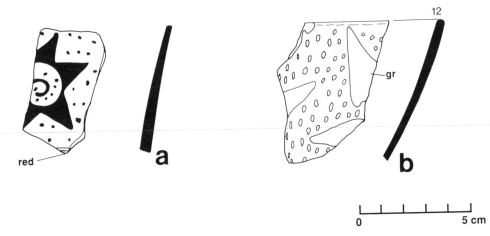

red

a

12

—gr

b

0   5 cm

Fig. 11.21 Pottery of the early Tiwanaku IV period from Lukurmata dwellings included the Tanware variants Starwares (a) and Gatoware (b).

(h) constricted waist keros.[7] This inventory includes most, but not all, of the red-slipped vessel types known from Tiwanaku.[8] Thus, only a subset of the Tiwanaku IV pottery used at Tiwanaku was appearing at the Lukurmata household level.

Summary of Household Activities

The artifacts associated with Structures 25–28 indicate that the types of activities associated with domestic architecture continued to be the same. Food preparation and consumption, basketry or hide working, spinning, weaving, hunting, manufacture and repair of cutting and scraping tools, and grinding activities continued as universal household tasks.

To this list might be added certain household ceremonies or ritual activities. Bone tubes, spoons, and spatulas were found with the Structure 25–28 occupation, indicating that these rituals continued to be carried out at the individual household level, despite the construction of the temple.

LUKURMATA IN REGIONAL PERSPECTIVE

With the expansion of the Tiwanaku polity, Lukurmata was no longer on the geographic edge of the Tiwanaku system, but deep in the Tiwanaku heartland. There were major changes in the heartland area surrounding Lukurmata during the Tiwanaku IV period, particularly in the adjacent plain known locally as the Pampa Koani, a vast expanse of raised fields and an important hinterland sustaining area for the nearby capital of Tiwanaku (Figure 11.22). The administrative requirements of this agricultural system may explain Lukurmata's growth into an important second-order center in the Tiwanaku polity.

Raised Field Agriculture

The Tiwanaku polity, like other native Andean civilizations, invested heavily in intensifying agricultural production through land reclamation and the spread of special agricultural practices (Kolata 1991; Moseley 1992). The best-documented Tiwanaku agrarian project is the massive Pampa Koani raised field system. In this low-lying, water-logged plain to the northeast of Lukurmata, some 7000 ha of raised fields were eventually built (Kolata 1991:109).

Systems of prehispanic raised fields have now been documented throughout the Lake Titicaca Basin. Experiments in both Peru and Bolivia have demonstrated that this indigenous form of agricultural production is many times more productive than dry field farming (Erickson 1988; Graffam 1990, 1992; Kolata 1986, 1991; Kolata and Ortloff 1989).

The altiplano raised fields consist of elevated planting platforms formed by excavating parallel canals and mounding the soil between them, usually with the help of sod bricks, on a gravel and cobblestone base to create a flat or slightly convex planting

---

[7] Most of these shapes are described by Bennett (1934). Convex bowls, a relatively rare Tiwanaku shape, are illustrated in Eisleb and Strelow (1980:Figures 155, 156, 159, 160). An example of the "constricted waist kero" is shown in Eisleb and Strelow (ibid.:Figure 76).

[8] The designations are Bennett's (1934).

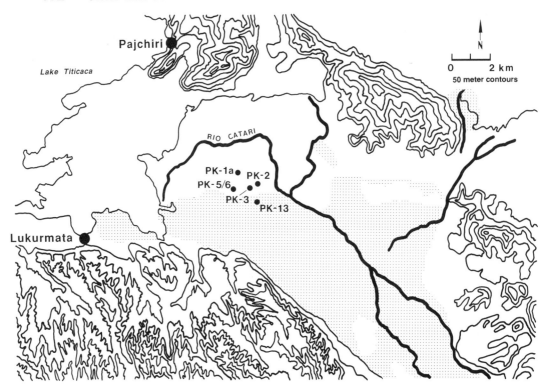

Fig. 11.22 Lukurmata and other Tiwanaku IV/V period sites on the Pampa Koani (adapted from Kolata 1986: Figure 3). Shading indicates extent of raised fields.

surface (Erickson 1988; Graffam 1990; Kolata 1983). Roughly half of a raised field is planting surface; the rest is made up of the canals or water-filled swales (Kolata 1986). The swales themselves form highly productive zones. In addition to providing a habitat for aquatic wildlife and edible plants, the sediment and algae that accumulate in the swales provide a yearly source of nutrient-rich, low alkaline organic material to serve as fertilizer for the fields (Erickson 1988; Kolata and Ortloff 1989).

The size and design of fields vary considerably. Most fields in the Pampa Koani have a planting surface of between 5 m and 15 m wide and up to 200 m in length (Kolata 1983). Some raised field groupings consist of sets of individual fields in parallel orientation, separated from one another by 3–5 m wide swales. Other field groupings, however, form complex interlocking or curvilinear patterns. A number of distinct patterns of raised fields have been recognized in the Titicaca Basin; the two most common are the "curvilinear" and "riverine" types (Denevan 1970, 1980; Kolata 1986; Lennon 1982, 1983; Smith et al. 1968).

Recent studies with reactivated prehispanic raised fields in the Pampa Koani have shown that their yield is far superior to modern, dry farming techniques. Test plots of potatoes planted in reconstructed raised fields several kilometers east of Lukurmata produced an average of 42,146 kg/ha, roughly three times the 14, 496 kg/ha average of improved agriculture with fertilizers, and roughly twenty times the traditional, shallow furrow, dry farming currently practiced by the population on the edge of the Pampa Koani (Kolata and Ortloff 1989; Kolata 1991:106–8, Tables 1–3).[9]

In addition to potatoes, the reactivated Pampa Koani fields have produced abundant yields of the native crops quinoa and cañiwa, as well as introduced crops such as broad beans, onions, and lettuce.

The effectiveness of raised fields has been attributed to a range of factors, recently summarized by Kolata (1991) in a review of Pampa Koani agricultural production. Among the proposed advantages that raised fields hold over dry fields are: (1) a better hydraulic regime with improved drainage and water conservation; (2) protection from salinization caused by the incursion of salty Lake Titicaca waters; (3) optimal position- ing of crop roots to water, so that moisture is maintained close to the roots, yet the root systems are protected from water logging (in land subject to wet season inundation and supersaturation); (4) improved soil fertility due to less nutrient leaching; and (5) better thermal properties, specifically, an enhanced heat storage capacity that mitigates the damage of the frequent altiplano frosts[10] (Denevan 1970; Erickson 1985, 1988; Kolata 1986; Kolata and Ortloff 1989).

The crippling frost that struck the Pampa Koani region in late February 1988 pro- vided dramatic support for the theory that heat conservation is one of the important benefits of raised fields. Temperatures as low as -5 C{{ring}} devastated potato fields around the Bolivian Titicaca Basin (Kolata and Ortloff 1989:259). Conventional po- tato fields adjacent to the reactivated fields then in operation suffered product losses of 70 percent to 100 percent. Fields located in hollows or depressions where cold air could settle were the most damaged. In contrast, the experimental raised fields experi- enced only minor damage, principally "frost burning" on potato plant leaves, particu- larly on plants at the edges of the planting platform (ibid.). Thus, the long-term advan- tages of raised fields over dry farming may not lie so much in a greater yield as in the increased buffering from temperature fluctuations—especially the endemic frosts of the altiplano wet season.

The raised fields were fed by a sophisticated hydraulic system of canals and aque- ducts. The principal water course in the Pampa Koani, the Río Catari, was diverted and artificially canalized to open up more land to raised field production and help prevent flooding of the Pampa Koani (Kolata 1991:116). A sophisticated canal by-pass system further aided in the handling of periodic flooding (ibid.).

The Pampa Koani, far from being the desolate, marginal environment that it now appears, would have been transformed through raised field agricultural systems into a tremendously productive region during the Tiwanaku IV period, capable of supporting a substantial population. Kolata (ibid.:111, Table 6) estimates that the Pampa Koani alone, with double cropping and 75 percent field utilization, could have provided enough food yearly for 105,000 to 410,000 people.

Kolata (1983, 1991) has persuasively argued that the scale and complexity of the hydraulic infrastructure, the potential for surplus production, and the existence of sim-

---

[9] Fertilizers were not used in these experimental fields, and weeding and cultivation took place in the traditional manner (Kolata and Ortloff 1989). It should be noted that some of the difference be- tween the two yields may result from the well-known "virgin-soil" effect; the raised fields had not been in cultivation for many centuries, whereas the traditional dry fields have been.

[10] Kolata and Ortloff (1989), Erickson (1988), and Kolata (1992) provide more detailed analyses of the heat storage properties of raised fields and their relation to frost protection.

ilar features in the Tiwanaku Valley indicate that the Pampa Koani raised field system represents a centrally directed, Tiwanaku state reclamation project (Graffam [1992] and Erickson [1988] have taken strongly opposed positions). With regard to the Tiwanaku state and the raised field systems of the Pampa Koani and elsewhere, Kolata (1991:121) observes: "Investment in landscape capital (terrace and irrigation systems, aqueducts, and dikes) that served the purpose of expanding or stabilizing regional agricultural production goes hand in glove with [a] strategy of direct elite (state) intervention. Economic surplus generated from these intensification projects, of course, was the pediment of their political power."

The Pampa Koani Settlement System

Most of the raised fields of the Pampa Koani are thought to have been built during the Tiwanaku IV period, although some fields date to the Tiwanaku III or post-Tiwanaku periods (Graffam 1992; Kolata 1986; Kolata and Ortloff 1989). The number of fields was far in excess of the needs of the population actually living on the Pampa Koani, and all but a fraction of the agricultural production from the raised fields was probably used to support the populations at Tiwanaku and Lukurmata (Kolata 1986:750; 1991).

Although little is known about settlement on the Pampa Koani prior to A.D. 400, the available evidence suggests that the residential population of the Pampa Koani grew significantly during the Tiwanaku IV period. Concurrent with this population increase was the construction of many raised fields and supporting irrigation systems, and the emergence of a four-tier settlement hierarchy (Figure 11.23). This settlement hierarchy consisted of two second-order centers, Lukurmata and Pajchiri, with public architecture complexes and substantial residential populations; nine residential platform mounds (some with limited public architecture);[11] and over a hundred individual habitation mounds (Graffam, personal communication).[12]

Lukurmata and its counterpart on the other side of the pampa, Pajchiri, are the largest sites associated with the Pampa Koani raised fields. Pajchiri has received little investigation, but it is similar to Lukurmata in several ways, including general topographic setting, large size, and possession of Tiwanaku-style public architecture. Like Lukurmata, Pajchiri overlooks the lake at the edge of the main area of raised fields. The

---

[11] This tier consists of large terraced platform mounds (Kolata 1983, 1986). Nine of these have been identified, ranging in size from 40 m × 30 m on a side and 1.75 m high, to 120 m × 75 m on a side and 3.75 m high (Kolata 1983; 1986:Table 1). The majority of them are clustered in the lower Pampa Koani, roughly 8 km northeast of Lukurmata. Most are quadrangular in shape, but PK-2 and PK-3 are L-shaped, with a narrow terrace extending from the main platform. Test excavations indicate that the largest mounds—the contiguous PK-5 and PK-6 platforms—were initially constructed during the Tiwanaku III period and then enlarged and remodeled during the Tiwanaku IV period. The other seven platform mounds also yielded some Tiwanaku III period pottery, but most of their ceramics are Tiwanaku IV-style.

[12] These generally appear as oval mounds, roughly 20 m × 13 m in area and 1 m high, frequently situated on the ends of raised fields. Excavation of extant mounds has revealed traces of domestic occupations including packed earth floors or living surfaces. Overall, however, the mound occupations do not appear to have had long-term occupations. Kolata (1986) reports Chiripa and Tiwanaku I-style ceramics from below several of these habitation mounds (such as PK-1[b]), but this material can probably be associated with premound occupations, rather than the mound itself.

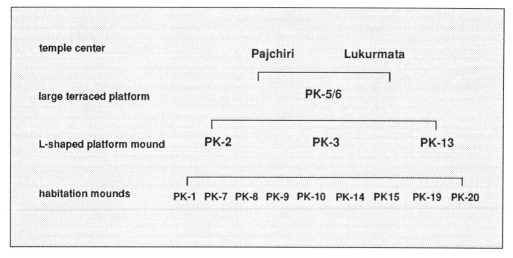

Fig. 11.23 Tiwanaku IV/V period settlement hierarchy in Pampa Koani based on site size and amount of public architecture (adapted from Kolata 1986: Figure 8).

Pajchiri complex covers roughly 30 ha, and consists of four distinct components: domestic terraces, a "fortress," a ceremonial precinct with monumental terraces, and a semi-subterranean temple. The sunken temple, with its ashlar masonry, its gate, and its stone staircase, is similar to those found at Lukurmata and Tiwanaku (Bennett 1934). Recent work at Pajchiri has revealed a system of large aqueducts similar in design and operation to examples at Lukurmata (Ortloff and Kolata 1989). Although some Tiwanaku III-style sherds have been recovered from the surface at Pajchiri, Tiwanaku IV-style polychrome pottery is much more common, indicating that Pajchiri was contemporary with Lukurmata.

The 6.5 ha of raised fields at Lukurmata itself (3% of the area of the site) could not have fed the entire community during the Tiwanaku IV period. Therefore, the bulk of the Lukurmata population was probably supported by the raised fields of the Pampa Koani system. Because many of these fields are within several kilometers of Lukurmata, most of the Lukurmata residents were probably involved in primary agricultural production. The smallest of the Pampa sites may represent families continuously responsible for guarding and weeding fields, while the highly labor-intensive agricultural tasks—planting, harvesting, and cleaning the canals or swales—seasonally involved most of the Lukurmata population.

Just as Lukurmata residents may have traveled out into the Pampa Koani for agricultural activities, so the inhabitants of the smaller Pampa Koani sites probably traveled to Lukurmata on occasion. The public architecture at Lukurmata suggests that one of Lukurmata's new functions was as a religious "central place," a regional center for ritual activity. Lukurmata would have been home to a temple staff, and visited by residents of outlying communities for important ceremonies.

Lukurmata probably also served as a regional mortuary center. We do not know if the individuals in the elite burial platform were Lukurmata residents. Perhaps the highest-status individuals from small, outlying communities in the Pampa Koani were taken to Lukurmata for burial.

Ceramic Style Affiliations

Although the range of Tiwanaku vessels represented in this occupation is much greater than the range of Tiwanaku vessels represented in earlier occupations (including the Structure 22–24 occupation), this does not necessarily mean that Lukurmata residents were now more closely tied to Tiwanaku. Our sample size of Tiwanaku IV vessels is much larger than that of Tiwanaku III vessel types, and larger sample sizes result in increased diversity in the sample.

It may be more significant that the entire known Tiwanaku III inventory is represented at Lukurmata. In contrast, only a portion of the broad range of Tiwanaku IV vessel types appears in the Structure 25–28 occupation. This may have been a matter of local preferences, or perhaps newly restricted access to Tiwanaku products. There is evidence that households in later occupations at Lukurmata had differential access to Tiwanaku pottery.

The increase in variety was almost exclusively restricted to decorated vessels. Does this mean that serving and hospitality functions at the household level were becoming more important? Or, that Lukurmata residents were absorbed into a Tiwanaku social order (entailing particular activities and forms of social marking) so that their household contents came to more closely resemble what might be found in a residence at the capital? Unfortunately, we do not have comparable data from an early Tiwanaku IV period domestic occupation at Tiwanaku itself.

The pottery found with the Structure 25–28 occupation also provides evidence that Lukurmata residents continued to have some form of interaction with other regions, if only through Tiwanaku-dominated exchange networks. Proportionally fewer non-Tiwanaku, nonlocal bowl fragments were found with the Structure 25–28 occupation than with the Tiwanaku III period occupations, further indicating that ties between Lukurmata and Tiwanaku were becoming more important than interaction between Lukurmata and other communities. If we assume that the Local Tradition pottery was not made locally, or at Tiwanaku, this process would also explain the rapid decline in the proportion of Local Tradition vessels in Lukurmata households.

SUMMARY

Did Lukurmata's evolution into a large, complex, second-order site result in a major transformation of household life there? Our sample size is small, but the Structure 25–28 occupation suggests that the answer is "no," at least for the ridge residents.

Despite the vast change in Lukurmata, and in Lukurmata's role in the Tiwanaku system, domestic life on the ridge remained much the same as it had been. The most striking difference between the Structure 25–28 occupation and previous occupations—the change from Tiwanaku III-style pottery to Tiwanaku IV-style pottery—was not accompanied by other changes in household organization. The continuity in the types of artifacts associated with residences indicates that a similar set of tasks continued to be part of the household domain. In short, the adoption of a new style of pottery, though highly striking from an archaeological perspective, represents at most a *sys-*

temic change, not a *transformational* change in the household system, or in the underlying structure and operation of the household.

The Structure 25–28 occupation illustrates the importance of complementary regional-and household-level approaches to interpreting change in past complex societies. The occupation demonstrates how change may take place at different levels of society; analysis at one level alone cannot provide a complete picture of societal change. In previous Lukurmata occupations, we have noted changes at the household level that were not accompanied by changes at the settlement level; in the Structure 25–28 occupation we see the opposite.

We can never really know why Lukurmata, and not some other site, grew to be a regional ceremonial-administrative center. Nothing about Lukurmata during the Tiwanaku III period suggests that the site was markedly different from the many other settlements that must have existed in the area, or that it was going to develop in this direction. Lukurmata may, for instance, have been a ceremonial center in the pre-Tiwanaku period. There is some evidence that the Lukurmata temple represents the rebuilding of an earlier structure (Bennett 1936; Bermann 1990). Was Lukurmata deliberately selected by the Tiwanaku rulers for development as a regional administrative center during the Tiwanaku IV period? The abruptness of its growth suggests so.

One of the attractions of Lukurmata may have been its location at one of the points where Lake Titicaca is closest to Tiwanaku: a straight-line distance of some 12 km (Rivera, personal communication). Lukurmata could have evolved as an important point of access to the lake and lake resources for the Tiwanaku capital.

Lukurmata may also have occupied a "strategic" position for controlling traffic in the Pampa Koani and the Taraco Peninsula. Its position at the point where the hills are very close to the Pampa would have allowed it to regulate any east-west traffic moving on the northern half of the Taraco Peninsula (a fact well recognized by the present-day Bolivian customs police).

Lukurmata may further have evolved as part of a central-place system. It appears to be one of three regional administrative centers located within a day's travel of Tiwanaku in each cardinal direction (the others would be the "port" of Iwawe to west of Tiwanaku, Khonko Wankani to the south; and an as yet unidentified site to the east).

Finally, Lukurmata may have been singled out for its distinctive landform; the Wila Kollu hill, on which the temple is located, is one of the few elevations in the Pampa Koani area. Even today, the hill is a widely used landmark by the Pampa Koani population. In addition to being a visually prominent point, the hill also provides a setting well above the limits of the periodic flooding by the lake.[13]

The hill may have made Lukurmata attractive to Tiwanaku for other reasons. As I have discussed, the entire south face of the hill was transformed into a terraform pyramid, the builders exploiting the natural hill to make the Wila Kollu landform an imposing ceremonial center. The massive Akapana pyramid at Tiwanaku represents similar exploitation of a natural hill (Kolata, personal communication).

---

[13] The recent disastrous rise in lake level (1985–89) covered the Pampa Koani and turned the Wila Kollu hill into an island.

12

Lukurmata at Its Height

After Structures 25–28 were abandoned, other residences were built nearby. The intensity of occupation on the ridge seems to have increased; less fill separates Tiwanaku IV period occupations than separated Tiwanaku III period occupations, and the Tiwanaku IV period structures themselves show more episodes of reflooring, probably to extend the uselife of structures. The increased density of settlement on the ridge may have prevented residents from simply building a new house nearby when the old one began to disintegrate.

The last occupation dating to the Tiwanaku IV period was at 60–64 cm below datum. Excavating 248 contiguous m² at this level revealed the remains of seven buildings (Structures 33–39) and associated hearths, burials, and outdoor activity areas (Figure 12.1). Figure 12.36 is an artist's reconstruction of how this occupation may have appeared. A contemporaneous house (Structure 42) excavated on the other side of Lukurmata makes possible some limited interhousehold comparisons.

A single carbon sample from an outdoor hearth on the ridge yielded a corrected, calibrated date of A.D. 840 ± 115. The Tiwanaku-style ceramics suggest a late Tiwanaku IV period or early Tiwanaku V period occupation.

SITE COMPOSITION

Covering some 120 ha, Lukurmata was divided into several discrete residential areas, with domestic occupation on the point to the north of the temple, the ridge to the west of the hill, and in the center of the site. Settlement continued to expand in the southern portion of the site during the Tiwanaku IV period, with the construction of broad, low terraces for houses and storage structures. Multiple excavations on the ridgetop allow us to estimate the maximum population for the ridge at this time as around three hundred individuals.[1]

The occupation of the late Tiwanaku IV period revealed several important changes in residential organization: (1) differences between houses in architectural styles; (2) an increase in residential density, with structures so closely packed as to be touching

---

[1] Each of the two patio groups I exposed covers approximately 160 m². Arbitrarily assuming that each patio group represents 10 people (5 for each structure with a hearth), calculating that 6000 m² of the ridge surface (not including terraces) would have been available for domestic occupation gives us a figure for the ridge of 370 individuals. The redgetop residential density figure cannot be extended to other residential areas of the site. Domestic organization took a very different form in at least one other area of the site (near Structure 42) and residential density in this part of the site would have been much lower.

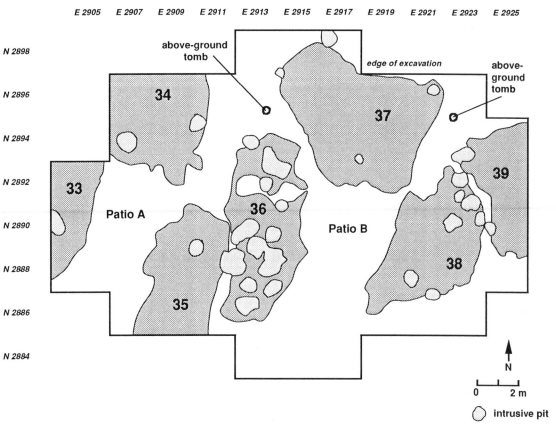

Fig. 12.1 Plan of Structure 33–39 occupation showing housefloors (dark shading), patio areas, and above-ground tombs.

one another; and (3) greater uniformity in spatial orientation, that is, buildings oriented to the cardinal directions. The most striking change, however, was the grouping of structures on the ridge to enclose small outdoor activity areas. This change in spatial organization was part of a significant shift in domestic life—the emergence of a new form of domestic unit, organized around patios. As can be seen in Figure 12.1, we exposed at least two such "patios" on the ridge: Patio A, formed by Structures 33, 34, and 35; and Patio B, formed by Structures 36, 37, and 38.

DOMESTIC ARCHITECTURE: PATIO B

Structures 36, 37, and 38 were completely excavated. Structure 38 was the oldest of the group. It had been refloored and remodeled several times, while maintaining the same general dimensions and floor plan. Although the three structures grouped around Patio B were similar to one another architecturally, they differed markedly in terms of interior features and contents.

Structures 38 and 36

Structure 38 was a rectangular structure, measuring 6 m × 4 m, with a entrance in the northwestern wall (Figure 12.2). The bright orange clay floor of the structure contained two large postholes near the center of the house, two hearths, and several large storage pits (Figure 12.3).

Unlike hearths in earlier houses, the hearths of Structure 38 were sturdy adobe con-

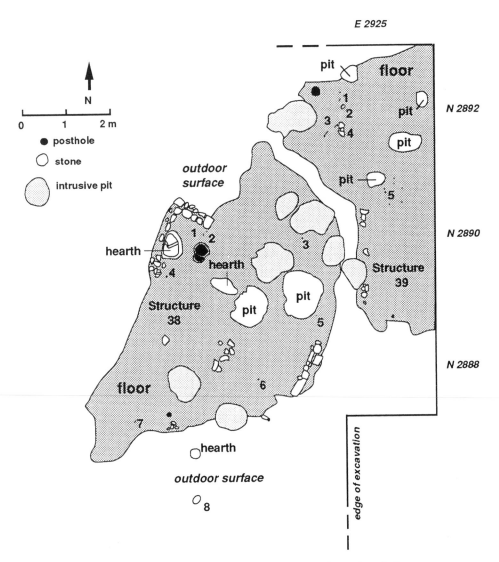

Fig. 12.2 Plan of Structure 38 and 39 floors with selected artifacts plotted. *Key, Structure 38*: (1) llama phalanges with drilled holes, (2) stone bead, (3) worked camelid bone, (4) ground stone ball, (5) worked camelid bone, (6) cone, (7) bone needle fragment and bone ring, (8) cache of cones (outside structure); *Key, Structure 39*: (1) needle fragment, (2) chunk of adobe with twig and cane impressions, (3) fragment of bone spoon, (4) spindle whorl, (5) lithic debitage.

Fig. 12.3 Floor of Structure 38 looking west. Walls in the foreground date to the post-Conquest colonial period.

structions. The larger of the two hearths consisted of a stone-and adobe-lined pit in the floor with a thick adobe collar extending 8–11 cm above the floor (Figure 12.4). A large stone fixed into the adobe divided the hearth into northern and southern chambers. Three large fieldstones in the southern chamber had probably served as pot rests. The hearth was full of carbonized llama dung, a common fuel on the altiplano, as well carbonized plant remains. The smaller hearth was not stone-lined, and it was single-chambered. It did not appear to have been used as intensively as the larger one.

In the eastern half of Structure 38 were two large storage pits. These pits, along with an intrusive tomb, can be seen in the center and left foreground of Figure 12.5. A number of large undecorated cooking pots were smashed at the bottom of the smaller of the two pits (shown partially bisected in Figure 12.5) perhaps by the house occupants when the house was abandoned. The larger pit was bell-shaped in profile and deeper, with a flat clay bottom 92 cm below floor level. The walls of the pit were unmodified clay, except for a section of the southwestern wall, which consisted of three rows of field cobbles laid in clay mortar.

We were surprised to find behind this wall a third pit that had been sealed the last time the house was refloored. The pit had been filled with soil and refuse, including camelid and fish remains, plainware and decorated pottery fragments, stone flakes, and chunks of burned clay and adobe. On the bottom of this pit were bones of a human adult: a right femur, right innominate, and a section of the right humerus. Since poor preservation cannot account for the incompleteness of the burial, this is a case of sec-

Fig. 12.4 Detail of Structure 38 floor showing wall foundation and double-chamber adobe hearth.

Fig. 12.5 Western edge of Structure 38 floor (white) and intrusive Tiwanaku V period tombs.

ondary burial (common at Tiwanaku), or the disturbance of an earlier grave, rather than refuse from a meal. A 5 cm × 6 cm sheet of beaten metal was lying under the bones.

Structure 36, forming the western side of Patio B, was very poorly preserved and riddled with intrusive tombs (Figure 12.6). It was somewhat longer and narrower than

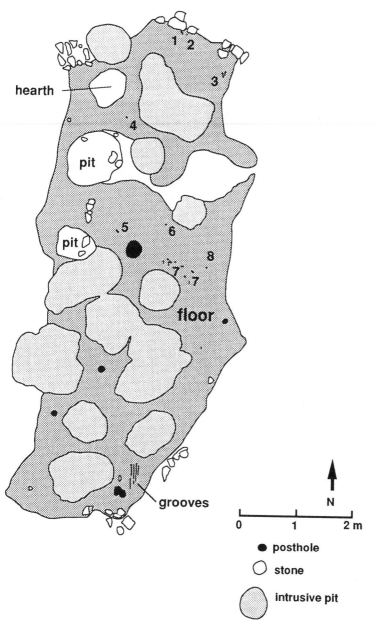

Fig. 12.6 Plan of Structure 36 floor with selected artifacts plotted.
Key: (1) bone needle fragment, (2) bone spindle whorl fragment, (3) fragments of three wichuñas, (4) shell bead, (5) wichuña fragment, (6) ceramic spindle whorl fragment, (7) lithic debitage, (8) decortication flake.

the other buildings of this occupation, and would have been rectangular in plan, measuring roughly 8 m × 3.5 m. Like Structure 38, the largest posthole was in the center of the building. Several smaller postholes were found near both ends of the structure. The entrance to the structure could not be located.

Only two major interior features could be identified: (1) a poorly preserved hearth filled with homogeneous gray ash, fish bone, fragments of burned adobe, and rock; and (2) a large storage pit, with a mouth diameter of 90 cm and a depth of 78 cm. This appears to have been empty when the house was abandoned.

Structure 37

Structure 37 formed the northern side of the patio. The plan of Structure 37 was difficult to determine because the preserved wall segments show that the edges of the floor do not mark the edges of the structure itself (Figure 12.7). An intrusive stone-lined drain ran through the middle of the floor. The "shadow walls" in the soil and the distribution of artifacts on the floor suggest that the building had straight walls, and may have been "L-shaped" with an extension to the northeast.

Unlike Structures 36 and 38, the Structure 37 floor contained no features other than small postholes near the edge of the floor and a very shallow refuse pit. This pit contained gray ash, fish remains, two bone bead fragments, and a fragment of camelid bone carved with zoomorphic designs.

DOMESTIC ACTIVITIES: PATIO B

The differences in features between Structures 36, 37, and 38 were also evident in house contents. Unlike the floors of Structures 36 and 38, the Structure 37 floor was not stained or charcoal-smeared, and exhibited little ash, bone fragments, or fragments from cooking vessels. The pottery assemblage of Structure 37 also differed from those of Structures 36 and 38. Fragments from a range of undecorated cooking vessels (ollas and open-mouth bowls of various sizes) and Tiwanaku-style decorated vessels (keros, open-mouth bowls, flaring-sided bowls) were found on Structure 36 and 38 floors. In contrast, most of the sherds on the Structure 37 floor were from a single vessel form represented only in that structure and in Structure 34. This vessel form was an undecorated, open-mouth bowl with thick walls and a flat bottom (Figure 12.8).

The lack of characteristic features and occupational debris on the floor of Structure 37 indicates that the structure was not used as a dwelling, or at least as a building in which the full range of domestic tasks was carried out. It may have been used for storage.

The enclosed Patio B measured roughly 22 m² (Figure 12.9). In some places, particularly near the sides of buildings, extensive use had packed the soil into a hard, discolored surface. Not surprisingly, the types of artifacts and features found in the patio area were similar to those found indoors. Most household tasks were probably performed outdoors, with houses used only for sleeping and carrying out activities during bad weather.

A number of patio features were excavated. Just east of Structure 38 was a hearth with a raised adobe basin. The adobe collar of the hearth would have supported cook-

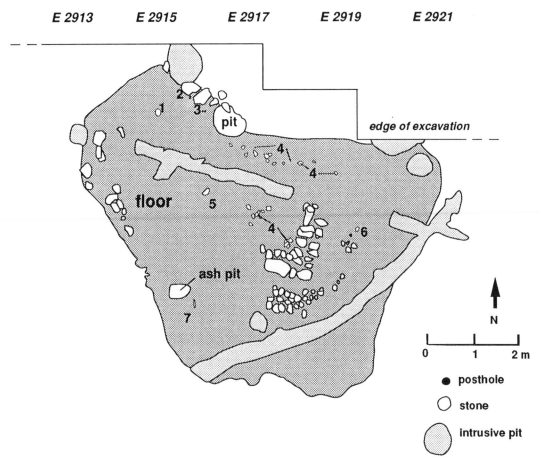

Fig. 12.7 Plan of Structure 37 floor with selected artifacts plotted. *Key*: (1) stone tablet (pot lid?), (2) cone, (3) two ceramic spoons, (4) thick-walled bowl fragments, (5) open-mouth bowl illustrated in Figure 12.8, (6) basalt ground stone hoe or ax, (7) bone scraper made from camelid femur.

ing vessels above the fire. The hearth contained a small amount of ash, small burned camelid bone fragments, and fire-blackened plainware sherds. Two shallow refuse pits were found in the northern margin. One contained only ash, but the other held large quantities of sherds and burned bone fragments.

Charred remains of maize kernels were found in several unsystematically collected flotation samples from the Structure 33–39 hearth and midden contexts (Hastorf, personal communication). Conventionally, Lukurmata would be considered above the elevation (roughly 3300 msl) at which maize can be grown, indicating its importation from lower elevations. The nearest maize-growing zone would have been roughly 75 km to the east. However, it is possible that maize was produced, if only in small quantities, in the Pampa Koani raised fields.

Overall, the artifact assemblage of Patio B was similar in many ways to the assem-

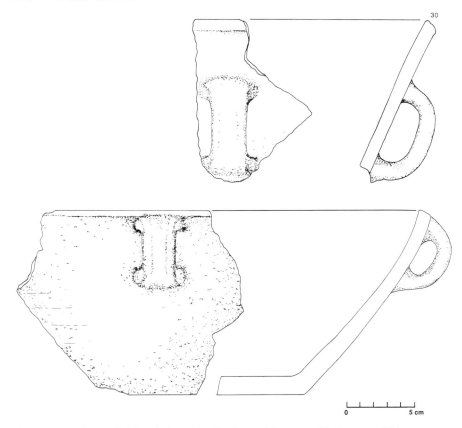

0   5 cm

Fig. 12.8 Thick-walled bowls found on the floor of Structure 37. Pottery of this type was found only with Structures 34 and 37.

blage of artifacts from previous domestic contexts in the Lukurmata sequence. The artifacts reflect continuity in basic domestic activities:

- food preparation and consumption (ash, charcoal, camelid, bird, and fish bones; remains of maize, quinoa, and potatoes; ground stones; and fragments of fire-blackened cooking pottery)
- sewing, hide working, or basketry (bone awls and needle fragments)
- spinning (spindle whorl fragments)
- weaving (wichuña fragments)
- production or repair of stone cutting tools (lithic debitage)
- grinding and scraping tasks (small mortars, bone scrapers)
- drug ingestion (bone snuff tubes)

The patio area provided evidence for a new household activity at Lukurmata, represented by a type of artifact not seen in previous occupations: a bone tool (10–15 cm in length) manufactured from the mandible of adult camelids. These tools, of unknown

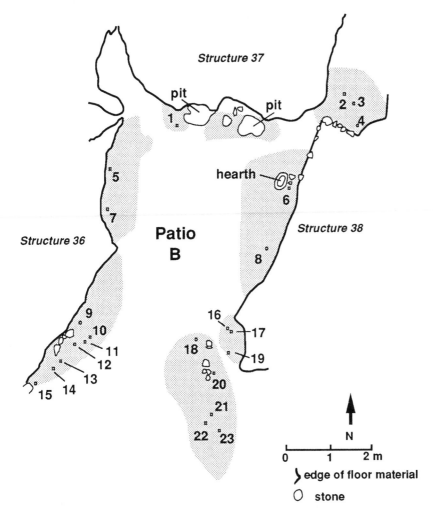

Fig. 12.9 Patio B surface with selected artifacts plotted. Shading indicates extent of preserved outdoor surfaces. Intrusive features not shown. *Key*: (1) broken mano, (2) metal pin fragments, (3) worked bone, (4) projectile point fragment, (5) spindle whorl fragment, (6) two stone balls, (7) bone awls, (8) camelid mandible tool production area, (9) camelid mandible tool, (10) projectile point fragment, (11) bead, (12) broken mano, (13) cone, (14) bone needle fragments, (15) bone scraper made from camelid rib, (16) marine shell bead, (17) biface, (18) wichuña fragment, (19) stone (basalt) ax or hoe, (20) antler tool (hoe?), (21) retouched flakes, (22) cones, (23) ground stone bowl fragment illustrated as Figure 12.32a.

use, were made by breaking off the ascending ramus above the mandibular angle and smoothing the bottom edge (Figure 12.10).

These camelid mandible tools are closely associated with occupations dating to the Tiwanaku IV and V periods at sites in the Tiwanaku settlement hierarchy. Identical tools have been found in sizable numbers at Tiwanaku (Kolata, personal communication; Rydén 1947:33), Khonko Wankani, Pajchiri, and Omo in Moquegua, Peru (Goldstein 1989:10). Tools of this type are not found in non-Tiwanaku sites, or in Tiwanaku III or post-Tiwanaku period occupations at Tiwanaku sites. The presence of these tools in a variety of geographic contexts (the coastal sierra site of Omo, lake-side Lukurmata, and inland Tiwanaku) suggests that they were not associated with specific lacustrine or altiplano adaptations.

The function of these tools remains unknown, although the wear on the bottom edge suggests a scraping function. A single specimen found at Omo in Moquegua, Peru (where preservation is better than at most Bolivian sites), was tied with wool twine to a fragment of wood hafting (Goldstein 1989:10). Stig Rydén (1947:Figure 5, *L* and *M*; Figure 16, *Q*) illustrates specimens from Tiwanaku. Rydén (ibid.:34) suggests that they were "probably used in pottery-making for smoothing the inner side of bulging vessels." The large number of camelid mandible tools found at Lukurmata, coupled with the lack of any evidence for ceramic production at the site, make such a specialized function unlikely.

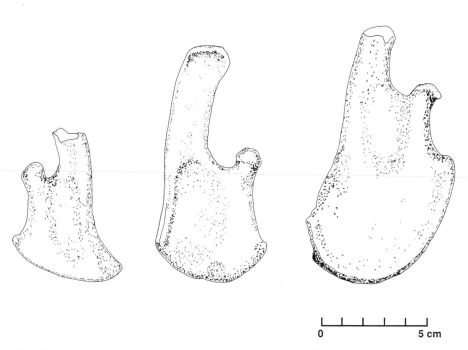

0   5 cm

Fig. 12.10 Examples of bone tools made from camelid mandibles found with the Structure 33–39 occupation. Manufacture of these tools was a household activity at Lukurmata, but their function is not known.

Workshops (the areas where an item was actually made) are rarely found by archaeologists. Instead, archaeologists generally find workshop dumps (Moholy-Nagy 1990). Both types of locations were found in or near Patio B. A production area of small splinters from camelid mandibles that might have been missed or overlooked in sweeping and cleaning was located near the edge of Structure 38. A dumping area outside the patio area proper contained larger pieces of camelid mandibles including broken-off sections of the lower mandible. We did not find the tools, presumably stone grinding tools, used to produce the mandible tools.

Because we do not know the function of these tools, it is not certain that their use was a household activity, but it appears as if their manufacture, at least, was carried out at the household level. Structures 36–38 were not the only structures where we found evidence of the production of these tools. Debris from their manufacture was also found with Structure 42, suggesting a universal household activity rather than specialized craft production by particular households.

DOMESTIC ARCHITECTURE: PATIO A

To determine if the arrangements of structures, differences between buildings, and distribution of household artifacts seen in the Patio B area were characteristic of patio groups, I investigated a second patio group immediately to the west of the Patio B group. Patio A was formed by Structures 33, 34, and 35.

Structure 35

This partially excavated structure formed the eastern edge of Patio A (Figure 12.11). Roughly 17 m^2 (or 85%) of the floor of this structure was exposed. The floor was similar in shape and size to that of Structure 36. Unlike many of the other buildings, Structure 35 did not have a large central posthole. A number of postholes were found near the edges of the floor, and the building was sufficiently narrow that the roof could have rested on the walls. The entrance could not be located.

The structure had the same types of features as Structure 38: a hearth and two large storage pits. The oblong hearth was stone-and adobe-lined with an adobe collar. A large, slightly bell-shaped storage pit contained faunal remains, fragments of pottery from utilitarian cooking vessels, and decorated Tiwanaku-style keros and flaring-sided bowls. A smashed cooking olla and several large fieldstones were found on top of this refuse.

Structures 33 and 34

Only 9 m^2 of the floor of Structure 33 was exposed (Figure 12.12). In construction techniques and materials the structural remains resembled the other buildings of the occupation. No major features were found in this floor, although a hearth may have been in the unexcavated portion of the floor. We located the edge of a shallow ash pit near the center of the floor.

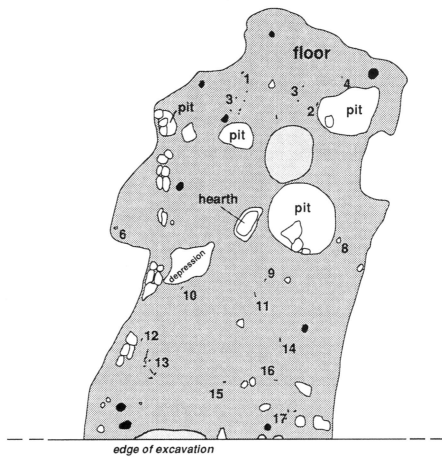

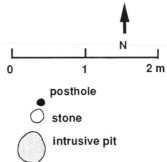

Fig. 12.11 Plan of Structure 35 floor with selected artifacts plotted. *Key:* (1) antler fragment, (2) obsidian flake, (3) lithic debitage (obsidian), (4) stone bead, (5) metal pin, (6) ground stone ball, (7) mano, (8) pecked cobble, (9) stone blade, (10) projectile point fragment, (11) worked camelid bone, (12) retouched flake, (13) worked camelid bone and bone splinters, (14) smoothed pebble, (15) obsidian flake, (16) chert flake, (17) lithic debitage.

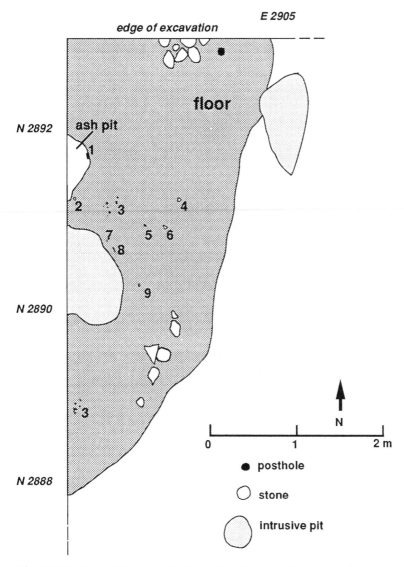

Fig. 12.12 Plan of Structure 33 floor with selected artifacts plotted.
Key: (1) bone needle, (2) stone cone, (3) lithic debitage, (4) pecked cobble,
(5) copper fragment, (6) broken mano, (7) spindle whorl fragment,
(8) copper pin fragments, (9) retouched flake.

The approximately 18 m^2 of Structure 34 may represent just over half of the total floor area (Figure 12.13). A central posthole was not found, but a number of smaller postholes ran near the center of the structure and around the edges of the floor. The entrance could not be defined. Like Structure 37, this building did not appear to have had major interior features other than postholes.

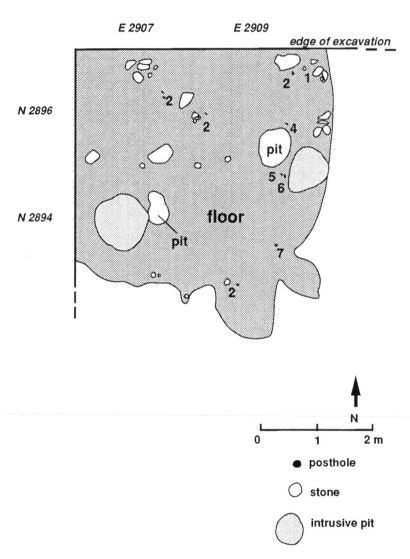

Fig. 12.13 Plan of Structure 34 floor with selected artifacts plotted. *Key*: (1) stone bowl, (2) thick-walled bowl fragments, (3) lithic core, (4) wichuña, (5) cone, (6) double cone, (7) obsidian projectile point.

DOMESTIC ACTIVITIES: PATIO A

The artifacts recovered from the floors of Structures 33 and 35 were similar in type and quantity to the artifact assemblage found in Patio B. They included fragments of cooking and decorated pottery; remains of camelid, fish, and bird bone; pieces of fire-cracked rock; broken grinding stones; stone scrapers; bone awl and needle fragments; spindle whorls; cones; bone scraper; debris from expedient stone tool making (chert and obsidian); and a broken projectile point (Structure 35). Items of adornment included bone beads and part of a metal pin (Structure 33).

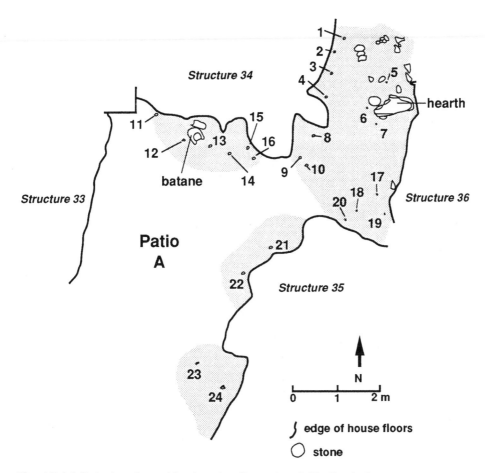

Fig. 12.14 Patio A surface with selected artifacts plotted. Shading indicates preserved outdoor surfaces. Intrusive features not shown. *Key*: (1) mica fragments, (2) bone needle fragments, (3) camelid mandible tool, (4) camelid mandible tool fragments, (5) bone needle, (6) cone, (7) cone, (8) chunk of obsidian, (9) exhausted core, (10) flakes and lithic debitage, (11) retouched flake, (12) cones, (13) lithic blade, (14) spindle whorl, (15) bone awl, (16) chipped stone scraper, (17) pecked cobble, (18) worked bone, (19) biface, (20) camelid mandible tool, (21) camelid mandible tool production area, (22) ground stone, (23) lithic debitage, (24) cone.

In contrast, the floor artifact assemblage of Structure 34 resembled the contents of Structure 37. Like Structure 37, the floor did not display a significant amount of ash, fish bones, fire-cracked rock, or small bone splinters. Pottery fragments on the floor of Structure 34 were from the distinctive type of thick-walled open bowl found in Structure 37, and larger utilitarian vessels, including the Pantini Orange jar with the raised punctate necklace. The features and contents of Structure 34 suggest use for special purposes (possibly storage) or for a restricted set of activities.

Patio A measured roughly 24 m^2 (Figure 12.14). Although we excavated much of this open area, an outdoor surface was only preserved in a few places. Food preparation and consumption were represented by a hearth located in the northeast corner of the patio area. This oblong feature was stone-and adobe-lined, with an adobe collar. Several cones and a bone needle fragment were found near the hearth. Nearby was a huge broken *batane* or grinding basin (weighing roughly 90 lbs).

As with Patio B, the debris from the preparation and repair of stone cutting tools was located in the western side of the patio. An area of roughly 2 m^2 yielded a relatively high density of small chipped stone debitage and flake tools.[2]

A concentration of camelid mandible bone splinters and teeth represented a third locus of domestic activity: the production of camelid mandible tools. This area was located on the eastern side of the patio south of the hearth. In addition to bone splinters, this area yielded a single broken (discarded) mandible tool fragment.

STRUCTURE 39

Part of a seventh structure (Structure 39) was exposed just east of Structure 38 in the central excavation on the ridge (Figure 12.2). The western half of the housefloor was excavated, roughly 12 m^2. It appeared that the structure would have been rectangular and measured approximately 6 m × 4 m. Organic staining and soot marks on the floor suggest that the structure had straight walls oriented north-south. We did not find a clear central posthole, but an irregular feature (35 m × 23 cm) in the northern section of the floor may have been a poorly preserved posthole. A number of smaller postholes were found around the edges of the floor. The entrance could not be defined. A chunk of burned adobe bearing impressions of reed or cane matting was found on the floor. Several small pits containing ash and one larger refuse or storage pit were found in the floor.

The artifacts on the floor suggest a residential function rather than a special-purpose one. The regularity in the grouping and orientation of domestic architecture on the ridge makes it probable that Structure 39 was part of another patio group to the east of the central excavation.

COMPARISON OF PATIOS A AND B

Excavation exposed two "patio groups" on the ridge, each covering roughly 160 m^2. Some of the structures located around the patio areas were dwellings, and were used

---

[2] The debris—which consisted mostly of angular fragments, decortification flakes, scaled and bipolar flakes—probably represents production of "expedient flake tools" rather than formal tools such as blades or bifaces (Parry 1987). A small exhausted core and a broken hammerstone were also found near this area.

for a broad range of domestic activities. Each patio group also included a structure used for nonresidential activities (Structures 34 and 37).

The occupants of each patio group organized household space in a similar manner. The two patio groups displayed an identical range of structure types, features, and artifacts, and a parallel spatial arrangement.

The spatial distribution of de facto refuse and features in the Structure 33–39 occupation presents an interesting pattern, although the incomplete preservation of the patio surfaces makes all interpretations tentative. The pattern suggests a single activity locus when certain tasks were performed outside, and dual loci (in the patio group) when the same task was performed indoors (i.e., in each residential structure). For instance, each dwelling had an indoor hearth, presumably used for cooking in inclement weather. But each patio displayed only one outdoor hearth, suggesting that when food preparation and consumption took place outside, it was shared by the inhabitants of both of the dwellings that faced the patio.

Similarly, manufacture of chipped stone tools was occasionally performed indoors by inhabitants of each dwelling in Patio Group B. However, only one clear locus of chipped stone tool manufacture was found outdoors in Patio B, suggesting that when this activity was conducted outdoors, it was done jointly by the patio group inhabitants.

CEREMONIAL ACTIVITIES: A RITUAL LOCUS

Early in the Tiwanaku IV period, the northern face of the ridge extending west from the temple hill was terraced and walled. A 5 m^2 excavation of the terrace surface in excavation unit N2886 E2855 exposed unique features: offerings of highly decorated pottery vessels and juvenile camelid. These features and the lack of normal occupational debris on the terrace suggest that the terrace was used for a limited set of ceremonial activities.

The top of the terrace was a level, unpaved surface of hard-packed soil 140–150 cm below the top of the ridge (Figure 12.15). It was fairly even and uniformly covered with a 3–5 cm thick layer of homogeneous gray ash of unknown origin. Although at one time this terrace must have had retaining walls to the north and south, we could not find traces of either. The preserved section of the terrace surface indicates that the terrace surface was at least 2 m wide. Despite several intrusive Tiwanaku V period or post-Tiwanaku period tombs, the terrace surface itself was well preserved.

There was no evidence of a domestic occupation on the terrace (Figure 12.16). Instead, it displayed an extraordinary assemblage of features and artifacts, including three separate offerings of an intact, modeled zoomorphic puma incensario. These vessels (not illustrated) were found upright in 50–60 cm deep, partially stone-lined pits near the northwest edge of the excavation unit. One of the vessels was filled with the burned remains of a plant tentatively identified as *tola* ("greasebush" or *Lepidophyllum quadrangulare*), a common plant in the region whose bitter root was in recent times eaten during the rainy season (La Barre 1948:53).

Fragments from a different form of vessel, a flat-bottomed open bowl decorated with pumas and condors, were also found buried as an offering in the terrace (Figure 12.17). Fragments from similar flat-bottomed open bowls (also decorated with pumas and condors) were found lying on the terrace surface. Two of these bowls appear to

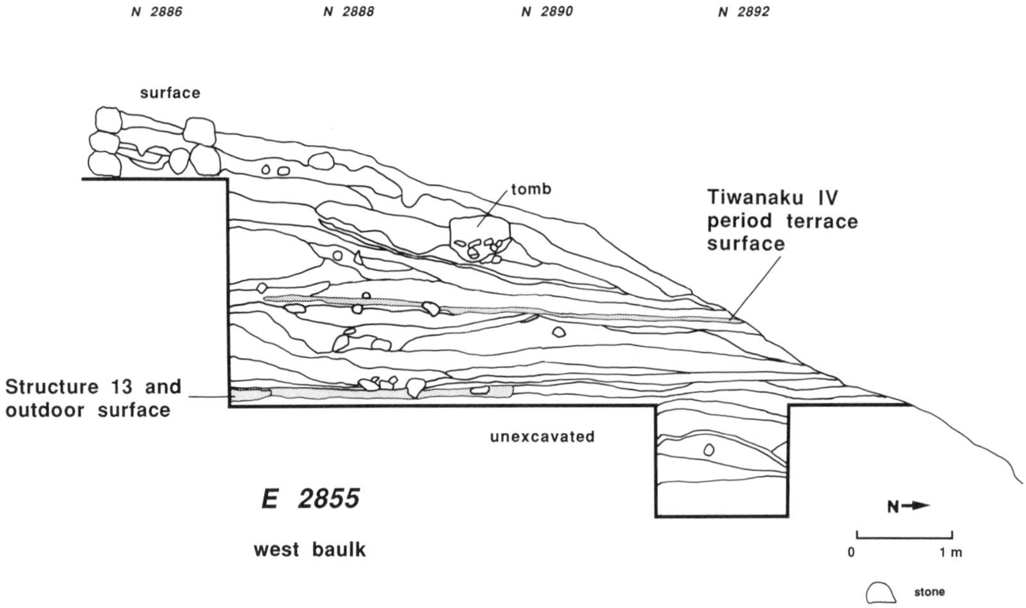

Fig. 12.15 Simplified profile of N2886 E2955 excavation unit showing stratigraphy on the north face of the ridge and the positions of Tiwanaku IV period terrace (shaded) and Structure 13.

Fig. 12.16 Plan of terrace surface (shaded) on the north face of the ridge with selected artifacts plotted. This section of the terrace was used for ceremonial activities. *Key*: (1) modeled feline vessel filled with burned plant material, (2) fragments of modeled feline vessel, (3) fragments of flat-bottom open bowl painted with feline motif shown in Figure 12.17, (4) fragments of modeled feline vessel, (5) fetal camelid, (6) fragments of flat-bottom open bowl painted with feline motif, (7) base of kero (interior coated with unidentified white substance), (8) pottery fragment decorated with painted feline, (9) bone carved with zoomorphic designs, (10) ornament of worked green stone, (11) bone carved with zoomorphic designs.

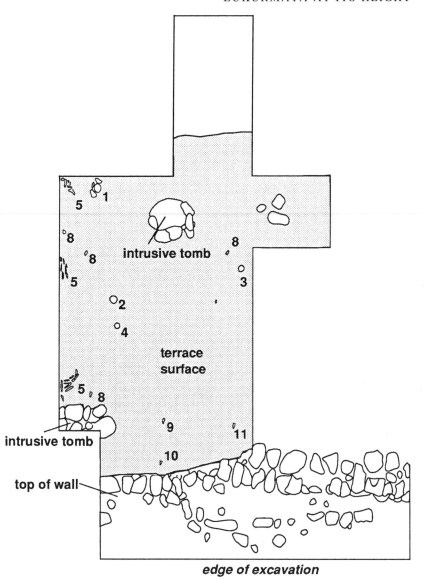

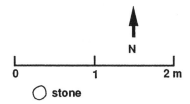

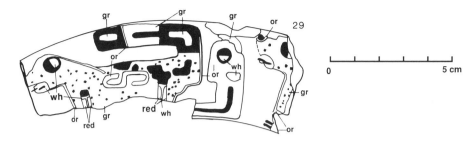

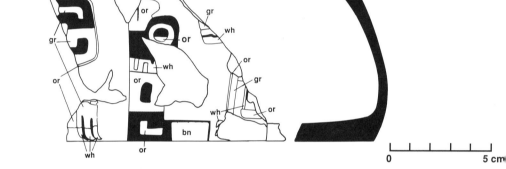

Fig. 12.17 Pottery fragment from terrace with puma and condor decoration on the rim interior and body exterior. Black, orange, brown, white, and gray painted decoration over polished red slip.

have been used as serving vessels. Fish remains (bone and scales) were found adhering to the interior walls and bottom of each.[3]

The burial of a fetal/infant camelid in a shallow pit was yet another typical terrace feature. Four examples of this offering were excavated.

Other artifacts found lying on the terrace included: a bone carved with zoomorphic designs; a piece of worked green ornamental stone; the base of a kero (decorated with the puma motif), the inside of which was coated with an unidentified white substance; fragments from at least six modeled puma incensarios; and fragments of Tiwanaku vessels elaborately decorated with pumas and condors. Pottery of the latter type was represented in significant numbers in only two other areas of Lukurmata: the "elite" tombs in the burial platform and in the jumble of small storage structures near Structure 42.

Overall, remains found on the terrace were strikingly different than those closely

---

[3] The only intact specimen of this bowl form found at Lukurmata was included as a grave-good in one of the high-status or elite tombs in the burial platform in the center of the site.

associated with domestic occupations. Particularly striking was the presence of the puma motif in the terrace ceramic assemblage. The fragments of modeled zoomorphic puma incensarios found on the terrace represent at least nine individual vessels. Fragments of pottery bearing painted puma designs represented at least six more vessels. Overall, 23 percent of the sherds in the terrace ceramic assemblage were decorated with a painted feline motif or were from feline-shaped vessels. In contrast, less than 0.05 percent of the sherds in ceramic assemblages associated with housefloors displayed a feline motif.

In summary, the northern terrace on the ridge appears to have been a spatially separate locus used for ceremonial or ritual activities involving offerings and serving activities. These activities involved "social display" Tiwanaku pottery of the type not used in day-to-day household activities.

OFFERINGS ELSEWHERE ON THE RIDGE

The remains of individual Tiwanaku IV-style zoomorphic puma incensarios were found deeply buried in several places on the ridgetop. Each offering consisted of a large (25–35 cm high) modeled, hollow-base, scalloped-rim puma. These vessels were not grave-goods, and were usually buried alone; in one case, a puma had been buried with a large, non-Tiwanaku vessel.

We could not determine if the offerings dated to the Structure 33–39 occupation because the outlines of the pits were not preserved, and most of these features were heavily disturbed. Stratigraphic evidence suggests that at least two of the offerings were made prior to the construction of Structure 26, or early in the Tiwanaku IV period. The other three offerings seem to date to somewhat later in the Tiwanaku IV period, indicating that rituals in residential areas involving these pottery forms continued throughout the Tiwanaku IV period.

MORTUARY ACTIVITIES

The tombs below the Structure 33–39 occupation indicated that mortuary activities had become part of Lukurmata household activities, at least to the extent that burials were placed in residential areas. Only one of the tombs (Burial 10) found in the main excavation on the ridge clearly dated to the Tiwanaku III period, suggesting that the pre-Tiwanaku pattern of *not* placing burials near or below houses continued during the Tiwanaku III period. In contrast, burial near structures apparently became more common during the second half of the Tiwanaku IV period.

Ridgetop Burials

On the basis of associated pottery and stratigraphic position, ten tombs found in the main excavation can be securely dated to the Tiwanaku IV period. In general, burials on the ridge during the Tiwanaku IV period were probably placed outside domestic structures.

Eight of these tombs were conventional below-ground burials, while two were elaborate, partially above-ground double-chamber stone cists. Each two partially above-

Fig. 12.18 Upper chamber of Burial 11, one of the two-chamber, above-ground tombs associated with the Structure 33–39 occupation.

ground tombs (Figure 12.1) consisted of two chambers: an above-ground cylindrical stone chamber roughly 40 cm high containing adult skeletal remains, and a lower, partially stone-lined chamber, 45 cm deep (Figure 12.18, Figure 12.21). The lower chamber of one tomb (Burial 11) contained an upright, partially intact, modeled llama incensario filled with ash (Figure 12.19, Figure 12.20).[4] The partially above-ground tombs (Burials 11 and 12) probably date to the late Tiwanaku IV period, but neither can be associated with a particular occupation.

No features similar to the partially above-ground tombs were found elsewhere at Lukurmata, although several of the higher-status burials in the platform (described below) displayed a different form of two-chamber arrangement.

The eight Tiwanaku IV period below-ground tombs on the ridge were rectangular or oblong in shape, averaging 50 cm × 90 cm long and 50 cm deep (Figure 12.22). Each had been lined and capped with stone slabs. Large grinding stones (batanes) had been used to cap four of the tombs. Each tomb contained the remains of a single adult, buried on its side in a flexed position, accompanied by few or no items. Grave-goods—

---

[4] Some of the burned vegetation in the vessel has been identified by Heidi Lennstrom and Melanie Wright of the University of Minnesota, as a plant known in Aymara as *wira q'uwa*, an herbaceous plant commonly burned today by the Aymara in ceremonies (Lennstrom, personal communication; van den Berg 1985:207). This may be the same plant that La Barre (1948:56) calls *q'oa*. La Barre (ibid.) further notes that *q'oa* refers to *Mentha pulegium* as well as several other plants of the Borreria and Rubiaceae families.

Fig. 12.19 Modeled llama incensario as found in the lower chamber of Burial 11. The animal's head had been deliberately removed.

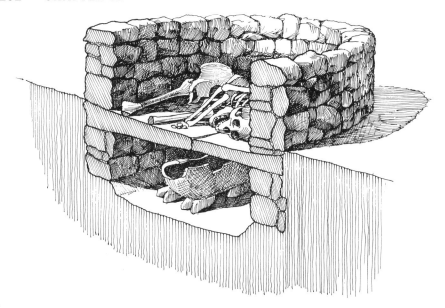

Fig. 12.20 Artist's reconstruction of Burial 11. The skeleton of an adult male was found in the upper chamber. The lower (subsurface) chamber contained a modeled llama incensario (Figure 12.19) and two large stone cones.

limited to a small number of utilitarian vessels and items of adornment—were found in only two of the tombs.[5] The Tiwanaku IV period tombs on the ridge had a different form than the circular cist tombs of the Tiwanaku V period and the post-Tiwanaku period slab tombs.

[5] One of these burials (Burial 13: N2896 E2913 Feature CB) consisted of the poorly preserved, disarticulated remains of an adult. Associated with the skeletal material were a bone carved with zoomorphic designs; a large metal pin; and twenty-nine small, pierced, flat sections of sodalite (some carved with geometric designs), probably the remains of a necklace. A Tiwanaku IV period tomb below Structure 37 (Burial 14: N2892 E2919 Feature 3) also contained the remains of a necklace. This tomb, oriented east-west, was rectangular, measuring approximately 47 cm × 71 cm wide and 50 cm deep (interior dimensions). One of the two capstones was a large batane or grinding stone. The fragments of a small, strap-handled, undecorated jar on top of these stones probably represented an offering. The base of this vessel contained an unidentified burned organic material. The walls of the tomb were constructed of two layers of flat slabs set on edge, although a second batane had been used as well. The flat floor of the tomb was not stone-lined. The tomb contained an adult buried in a flexed position with the head to the east. A poorly preserved metal (copper?) pendant with circular sodalite inlay was found in the chest area. A nearby tomb (Burial 15: N2892 E2919 Feature 4) displayed a similar construction style. It was also oriented east-west, measuring 89 cm × 54 cm wide and 50 cm deep. This tomb had been capped with two grinding stones, but no pottery offering was found on these. The walls were made up of a layer of small slabs resting on a layer of larger slabs. The floor of the tomb was not stone-lined. The tomb contained an adult male, with an artificially deformed cranium. The individual had been buried in a flexed position, on its right side, with the head to the west. No grave-goods were found.

Fig. 12.21 Upper chamber of Burial 12.

Fig. 12.22 Tiwanaku IV period tomb (Burial 20) below the floor of Structure 36. Flexed body position and tomb construction are typical of Tiwanaku IV period burials at Lukurmata.

Burials in the Central Platform

Fourteen Tiwanaku IV period tombs were excavated in the platform in the center of the site. These tombs differed in form and grave-goods from those on the ridge. The range and quantity of artifacts from these tombs suggest that this area served as a cemetery for higher-status individuals, both adults and juveniles. Each tomb consisted of a stone-capped circular shaft or pit, with a horizontal circular bench near the base of the tomb. Several of the tombs had a small chamber adjacent to the shaft (Janusek and Earnest 1988).

Each tomb contained a single individual, with the majority of the burials appearing to be adults. Individuals were buried in a seated and flexed position, usually facing north (ibid.). The basic assemblage of grave-goods accompanying each platform burial included the following:

- two or more polished blackware or polychrome Tiwanaku IV-style vessels
- intact bones from camelid, deer, or dog (placed in the tomb as offerings)
- stone tools or items of personal adornment made from imported materials such as obsidian or sodalite, craft items (metal or bone hair/clothing pins),
- small unfired clay pots and zoomorphic figurines[6]

Mortuary patterns of the late Tiwanaku IV period at Lukurmata suggest social differentiation in the placement of burials and associated grave-goods. Individuals of relatively lower status and children were buried in residential contexts—near or below dwellings. Adults of relatively higher social status were buried in the platform near the center of the site, with a much wider range and quantity of grave-goods.

TIWANAKU IV PERIOD DOMESTIC TERRACES

The ridgetop patio groups were not the only form of domestic organization at Lukurmata at the close of the Tiwanaku IV period. An example of a contemporary but different type of residence was excavated on one of the artificial terraces roughly 600 m to the south of the ridge. While the ridgetop domestic occupation was near Lukurmata's civic-ceremonial core, Structure 42 was located on a far hillslope near the southern edge of the site (Figure 12.23).

This hillslope still exhibits traces of broad, low, stone-faced terraces approximately

---

[6] Two tombs provide an indication of the range of grave-goods associated with these burials. The first of these tombs excavated (N2579 E3152 Tomb 1) held the fewest grave-goods. It consisted of a circular shaft roughly 80 cm in diameter and 120 cm deep. Above the large, flat capstones of the tomb was an intact Tiwanaku IV-style modeled, hollow-base puma incensario, upright, and filled with unidentified burned plant matter. Below the capstones, in the unmodified tomb chamber was a black-on-red flaring-sided bowl. The poorly preserved skeletal material represented an old adult. The orientation of the individual could not be determined. Fragments of an incised, polished blackware kero were found on the base of the tomb. A more elaborate tomb (Tomb 4 in N2553 E3133) contained an adult in a seated and flexed position facing northeast (Janusek and Earnest 1988). This individual was buried in a "benched" tomb. Grave-goods included parts of an adult camelid (skull, three limbs, ribs) and a set of deer antlers (ibid.). The remains of a large rodent (possibly vizcacha) found in the tomb may not represent actual grave-goods. Other grave-goods included two small unfired clay vessels, a small undecorated olla, and a elaborate Tiwanaku IV-style polychrome flat-bottom bowl (ibid.).

Fig. 12.23 View south from the main excavation on the ridge showing excavation of raised fields and location of Structure 42 (arrow).

1 m high and 3–4 m deep. We chose to excavate in an area of the hillslope with high surface artifact density and well-preserved terraces.

The surface of one terrace was nearly exposed in its entirety. On it we found the remains of two structures, one of which (Structure 42) was completely excavated. Structure 42 was located on the upper terrace (i.e., above the retaining wall or terrace face). Only part of the second structure on the terrace below was excavated.

Structure 42 stood at the western end of a 40 m long terrace. The 1987 excavation of the entire surface of this terrace exposed a maze of small enclosures, elaborate drainage systems, refuse pits, and stairways, as well as several burials. Structure 42 proved to be the only house on the terrace. No outdoor surfaces comparable to the patio areas of the ridgetop occupation were located.

The ceramics associated with Structure 42 indicate an occupation contemporaneous with the Structure 33–39 occupation on the ridge—a late Tiwanaku IV period or early ninth-century A.D., date. This chronological placement was supported by a single radiocarbon date of material taken from the Structure 42 hearth (A.D. 818 ± 110).

Structure 42 was a circular structure with an interior diameter of 3 m. The original floor had consisted of the usual layer of poured clay mixed with gravel and some sand. As with other Lukurmata domestic architecture, fieldstones in a mud mortar served as a foundation for mud brick or cut sod walls. The foundations consisted of two rows of unmodified fieldstone, and were preserved to a height of 50 cm above the original floor (Figure 12.24).

Fig. 12.24 Structure 42, a second style of a Tiwanaku IV period house. Looking south with the baffled entrance visible on the right side of the structure.

There was little evidence to indicate the nature of the house roof. A single posthole was found in the southern portion of the original floor. The roof was probably conical in form and supported primarily by the walls. An elaborate, shielded entrance opened to the west.

Three large features were found on the Structure 42 floor: a hearth, an adjoining ash pit, and a small storage/refuse pit. The single-chamber hearth was located against the south wall of the house. Like the hearths in the ridgetop structures, it was a stone- and adobe-lined oval, with a collar extending above the floor. Three large triangular stone slabs found in the hearth probably served as a pot rest. The hearth was filled with ashy soil and contained fire-blackened fragments of cooking pots, burned plant material (including charcoal), and fragments of camelid, fish, and bird bone. Adjacent to the hearth was a stone-ringed ash pit filled with a compact, homogeneous, greasy gray ash.[7] The third feature, a pit located against the northeast wall of the house, had been dug just before the house was abandoned (Figure 25).[8]

---

[7] Among the items recovered were burned plainware sherds, two small cones (one ceramic, the other of stone), fragments of camelid bone, chunks of burned adobe, and hundreds of fish bones (ribs, vertebrae, and cranial bones). Again, no camelid dung was found. In the southern corner of the ash pit was a 7 cm × 9 cm section of decayed, partially carbonized wood.

[8] This vertical-walled pit was circular in plan, with a mouth diameter of 28 cm and a depth of 26 cm. Neither adobe- nor stone-lined, it contained two distinct layers of fill. The upper layer of loamy clay contained the toe bones of a large bird, chunks of red pigment, and the lower section of an adult camelid mandible. The lower stratum of the pit consisted almost entirely of ash and pulverized camelid bone.

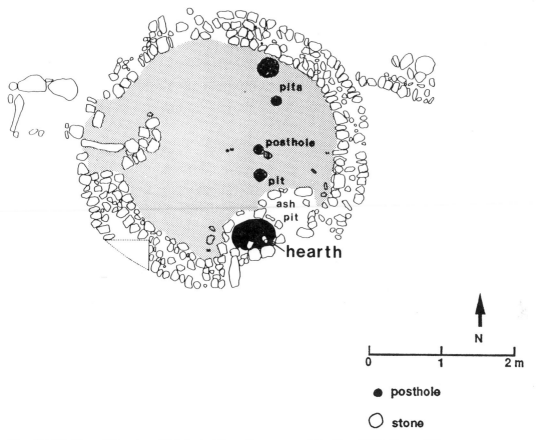

Fig. 12.25 Plan of Structure 42 (adapted from Bermann and Graffam 1989: Figure 33).

The original clay floor also displayed a number of circular depressions 12–15 cm in diameter and 2–5 cm deep. These shallow basins may have been produced by the weight of large storage vessels or grinding stones (batanes) of the type seen outside Structure 34.

STRUCTURE 42 DOMESTIC ARTIFACTS

The artifacts associated with Structure 42 included fragments of plainware cooking vessels and decorated Tiwanaku-style vessels (keros and open-mouth bowls); fragments of camelid and fish bone; fragments of bone needles and wichuñas; a spindle whorl; a stone "pot lid"; cones; broken grinding stones (Figure 12.32); a bead; and debris from stone tool making (debitage and cores, both obsidian and chert). Several intact camelid mandible tools and the debris associated with their making (bone splinters and broken-off lower mandible sections) were also recovered.

Despite the marked differences in architectural style, the range of features and contents of Structure 42 are similar to the residential structures of the ridgetop, suggesting that the Structure 42 occupants performed many of the same household activities.

These included cooking and eating, weaving, basketry or hide working, grinding activities, production of small flake tools, and manufacture (and use?) of the camelid mandible tools.

The complex jumble of enclosures and associated artifacts that characterize most of the terrace surface have no equivalent in the ridgetop occupation. This indicates that while households in each part of the site may have performed a similar set of basic household activities, they varied in other tasks. Further differences in household life are indicated by the small size of Structure 42 (less than 8 m^2) in comparison with the ridge houses. Finally, the Structure 42 household life does not seem to have been focused around a patio. Together, all this suggests that household life was organized very differently than on the terraces, that this was a different form of "household system."

Because of the high proportion of associated decorated pottery, many archaeologists would be quick to identify Structure 42 as an "elite" residence. However, we would expect "elite" residences to be larger than nonelite dwellings and to show greater investment in architectural elaboration or construction materials.

Social organization in prehistoric state societies is too complex to be captured in such simple, social status dichotomies as elite versus nonelite. Characteristically, states exhibit a huge range of social statuses and roles, and these are not likely to be completely reflected in decorated pottery preferences. In this case, the humble, rather prosaic household system juxtaposed with the storage complex and its contents suggest something other than simly an "elite" residence. Perhaps Structure 42 represents the dwelling of a noble's retainer.

DOMESTIC CERAMIC ASSEMBLAGES IN THE LATE TIWANAKU IV PERIOD

Households of the Structure 33–39 occupation used a range of undecorated pots for both cooking and storage, and a small number of Tiwanaku-style decorated vessels (Figures 12.26–12.32) and nonlocal, non-Tiwanaku bowls for serving.

By the time of the Structure 33–39 occupation, the Local Tradition that had characterized utilitarian household pottery at Lukurmata for centuries had vanished. As discussed in the previous chapter, Local Tradition pottery had declined markedly in frequency by the Structure 25–28 occupation, although Lorokea vessels, such as the annular-base bowls, continued to be used by households of the middle Tiwanaku IV period. No Lorokea pottery was found with the Structure 33–39 occupation.

The Structure 33–39 domestic pottery assemblage also revealed a decrease in the quantity and range of Tiwanaku decorated pottery appearing in ridgetop household units. Fragments from Tiwanaku decorated pottery averaged 23 percent of the domestic ceramic assemblage in the Structure 25–28 occupation, but by the Structure 33–39 occupation they averaged only 8 percent of the domestic assemblage. The drop in the variety of Tiwanaku decorated pottery in ridge households was less dramatic, but can be observed by comparing the forms of red-slipped vessels in each occupation. At least twelve distinct forms were represented in the Structure 25–28 occupation. In contrast, only seven forms are represented in the Structure 33–39 occupation.

Accompanying this change was a shift in the relative proportions of different vessel types. In the Structure 25–28 occupation, 87 percent of the red-slipped fragments were

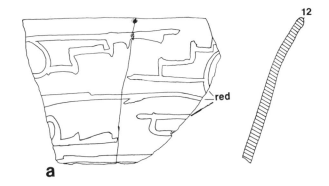

a

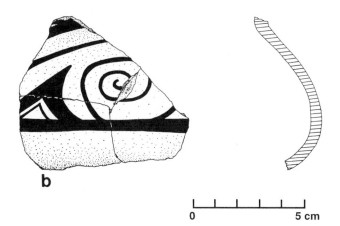

b

Fig. 12.26 Pottery fragments from the floor of Structure 38: (a) non-Tiwanaku-style red-on-gray bowl fragment, possibly an import from the Potosí region; (b) round-base open bowl fragment with "volute" motif.

Fig. 12.27 Round-base open bowl with "volute" motif found on an outdoor surface to the south of Structure 34.

0   5 cm

0   5 cm

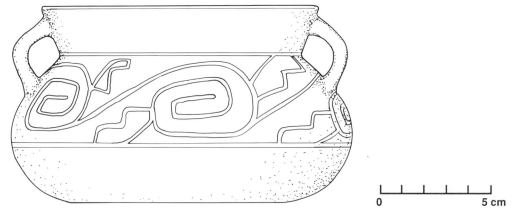

Fig. 12.28 Round-base open bowl found on the floor of Structure 37.

Fig. 12.29 Everted bowl from the floor of Structure 35 with decoration on interior of rim.

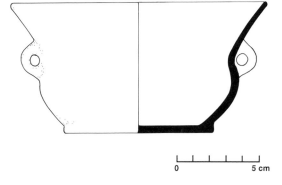

Fig. 12.30 Common utilitarian pottery shapes used by Tiwanaku IV, V, and post-Tiwanaku period Lukurmata households.

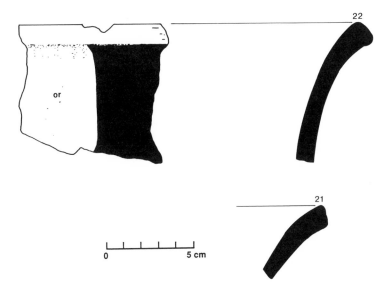

Fig. 12.31 Rim and neck of Pantini Orangeware storage vessels.

Fig. 12.32 Ground stone items from the Structure 33–39 occupation: (a) bowl fragment, (b) mortar, (c) grinding stone or *bolas* stone.

from the keros, flaring-sided bowls, or open-mouth bowls. In the Structure 33–39 occupation, 98.5 percent of the red-slipped sherds were from these three vessel types.

These shifts indicate that over time, the households on the ridge used a smaller range of Tiwanaku pottery, and acquired more of the three most common Tiwanaku forms (keros, flaring-sided bowls, and open-mouth bowls) and less of the more exotic shapes.

Intrasite Differences in Ceramic Assemblages

The terrace area and the ridge occupations displayed different quantities and varieties of Tiwanaku red-slipped pottery. Averaging the percentage of red-slipped fragments in excavation lots immediately above and below the Structure 33–39 and Structure 42 occupations gives us a figure for the ridge occupation of 8 percent red-slipped sherds; for the terrace, 20 percent red-slipped.[9]

There were also differences in the variety of Tiwanaku vessels found in each area, with a greater range of Tiwanaku IV forms represented in the terrace area. In addition to the twelve forms seen in the Structure 25–28 occupation, the terrace area contained three additional forms. Like the ridge occupation, keros, flaring-sided bowls, and open-mouth bowls were the most common forms in the terrace occupation, but the more exotic forms made up a larger proportion of the overall Tiwanaku-style assemblage.

In general, the terrace deposits contained greater quantities and varieties of imported

[9] This does not, of course, necessarily indicate that households on the ridge had greater access to Tiwanaku pottery. Many other explanations for the difference in representation are possible, including simple differences in discard patterns.

prestige-goods, including Tiwanaku decorated pottery. The terrace inhabitants of the later Tiwanaku IV period may have been intermediaries in the flow of pottery from Tiwanaku to the ridge households. Alternatively, the emergence of different social statuses at Lukurmata may have been marked by differences in social role marked by pottery preferences and use, with the relatively lower-status households on the ridge restricted to common forms, largely decorated with geometric designs.

Non-Tiwanaku Imports

Households at Lukurmata had always used a small amount of decorated, imported pottery that was not Tiwanaku in style (Figures 12.33–12.35). The Structure 33–39 households were no exceptions. Among the non-Tiwanaku-style pottery fragments

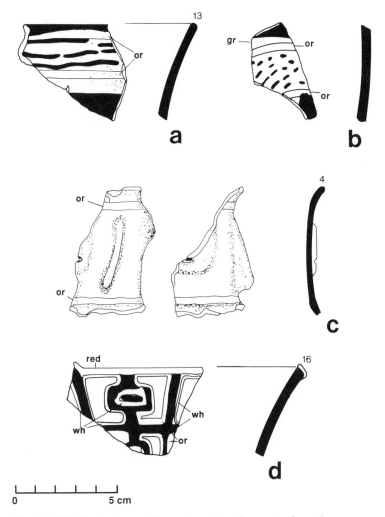

Fig. 12.33 Nonlocal, non-Tiwanaku pottery fragments from the Structure 33–39 occupation: (a, b, c) Juruquilla-style ceramics from Western Potosí?, (d) Mojocoya-style pottery from Cochabamba or Chuquisaca.

Fig. 12.34 Fragments of Mizque-style pottery from Cochabamba.

Fig. 12.35 Imported pottery used by Structure 33–39 occupations at Lukurmata. Ibarra-Grasso and Lewis (1986:226–31) refer to pottery of this style as "Nazcoide," but it is probably from southern Cochabamba or northern Chuquisaca.

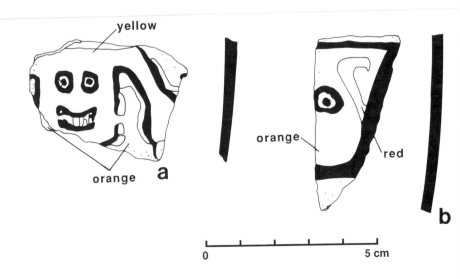

found with the Structure 33–39 occupation were small quantities of Mizque-, Yam-para-, and Mojocoya-style ceramics (Branisa 1957; Ibarra Grasso and Lewis 1986; Rydén 1956).[10] Each of these styles represents a poorly defined archaeological culture or ceramic tradition of the southern Cochabamba–northern Chuquisaca region. The Juruquilla-style pottery found with Structure 38 represents a highland western Potosí ceramic tradition. These non-Tiwanaku ceramics indicate contact (probably indirect) between Lukurmata residents and populations in the eastern lowlands and to the south of Tiwanaku.

There is no evidence that any of these imported vessels were used for cooking. The fragments of the imported vessels primarily represent open bowl or goblet forms, and none displays evidence of fire blackening or burning. As documented in earlier chapters, non-Tiwanaku imported bowls appear to have been used exclusively as serving vessels by pre-Tiwanaku and Tiwanaku III period residents of Lukurmata. The imported pottery of the Tiwanaku IV period was probably used in a similar manner.

In discussing the Tiwanaku-style pottery found in domestic contexts at the site of Omo, Peru, Goldstein (1989:66) argues that at Omo, "household serving functions were entirely fulfilled by Tiwanaku fineware ceramics." He (ibid.:141) further suggests that the use of these material symbols was an important means through which the Omo inhabitants "created" and maintained their Tiwanaku cultural identity. If pottery had this function in Tiwanaku society, the continued use of non-Tiwanaku serving vessels at Lukurmata could indicate that the local residents maintained some degree of local identity or tradition, distinguishing themselves from Tiwanaku.

SUMMARY

During the late Tiwanaku IV period, the ridge was primarily a residential area, with closely packed structures arranged to form patio groups (Figure 12.36). The ridge was also used for a limited number of burials and ceremonial offerings. Not all of the ridge was used for settlement. Excavation suggests that the terrace on the northern face of the ridge was used for ritual activities.

Some of the structures located around the patios were dwellings, and were used for a broad range of domestic activities. However, each patio group also included a structure used for an unknown, nonresidential purpose, probably storage.

This spatial grouping of houses, and their uniform cardinal orientation, are evidence of an increasingly formal division of space in the Lukurmata residential areas. The patio groups may represent a set of structures used by a single household, as the Aymara residents at Lukurmata do today. However, the presence of hearths in two structures of Patio B groups suggests that the patio group housed an extended family.

Changes in Lukurmata Domestic Organization

Most activities were conducted outdoors in the patio area, with the occupants of each patio group cooperating in or sharing certain tasks, but apparently not sharing others. The range and style of artifacts used in household activities exhibited a great

---

[10] The materials that Ibarra Grasso and Lewis (1986) classify as "Nazcoide" are now generally called "Mizque."

Fig. 12.36 Artist's reconstruction of the Structure 33–39 occupation showing patio groups, outdoor hearths, and above-ground tomb (Burial 11).

deal of continuity with earlier occupations, and many productive tasks seen in previous occupations (spinning, weaving, basketry or hide working, grinding activities, manufacture and repair of stone tools) continued as universal household activities.

However, the Structure 33–39 household activities also display significant shifts from the Structure 25–28 pattern. Some of these shifts involved changes in the range of activities: the adoption of ritual activities involving the burial of modeled puma vessels; placing tombs near or below residences; and introduction of a new activity involving manufacture/use of camelid mandible tools. Other shifts involved changes in the organization or scale of activities: a sizable increase in storage capacity at the individual household level; and reorganization of activities inherent in the formation of patio groupings.

The Structure 33–39 occupation represents the most extreme change in household life at Lukurmata if we measure such change in terms of simultaneous shifts in many dimensions of the household unit. Taken together, these shifts indicate a transformation of the household "system," or of the underlying principles of household organization.

Because there were no concurrent changes at the site or regional level, it is difficult to relate this household change to larger processes. However, several of the changes—the increased storage (and perhaps production) and the new mandible tool industry—may be signs of Tiwanaku's intrahousehold surplus production strategies, as I suggested in Chapter 2. The Structure 33–39 occupation represents the culmination of a trend of increasing storage at the household level. Increased household storage (as seen in the Structure 14–18 occupation) appeared at the time when Lukurmata was incorporated into the Tiwanaku polity, perhaps in response to the demands of the overarching Tiwanaku political economy. If so, the late Tiwanaku period occupations would suggest increasing surplus production demands on Lukurmata households, peaking with the Structure 33–39 occupation.

Changes in Interaction with the Tiwanaku System?

The pottery assemblage of the Structure 33–39 occupation provides evidence of a change in the relationship between Lukurmata households and the overarching Tiwanaku system. The decline in the amount and variety of Tiwanaku IV-style pottery in the ridge households indicates that the residents were no longer acquiring the full range of Tiwanaku items. Vessels with elaborate Tiwanaku iconography appear in the ridge household units, so the residents apparently were not rejecting Tiwanaku ideology. Nor does the decline mean that the residents were precluded "access" to the full range of pottery, except perhaps in the economic sense. The highly decorated Tiwanaku pottery may have been a measure of "wealth" rather than social identity, and simply too expensive for ridge residents (Smith 1987).

Implications for Investigating Household Change

The changes displayed by the Structure 33–39 occupation illustrate the utility of the "local perspective" in interpreting past social change. In this case, significant change at the household level was not associated with major changes at the site or regional level. As far as we know, Lukurmata had become a secondary center in the Tiwanaku state settlement hierarchy long before the Structure 33–39 occupation. This might suggest that local-level (rather than regional-level) pressures or stimuli led to a transformation in household life. I have argued elsewhere, for instance, that the Structure 33–39 occupation changes can be interpreted as an increase in the "complexity" of the household unit—a typical feature of archaic urbanization (Bermann n.d.).

The Structure 33–39 occupation represents a dramatic change in the organization of the Lukurmata household. Change of this magnitude, perhaps to extended family groupings, would be viewed by many social historians or anthropologists as representative of a fundamental adaptive shift to new ecological or economic circumstances (Wilk 1990), or even a change in "ethnic" identity (Stanish 1989a). That this household-level shift was not matched by changes at other levels (and vice-versa in the Structure 25–28 occupation) suggests that at least some changes for Lukurmata households were not causally linked to the Tiwanaku system.

Several dimensions of the household (number of structures, storage capacity, interaction with Tiwanaku) seem to have changed gradually throughout the Tiwanaku period at Lukurmata. Other changes, however, such as the shift in spatial grouping to a patio pattern, may have been more abrupt. If so, it may indicate that the social organization of production, household membership and residential patterns were the most stable elements of domestic organization, or the most resistant to change. However, the appearance of a late Tiwanaku IV period shift to a patio pattern may be an artifact of investigation; we may not have excavated large enough areas of earlier occupations (such as the Structure 7 or Structure 9–10 occupations) to be able to recognize patio groupings.

13

Lukurmata's Decline during the Tiwanaku V Period

The population of Lukurmata appears to have declined sharply during the Tiwanaku V period (A.D. 800–A.D. 1200). No housefloors dating to this period were found at Lukurmata, but the presence of surface artifacts and features from the Tiwanaku V period show that a residential population remained at the site. It is difficult to measure the extent of the population drop at Lukurmata, and the focus of domestic occupation may have shifted from the ridge to other areas of the site. The public architecture at the site may have been abandoned as well. Midden accumulated on the central burial platform, and there is some evidence that the temple fell into disuse.

The Structure 33–39 floors represent the last clear evidence of domestic occupation on the ridge for centuries. After these buildings were abandoned, people may have continued to live on the ridge, but the density of occupation was much lower than it had been.

Features dating to the Tiwanaku V period at Lukurmata include burials and refuse pits. Burials and several small refuse pits were found in the main excavation on the ridge. A larger pit, described below, was found in an excavation to the south of the temple hilltop. Carbon collected from Level 18 of this feature provided a calibrated and corrected date of A.D. 1045 ± 100.

A TIWANAKU V PERIOD REFUSE PIT

A 14 m² excavation in the swale south of the temple hill (Bennett's Section K, see Figure 11.9) exposed a 2.5 m depositional sequence with post-Tiwanaku and Tiwanaku V-style materials and features including a large refuse pit and two outdoor activity surfaces. No house remains were exposed in this excavation, but the extensive domestic debris suggests that houses had been located nearby. The contents of the pit suggest strong continuities with the Tiwanaku IV period occupations in domestic activities and materials.

The refuse pit was 1.9 m in diameter and 85 cm deep, with a stratified fill ranging from ashy midden to aeolian material. Artifacts from the pit suggest that it was a receptacle for household debris including material cleaned from hearths. Items from the pit included fragments of animal bone and pottery, stone cones, projectile points, gray obsidian flakes and debitage, bone needles and wichuñas, and ground stone items (hammerstones, balls).

The pottery assemblage from the pit strata was not markedly different from that of the Structure 33–39 occupation: pieces of Pantini Orangeware jars (with raised punctate necklaces), various smaller jar forms, and open-mouth ollas common in the Structure 33–39 occupation (Figures 13.1 and 13.2). Tiwanaku-style pottery was less common than in the Structure 33–39 ridge occupation, and most fragments were from vessels decorated in the Tiwanaku V-style. Fragments of nonlocal, non-Tiwanaku-style vessels were also recovered from the pit (Figure 13.3).

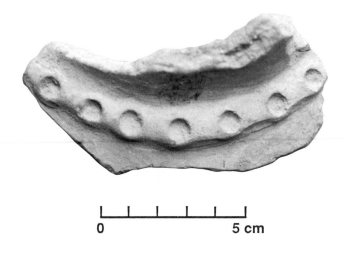

Fig. 13.1 Fragment of Pantini Orangeware jar showing typical raised punctate necklace decoration.

0   5 cm

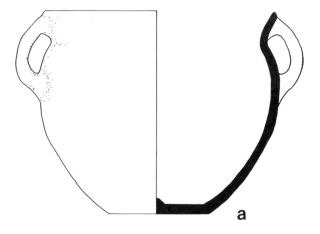

a

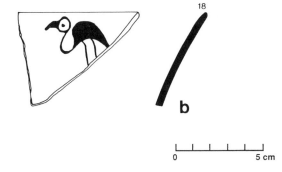

18

b

0   5 cm

Fig. 13.2 Tiwanaku V-style domestic pottery: (a) undecorated olla, (b) interior decoration of flaring-sided bowl.

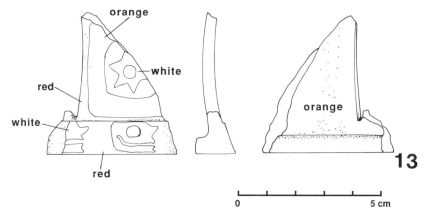

Fig. 13.3 Fragment of non-Tiwanaku-style pottery from the Tiwanaku V period refuse pit in Section K.

MORTUARY ACTIVITIES

Two clusters of tombs tentatively dating to the Tiwanaku V period were identified in the central excavation on the ridge, suggesting that during the Tiwanaku V period individuals were buried in small, discrete cemeteries (see Figure 14.2).[1]

Each of the nine tombs consisted of a 0.5–1.0 m deep, bell-shaped pit, often with a collar of fieldstones ringing the tomb mouth. Several of the tombs were partially stone-lined. The cap of the tomb had probably been just below the original ground surface. Similar Tiwanaku V period tombs have been excavated at Wakuyo (Perrin 1957).

Tombs were capped with from two to five large stone slabs, with smaller stones used as chinking. Roughly half of the tombs were capped with dressed andesite blocks. The presence of the dressed andesite blocks is of particular interest. Andesite is not a local material, and it is hard to imagine that it would be brought into Lukurmata simply to aid in capping tombs. Much more likely is that a nearby source of the blocks was at hand.

The public architecture at Lukurmata, partially constructed of such blocks, would have provided this source. To the west of the Lukurmata temple was a structure modeled on the Kalasasaya at Tiwanaku, and probably built in the same "pillar and sillar" construction style in which the space between large, upright pillars is filled with smaller, dressed blocks. The "pillars" of the Lukurmata structure remain in situ, but the smaller blocks are not with them. The removal of blocks by Tiwanaku V period inhabitants strongly implies that the temple was no longer in use. A striking parallel has been documented at another Tiwanaku temple site, that of Omo in the Moquegua Valley, Peru (Goldstein 1993:43). The cut stones of the Omo temple were eventually robbed

---

[1] The lack of diagnostic grave-goods made it difficult to distinguish Tiwanaku V burials from post-Tiwanaku burials at Lukurmata. Three of the nine tombs contained Tiwanaku V-style pottery. The other six were assigned to the Tiwanaku V period on the basis of stratigraphic evidence. An additional seven tombs may date to Tiwanaku V, but were not considered as such because they lacked temporally diagnostic grave-goods and the stratigraphic evidence for their date was ambiguous. These seven tombs have been counted as post-Tiwanaku period tombs.

for use in Chen Chen phase tombs by a local population that continued to maintain Tiwanaku ceramic styles and mortuary patterns. Unfortunately, the tombs with blocks at Lukurmata are not those that contained Tiwanaku V-style vessels as grave-goods, so we cannot be completely certain that stones were robbed from the temple during the Tiwanaku V period.

Several of the tombs contained more than one individual, and tombs did not contain a uniform set of grave-goods. In the five cases in which orientation of the body could be determined, the individual had been buried in a seated and flexed position facing east. Rather than discussing each of the nine tombs in detail, I will briefly describe three of the better-preserved tombs.

Burial 21

This tomb in the eastern cluster was a slightly bell-shaped pit (48 cm × 51 cm in diameter and 51 cm deep) that contained the remains of three adults. The tomb was not stone-lined and did not display a stone collar or capstones, although these may have been lost to modern plowing. Each individual had been buried in a seated and flexed position facing east. All exhibited similar artificial cranial deformation. One of the individuals was clearly older than the other two, and at least one individual was male. The cranium of the older individual displayed a partially healed trepanation in the left frontal bone. Poor preservation prevented us from determining if each skeleton had been complete at the time of burial, and the two younger individuals may have represented secondary burials. No grave-goods were found.

Burial 23

This was a simple bell-shaped pit without a stone collar or lining. This tomb was lower in the fill than the two described above, and may have been slightly older. The pit had a mouth diameter of 48 cm, a maximum width of 80 cm, and a depth of 94 cm. The tomb contained the remains of a child (8–12 years old) who had been placed in a seated and flexed position facing northeast. The cranium exhibited the same style of artificial deformation as the individuals of Burial 21.

Grave-goods included two ground stone objects, bone tools, and pottery. One of the stone items was a cube of worked stone (12 cm along a side) with a shallow, 1 cm wide groove along one side and two 3 cm deep conical depressions in another. The function of this object is unknown, but it resembles the arrow shaft-straighteners of prehistoric North America. The other stone artifact was a large (31 cm × 18 cm × 2 cm) disk-shaped slab of stone with a 6 cm diameter hole near one end.

Directly on the floor of the tomb, below the skeleton, was a kit of five bone weaving tools (wichuñas) of progressive sizes ranging from 8 cm to 19 cm in length (Figure 13.4). Other grave-goods included three pots, one relatively intact. West of the body were the fragments of a Tiwanaku V-style kero lying on its side. An intact, straight-sided Tiwanaku V-style cup was upright next to it. The inside of this vessel was coated with several layers of a white, plaster-like substance. The remains of a second Tiwanaku V-style kero were southwest of the skeleton. All three vessels can be assigned on a stylistic basis to the late Tiwanaku V period.

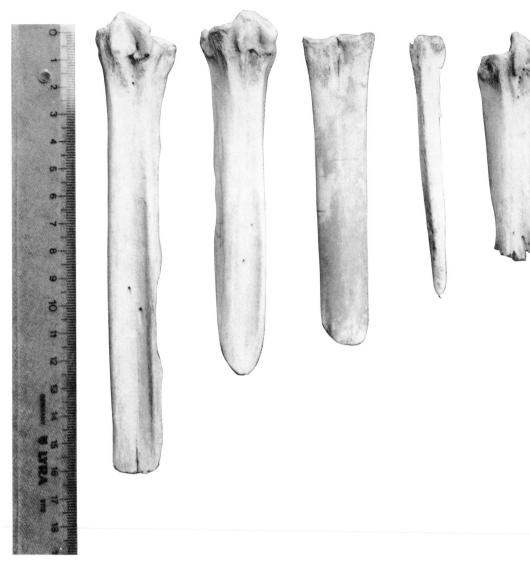

Fig. 13.4 Burial 23 grave-good: a set of wichuñas or weaving tools.

Burial 27

This tomb consisted of a stone-capped, bell-shaped pit, with a partially preserved fieldstone collar. One of the stones making up the collar was a dressed block of andesite. The tomb had a mouth diameter of 42 cm, a maximum width of 65 cm, and a depth of 44 cm. The tomb was partially filled with 10 cm of water-deposited soil. Lying on top of this fill were two intact Tiwanaku V-style vessels: a flaring-sided bowl and a squat, polychrome kero decorated with pumas. This vessel is early Tiwanaku V period in style. Preservation of the human remains was extremely poor. The burial was represented only by scattered bone fragments, including fragments of adult molars.

LUKURMATA IN REGIONAL PERSPECTIVE

Although Lukurmata was in decline by the Tiwanaku V period, this was the period when the Tiwanaku state reached its greatest extent and emerged as a true empire. Tiwanaku V-style materials are spread from the Pacific coast to the Cochabamba lowlands on the eastern slope of the Andes. We do not how the apparent drop in population at Lukurmata relates to changes in the size or distribution of the population in the Pampa Koani region as a whole. The limited investigation that has been done at sites in the Pampa Koani suggests that occupation continued at the smaller mounds during the Tiwanaku V period, and the Pampa Koani remained Tiwanaku's "breadbasket" (Graffam, personal communication; Kolata 1986).

A possible explanation for the partial abandonment of Lukurmata during the Tiwanaku V period is the growth of the site of Tiwanaku. The capital itself may have taken over direct administration of the Pampa Koani, since the Pampa Koani is easily within a day's roundtrip travel from the capital.

Studies of the evolution of regional settlement hierarchies in several other areas of state formation suggest that as the state capital grows, second- or third-order centers close to the capital may decline. This pattern has been observed in the evolving settlement around Teotihuacán in the Valley of Mexico (Parsons 1974), the abandonment of the lower-order sites surrounding Uruk in the Late Uruk period (Adams and Nissen 1972:87–88), and the decline of centers in the Central area around Monte Albán during the II Period (Kowalewski 1983:148). The changes in the settlement around Monte Albán described by Stephen Kowalewski (1983:110) may also have characterized settlement shifts around Tiwanaku at start of the Tiwanaku V period .

Browman (1981) has argued that the Tiwanaku state was substantially reorganized at a regional level in the ninth or tenth century. Increasing centralization of administration at Tiwanaku may have been part of this process. The results of the recent regional survey of the Tiwanaku Valley also seem to confirm an extensive reorganization of settlement, agricultural production, and settlement hierarchy at the start of the Tiwanaku V period (Albarracin-Jordan and Mathews 1990).

If Lukurmata's administrative role in the Tiwanaku system that had led the settlement to grow from a small village to a large center during the Tiwanaku III and IV periods, the loss of this role during the Tiwanaku V period may have caused the process to reverse itself, leading Lukurmata to revert to the kind of community it had been in pre-Tiwanaku times. The excess population, representing a temple staff, elites and their retainers, or those overseeing Pampa Koani production, moved back to the capital or to other sites. Residents of the Pampa Koani may have continued to visit the temple at the now largely abandoned Lukurmata, perhaps for offerings and human burials.

SUMMARY

During the Tiwanaku V period, the size of the Lukurmata residential population appears to have declined sharply, the ridge may have been abandoned, and the public architecture may have fallen into disuse. The size and areal extent of the Tiwanaku V period occupation at Lukurmata could not be determined, but information from the systematic surface collection suggests that the focus of settlement shifted from the old core of the site (on the ridge) to the swale south of the temple and to the northern side of the temple hill during the Tiwanaku V period.

14

The Post-Tiwanaku Period at Lukurmata

The earliest post-Tiwanaku period occupation found in the ridgetop excavation was represented by the partially preserved remains of a single house, Structure 43, and associated outdoor features at 40–45 cm below datum, a short distance below the modern plow zone. A large number of post-Tiwanaku period tombs were also excavated. Mollo-style pottery (a post-Tiwanaku period "culture" centered to the east of Lake Titicaca) associated with the structure and several of the tombs helped to fix the date of this occupation between A.D. 1200 and A.D. 1300.

SITE COMPOSITION

There was little settlement on the ridgetop during the post-Tiwanaku period, and Lukurmata was probably once again a hamlet or small village. Although we excavated in excess of 350 m² on the ridge, only one structure dating to the immediate post-Tiwanaku period was found (Figure 14.1). This ridgetop occupation is older than a small group of post-Tiwanaku period structures excavated to the north of the temple hilltop (Wise 1989).

DOMESTIC ARCHITECTURE

Roughly two-thirds of Structure 43 was excavated; the rest had not preserved. Defining the floor was difficult, particularly near the center of the structure. Structure 43 had been rectangular in plan, measuring 4.2 m on one side and 4.6 m on another. The floor consisted of the familiar 2–4 cm thick layer of prepared clay mixed with sand. Short alignments of fieldstones represented the base of mud brick or cut sod walls. Unlike most earlier structures, the floor of Structure 43 had been poured after the construction of the walls. Postholes were found in two of the corners of the floor. A 1.2 m long extension of floor material from the northeast side of the structure probably represented a short entrance.

DOMESTIC ACTIVITIES

Three large features were found in the floor: a hearth (an unlined basin scraped into the floor) and two refuse pits. Most of the floor artifacts were found in the western half of the structure, clustered around the hearth and ash pit. Just to the west of the hearth was a concentration of fish bone (*Orestias* sp.). Bone fragments from camelid and bird were also found on the floor, as was a section of bone, probably a section of camelid metatarsal, with longitudinal cut marks. Other floor artifacts included a groundstone

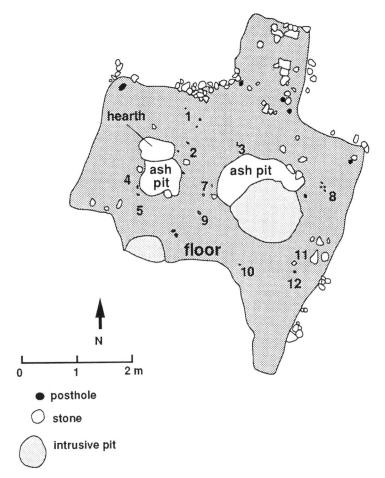

Fig. 14.1 Plan of Structure 43 floor with selected artifacts plotted. *Key*: (1) obsidian flake, (2) burned cone in clay, (3) bihemispherical ground stone, (4) wichuña fragment, (5) worked bone, (6) bone needle, (7) quartz crystal, (8) worked llama rib fragments, (9) stone scraper, (10) cone, (11) bowl fragments, (12) cone.

"double-cone," a stone scraper, obsidian flakes and debitage, and fragments of plainware and decorated pottery. The floor also yielded three stone cones, one partially encased in burned clay.

Two small sections of an associated outdoor activity area were exposed. Each consisted of roughly 4 m² of stained and hard-packed sandy surface. Fragments of utilitarian pottery, including a large part of a fire-blackened open-mouth bowl or olla, camelid and fish bone, a chert knife that may have once been hafted, a spindle whorl, obsidian debitage, and a small ground stone ball of unknown use were found in the area to the northwest.

Two small hearths were found in a second patch of outdoor surface to the east. Associated with these were plainware and decorated pottery fragments; bone fragments of camelid, fish, and bird; a broken grinding stone or mano; and the base of a broken obsidian projectile point. The fragments of two storage vessels or water jars were found near the house wall.

Like previous domestic pottery assemblages, the sherds associated with the Structure 43 occupation represent a range of both plainware and decorated forms. The Structure 43 assemblage contained proportionally less decorated pottery and a smaller range of vessel shapes than Tiwanaku period assemblages.

POST-TIWANAKU PERIOD OFFERINGS

A post-Tiwanaku period ritual/mortuary activity was the burial of large jars. We found four jars in the ridge excavation, and a fifth in the platform in the central section of the site. None of these jars was deeply buried; in fact, one of the ridgetop specimens had been shattered by modern plowing.

Four of the features consisted of a single intact, globular jar, resembling both the Tiwanaku period Pantini Orangeware vessels and Mollo "aryballus-like" fermentation or water jars (Rydén 1957). Each of the buried vessels displayed two strap-handles at midbody, a short, cylindrical neck, and a raised, punctate necklace.

Each vessel also contained the fragments of a complete, decorated bowl broken to fit through the jar neck, and four to seven chipped stone bifaces of red or white quartz. The broken bowls are post-Tiwanaku period in style, with black painted decoration taking the form of interior pendant loops or wavy horizontal lines. Identical bowls were also found as grave-goods in several of the post-Tiwanaku period tombs. Only one of the jars—the one damaged by modern plowing—contained human skeletal remains. Found in this vessel were the bones of a infant less than a year old, a black obsidian biface, and the fragments of a decorated bowl. This form of burial is similar to post-Tiwanaku period features at the Cochabamba site of Colcapirhua (Bennett 1936:371).

Similar offerings of large jars have been found at archaeological sites east of Lake Titicaca. Rydén (1959) found fourteen buried jar offerings at Cayhuasi, a Tiwanaku V period and post-Tiwanaku period site approximately 240 km southeast of Lukurmata in the Department of Oruro. The Cayhuasi "libation spot" consisted of a cluster of intact, two-handled aryballoid vessels, several found standing upright. Most of these had been "capped" with post-Tiwanaku style bowls, and contained the fragments of a second, complete bowl. In the base of several of the larger vessels Rydén (ibid.:101) found a thin residue, possibly from maize beer. Citing the early chronicler Poma de Ayala, Rydén (ibid.) suggests that the area was used for postmortem offerings.

MORTUARY ACTIVITIES

Sixty-five of the tombs found in the main excavation on the ridge were tentatively dated to the post-Tiwanaku period (Figure 14.2). While the Tiwanaku V period tombs seem to have been grouped in two clusters, the post-Tiwanaku period tombs were scattered across the main excavation on the ridge. Some post-Tiwanaku period burials were placed in a simple, unmodified pit, but most were placed in a tomb with some stone architecture. Two distinct types of post-Tiwanaku period cist tombs could be distinguished: circular tombs and slab tombs. Circular tombs had stone collars, were

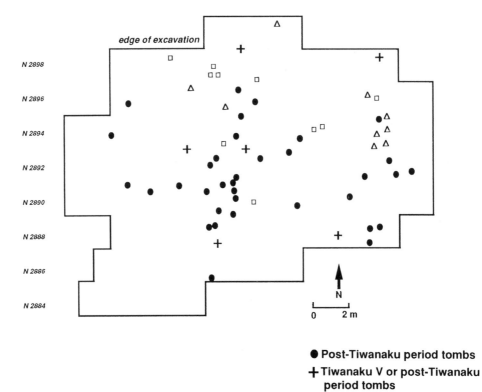

Fig. 14.2 Distribution of Tiwanaku IV, V, and post-Tiwanaku period tombs in the main ridge excavation.

occasionally partially stone-lined, and usually had large capstones. The circular tombs had slightly bell-shaped pits and were 0.75–1 m deep. Slab tombs were quadrangular or polygonal in shape, lined with stone slabs set on edge, and not as deep as circular tombs. Slab tombs were also capped with large, flat stones.

Tombs of each type usually contained the remains of a single individual, but several burials of multiple individuals were found. The dead were generally placed in a seated and flexed position, facing east or northeast. The position of the skeletal remains suggests that the individuals were wrapped and tied when placed into the tomb. The ridge-top burials exhibited no bias for adults; infant and child burials were common. Over half of the more architecturally elaborate tombs (those with stone architecture) contained adults (66%). In contrast, adults were found in only 44 percent of the simple pits lacking stone architecture. However, this difference is not statistically significant (Chi-Square = 3.463, df = 1, p. = .0627). Neonates and infants were generally buried in shallow holes covered with a large rock. One of the seven neonate/infant burials dating to the post-Tiwanaku period was in a tomb of the circular or slab variety. Nearly all of the preserved crania, child and adult, displayed one of two styles of artificial cranial deformation. One style of deformation is that pictured in Figure 5.8. The other style of deformation is shown in Figure 14.3. However, there does not appear to be any relationship between cranial deformation style and tomb style. The post-Tiwanaku period tombs did not exhibit a great deal of consistency in the quantity or range of grave-goods; most of the tombs lacked grave-goods of any kind.

Circular Cist Tombs

Thirty-four (52%) of the post-Tiwanaku period burials were in circular cist tombs. Of the nine tombs with grave-goods (26%), eight contained post-Tiwanaku period pottery. The individual had been buried facing east in 88 percent of the cases in which body orientation could be determined. Poor preservation prevented determination of the age of the individual in some cases, but adults made up 66 percent of the burials for which the individual's age could be determined.

Slab Tombs

Nine slab-lined tombs were found in the main excavation. Six contained adults. Body orientation could be determined in six cases, and showed four individuals facing east, two facing west. Grave-goods were found in four of the tombs.

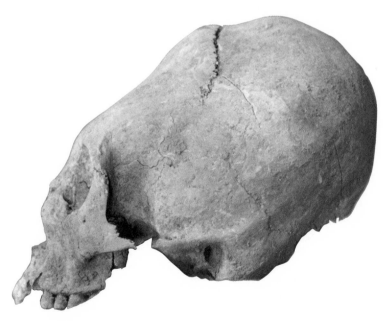

Fig. 14.3 Post-Tiwanaku period artificial cranial deformation: N3039 E3116 Feature 1.

Other Burials

Only three of the twenty-two burials without tomb architecture were accompanied by grave-goods. These burials were frequently disturbed, incomplete, or poorly preserved. In some cases, they were represented by only a handful of bone fragments, making statistical comparisons with the stone-tomb burials difficult.

An example of this type of burial was Burial 30, located near the eastern edge of the main excavation (Figure 14.4). This burial was found just below the plow zone, and modern plowing may explain the lack of tomb architecture. Nevertheless, the skeletal remains themselves were well preserved and remained articulated. They represented an adult male buried in a flexed position, lying on his right side with his head to the west. Unlike many of the post-Tiwanaku period burials, his skull had not been artificially deformed. To one side were two small pots, one containing fragments of eggshell and the remains of a guinea pig. A cache of eleven stone cones to the north of the skeleton may have also been associated with the burial.

Fig. 14.4 Burial 30 was accompanied by two vessels, stone cones and a guinea pig.

Burial Summary

Overall, there was no significant variation between slab and cist tombs in body orientation, selection for adults, or grave-goods. There was, however, an intriguing difference between the two types of tombs. A large grinding stone (batane) made up part of the lining or cap of seven of the nine slab tombs. In contrast, only five of the cist tombs displayed a batane (Chi-Square = 14.071, df = 1, p = .0002). Perhaps when an individual died, the family grinding stone was used in tomb construction.

It is not known if the two post-Tiwanaku period tomb styles at Lukurmata reflect chronological differences, social or ethnic preferences, or the circumstances of death. Tombs of both types are found elsewhere in the region. The Lukurmata slab tombs closely resemble those found at highland and non-altiplano "Mollo" sites such as Piñiko, Markopata, Kellikani, and Jutaraya. However, the Lukurmata tombs differ in type and quantity of grave-goods, and in use of batanes as construction materials (Ponce 1957a; Rydén 1957). The tombs found at the Mollo capital of Iskanwaya themselves are not of the slab type (Ponce 1980).

LUKURMATA IN REGIONAL PERSPECTIVE

By the thirteenth century A.D., Tiwanaku materials had disappeared from the southern Andes, although pottery forms and iconography derivative of the Tiwanaku styles continued to be used in many areas. Taking the place of this stylistic "horizon" was a host of different ceramic complexes, each of much more limited geographic distribution. The post-Tiwanaku period was characterized by the existence of many small, competing polities (often referred to as kingdoms or *señorios*). Some of the ceramic complexes are known to correspond to specific kingdoms.

Coinciding with the disappearance of Tiwanaku-style materials from the southern Andes was the depopulation of the capital site. Unlike other imperial capitals, which apparently went through a long period of slow decline, Tiwanaku seems to have been virtually abandoned in a short space of time, leaving only a small, thinly scattered residential population. Once the most powerful center in the southern Andes, Tiwanaku after A.D. 1200 was no longer a site of any political consequence. The post-collapse pottery found at Tiwanaku shows that there, as elsewhere in the Andean highlands, the elaborate Tiwanaku corporate art styles and iconography were quickly and completely abandoned. The most powerful and common elements of the Tiwanaku corporate art style—the Front Face Deity, the puma, the condor—would not appear again in the altiplano.

The causes underlying the collapse of the Tiwanaku polity remain poorly known. One factor in Tiwanaku's decline may have been the failure of Tiwanaku's massive systems of intensive agriculture, including the raised fields of the Pampa Koani. Recent analysis of paleoenvironmental markers from the Peruvian Quelccaya ice cap and Lake Titicaca sediments seem to indicate significantly lowered rainfall in the south-central Andes between A.D. 1000 and A.D. 1400 (Ortloff and Kolata 1993; Thompson et al. 1985, 1988). Ortloff and Kolata (1993:195) argue that such a climatic shift led to "chronic drought conditions," leading to the collapse of the agrarian systems on which the Tiwanaku polity depended.

Raised field systems, while better able to withstand periods of drought than other forms of agriculture, are also ultimately vulnerable to water shortages (Ortloff and Kolata 1993:211). The onset of a long drought, sharply curtailing agricultural production in the Pampa Koani's raised fields, may account for the movement of population out of Lukurmata following the Structure 33–39 occupation.

The collapse of the Tiwanaku political formation was accompanied by massive abandonment of the Pampa Koani and the extensive raised field systems (Kolata 1986). A much reduced and dispersed occupation continued, cultivating individual fields on a smaller scale (Graffam 1992). Many Pampa Koani residents appear to have moved to higher ground and begun to practice terrace agriculture. Kolata (1986:751) notes that "the apparent virtual abandonment of the Pampa Koani after Tiwanaku V times stands in sharp contrast with the substantial post-Tiwanaku period occupations and agricultural constructions along the adjoining mountain slopes north of the modern village of Ayagachi, and on the nearby peninsula of Cumana." Similar post-Tiwanaku period sites have recently been located closer to Lukurmata on the high areas overlooking the Pampa Koani near the community of Korila (Stanish, personal communication).

The archaeological evidence from the post-Tiwanaku period at Lukurmata suggests that the resident population was not closely tied to any major center. This is not very surprising; certainly there were no demographic concentrations comparable to Tiwanaku in Bolivia during the post-Tiwanaku period, nor were there political formations of the scale or complexity of the Tiwanaku polity. The post-Tiwanaku period polities of Bolivia were small, loosely integrated, kin-based señorios (Abercrombie 1986). Pottery stylistically associated with several different post-Tiwanaku period señorios (Mollo, Omasuyo, Lupaca, Pacajes) occur in the post-Tiwanaku period occupation at Lukurmata (Bermann 1990; Graffam 1988, 1992; Wise 1989). Some of this pottery is illustrated in Figures 14.5–14.7. Therefore, while we cannot rule out Lukurmata's inclusion in larger political units during the post-Tiwanaku period, none appears to have truly "controlled" Lukurmata or the Lukurmata area (see Graffam 1988 for an opposing view). Lukurmata, as it had been prior to the emergence of the Tiwanaku state, was probably for all intents and purposes relatively autonomous politically, a small community loosely tied to neighboring sites through exchange and kinship.

The Structure 43 occupation does not provide enough evidence to assess Lukurmata's participation in post-Tiwanaku interregional exchange systems. The type-site of Mollo-style pottery is the site of Iskanwaya (Figure 1.2). The relatively large quantities of Mollo-style pottery in Lukurmata tombs suggest that interaction with populations on the eastern slopes of the Andes continued to be important to Lukurmata residents. The styles of imported decorated pottery at Lukurmata suggest that residents interacted with populations to the south as well. Yet the only nonlocal material, other than pottery, found with the Structure 43 occupation was the obsidian and this is the same color as that found in earlier occupations (Hoya de Titicaca type).

Regional interaction for Lukurmata residents was probably far different during the post-Tiwanaku period than it had been during the Tiwanaku IV and V periods. Formerly, long-distance trade, and perhaps even local exchange, took place in the context of a larger political system, with most materials channeled through the imperial capital

Fig. 14.5 Post-Tiwanaku period bowl.

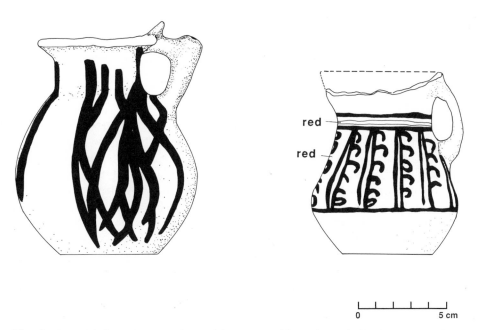

Fig. 14.6 (a) Mollo-style spouted vessel from a post-Tiwanaku period Lukurmata tomb,
(b) Omasuyo-style (?) vessel from a post-Tiwanaku period Lukurmata tomb.

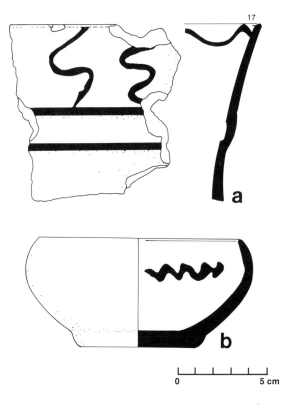

Fig. 14.7 (a) Mollo-style flaring-sided banded bowl from midden context, (b) bowl from a post-Tiwanaku period Lukurmata tomb.

and local elite households. In contrast, exchange during the post-Tiwanaku period was probably fairly direct, conducted between individual households.

SUMMARY

The Structure 43 occupation suggests that with the collapse of the Tiwanaku state, domestic organization returned to something very close to the pre-Tiwanaku pattern. Just as the community as a whole returned to being a small settlement of dispersed homesteads, so the household unit once again included a single, all-purpose structure. It is difficult to evaluate the lasting effects Tiwanaku may have had on Lukurmata households, but the activities introduced into the household during the Tiwanaku period—represented by the mandible tools, the zoomorphic incensarios and hallucinogenic complex, the special-purpose structures and the thick-walled bowls—disappeared with the dissolution of the Tiwanaku system.

The range of artifacts associated with Structure 43 were similar to those found with much earlier houses at Lukurmata, indicating that many of the same types of activities continued as domestic tasks. Food preparation and consumption, spinning, weaving, basketry or hide working, grinding activities, manufacture of flake cutting tools, and the unknown activity represented by the cones remained basic household tasks. This continuity extended to the actual style of many items, which were indistinguishable from specimens from the pre-Tiwanaku period occupations.

Clearly, however, the domestic occupation at Lukurmata did not continue in a "Tiwanaku-derived pattern" after Tiwanaku collapsed. A basic set of household activities continued, but household activities and domestic organization must have differed markedly in other ways. That Structure 43 was an isolated structure and not part of a patio group implies a different social context for household activities, perhaps with fewer shared activities. It also may indicate that the composition of the residential group changed, perhaps from an extended family to a conjugal family.

The shift from the patio group back to a single, all-purpose dwelling may be the household-level equivalent of the regional post-Tiwanaku period "balkanization": a shift to a lower integrative level between societal parts. If patio groups represented some form of suprahousehold organization, or some degree of cooperation between households, the Structure 43 occupation may represent a loss of this integration and a return to the "basic" nuclear household as the fundamental residential and productive unit.

15

Conclusion: Lukurmata Households and the Tiwanaku State

It remains for me to justify one last choice: that of introducing everyday life, no more, no less, into the domain of history. Was this useful? Or necessary? Everyday life consists of the little things one hardly notices in time and space. The more we reduce the focus of vision, the more likely we are to find ourselves in the environment of material life: the broad sweep usually corresponds to History with a capital letter, to distant trade routes, and the networks of national or urban economies. (. . .) The ways people eat, dress, or lodge (. . .) are never a matter of indifference. And these snapshots can point out contrasts and disparities between one society and another which are not all superficial.

(Braudel 1981:29)

The study of Andean prehistory has been shaped by a "capital-centric" perspective that treats smaller sites merely as ahistorical components of larger political formations, and larger formations themselves as highly stable, integrated, and unified systems. While capitals are interesting, we have to remember that each capital is unique and is rarely representative of the way the majority of the population was living. Similarly, while study of social macroprocesses is important, the Lukurmata sequence demonstrates that household life can display an "evolution" of its own, independent of state- or regional-level processes.

The questions of where and how these "evolutions" shape each other, or how levels of society articulate with each other, are important to understanding any society. Much of anthropology has been concerned with the "integration" and composition of social systems, the means by which the smaller units of society (such as families) are incorporated into larger units or formal organizations.

Despite this interest, there has been little study in Andean archaeology of the relationship between household and state. The effects of state formation, imperial expansion, and economic integration on the individual household are seldom seriously addressed.

The Need for Diachronic Approaches to Domestic Remains

Archaeologists have studied prehispanic residences in a variety of ways. Domestic remains have been analyzed to reconstruct formation processes, identify prehistoric domestic activities, or determine the ethnic identity or social status of the occupants. Comparison of prehistoric dwellings and their contents has been important in reconstructions of intra- and intersite differences in status, craft production, and access to resources.

As important as these approaches to domestic remains are, their inherently synchronic nature limits their usefulness when it comes to understanding the effects of larger sociopolitical processes at the individual household level. If we simply compare contemporaneous subordinate sites, we limit explanations of their differences to various forms of interaction with the capital. We ignore each site's previous function and history. Regional syntheses founded on synchronic comparisons view the capital as the only source of change, and explain all developments (and intersite variation) with reference to capital-dominated administrative or economic processes. This assumption, already prevalent in much of anthropology, implicitly poses the relationship between small sites and larger capitals as one between *statics* (village life, peasant society, traditional culture) and *dynamics* (capitalist system, expansive state; Abercrombie 1986:1).

Synchronic approaches need to be complemented with diachronic studies, studies of change through time. Comparing the sequence of changes in household organization to the sequence of changes in a site's overall role in the larger system provides a more direct view of how participation in larger systems affected the way people lived. Such an approach will provide information critical to reconstructing the varying ways in which constituent populations may have been incorporated into overarching political formations. The Lukurmata sequence suggests that not all changes at the household level were the result of shifts in interaction with a larger system. Nor were each of the macrolevel changes, usually the central concern of archaeologists, accompanied by shifts at the household level.

Continuity and Change: Different Lines of Evidence

Household archaeology provides a perspective on Lukurmata's evolution different than that yielded by approaches operating at the site or regional level. In a roughly parallel manner, if the three subhousehold lines of evidence I discussed in Chapter 2 (domestic architecture, house contents, and style of associated pottery) are considered independently, each also provides a different picture of change over time in household life (Bermann 1993).

The artifacts associated with houses changed the least through time. Similarities in artifact assemblages between houses of the same and different periods suggest that certain tasks were performed throughout the entire span of domestic occupation at Lukurmata. These tasks included food preparation and consumption, spinning, weaving, basketry, hide working, and manufacture of stone cutting and scraping tools. These were universal domestic activities carried out by each household, and artifacts relating to these activities were found in each house from every period of occupation regardless of house shape or size.

If we had excavated at Lukurmata and found no housefloors or other architectural remains, but only the artifacts once associated with houses, what would our picture of household life over a 1500-year period be? It would be one of tremendous stability with little or no change in domestic activities. Although we might note some changes in artifact style, these changes would be overshadowed by the long continuity in the types of items associated with houses.

If we consider the two lines of evidence (domestic architecture and house contents) in conjunction, noting changes in the size of floor area or in the spatial distribution of artifacts in relation to architecture, it is clear that domestic activities did change in significant ways over time, even though a particular set of tasks remained basic to the household. This change may have been in the allocation of space and the appropriate place to carry out specific tasks, or in the importance accorded particular activities.

If we had recovered only ceramics, we might have gotten a very different picture of the pace of change in household life at Lukurmata. We would have seen a period during which household pottery changed very little, followed by a period of abrupt changes (particularly in decorated pottery) with the appearance of Tiwanaku III- and IV-style materials. Thus, the ceramic evidence would suggest a long period of stasis in household life followed by extensive and dramatic changes, perhaps even "population replacement." In fact, the most striking changes in household ceramics (associated with the Structure 25–28 occupation) were not accompanied by shifts in residential design or in household activities.

Over time, the greatest amount of change was exhibited in domestic architecture. This change was not in building materials or construction techniques; these hardly varied during Lukurmata's prehispanic occupation and, in fact, still characterize Aymara households today. Instead, changes took place in the shape, size, grouping, layout, and variety of residential architecture. These changes included an increase over time in house size (or in the amount of interior area used by households), the formation of patio groups, and an increase in the varieties of buildings used by households.

The sequence of domestic architecture might indicate that household life was not as static as the continuities in household artifacts suggest, nor as subject to abrupt change as suggested by the ceramic evidence. If we had recovered only architecture without artifacts, the history of Lukurmata would appear to have been characterized by uneven, but continuous change, with rapid, major shifts in residential organization followed by periods of slower change. On the other hand, there was impressive continuity in construction materials and techniques. As we have seen, not every change in domestic architecture was accompanied by shifts in other aspects of domestic life.

Taken together, these three lines of evidence (changes in architecture, house contents, and pottery styles) reveal the complexity of the evolution of household life at Lukurmata.

Lukurmata Evolutionary Sequence: The "Capital-Centric" Perspective

One way of placing the evolution of household life at Lukurmata in a larger context is to divide its prehistory into phases based on its position within the larger Tiwanaku settlement hierarchy, as well as the style of Tiwanaku pottery at the site. This division yields a "capital-centric" division of Lukurmata's development—in essence, an "external" view of Lukurmata from the perspective of the Tiwanaku capital.

Lukurmata's development can be divided, successively and with approximate dates, as follows: (1) independent hamlet; (2) frontier village; (3) second-order center; and (4) postimperial hamlet.

Independent Hamlet (100 B.C.–A.D. 200)

Lukurmata during this phase was an undifferentiated residential site, and may not have been part of a larger political unit. There was no evidence for any degree of social differentiation or craft specialization. There was little diachronic change in the household unit, and household activities consisted of a limited range of productive tasks. The household unit itself contained only one structure. Interaction with other sites was organized on a household basis. There is no evidence for participation in long-distance exchange networks.

Frontier Village (A.D. 200–A.D. 700)

Lukurmata was probably a lower-order site in the Tiwanaku settlement hierarchy during this phase, which roughly corresponds to the Tiwanaku III period. There is no evidence of public architecture at the site. The representation of non-Tiwanaku, imported ceramics in Lukurmata households reached its peak during this phase, suggesting considerable interaction with communities other than Tiwanaku.

The large percentage of nonlocal pottery in Lukurmata households may reflect Lukurmata's geographic position on the edge of the Tiwanaku polity, where the site could have served as a center for interaction with external groups. Several studies have suggested that chiefly level societies are seldom more than one day's travel in diameter, allowing chiefs to visit the outermost point of their domain and return to the center in less than a single day (Helms 1979; Spencer 1982:7). Lukurmata, five hours on foot from Tiwanaku, fits neatly into this range.

If a chiefly polity at Tiwanaku was directly attempting to stimulate surplus production by Lukurmata households, we should expect to see an increase at Lukurmata in tools or productive facilities, or a reorganization of craft production and/or subsistence activities.

There was no evidence during the Tiwanaku III period for a significant increase in the relative proportion of tools (agricultural implements or spinning and weaving items). Additionally, the Tiwanaku III period Lukurmata houses displayed great continuity in the variety of household artifacts, indicating that mobilization of surplus did not involve changes in the range of household activities. This would rule out "disarticulated" production as well (see Chapter 2). But there were several shifts in the household unit consistent with a "focus change" strategy of surplus mobilization. This strategy involved changes in the organization of, or emphasis placed on, particular activities, rather than the appearance of new activities.

Two important changes in the household unit occurred: one in the fourth century A.D., the other in the seventh century A.D. The earlier shift, seen in the Structure 14–18 occupation, coincided with the appearance at the household level of significant amounts of Tiwanaku III-style decorated pottery. As prestige items, this pottery may mark attempts by an elite stratum to stimulate production. The Structure 14–18 occupation marked a shift from a household unit with a single, all-purpose structure to a multibuilding household unit. Household units now included a structure used as a dwelling, and a second structure, used for unknown activities, perhaps storage. Internal storage features appeared in Lukurmata structures for the first time.

Later change in the household unit, at the end of the Tiwanaku III period (seventh century A.D.), suggests a trend toward special-purpose domestic architecture. Structure 24 was clearly a specialized structure, probably used for storage. The appearance of structures specifically designed for storage purposes denotes the increasing importance or institutionalization of storage activities at the household level.

Overall, this evidence for increasing storage during the Tiwanaku III period suggests stimulated production following a "focus change" strategy. While we cannot be certain that this was the result of Tiwanaku's demands on producing units, the increase through time of Tiwanaku prestige-goods in Lukurmata households suggests that the processes were related.

Second-Order Center (A.D. 700–A.D. 900)

Lukurmata grew explosively in this phase. At the regional level, the years between A.D. 400 and A.D. 800 saw the transformation in the scale and complexity of the Tiwanaku polity. I have argued elsewhere that the regional changes in the Tiwanaku polity early in the Tiwanaku IV period are consistent with a process of state formation (Bermann 1990). Lukurmata's new size and public architecture mark it as a second-order center in the Tiwanaku settlement hierarchy during this phase (Kolata 1986). In addition to the construction of public architecture, this phase saw an increase in site complexity, with increased site functions (administrative, ceremonial, mortuary) and increased spatial segregation of functionally distinct areas. Segregated residential areas appeared as well. This segregation included the construction of formal barriers such as walls and features to limit access to high-status or ceremonial spaces. Residential and mortuary patterns indicate increased social differentiation and differential access to exotic or highly valued goods. The greater range of activities and occupant statuses at Lukurmata is reflected in increased variation in domestic architectural forms.

Yet there is no evidence that the emergence of Lukurmata as a secondary center in the seventh century A.D. was associated with major shifts in household production. The site-level transformation was accompanied by two changes at the individual household level.

The first change was the disappearance of the specialized storage structure from the household unit. The last Tiwanaku III period occupation had such a structure (Structure 24); the subsequent occupation did not. The abandonment of Structure 24 is evidence for changes in storage patterns at the beginning of the Tiwanaku IV period. This change is consistent with the surplus mobilization strategy consisting of direct appropriation of surplus (Strategy A4). In this strategy, household storage or "replacement fund" is moved from households to suprahousehold bodies. Storage may have shifted from the household domain to the small complex of storage facilities found on the domestic terracing along the southern margin of Lukurmata (associated with Structure 42).

Other changes in Lukurmata households during the early Tiwanaku IV period involved shifts in ceramic-style preferences and in ritual/religious activities using zoomorphic incensarios. These changes suggest that incorporation into the Tiwanaku polity involved changes in the social or ideological domain, rather than the economic sphere alone.

The early Tiwanaku IV period changes at the site level suggest extrahousehold strategies of surplus mobilization, in the form of labor services. The massive modification of the Lukurmata temple hill, and the construction of monumental architecture, suggest organization of Lukurmata residents for labor projects. The other line of evidence indicative of extrahousehold surplus mobilization is the raised field system of the Pampa Koani. The complexities of the necessary canal system, the canalization of the river bisecting the Pampa, the causeways, and the large mounds and public architecture sites, all suggest a state-founded and-organized agricultural project. The Pampa never had a large resident population, and labor was probably provided by the residents of large adjacent sites such as Lukurmata and Pajchiri.

With a productive potential far beyond that needed by the Pampa and Lukurmata populations, Pampa production could only have been intended to support the demographic concentration at Tiwanaku. In their labor investment and high-yield potential, the Pampa fields obviously represent something more than "for-use" production. Similar agricultural features may be typical of archaic states in which state wealth is generated, at least in part, through large-scale productive projects outside the traditional domestic economy. These often involved extensive irrigation and landscape modification, or application of new productive technologies. In the case of the Inca, such projects on crown lands were worked largely by mobilized (mit'a) labor, rather than permanent (or attached) residents. Although further investigation is necessary, it is likely that the Pampa Koani fields were worked the same way.

Extensive changes in the household unit occurred near the end of the Tiwanaku IV period, in the ninth century A.D. These changes, seen in the Structure 33–39 occupation, suggest shifts in household production. There was an increase in the overall "complexity" of domestic organization at Lukurmata. Specifically, we see an increase in: (1) the range of features and artifacts making up the household unit; (2) the range of household activities; (3) the formal spatial division of these activities; and (4) the variation between household units in architecture, activities, and access to certain items.

Patio groups emerged, containing one or more residential structures and one used for special purposes. The Structure 33–39 occupation provides evidence for production involving new activities (perhaps organized at the suprahousehold level). The camelid mandible tools and new thick-walled bowls of the Structure 33–39 occupation are the archaeological indications of this type of change in the range of household activities. These remains represent new tasks added to household activities, and in the case of the mandible tools, one clearly associated with the Tiwanaku polity (even though we do not know what it was). Spatial artifact distributions suggest that the patio groups themselves functioned as units of production for whatever activities involved this new form of pottery and the camelid mandible tools.

I suggest that the late Tiwanaku IV period changes in household activities were related to the demands of the Tiwanaku political economy. Changes in the "complexity" of household organization may be related to Lukurmata's evolving role in the Tiwanaku settlement hierarchy. Michael Whalen's (1988:269) analysis of changes in household organization during the Early and Middle Formative in Oaxaca suggests a parallel process, with the development of larger, more complex, and more formally defined residential units accompanying the increase in complexity of the regional settlement hierarchy. While there is evidence for concomitant agricultural intensification, Whalen (ibid.:287) suggests a noneconomic explanation for these household unit changes, that of response to scalar stress—the organizational stress taking place in groups "that increase[s] their size without altering their organization." The creation of a new organizational level (such as suprahousehold groupings) increases the integration and manageability of the system (Johnson 1982; Whalen 1988). This type of reorganization should also be an administrative goal of an elite stratum interested in implementing tight political control or organizing household and suprahousehold productive activities.

As I will discuss below, the evidence suggests intrahousehold surplus mobilization by the Tiwanaku polity during both the Tiwanaku III and IV periods. Chiefly (Tiwanaku III period) mobilization involved a "focus change," a reorganization of productive activities. In contrast, state mobilization, at least at the end of the Tiwanaku IV period, involved direct appropriation of surplus and the addition of new household activities to household production. The Pampa Koani fields and the public architecture at Tiwanaku suggest the operation of extrahousehold mobilization strategies (probably of labor) during the Tiwanaku IV period.

Postimperial Hamlet (A.D. 1200–A.D. 1300)

Lukurmata at this stage was once again an undifferentiated residential hamlet, relatively autonomous and not tightly linked to other centers. There is no evidence that the collapse and abandonment of Tiwanaku was followed by political integration of the region. Public architecture at the site had been abandoned (except for interment of burials) and the resident population may have been less than one hundred persons.

If many of the earlier changes in household organization were connected to Lukurmata's participation in a system in which surplus was demanded from producing units, the dissolution of this system (and surplus demands) should result in the household "reverting" to something very similar to what it had been. The household unit of the postimperial phase should resemble that of the independent hamlet phase, prior to Lukurmata's incorporation into larger political units. Structure 43 meets these expectations. Household units during this phase once again included a single, small all-purpose structure, and productive activities were restricted to the same domestic tasks performed by pre-Tiwanaku period households.

AN ALTERNATIVE EVOLUTIONARY SEQUENCE: THE "LOCAL PERSPECTIVE"

Many of the major changes in household life at Lukurmata did not coincide with the "capital-centric" phases presented above. This dissonance is one of the more interesting aspects of Lukurmata's evolution, and has larger implications for archaeological approaches to social change. If Lukurmata's history is outlined with the household unit as the only line of evidence, the Lukurmata occupation is divided into very different chronological segments. This is shown in Figure 15.1, in which I have presented, side-by-side, how an archaeologist might subdivide Lukurmata's prehistory from both the "capital-centric" perspective and the "local perspective."

The "capital-centric" chronology is based on regional processes—shifts in the overarching Tiwanaku polity, Lukurmata's evolution in the settlement hierarchy, and changes in regionally distributed pottery styles. In fact, the "capital-centric" chronology depicts how I might have subdivided Lukurmata's prehistory if I had excavated only middens and public architecture, and not house remains. The "local perspective" chronology uses household remains as the unit of analysis, and reflects changes in the household "system."

The First Phase of the "local perspective" chronology lasted from 100 B.C. to A.D. 250. The household unit of this phase included a small dwelling with an indoor hearth, a larger outdoor hearth, and outdoor activity areas. Universal household activities included cooking and eating, spinning and weaving, basketry, hide working, scraping tasks, expedient stone tool flaking, and serving activities around the outdoor hearth. The Structure 2–3 occupation saw shifts in architectural and pottery styles, but not in floor area, house contents and features, or domestic activities.

The Second Phase (A.D. 250–A.D. 350) is marked by the first major change in household activities or morphology. Structures 9 and 10 were several times larger than earlier houses, and had circular plans. This shift may have reflected a change in the organization of activities, the time committed to indoor tasks, or a change in household composition. There is no indication of ties with Tiwanaku, so these changes may have had local stimuli. The range of household activities was similar to that of the First Phase. Tiwanaku III-style pottery began to appear at Lukurmata near the end of this phase.

The Third Phase (A.D. 350–A.D. 450) is marked by another shift in the household unit: individual structures became smaller, and household units now included two or more structures. One or more of these structures served as dwellings, while another structure of the household unit (one example was Structure 17) was used for a different, limited set of activities, such as storage.

This was the first appearance of a sequence of structures in the Lukurmata household not used for the full range of domestic tasks. The total interior floor area for a Third Phase household unit is slightly greater than that of the Second Phase household unit, but it is possible that activities formerly carried out in one structure were now divided among several buildings. The domestic artifact assemblages indicate continuity between the Second and Third Phases in the range of household activities, despite the change in the use of space, architectural composition of the household unit, and style of pottery used by the household.

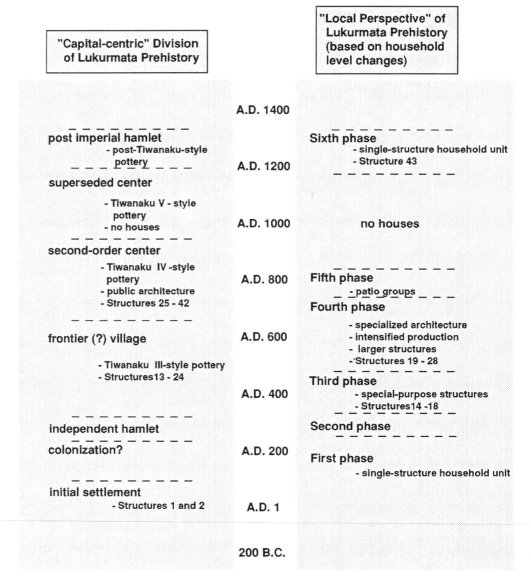

Fig. 15.1 Contrasting perspectives on Lukurmata prehistory: the "capital-centric" versus the "local perspective."

The Fourth Phase (A.D. 450–A.D. 750) is represented by three occupations (Structure 19, Structures 22–24, Structures 25–28). There was strong continuity in most domestic activities during this phase, although two new activities may have been adapted by the household: hallucinogenic drug usage and a ritual activity involving Tiwanaku-style zoomorphic incensarios. Domestic architecture did not change much during this phase, with each occupation displaying large, all-purpose structures nearly identical to one another in form and contents.

One shift in the household "system" was the appearance of not just "special-pur-pose" structures but a specialized structure in the form of Structure 24. This may have continued in use during the subsequent occupation (some of its walls were standing during the later occupation). No specialized structures were found in occupations after the Structure 25–28 occupation, suggesting changes in domestic storage patterns. This may mark the operation of new surplus mobilization strategies.

The Fifth Phase (A.D. 750–A.D. 850) is marked by the formation of patio groups consisting of three structures (two dwellings and a "special-purpose" building) ar-ranged to enclose an open space used for universal household activities as well as for new craft activities (including camelid tool making). The household unit of this phase also included burials placed under or near housefloors. A different form of contempo-rary household unit, including a small, circular dwelling, was found in another area of the site.

No domestic structures pertaining to the Sixth Phase (A.D. 850–A.D. 1200) were excavated, so little is known of domestic occupation during this time. The materials recovered from refuse features suggest continuity in the style and variety of household artifacts.

The Seventh Phase (A.D. 1200–A.D. 1300) is signaled by a striking shift in the com-position of the household unit similar to those of the First or Second Phase. The only household unit exposed (Structure 43) consisted of a single, all-purpose structure with features and contents indicative of a narrow range of basic tasks.

Comparing the "capital-centric" and "local perspective" chronologies reveals that several changes in the household unit more or less coincided with the appearance of particular Tiwanaku pottery styles at Lukurmata. This temporal association suggests that incorporation into the Tiwanaku system may have led to the change in household organization seen in the Third Phase—the addition of special-purpose structures to the household unit. The emergence of Tiwanaku as a state (loosely marked by the appear-ance of Tiwanaku IV-style pottery) more or less coincided with the beginning of the Sixth Phase.

At the point when Lukurmata was changing the most as a settlement—the beginning of the Tiwanaku IV period—individual households showed little change in architec-ture or activities. The only difference between the terminal Tiwanaku III period occu-pation and the first Tiwanaku IV period occupation was the absence of specialized structures in the latter. The dwellings of each occupation and their contents were nearly identical. On the other hand, the changes in the household unit seen in the Second Phase structures predated interaction with Tiwanaku, and may have resulted from local pressures or trends. Such changes remind us that Lukurmata, like all smaller sites, was a dynamic community in its own right.

Tiwanaku Political Economy and Lukurmata Evolution

In Chapter 2 I argued that Tiwanaku's demands for surplus production might lead to changes in Lukurmata households. These changes might be identified by the concur-rence of change (changes in household production coinciding with changes in the scale of the Tiwanaku polity) or by changes indicative of increased surplus production. Does the evidence from Lukurmata suggest surplus mobilization by the Tiwanaku polity? If so, we would expect to see: (1) a change in tools or productive facilities on initial incorporation into the Tiwanaku polity; (2) a change in household production patterns when Tiwanaku became a state; and (3) a change in household production patterns after Tiwanaku's collapse.

The Lukurmata household evidence is ambiguous at many points. Nevertheless, the Tiwanaku III and IV periods meet expectations 1 and 3. If an increase in storage capacity is a measure of surplus production, the Structure 14–18 occupation (marked by the appearance at the household level of large quantities of Tiwanaku III-style materials) suggests that changes in household production coincided with incorporation into the Tiwanaku polity.

After the Tiwanaku state collapsed, the household unit "reverted" to what it had been in pre-Tiwanaku times—a single-structure household unit with limited storage (Structure 42).

The *concurrence* of change would suggest that these shifts in domestic organization were linked to the political economy of the Tiwanaku polity. The *nature* of the changes represented by the Structure 33–39 occupation also suggests shifts in household production linked to Tiwanaku political economy, with an increase in storage, possible suprahousehold production of particular goods, and the production of the Tiwanaku-associated camelid tools.

If we accept that these changes at the household level resulted from Tiwanaku's demands for surplus production, two additional questions present themselves: Were intrahousehold or extrahousehold strategies used? What does this reveal about Tiwanaku as a prehispanic polity, particularly in comparison to the Wari and Inca states?

TIWANAKU IN COMPARATIVE PERSPECTIVE

The changes in the Lukurmata household sequence provide insight into Tiwanaku surplus mobilization strategies. If these strategies are explicable as components of wider modes of administration and control, then the household changes also provide insight into the nature of the Tiwanaku polity (D'Altroy 1987a).

Capital-centered political formations can dominate subject populations in a variety of ways. Domination may be through direct rule in which subject territories are tightly integrated into the state's political system, and are administered from the center by administrators who largely supplant local elites (D'Altroy 1987a:6, 1992; Hassig 1985; Luttwak 1976). This form of direct or "territorial" rule is characteristic of imperial states (Doyle 1986; Schreiber 1992:15).

Alternatively, rule of subject populations can be indirect; subject territories are controlled through patronage of local rulers or through manipulation of locally important institutions (D'Altroy 1987a:6; Luttwak 1976; Paynter 1982). This form of indirect or "hegemonic" rule is typical of polities in which a single powerful capital or metropole controls a collection of client states (D'Altroy 1987a, 1992; Hassig 1985; Luttwak 1976; Schreiber 1992:14).

The Wari and Inca Empires: Models of Territorial Control

A territorial mode of control goes beyond the addition of another level of decision making, or the formation of relationships between regional elites. It involves *appropri-*

ation of local decision making by centralized institutions. Therefore, it also involves an extension of centralized decision making or administrative machinery into the subject area (D'Altroy 1987a; Schreiber 1992). Archaeological correlates of this type of direct administration include new levels added to the administrative settlement hierarchies, specialized architecture relating to administrative functions, residences of transplanted officials, even architecture (fortresses or barracks) signaling a military presence (D'Altroy 1987a, 1992).

The territorial mode of integration, often involving a reorganization of local hierarchy and settlement, requires considerable investment on the part of the imperial core. Therefore, it is commonly associated with heavy extraction of resources from the subjugated area (D'Altroy 1987a; Hassig 1985). Resources may be extracted through stimulating surplus production by local producing units (intrahousehold strategies), or through large-scale state-run projects (extrahousehold strategies). The form that surplus mobilization takes generally is determined by centralized governing institutions or the rulers at the capital.

The Middle Horizon period Wari empire (A.D. 400–A.D. 1000) and the later Inca empire (A.D. 1400–A.D. 1534) are excellent examples of political formations based largely on the territorial mode of control, although each, in particular times and places, also pursued hegemonic strategies (Schreiber 1992). These polities left a remarkably similar regional pattern of public architecture, consisting of a complex framework of administrative centers with standardized and highly distinct "imperial-style" (state-associated) architecture, linked through a framework of roads, way-stations, forts, barracks, and production/storage complexes. This regional framework is the archaeological correlate for a system of direct rule and territorial control that saw the state directly administering local populations.

In a recent comprehensive overview of the Inca empire, D'Altroy (1992) has outlined at length the nature of Inca territorial control. He concludes that a number of factors led the Inca to pursue a territorial strategy throughout the Andean highlands, characterized by the construction of imperial administration centers (such as Hatun Xauxa or Húanuco Pampa), fortresses and other forms of public works, state investment in agrarian intensification, and the application of the famous Inca decimal system of administration (ibid.:217).

In an equally comprehensive overview of the Wari empire, Katharina Schreiber (1992) has documented a comparable regional pattern. The Wari regional settlement pattern reflects, as Isbell (1988:189) notes, a provincial administrative structure and political economy that constitutes a forerunner of the later "Inca mode of production." The Wari regional pattern included a network of state-administrative centers (such as Jargampata, Jincamocco, and Pikillaqta) with storehouses and barrack-like facilities, all linked by a system of roads and fortresses (Isbell 1988:189; Isbell and Schreiber 1978; see especially Isbell and McEwan 1991 and Schreiber 1992).

Incorporation into the Wari and Inca polities led to similar consequences for subject populations—a reflection of the shared territorial mode of control. Excellent diachronic archaeological studies at the regional level (including Schreiber's [1987b] study of the Carahuarazo Valley and [1992] monograph on Wari imperialism) have shown that both Wari and Inca conquest frequently involved: (1) construction of a state-associated administrative center in the subject area; (2) alterations or leveling of the preexisting local political order; (3) imposition of an "Inca mode of production";

and (4) attempts to increase local production, sometimes through resettlement of the local population (D'Altroy 1992; Isbell 1988; Isbell and Schreiber 1978; Moseley 1992; Schreiber 1987b, 1992).

Many prehistoric states throughout the world appear to have been predominantly "territorial" in mode of control and integration (Doyle 1986). However, this interpretation may stem in part from the ease of recognizing a territorial strategy archaeologically. Indeed, it is usually the material manifestations of this mode of control (roads, forts, hierarchies of state-associated architecture, administrative buildings in the style of the capital) that allow archaeologists to recognize archaic states at all (Schreiber 1992). Archaic states that rely on alternative forms of integration, such as a hegemonic strategy, will be much more difficult to recognize archaeologically.

A hegemonic mode of control, which does not involve close administration of local units or populations by state institutions, is unlikely to be accompanied by the material manifestations of territorial control. Hegemonic control is implemented through client local elites who may be rewarded by valued goods from the state, affiliation with the elite stratum of the state, or state backing in local power struggles. Client local elites may accumulate imperial goods, dominate exchange with the state, and emulate the state ruling stratum in the material marking of social status and identity (dress, decoration, serving activities, house style, etc.).

What type of archaeological pattern would a "hegemonic empire," or one based on indirect rule, produce? It is a difficult question; in some cases the lack of evidence for territorial control has been treated as evidence of hegemonic control. It would also be difficult to distinguish hegemonic control of a subject region from the operation of a prestige-good economy in a politically independent region. Politically independent rulers may acquire materials from a political capital, and adopt the styles of the capital, to bolster or enhance their own local status. Edward Schortman and Patricia Urban (1987:72) have described this process as an ideological "convergence," in which local elites identify with the "social, ideological, and proxemic patterns" of the rulers of the larger political system. Not only might hegemonic control and a prestige-good economy leave a similar archaeological signature, but in some cases the formation of a prestige-good economy may be a component of hegemonic control.

In the hegemonic mode of control, the imperial core makes a lower investment in administration, seeking limited extraction of resources (D'Altroy 1987a, 1992; Hassig 1985; Luttwak 1976). Therefore, hegemonic control is not likely to have been accompanied by a buildup of administrative machinery (Wari/Inca-type storage complexes or barracks, for instance). The form that local intensification or surplus mobilization takes will be left in the hands of local paramounts or institutions, but the hegemonic mode of control may involve both intrahousehold and extrahousehold surplus mobilization strategies. Although local elites might stimulate surplus production of particular items, this stimulation would not result in great reorganization or distortion of traditional modes of production.

In both territorial and hegemonic modes of control, interaction with the capital is channeled through some, but not all, sites. In the territorial mode of control, these sites evolve and function as second-order administrative centers. In the hegemonic mode of control, interaction is more likely to be channeled through preexisting centers, usually paramount seats. This should not involve major transformations at the site level, although a change in the size and status of the paramount's household and retainers might be one manifestation. Local rulers in turn, would stimulate surplus production from local households. Thus, what we might see would be changes at the household level, with little evidence of change or processes of control at the regional level. "Local perspective" investigation at the household level at sites with Tiwanaku materials will be critical to documenting whether this mode of control characterized the Tiwanaku polity (Stanish 1992:83).

Tiwanaku: A Different Type of Political Formation?

It has long been recognized that two powerful civilizations, Wari and Tiwanaku, dominated between them the Andean highlands during the Middle Horizon period (A.D. 600–A.D. 1000). The marked differences between the archaeological records left by the two civilizations have led scholars to see the polities as fundamentally different in character and degree of political integration. The Wari polity has been viewed as a secular empire on the model of the Inca polity (or, for that matter, the Roman empire). The Tiwanaku political formation, conversely, has often been viewed as a powerful religious system, or, in Browman's (1984:124) "altiplano" model, as the urban head of a loosely linked network of semi-independent centers, a "hegemony."

In contrast to the archaeological records left by the Wari and Inca, that of the Tiwanaku system does not immediately lend itself to facile interpretation. The Tiwanaku polity lacks virtually all of the archaeological correlates of a territorial mode of control. Tiwanaku military garrisons, forts, specialized administrative centers, and large-scale storage facilities have yet to be discovered. There are no secular Tiwanaku architectural forms associated with administrative personnel, or politico-economic decision making, comparable to the imperial Inca *tambos* and *colcas*, or the Wari barracks and rectangular enclosures (Isbell and McEwan 1991). The semi-subterranean temples and Kalasasaya-like enclosures found at a handful of sites are the only Tiwanaku public architectural forms now known for second- or third-order sites in the Tiwanaku settlement hierarchy.

Because Tiwanaku lacks a regional archaeological pattern analogous to that of the Wari and Inca polities, a variety of hypotheses concerning the nature and degree of the integration of the Tiwanaku polity can be proposed. One hypothesis is that the Tiwanaku polity was simply much smaller than the expansive Wari state, and that the Tiwanaku rulers really only controlled, "through a centralized, hierarchical, and theocratic organization" (Isbell 1988:177) that which I have described as the Tiwanaku "core" area in the Lake Titicaca Basin, an area extending 15–70 km from the capital in any direction (Isbell 1988:177). Outside of this area, the Tiwanaku rulers maintained a system of trade and hegemonic relationships, and perhaps the occasional colony, such as at Omo in the Moquegua Valley, Peru.

If this were the case, better interpretive analogues for the Tiwanaku polity might be the post-Tiwanaku period Aymara kingdoms, political formations with large, highland capital sites that did not control contiguous territory (Stanish 1992). One element of this hypothesis might involve distinguishing between north-central and south-central Andean traditions of statecraft. Just as the central Andean Inca polity resembled the earlier north-central Andean Wari polity, so perhaps the Tiwanaku polity and Aymara kingdoms to the south represented manifestations of a tradition of statecraft indigenous to the southern Andes.

Alternatively, Tiwanaku might be compared to the city of Teotihuacan in the Valley of Mexico that dominated much of central Mesoamerica between A.D. 1 and A.D. 600. The Teotihuacan state consisted of a vast city, with a massive residential population and set of public architecture, supported by a huge and well-organized, sustaining hinterland (Blanton et al. 1981). However, the Teotihuacan polity itself was a city-state, rather than an imperial state. The Teotihuacan polity lacked a true empire; there is little evidence that its direct political control extended beyond the Valley of Mexico (Sanders 1974). The Teotihuacan regional settlement pattern does not include the provincial centers, forts, roads, and other features of control reflecting the administration of an empire (Fiedel 1987:278). In this regard, the Teotihuacan state differed from the contemporaneous Zapotec state to the south that ruled in a territorial mode, with its state administration spread through a regional system of secondary and tertiary centers (Blanton et al. 1981:233). In contrast, the institutions of administration in the Teotihuacan polity, as Richard Blanton et al. (ibid.) note, were concentrated in the city itself. Teotihuacan probably dominated its neighbors through a combination of commercial power, religious authority, and punitive military expeditions. Teotihuacan-style materials, such as the famous Thin Orangeware pottery, are found at many distant sites. As in the Tiwanaku case, the existence of such materials at distant sites has led some scholars to argue that such sites must represent colonies (Blanton et al. 1981:141; Sanders 1978).

Another hypothesis is that the Tiwanaku state really was comparable to the Wari state in degree of political integration, modes of control, and geopolitical strategy. However, in the Tiwanaku case, these characteristics were not manifested in the same types of administrative architecture as in the Wari or Inca polities, thus leaving a very different archaeological record. Nonetheless, the Tiwanaku polity and archaeological record can still be examined using Wari and Inca analoges, and modeled in terms of levels of administrative hierarchy, colonies, and regional strategies (Goldstein 1989; Kolata 1986, 1991).

The Lukurmata household unit evidence, together with Pampa Koani archaeological remains, lend some support to this hypothesis. As with the Sausa absorption by the Inca, involvement in the Tiwanaku system was accompanied by changes in productive patterns at the individual household level, at least in Lukurmata. The nature of these changes is consistent with mobilization of surplus. These household-level changes suggest that Tiwanaku—like other Andean polities—was a political formation extracting surplus from producing units to meet the costs of administration or regulation.

The Tiwanaku mode of control may not have resulted in complete submersion or alteration of local patterns and traditions. There may have been a great deal of continuity in domestic organization and household productive patterns at other "Tiwanaku" sites. These pre-Tiwanaku local patterns would have shaped the incorporation of local populations into the Tiwanaku political economy, resulting in the regional variation in the distribution of Tiwanaku-style remains. Thus, Tiwanaku may have directly mobilized surplus from all subject households, but the strategy used by rulers, and the form the mobilization took, may have depended on local, preexisting production patterns.

From this perspective, the great regional variation in Tiwanaku-style remains in the southern Andes does not indicate that Tiwanaku was something less than an imperial state, but only that the Tiwanaku polity may have been integrated differently from the Wari or Inca polities, particularly at the regional level.

It would be difficult, using regional approaches, to recognize the Inca state without the roads, forts, tambos, colcas, and distinctive Cuzco pottery. Imagine "peeling away" these highly distinctive, pan-regional elements of Inca administration from the Andean archaeological record. This would reveal "underneath" a heterogeneous pattern of local and regional diversity, one very similar to the Tiwanaku regional archaeological record. Diachronic study would still show that the Inca affected household and community organization, but without the regional pattern of distinctive and uniform Inca administrative architecture archaeologists would have difficulty linking these changes to state policies or actions.

Yet another possibility is that the Tiwanaku regional archaeological record differs markedly from that of the prehispanic territorial states because the underlying nature and integration of the Tiwanaku political formation were quite different, perhaps consisting of one of the alternative native forms of sociopolitical organization that have been documented ethnohistorically in the Andes (Netherly 1984, 1990; Murra et al. 1986; Platt 1987). In a challenging consideration of the Tiwanaku polity, Albarracin-Jordan (1992) has suggested that the Tiwanaku political formation may have been fundamentally different in structure and operation than territorial polities or expansive states such as that of Wari or the Inca. Instead of an empire organized along Roman or Inca lines, Albarracin-Jordan suggests that the Tiwanaku "polity" actually consisted of a complex system of nested indigenous social units (*ayllus*) linked through extensive kinship and religious ties and a hierarchy of leadership. Tiwanaku may have been a uniquely Andean sociopolitical formation rather than a centralized state in the Western (or Wari/Inca) sense (Wallace 1980). Attempting to interpret the Tiwanaku archaeological record with models derived exclusively from the Wari or Inca states, or Near Eastern archaeology, will result in a distorted reconstruction of the Tiwanaku phenomenon (Albarracin-Jordan, personal communication).

The Lukurmata research suggests that although the Tiwanaku polity differed from the territorial Wari and Inca polities at the regional level, these political formations may have had more in common in terms of political economy than currently recognized, at least in the Tiwanaku core area. The changes in Lukurmata households are consistent with the demands of territorial states, but the Tiwanaku polity may have met the same objectives (surplus mobilization to meet costs of regulations) through somewhat different means of control and administration.

At the regional level, Tiwanaku does not appear to have been a polity based on territorial control. Instead, as Browman (1980) has proposed, the regional distribution of Tiwanaku remains suggests, at most, a loosely integrated, hegemonic political formation.

A different conclusion, however, is produced by the Lukurmata household sequence. The evolutionary trajectory of Lukurmata suggests that the Tiwanaku polity may have been more territorial in mode of control than previously thought—at least in the core area around the site of Tiwanaku itself.

That Tiwanaku governance was, in some areas, territorial in mode is suggested by the investment in "high-extraction," extrahousehold projects such as the Pampa Koani raised fields. Here productive installations are associated with a concentration of public architecture (at Lukurmata, Pajchiri, and sites in the Pampa), corporate construction projects (causeways and canals), suggesting direct Tiwanaku administration of Pampa production (Kolata 1991).

Like the Sausa households under Inca rule described by Hastorf (1990), Lukurmata household unit changes suggest both intra- and extrahousehold mobilization strategies. For both Sausa and Lukurmata households, incorporation into the larger system and subsequent surplus mobilization involved a "focus change." In other words, in both the Inca and Tiwanaku cases, state wealth was not completely generated outside of the traditional domestic economy. Like the Inca, Tiwanaku political economy apparently did not leave the "larder of the peasant . . . untouched" (Murra 1980:79).

Directions for Future Research: The Need for Complementary Approaches

Previous research on Tiwanaku as a polity has focused on the presence of Tiwanaku-style materials at sites throughout the southern Andes without truly exploring the processes that accompanied their distribution (Stanish 1992). Domestic contexts at these sites have not been investigated, making it impossible to determine if the appearance of Tiwanaku-style materials was accompanied by changes in household organization or in the local economy. The Lukurmata sequence demonstrates that significant changes in domestic organization may not be recoverable through surface investigation, visible in burial patterns, or approachable with stylistic artifact analysis. Some of the most significant changes in the Lukurmata household unit did not involve changes in the style or quantity of artifacts; they did not, in fact, involve Tiwanaku-style materials at all. The lesson is clear: if we examine only the presence, varieties, or relative quantity of Tiwanaku-style materials in peripheral areas in order to measure participation in the Tiwanaku system, we can never arrive at a full or accurate understanding of the nature and effects of participation in the system. Increasingly detailed inventories of Tiwanaku-style items in peripheral regions, or more interregional comparisons of Tiwanaku-style artifact inventories, can ultimately tell us relatively little about the regional integration and organization of the Tiwanaku polity. In short, documenting the impact of participation in the Tiwanaku system at the local level requires study of settlement organization and household life before and after the appearance of Tiwanaku-style materials. Because the Tiwanaku polity lacks Inca-style administrative correlates, such studies will be especially critical for gaining an understanding of the Tiwanaku political formation.

A corollary of the above observation is that an understanding of the Tiwanaku polity must be based on activities rather than materials. Participation in the Tiwanaku system cannot be approximated in terms of objects, only in terms of underlying socioeconomic patterns (Stanish 1992). As Stanish (ibid.:74) has correctly noted, "the simple comparison of diagnostic ceramic types is an inadequate method for assessing regional political affiliations and the nature or complexity of economic networks."

I argue that we must go one step further. Understanding the effects of interaction with Tiwanaku on local populations is basic to assessing the nature of the Tiwanaku polity itself, and the role that interaction with Tiwanaku played in the cultural evolution of outlying populations. Such an assessment must be based on information drawn from diachronic investigation of continuities at the household and site levels. These types of studies, comparing preimperial and imperial patterns for the Wari and Inca polities (Costin and Earle 1989; D'Altroy 1987a, 1987b; Hastorf 1990a; Schreiber

1987b, 1992), have proven to be of immense value in arriving at a more sophisticated understanding of these prehispanic states. But only recently have comparable studies been undertaken for the Tiwanaku polity (Albarracin-Jordan and Mathews 1990; Stanish n.d.).

The research at Lukurmata was the first to examine Tiwanaku's impact on a community and its component households. Future studies, inside and outside the Tiwanaku "core" area, should reveal to what extent, and in which regions, the Tiwanaku system operated as an imperial state on the Wari model (as Stanish's [n.d.] research in Puno, Peru, suggests), or as the "altiplano" model polity suggested by Browman (1984).

The Lukurmata household unit sequence shows that incorporation into the Tiwanaku "sphere" involved more than acquisition of Tiwanaku-style materials by Lukurmata residents. The relationship between the population of Lukurmata and the site of Tiwanaku was more than "ideological influence" or "exchange." Such simplistic and relatively ethnocentric terms, although still commonly used in Andean archaeology, do little more than caricaturize the complex and dynamic Lukurmata–Tiwanaku relationship.

In summary, the archaeology of the Tiwanaku political formation lacks many of the material correlates of statecraft characteristic of the best-known Andean polities. Yet at the same time, the Tiwanaku polity engaged in some similar activities, such as massive agrarian projects. At the site and household levels, the Tiwanaku polity displays several close parallels to the Wari and Inca empires. However, at the regional level, the Tiwanaku polity seems to have been integrated quite differently than the Wari and Inca empires, lacking in particular the extended administrative hierarchy and the elements of a "territorial" mode of control. In differing from the Wari and Inca polities, Tiwanaku is a valuable reminder that prehispanic statecraft in the Andes could, and probably did, take more than one form.

The Inca have served as a powerful comparative template for understanding many prehispanic Andean polities, but we must not assume that the Inca polity represented the only kind of state to exist prior to the arrival of Europeans. The Inca state should not be used as the standard against which to measure or define other prehispanic political formations. Recognition of other types of state organization may require different lines of evidence (domestic remains, for instance), and the use of other ethnographic or historical analogues.

Summary Implications of this Study

I have interpreted the Lukurmata sequence of domestic remains as revealing: (1) a shift from a simple household unit with a limited range of productive activities to a household unit showing signs of having its production increased as it entered the Tiwanaku system; (2) a subsequent shift to more complex and differentiated household units when Lukurmata became a second-order center in the Tiwanaku state; and (3) a return to a simple household unit after the state system collapsed. This development of Lukurmata household units as well as contemporaneous site and regional development suggest that surplus mobilization was a significant part of the Tiwanaku political economy. Although the number of household units excavated is insufficient to document the complete range of mobilization strategies in operation, both intra- and extrahousehold strategies appear to have been used.

At the same time, however, the Lukurmata household unit sequence demonstrates that the incorporation of communities outside the capital into larger political units may have little or no effect at the household level. The similarities between the terminal Tiwanaku III period and early Tiwanaku IV period structures and their contents indicate that the Lukurmata households' interaction with the Tiwanaku III period polity was little different from their interaction with the Tiwanaku IV period state, at least initially. One interpretation of this continuity in household life is that the differences between the Tiwanaku III polity (perhaps a chiefdom) and the vastly larger and more complex Tiwanaku IV polity (a state) may not be very important at the household level. Furthermore, the most striking shift in domestic organization occurred late in the Tiwanaku IV period, implying that as yet unknown processes had greater impact at the Lukurmata household level than did either initial incorporation into the Tiwanaku polity or the regional-level transformation in the Tiwanaku polity early in the Tiwanaku IV period.

If nothing else, the fact that household changes did not always coincide with changes in ceramic styles should cause us to reevaluate our ideas concerning the recognition of societal change in the archaeological record, and the need for complementing regional approaches with comparable studies at the subregional level.

The emphasis on regional approaches in archaeology has greatly added to our knowledge of prehistoric polities and how they evolve, but it has also left us with only a partial view and only a general understanding of these societies. The emphasis on regional approaches has inevitably led to construction of an Andean past in which regional orders, macrolevel changes, and the "rise and fall" of states are presented as the most important elements of Andean prehistory.

Andean archaeology has long tended to equate significant processes of change in the past with shifts in regional patterns. The adequacy of this perspective should be challenged. The great states may not have been as homogeneous or as integrated as we have often assumed, making the recognition of historical continuities at many levels critical to understanding the archaeological record presented by the prehispanic polities.

The goal of a "local perspective" is not to arrive at generalizations for household change that are comparable or parallel to observed regional-level processes. Nor should the "local perspective" have as its goal the treatment of a single site as a "microcosm" of larger systems. We should not interpret the archaeological record as the independent evolution of many settlements, or set out to recast Andean prehistory in the Indian image of timeless villages (see Chapter 1). Household archaeology cannot replace regional study.

Instead, I have suggested that documentation of regional shifts is only one method of examining social change in the past. Regional studies do not provide equal insight into all dimensions of social change. Each "version" of prehistory—regional, "capital-centric," "local," or household—can capture only part of the complex process of social change. Focusing on one to the exclusion of others will result in a distorted and incomplete prehistory (Roseberry 1991:41). The goal of the "local perspective" is to provide a complementary paradigm that will lead to a more balanced view of prehistoric societal change. Research at alternative spatial scales will illuminate processes of change and evolution in past societies not visible to regional approaches alone. By developing and integrating alternative perspectives, we will also become more aware of the biases inherent in every approach, and how these biases shape our research.

An Andean archaeology focused on local diachronic development and on household-level changes, rather than on ceramic style distributions, would generate a very different view and understanding of Andean prehistory. Whether this "household" understanding is "more important" than the current one depends partly on which aspects of social life are considered important. Ultimately, the "enduring structures of domestic life" may be more useful for forging an understanding of past societal evolution than designs on pots (Braudel 1981). In arguing for complementary approaches, I am saying that, at the least, household evolution is a line of evidence that deserves to be considered.

SYNTHESIS

The main points raised by this study are as follows.

1. A focus on households provides a different perspective on evolution and social change at second- and third-order sites in regional hierarchies. Comparing the timing and nature of change at the household level to changes in site structure and changes in participation in the overarching system reveals that changes at the household level are not congruent with changes at higher social levels.

2. Different aspects of domestic life (the architecture of dwellings, household technology or contents, preferences in pottery style), if considered individually, provide different pictures of change over time at the household level. This fact has important implications for the formulation of appropriate research methodologies. If we exclusively excavate house remains, midden areas, mortuary contexts, or public architecture, we may develop distorted reconstructions of diachronic change at sites, since any one of these contexts might present a unique sequence of change over time. These different lines of evidence need to be integrated to arrive at a meaningful understanding of change in prehistoric societies.

3. There was a significant amount of continuity in household organization, regardless of the degree of Lukurmata's incorporation into larger political units. There were also important changes in household organization resulting from Lukurmata's interaction with the Tiwanaku system. Continuity and change coexist, and both are significant and deserving of study. Although continuity is often less exciting to archaeologists than sweeping changes, the long persistence of many aspects of Lukurmata household life, the long continuities in what people did every day (universal household activities) have important implications for understanding the prehispanic household as an adaptive unit.

4. Lukurmata was a dynamic settlement in its own right; not all changes in household life were the result of interaction with Tiwanaku. This perspective contrasts with "capital-centric" approaches that treat only the capital as dynamic, while smaller sites are thought to be passive dependents, "microcosms" of the capital.

5. Mobilization of surplus appears to have been an element of Tiwanaku political economy. The Lukurmata household sequence suggests that such mobilization occurred via intra- and extrahousehold strategies. Surplus mobilization by overarching political bodies may have been an important stimulus for household change at Lukur-

mata. When Tiwanaku collapsed, the Lukurmata household unit "reverted" to a pre-Tiwanaku period pattern, resembling household units at Lukurmata prior to the site's incorporation into the Tiwanaku polity.

THE Lukurmata research has increased our understanding of the Tiwanaku polity in several ways. These can be summarized in the following four points.

1. The Pampa Koani raised fields, the evolution of Lukurmata as a settlement, and the sequence of household change at Lukurmata suggest large-scale surplus mobilization by the Tiwanaku polity during the Tiwanaku IV period. These changes support the idea that the Tiwanaku political formation was, in fact, a state rather than simply a trade or religious network.

2. The evolution of Lukurmata and the Pampa Koani indicate territorial rather than hegemonic control of at least some domains by the Tiwanaku polity. Yet this was a "territorial" pattern of control (i.e., direct administration, high extraction) lacking the material correlates most commonly believed by archaeologists to be indicators of such control. It is the lack of these Wari/Inca-type territorial elements (large-scale storage complexes, specialized sites) that has made it difficult to recognize Tiwanaku as an imperial state. The evolution of Lukurmata and its households suggests that these mobilization strategies may have existed.

3. Household and community data suggest that the Tiwanaku and Inca polities may have mobilized surplus from producing units in similar ways. If only regional data were examined, the two polities would appear very different, perhaps leading to the conclusion that Tiwanaku was a "hegemonic" polity, in contrast to the Inca territorial mode of control.

4. The Tiwanaku state achieved the same ends (increased surplus production) as the Wari and Inca polities, but with somewhat different means. It maintained a high extraction system, without many of the "typical" material correlates (specialized sites and architecture) that characterized such a system in other prehistoric states. The archaeology of the Tiwanaku polity therefore suggests that the Wari/Inca form of organization was not the only mode of regional integration in the prehispanic Andes.

CONCLUSION

Upon analysis, any archaeological record spanning a long period will reveal some change through time in the composition of artifact assemblages or in artifact styles. As Rogers (1990:102) has noted, this inherent change, "coupled with analogies and assumptions about culture change (often remaining implicit), form the basis of archaeological studies of cultural change." A first step in reconstructing prehistoric social change is identifying points of change in the material record, usually with reference to particular categories of archaeological remains (ibid.:103). In Andean archaeology, the categories of material remains used to define social change have generally been limited to pottery styles or aspects of regional settlement patterns. Implicit assumptions about the significance of pottery style preferences, and a "capital-centric" perspective, have long guided interpretation of prehispanic Andean social change. However, the actual connection between social changes in Andean prehistory and changes in either category of material remains (pottery or regional settlement patterns) is far from clear. This lack of clarity is due in part to a failure to examine in a systematic fashion the relationship between changes in material remains and cultural change (Rogers 1990). It is also the result of not utilizing alternative measures of change (such as domestic remains), or of not comparing the timing and nature of change at different societal levels.

As this volume demonstrates, our knowledge of life at one societal level in the prehispanic south-central Andes—that of the household—is still rudimentary. The type of "local perspective" investigation I conducted at Lukurmata has not been attempted elsewhere in the region. As a consequence, my own interpretations are limited by the lack of comparative information from other sites. Much household archaeology has focused on exposing large numbers of contemporary structures in order to reconstruct synchronic sociopolitical organization. While a "local perspective" is unorthodox in Andean archaeology, I hope excavations that trace the development of communities over long periods of time will be more common in the future.

My interpretations of the Lukurmata data have other limitations. Excavation of house remains is time-consuming. As a result, most investigations, mine included, are only able to gather information on a few dwellings, limiting the scope of generalizations and making all conclusions tentative. I was extremely fortunate to encounter at Lukurmata an area with a long sequence of superimposed housefloors. But while this sequence provided a unique diachronic perspective, the synchronic variation in the residential occupation at Lukurmata remains relatively unexplored.

In this volume I have argued that domestic remains are:

- a class of evidence that, of itself, can be used to address broad issues of cultural evolution.
- a line of archaeological evidence essential for exploring patterns, relationships, forces, and processes not readily apparent at the regional level.
- natural units of analysis for measuring the nature and degree of "tradition" (cultural continuity) and cultural change.

Household archaeology in other parts of the world has demonstrated its potential, but in Andean archaeology, domestic remains are frequently still considered little more than handy containers for decorated pottery, material markers of ethnic or cultural "identity," materials for reconstructing household activities, or a convenient setting in which to examine archaeological formation processes. Only within the past decade have Andean archaeologists begun to use domestic remains to address broad questions of sociopolitical evolution and culture change (Bawden 1982, 1990; Costin and Earle 1989; Hastorf 1990a, 1990b; Stanish 1992).

Preconceptions about prehispanic households and their relationships to larger political orders, often based on ethnographic analogy and accompanied by (in Roseberry's phrase) "formulaic references to the household as a unit of production," have led archaeologists away from fully exploring the nature of prehispanic households, intrahousehold dynamics, the relationships between households, and the place of households in larger sociopolitical and adaptive frameworks (Roseberry 1991:22).

The purpose of this study is *not* to argue that any house forms were "typical" of a particular period of settlement at Lukurmata. We did not excavate a large enough sample of structures to allow this conclusion. Nor was the sample of dwellings large enough to compensate for the natural variation inherent in the household cycle. Two very different household units may represent a similar household at different stages in the household cycle (Hirth 1993; Sheehy 1991; Tourtellot 1988). Instead, I have tried to show how a set of domestic remains can be variously interpreted so as to provide new insights into prehispanic social change that complement traditional site- and regional-level approaches. A household archaeology that treats households as historically structured, culturally meaningful units integrated into larger systems will refine our understanding of social change and cultural evolution.

APPENDIXES

I

Tabular Household Data: Features and Artifacts Used in Analyzing Lukurmata Domestic Occupations

Feature	Use	Area Excavated (m²)	Estimated Interior Area (m²)	Indoor Hearth Area (ct.)	Indoor Hearth Area (m²)	Indoor Pits (ct.)	Pit Vol. (m³)	Ceramic ct.	Ceramic wt. (g)	Faunal ct.	Faunal wt. (g)
1	housefloor	9.7	14	0	–	0	–	7	36.	16	45.
37–1	outdoor surface	20.0						88	627.	129	660.
37–2	hearth	.04									
37–3	refuse pit	.08 m³									
37–4	refuse pit	.07 m³									
3	housefloor	2.7	8.5	0	–	0	–	28	189.	33	47.
4	housefloor	0	–	–	–	–	–				
35–1	outdoor surface	9.40						64	416.	98	265.
35–2	outdoor surface	3.20						55	202.	46	109.
35–3	Hearth A	.07						5	12.	8	20.
35–4	Hearth B	.09						2	5.	5	18.
35–5	Hearth C	.32						34	398.	9	11.
35–6	midden	2.00						181	1176.	209	1045.
7	housefloor	8.4	9.3	?	–	0	–	16	120.	21	124.
35–1	hearth	.39 m³						74	1033.	88	329.
9	housefloor	15.53	16	1	.16	0	–	94	879.	91	634.
10	housefloor	3.75	–	–	–	–	–	11	75.	16	82.
30–1	refuse pit	.08						16	77.	6	24.
30–2	refuse pit	.10						7	39.	48	148.
30–3	refuse pit	.28						40	220.	27	198.
30–4	refuse pit	.18						5	45.	2	5.
30–5	outdoor surface	3.0						53	647.	16	105.
30–6	outdoor surface	3.0						41	202.	23	119.
13	floor/ surface										
14	housefloor	11.7	13	1	.23	1	.07	34	287.	23	145.
15	housefloor	6.7	–	–	–	–	–	51	810.	36	250.
16	housefloor	13.9	16	1	.13	1	.02	31	310.	20	89.
17	housefloor	9.9	12	–	–	1	.10	29	353.	3	17.

Feature	Use	Area Excavated (m²)	Estimated Interior Area (m²)	Indoor Hearth Area (ct.)	Indoor Hearth Area (m²)	Indoor Pits (ct.)	Pit Vol. (m³)	Ceramic ct.	Ceramic wt. (g)	Faunal ct.	Faunal wt. (g)
18	housefloor	1.5	–	–	–	–		10	141.	6	50.
28–1	clay pit	.72						0	–	0	–
28–2	midden/ surface	1.80						234	2806.	73	373.
28–3	midden/ surface	3.40						202	1880.	331	1423.
28–4	outdoor surface	0.80						15	113.	22	78.
28–5	outdoor surface	1.50						37	155.	87	367.
28–6	hearth	.18									
19	housefloor	22.1	20	1	.20	0	–	49	985.	40	90.
20	housefloor	3.3	–	–	–	–	–	7	128.	9	25.
21	housefloor	1.0	–	–	–	–	–	0	–	0	–
26–1	outdoor surface	6.0						313	2577.	170	1204.
22	housefloor	16.8	28.0	1	.25	–	–	68	496.	133	612.
23	housefloor	14.5	19.5	1	.22	–	–	40	324.	51	205.
24	housefloor	3.9	6.0	0	–	0	–	4	27.	2	12.
24–1	hearth/pits	3.70						154	1878.	117	276.
24–2	outdoor surface	1.80						30	130.	41	184.
24–3	outdoor surface	.40						12	62.	7	18.
24–4	midden	.90 m³						306	2900.	482	2080.
24–5	pit	.80						14	96.	48	221.
24–6	pit	.60						2	12.	3	11.
24–7	pit	.20						3	10.	9	62.
24–8	pit	.20						12	171.	27	124.
24–9	pit	.20						9	19.	21	133.
25	housefloor	4.4	–					12	82.	11	35.
26	housefloor	24.0	31.5	1	.13	2	.15	63	951.	66	179.
27	housefloor	25.0	37.5					47	672.	79	245.
28	housefloor	5.2	–					17	110.	9	49.
23–1	outdoor surface	4.8						12	122.	5	27.
23–2	midden	3.5						731	11542.	254	1014.
23–3	midden	10.2						1890	11398.	1092	3083.
23–4	midden	3.7						239	1601.	270	805.
23–5	outdoor surface	4.0						31	146.	16	75.

Feature	Use	Area Excavated (m²)	Estimated Interior Area (m²)	Indoor Hearth Area (ct.)	Indoor Hearth Area (m²)	Indoor Pits (ct.)	Pit Vol. (m³)	Ceramic ct.	Ceramic wt. (g)	Faunal ct.	Faunal wt. (g)
33	housefloor	7.6	–	–	–	–	–	69	686.	88	379.
34	housefloor	16.0	–	–	–	–	–	41	1218.	23	53.
35	housefloor	14.6	–	1	.12	2	.54	288	5127.	341	1360.
36	housefloor	14.1	31.5	1	.28	1	.66	84	488.	64	192.
37	housefloor	24.8	35.0	0	–	0	–	23	814.	18	49.
38	housefloor	17.1	26.0	2	.52	2	1.12	117	1832.	60	152.
39	housefloor	9.91	–	–	–	–	–	35	168.	73	132.
42	housefloor	6.3	7.0	1	.20	0	–				
20–1	terrace										
20–2	Patio B	14.5	24.0	1	.19	–	–	164	574.	254	1169.
20–3	Patio A	11.1	22.0	1	.20	–	–	389	3008.	423	2116.
20–4	outdoor surface	3.5						90	1249.	137	433.
20–5	outdoor surface	1.1						59	401.	23	164.
20–6	outdoor surface	2.0						121	640.	61	219.
20–7	midden	3.4						688	12944.	705	8530.
20–8	refuse pit	.02						3	21.	6	18.
20–9	refuse pit	.03						10	31.	18	45.
20–10	outdoor hearth	.04						4	44.	6	20.
20–11	refuse pit	.26						13	174.	77	145.
20–12	refuse pit	.27						55	502.	47	92.
43	housefloor	10.3	21.5	1	.21	0	–	277	2198.	134	407.
4–1	outdoor surface	2.0						9	62.	11	37.
4–2	outdoor surface	2.3						45	1345.	16	33.
4–3	outdoor hearth	.12						6	17.	3	8.

11

Faunal Remains from Lukurmata
Domestic Occupations

(a) BONE COUNTS AND PERCENTAGES

Occupation[a]	Camelid/Deer		Bird		Other		Unknown	
	ct.	%	ct.	%	ct.	%	ct.	%
1	115	(79.3)	21	(14.5)	6	(4.1)	3	(2.1)
3–4	321	(78.7)	69	(16.9)	9	(2.2)	9	(2.2)
7	81	(80.2)	14	(13.8)	5	(4.9)	1	(0.9)
9–10	184	(80.3)	29	(12.7)	6	(2.6)	10	(4.4)
14–18	549	(91.3)	26	(4.3)	17	(2.8)	9	(1.5)
19	199	(90.9)	8	(3.7)	9	(4.1)	3	(1.4)
22–24	895	(95.1)	29	(3.1)	11	(1.2)	6	(0.6)
25–28	1755	(97.4)	24	(1.3)	21	(1.2)	2	(0.1)
33–39	2356	(97.2)	46	(1.9)	13	(0.5)	9	(0.4)
43	142	(86.6)	15	(9.1)	6	(3.7)	1	(0.6)

[a] Included for each occupation are faunal remains from floors, floor contact zones, associated features, and associated deposits.

(b) PERCENTAGE OF BIRD BONE BY OCCUPATION

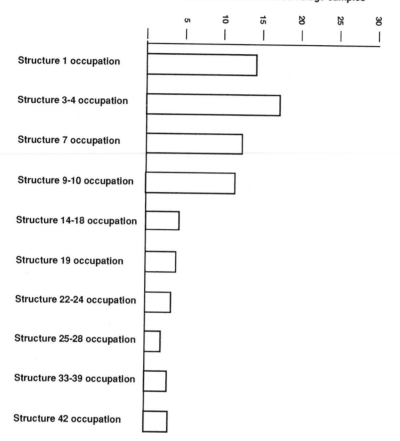

III

Radiocarbon Dates from Lukurmata
Domestic Contexts

Lab #	Material	Context	Corrected Age	Calibrated Date
SMU 2164	carbon	below floor of Structure 38 (N 2890 E 2921, Level 20)	2100 ± 240 B.P.	180 ± 290 B.C.
SMU 2116	carbon	refuse pit outside Structure 1 (N 2896 E2915, Level 37)	2000 ± 60 B.P.	20 ± 80 B.C.
SMU 2118	carbon	floor of Structure 11 (N 2896 E 2915, Level 29)	1620 ± 70 B.P.	430 ± 80 A.D.
SMU 2120	carbon	refuse pit outside Structure 13 (N2886 E2855)	1750 ± 250 B.P.	270 ± 280 A.D.
ETH 3177	wood frag.	below floor of Structure 29 (N 2888 E 2929, Level 23)	1340 ± 95 B.P.	680 ± 80 A.D.
ETH 3174	woody plant	outdoor hearth west of Structure 38 in Patio B	1180 ± 80 B.P.	840 ± 115 A.D.
ETH 3180	carbon	hearth below Tiwanaku V period outdoor surface (N 2859 E 3110, Level 18)	990 ± 95 B.P.	1045 ± 100 A.D.
SMU 1920	carbonized loam and carbon	Structure 42 hearth	1201 ± 96 B.P.	818 ± 110 A.D.

Calibration of radiocarbon to dendroyears from Stuiver and Pearson 1986. Dates are according to Libby half-life subtracted from A.D. 1950.

IV

Regional Time Chart

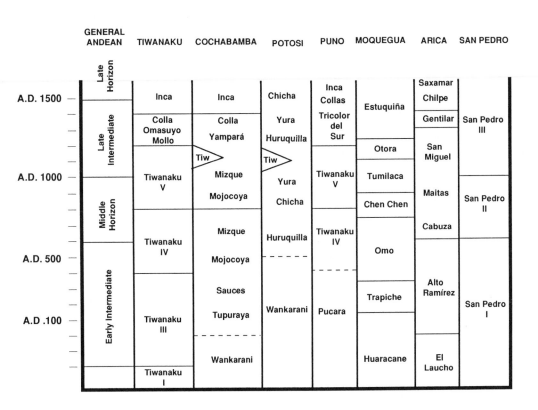

	GENERAL ANDEAN	TIWANAKU	COCHABAMBA	POTOSI	PUNO	MOQUEGUA	ARICA	SAN PEDRO
A.D. 1500	Late Horizon	Inca	Inca	Chicha	Inca Collas	Estuquiña	Saxamar Chilpe	
	Late Intermediate	Colla Omasuyo Mollo	Colla Yampará	Yura Huruquilla	Tricolor del Sur		Gentilar	San Pedro III
		Tiw	Tiw Mizque	Tiw Yura		Otora	San Miguel	
A.D. 1000		Tiwanaku V	Mojocoya	Chicha	Tiwanaku V	Tumilaca	Maitas	San Pedro II
	Middle Horizon					Chen Chen		
		Tiwanaku IV	Mizque	Huruquilla	Tiwanaku IV		Cabuza	
A.D. 500			Mojocoya	– – – –		Omo		
	Early Intermediate		Sauces	Wankarani	Pucara	Trapiche	Alto Ramírez	San Pedro I
A.D. 100		Tiwanaku III	Tupuraya					
			– – – –					
			Wankarani			Huaracane	El Laucho	
		Tiwanaku I						

Field Designations of Burials Mentioned in the Text

Burial Designations Used in This Volume	1986–87 Field Designations			Burial Designations Used in This Volume	1986–87 Field Designations		
1	N2892	E2919	Feature 5	22	N2892	E2923	Feature 2
2	N2892	E2919	Feature 7	23	N2892	E2923	Feature 3
3	N2892	E2919	Feature 6	24	N2892	E2923	Feature 4
4	N2892	E2919	Feature 9	25	N2894	E2923	Feature 2
5	N2892	E2919	Feature 8	26	N2894	E2923	Feature 5
6	N2896	E2915	Feature 11	27	N2894	E2911	Feature 10
7	N2888	E2917	Feature 10	28	N2894	E2913	Feature 1
8	N2892	E2919	Feature 10	29	N2898	E2917	Feature 5
9	N2886	E2917	Feature 10	30	N2890	E2925	Feature 1
10	N2894	E2915	Feature 12	32	N2894	E2923	Feature 1
11	N2896	E2913	Feature 5	34	N2894	E2915	Feature 2
12	N2894	E2913	Feature 3	35	N2894	E2915	Feature 5
13	N2896	E2913	Feature CB	36	N2890	E2913	Feature 8
14	N2892	E2919	Feature 3	37	N2892	E2913	Feature 2
15	N2892	E2919	Feature 4	39	N2896	E2915	SW
16	N2888	E2915	Feature 9	40	N2894	E2913	Feature 2
17	N2892	E2917	Feature 10	47	N2898	E2915	SW
18	N2896	E2915	Feature 23	48	N2888	E2913	Feature 5
19	N2896	E2909	Feature 30/10	49	N2888	E2915	Feature 5
20	N2892	E2913	Feature 5	51	N2896	E2915	Feature 10
21	N2892	E2923	Feature 1				

VI

Ceramic Descriptions

Fig. 4.3   PASTE AND TEMPER: Orange color, fully fired, medium grained, well-knit. Temper consists of 0.3–0.8 mm sand.
SURFACE TREATMENT: Orange (2.5YR 5/6) wiped, no slip.

Fig. 4.4   *Lorokea Fiber*
Fig. 4.5   PASTE AND TEMPER: Dark gray brown (5YR 2.5/2) color, gray core, fine
Fig. 4.6   grained, medium-knit. Temper consists of 0.5–0.8 mm vegetable fiber, mica.
Fig. 4.7a   SURFACE TREATMENT: Exterior and interior surfaces range from dark brown to very dark gray in color, unslipped, roughly smoothed.

Fig. 4.7b   *Thin Redware*
PASTE AND TEMPER: Red orange (7.5YR 3/0) or orange (5YR 6/6) color, gray black core. Paste of the smaller versions is fine grained and well knit. Paste of the larger bowls is slightly more porous. Temper consists of 0.3–1.0 mm vegetable fiber and 0.1–0.3 mm gold mica.
SURFACE TREATMENT: Exterior and interior surface colors range from orange (5YR 6/6) to orange brown (5YR 4/3), unslipped, wiped.

Fig. 5.4   *Tiwanaku I-Style Red-on-Chestnut Bowls*
PASTE AND TEMPER: Light orange brown (2.5YR 5/6–7.5YR 6/4) color, light gray core, fine grained, slightly porous. Temper consists of fine sand, and red, white, and gray mineral fragments.
SURFACE TREATMENT: Dark red (10R 4/6) burnished slip over light orange brown (2.5YR 5/6) paste on exterior. Interior is unslipped, wiped.
DECORATION: Some specimens have a dark gray horizontal line below the band of red slip on the exterior.

Fig. 5.5a   PASTE AND TEMPER: Orange (2.5YR 5/6) color, fully fired, medium grained, well-knit. Temper not visible.
SURFACE TREATMENT: Orange (2.5YR 5/6) burnished exterior, no slip. Interior is unslipped, wiped.
DECORATION: Incising and black (2.5YR 2/0) paint.

Fig. 5.5c   PASTE AND TEMPER: Light brown to dark gray, fine grained, well-knit. Temper consists of 0.2–1.0 mm gold mica, sand.
SURFACE TREATMENT: Gray brown (10YR 3/2) polished exterior slip. Interior is unslipped, wiped, and displays paja marks.
DECORATION: Paint-filled incising

not   *Queruni Orangeware*
illustrated PASTE AND TEMPER: Bright orange (10YR 7/3) color, fully fired, fine grained, compact, well-knit. Temper consists of 0.2 mm gold, white, mineral fragments (sand?).
SURFACE TREATMENT: Orange (5YR 5/4–2.5YR 5/6) roughly smoothed or wiped, often with horizontal wiping marks, exterior and interior.

Fig. 5.8   PASTE AND TEMPER: Orange (5YR 6/6) color, gray core, fine grained, well-knit. Temper consists of 0.2–5.5 mm sand (?).
SURFACE TREATMENT: Dark red (10R 4/6) burnished slip on exterior to within 2 cm of vessel base. Remainder of vessel exterior is orange (5YR 6/6) unslipped, slightly burnished. Interior has red slip just below vessel lip. Remainder of interior is orange (5YR 6/6) unslipped, slightly burnished.

Fig. 5.10   PASTE AND TEMPER: Orange (10R 4/6) color, fully fired, medium grained, well-knit. Temper consists of 0.8–6.0 mm vegetable fiber, 0.2–1.0 mm gold mica.
SURFACE TREATMENT: Exterior has light orange (10R 4/6) wash or slip smoothed over the "wings" and "upper back." Remainder of exterior is light orange brown (2.5YR 5/6), unslipped, smoothed.
DECORATION: Plastic modeling.

Fig. 8.11   *Cutini Creamware*
Fig. 8.12   PASTE AND TEMPER: Red brown (2.5YR 5/6) color, black core, medium grained, medium-knit, slightly porous. Temper consists of coarse, 1.3–13.3 mm vegetable fiber.
SURFACE TREATMENT: Very light brown (7.5YR 7/4) smoothed slip on exterior. Interior is the color of the paste (2.5YR 4/4–2.5YR 5/6), unslipped, wiped.
DECORATION: Dark brown (5YR 2.5/2), red (5YR 4/4), and orange (7.5YR 5/8) painted nongeometric designs on exterior. Specimen shown (a large jar) exhibits plastic decoration in the form of a raised midbody plaque (8 cm x ? cm).

Fig. 8.14   *Tiwanaku III Polychrome*
Fig. 8.15   PASTE AND TEMPER: Light brown (7.5YR 7/4 or 7.5YR 6/4)
Fig. 8.16   color, fully fired to a light gray core, fine grained, well-
Fig. 8.17   knit to slightly porous. Temper consists of 0.5–1.0 cm fragments of a
Fig. 8.19   soft red mineral, and gold mica.
SURFACE TREATMENT: Light brown (7.5YR 7/4), unslipped, slightly burnished to polished.
DECORATION: Black (2.5Y 2/0), white (10YR 8/1), dark brown (2.5YR 3/2), red (7.5R 3/6), and orange (2.5YR 5/8) painted designs (step, antler, and interlocking triangle). Decoration applied prior to burnishing.

Fig. 8.18   PASTE AND TEMPER: Light brown (7.5YR 7/4) color, gray core, fine grained, well-knit with occasional air pockets. Temper consists of 0.2–1.5 mm soft red mineral.
SURFACE TREATMENT: Light brown (7.5YR 7/4) polished, unslipped exterior and interior.
DECORATION: Black (2.5Y 2/0) and white (10YR 8/1) painted geometric design (interlocking triangles).

Fig. 8.20   PASTE AND TEMPER: Very light brown (7.5YR 7/6) color, gray core, fine grained, well-knit with occasional air pockets. Temper consists of 0.3–1.2 mm gold mica and soft red mineral.
SURFACE TREATMENT: Light brown (7.5YR 7/6) polished, unslipped exterior; light brown (7.5YR 7/6) rough interior.
DECORATION: Dark brown (2.5YR 3/2), red (7.5R 3/6), orange (2.5YR 5/8), and white (5YR 8/1) painted geometric design (interlocking triangle).

Fig. 8.22a   PASTE AND TEMPER: Brown orange (5YR 5/6) color, dark gray core, medium grained, poorly knit. Temper consists of 1.7–6.4 mm vegetable fiber, 0.2–1.0 mm gold mica.

SURFACE TREATMENT: Brown orange (5YR 5/6), unslipped roughly smoothed exterior and interior with fiber burnouts.

DECORATION: Raised band and punctations made with the end of a reed.

Fig. 8.22b   *"Imitation" Tiwanaku III Polychrome*
PASTE AND TEMPER: Light brown (7.5YR 7/4) color, black core, medium grained, slightly porous. Temper consists of 2.0–6.5 mm vegetable fiber, 0.2–1.1 mm gold mica.

SURFACE TREATMENT: Orange (2.5YR 4/8) burnished slip on exterior. Light brown (7.5YR 7/4) smoothed, unslipped interior.

DECORATION: Dark brown (2.5YR 3/2), red (10R 4/8), and white (7.5YR 8/4) painted geometric design (interlocking triangle).

Fig. 9.5a   *Tiwanaku III Ceremonial Burner*
Fig. 9.5b   PASTE AND TEMPER: Dark gray (7.5YR 7/0) color, fully fired, fine grained, well-knit. Temper consists of 0.3–1.0 mm gold mica, soft red mineral.

SURFACE TREAMENT: Orange (7.5YR 7/4) to gray (7.5YR 4/0) smoothed, unslipped exterior and interior.

DECORATION: Prefiring grooving of geometric designs (step) filled with red, white, or orange paint.

Fig. 10.6   PASTE AND TEMPER: Orange (5YR 6/6) color, gray core; fine grained, medium-knit. Temper consists of 0.9–2.8 mm vegetable fiber, 0.3–0.5 mm white mineral and gold mica.

SURFACE TREATMENT: Dark red (10R 4/6) burnished slip exterior. Orange (5YR 6/6) unsmoothed, unslipped interior.

DECORATION: Black (5YR 2.5/2), white (10YR 8/1), orange (2.5YR 6/8), gray (N5/) paint.

Fig. 11.2   *Tiwanaku V Polychrome*
PASTE AND TEMPER: Orange (2.5YR 6/4) color, slight gray core; medium grained; medium-knit paste. Temper consists of 0.2–0.4 mm gold mica.

SURFACE FINISH: Red (10R 4/6) burnished slip on exterior. Red slip extends partway down interior, remainder of interior is orange (2.5YR 6/4) smoothed, unslipped.

DECORATION: Black (5YR 2.5/1) and orange (2.5YR 6/8) paint depicting head of Staff God.

Fig. 11.3a   *Tiwanaku Polished Blackware*
PASTE AND TEMPER: Yellow gray (10YR 5/4) color, fully fired; fine grained, well-knit. Temper consists of 0.3–0.5 mm white mineral and gold mica.

SURFACE TREATMENT: Black (2.5Y 2/0) polished, unslipped exterior. Wiped, unslipped interior.

Fig. 11.3b   PASTE AND TEMPER: Light orange brown (5YR 7/6) color, fully fired, fine grained, well-knit. Temper consists of 0.1–0.3 mm gold mica.

SURFACE TREATMENT: Red (2.5YR 4/4) burnished slip exterior and interior.

DECORATION: Black (7.5YR 2/0) paint.

Fig. 11.5   *Tiwanaku IV Polychrome*
PASTE AND TEMPER: Dark orange (5YR 6/6) color, fully fired, fine grained, well-knit. Temper consists of 0.1–0.3 m gold mica.

SURFACE TREATMENT: Gray (2.5YR 4/0) highly burnished slip on exterior. Dark orange (2.5YR 5/6) burnished, unslipped interior.

DECORATION: Orange (2.5YR 6/8) and dark red (2.5YR 2.5/2) painted anthropomorphic design (Sacrificer).

Fig. 11.6   *Tiwanaku IV Polychrome*
PASTE AND TEMPER: Light orange brown (5YR 7/6) color, fully fired, fine grained, well-knit. Temper consists of 0.1–0.3 m gold mica.
SURFACE TREATMENT: Red (2.5YR 4/4) burnished slip on exterior. Dark orange (2.5YR 5/6) burnished, unslipped interior.
DECORATION: Orange (2.5YR 6/8), white (5YR 8/1), gray (5YR 4/1), and black (7.5YR 2/0) painted zoomorphic design (feline).

Fig 11.18   PASTE AND TEMPER: not visible
SURFACE TREATMENT: Red orange (5YR 6/6) slip on exterior and interior.

Fig.11.19   *Lillimani Creamware*
PASTE AND TEMPER: Buff to very light brown (7.5YR 7/4) color, often a gray core, medium grained, poorly knit and porous, occasional air pockets. Temper consists of crushed sherds and 0.3–1.0 mm black and white mineral.
SURFACE TREATMENT: Buff or very light brown (5 YR 7/3–7.5YR 7/4), smoothed to slightly burnished, slipped exterior. Gray-brown (10YR 5/1) wiped, unslipped interiors, often with visible wiping marks.
DECORATION: Black (5YR 3/2), dark brown (2.5 YR3/2), and orange (2.5YR 4/8) painted short curvilinear segments and very dark brown to black straight lines ranging from 0.5 cm to 1.5 cm wide.

Fig. 11.20
Fig. 11.21   *Tanware*
PASTE AND TEMPER: Very light brown (7.5YR 7/4) color, fully fired, fine grained, slightly porous. Temper consists of 0.3–0.9 mm gold mica, but 15 percent of simple volute design flaring-sided bowls have soft red mineral temper as well.
SURFACE TREATMENT: Very light brown (7.5YR 6/6), smoothed, unslipped exterior and interior. Simple volute design flaring-sided bowls frequently have a red (2.5YR 7/4), burnished slip on the interior. The "Starwares" variant displays an orange (5YR 6/6) burnished slip on exterior and interior.
DECORATION: On the basis of painted decoration, usually limited to the vessel exterior, the Tanwares can be divided into four variants: (1) Gatoware Variant (Figure 11.20b)—simple black (7.5YR 3/0) dots and triangles; (2) Simple Volute—volute motif in orange (5YR 6/8) and black (2.5YR 2.5/0); (3) Starwares Variant (Figure 11.20a)—complex, polychrome volute-star motif in red (10R 3/6), black (5YR 2.5/1), and (occasionally) white; and (4) 3–4-II Variant—polychrome "sun" figures in black, orange, and (occasionally) white. This design is an elaboration of the Simple Volute design.

Fig. 12.6a   *Non-Tiwanaku*
PASTE AND TEMPER: White (5YR 7/1) fully fired, fine grained, medium-knit. Temper consists of 0.3–0.7 mm black mineral.
SURFACE TREATMENT: Gray white (5YR 7/1) burnished, unslipped exterior and interior.
DECORATION: Orange-red (2.5TY 4/1) paint.

Fig. 12.6b   *Tiwanaku IV Black-on-Red*
PASTE AND TEMPER: Gray orange (5YR 7/4) fully fired, medium grained, well-knit. Temper consists of 0.3–0.5 mm gold mica.

SURFACE TREATMENT: Red (10R 4/6) highly burnished slip exterior. Orange (5YR 7/6) wiped, unslipped interior.
DECORATION: Black (10YR 2/1) painted design (volute).

Fig. 12.9   PASTE AND TEMPER: Brown orange (5YR 6/6) color, fully fired, medium grained, slightly porous.
SURFACE TREATMENT: Orange red (10R 4/8) polished slip exterior. Orange (5YR 6/6) burnished, unslipped interior.
DECORATION: Black (5YR 2.5/1) painted decoration on interior of neck.

Fig. 12.11   *Pantini Orangeware*
PASTE AND TEMPER: Orange (5YR 6/6) color, slight gray core, medium grained, well-knit. Temper consists of 0.2–1.5 mm gold mica.
SURFACE TREATMENT: Orange red (10R 5/8) smoothed slip exterior. Orange (5YR 6/6) smoothed, unslipped exterior.
DECORATION: Black (2.5YR 5/0) paint.

Fig. 12.15 a   PASTE AND TEMPER: Light yellow brown (7.5YR 7/4) to orange color, medium to coarse grained, poorly knit, porous paste. Temper consists of 0.4–1.0 gold mica and sand.
SURFACE FINISH: Light yellow brown (7.5YR 7/4), smoothed, unslipped interior and exterior.

Fig. 12.15b   PASTE AND TEMPER: Orange brown (7.5YR 6/4) color, fully fired, coarse grained, medium-knit. Temper consists of 0.4–1.0 gold mica and sand.
SURFACE FINISH: Whitish gray (7.5YR 5/0) wash on wiped, unslipped exterior. Orange brown (7.5YR 6/4) wiped, unslipped interior.

Fig. 12.17   PASTE AND TEMPER: Orange (10R 6/6) color, fully fired, medium grained, medium-knit.
SURFACE TREATMENT: Red orange (10R 5/8) burnished slip exterior. Slip extends over rim interior. Remainder of interior is orange (10R 6/6) smoothed, unslipped.
DECORATION: Black (2.5Y 2/0) painted volute design.

Fig. 12.18   PASTE AND TEMPER: Orange (10R 6/6) color, fully fired, medium grained, medium-knit.
SURFACE TREATMENT: Yellow brown (7.5YR 7/4) to orange burnished slip exterior. Dark orange (2.5YR 5/6) burnished slip inside rim and neck. Remainder of interior is orange (10R 6/6) smoothed, unslipped.
DECORATION: Dark red brown (10R 3/2) painted volute design on exterior. White (5YR 8/1) painted loops on interior of rim, neck.

Fig. 12.24   *Tiwanaku IV Polychrome*
PASTE AND TEMPER: Orange (5YR 6/6) color, fully fired, fine grained, well-knit. Temper consists of 0.2–1.0 mm gold mica.
SURFACE TREATMENT: Dark red (10R 4/6) polished slip exterior and interior.
DECORATION: Gray (5YR 5/2), orange (5YR 5/6), white (5YR 8/1), and black (7.5YR 2/0) painted zoomorphic designs (felines and condors).

Fig. 12.26   PASTE AND TEMPER: Orange (5YR 6/6) color, fully fired, fine grained, well-knit. Temper consists of 0.2–1.0 mm gold mica.
SURFACE TREATMENT: Orange (2.5YR 5/8) burnished exterior and interior.

DECORATION: Yellow (7.5YR 7/6), black (7.5YR 2/0), red (10R 3/6), and gray (2.5Y 2/0) paint.

Fig. 12.33a *Juruquilla*
Fig. 12.33b PASTE AND TEMPER: Light gray (10YR 6/2) color, fully fired,
Fig. 12.33c medium grained, well-knit. Temper not visible.
SURFACE TREATMENT: Light gray (10YR 6/2) unslipped exterior and interior.
DECORATION: Faded black (2.5YR 2.5/0) and orange (2.5YR 5/8) paint.

Fig. 12.33d *Mojocoya*
PASTE AND TEMPER: Gray brown (10YR 6/3) color, fine grained, slightly porous. Temper not visible.
SURFACE TREATMENT: Brown (5YR 3/3) unslipped exterior and interior.
DECORATION: Black (5YR 2.5/2), yellow-white (10YR 8/3), orange (5YR 5/6), and red (5R 3/3) paint.

Fig. 12.34 *Mizque Polychrome*
PASTE AND TEMPER: Orange to orange brown (7.5YR 6/6) color, fully fired, medium grained, medium-knit, slightly porous. Temper not visible.
SURFACE TREATMENT: Orange (2.5YR 6/8) smoothed slip exterior and interior of rim. Remainder of interior is orange (2.5YR 6/8) smoothed, unslipped.
DECORATION: Dark purple (5R 3/3), white (10YR 8/3), and black (2.5YR 2.5/0) paint.

Fig. 12.35a *Mizque (Nazcoide)*
PASTE AND TEMPER: Orange (7.5YR 6/6) color, slight gray core, medium grained, well-knit. Temper not visible.
SURFACE TREATMENT: Dark orange (2.5YR 4/6) burnished slip on exterior. Orange (7.5YR 6/6) smoothed, unslipped interior.
DECORATION: Yellow gray (5YR 6/4), white (10YR 8/1), and black (5YR 2.5/1) painted zoomorphic design.

Fig. 12.25b *Mizque (Nazcoide)*
PASTE AND TEMPER: Orange (7.5YR 6/6) color, slight gray core, medium grained, well-knit. Temper not visible.
SURFACE TREATMENT: Dark orange (2.5YR 5/4) burnished slip on exterior and interior.
DECORATION: Yellow orange (7.5YR 7/8) and black (2.5Y 2.5/1) paint.

Fig. 13.1 *Vilamaya Buffware*
PASTE AND TEMPER: Orange brown (5YR 6/4) color, fully fired, medium grained, poorly knit, porous with air pockets. Temper consists of 0.3–0.8 mm white, gray, black sand or crushed quartz.
SURFACE TREATMENT: Orange brown (5YR 6/4) to orange (5YR 7/6) slightly burnished, unslipped exterior and interior.
DECORATION: Punctated raised necklace around vessel shoulder.

Fig. 13.2 PASTE AND TEMPER: Light orange to gray color, fully fired, fine grained, air pockets. Temper not visible.
SURFACE TREATMENT: Red (19R 4/4) smoothed slip on exterior. Orange (2.5YR 6/8) smoothed slip on interior.
DECORATION: White (10YR 8/3) and orange white (5YR 7/6) painted decoration on exterior (stars and camelid skulls).

Fig. 13.3a — PASTE AND TEMPER: Orange (7.5YR 6/6) color, slight gray core, fine grained, occasional air pockets. Temper consists of 0.5–0.8 mm gold mica.
SURFACE TREATMENT: Orange (7.5YR 6/6) wiped, unslipped exterior and interior.

Fig. 13.3b — *Tiwanaku V Black-on-Orange*
PASTE AND TEMPER: Orange red (10R 4/6) color, fully fired, fine grained, medium-knit. Temper consists of 0.2–0.6 mm gold mica.
SURFACE TREATMENT: Orange red (10R 4/6) burnished slip on exterior and interior.
DECORATION: Black (7.5YR 2.0) painted zoomorphic designs (flamingo).

Fig. 14.7a — *Mollo*
Fig. 14.8a — PASTE AND TEMPER: Orange (2.5YR 4/8) color, fully fired, medium grained, well-knit. Temper consists of 0.6–1.0 gold mica and unidentified black mineral.
SURFACE FINISH: Orange (2.5YR 4/8) smoothed slip on exterior, part of interior. Remainder of interior is orange (2.5YR 4/8), wiped unslipped.
DECORATION: Black (2.5YR 3/0) paint. Plastic decoration of jars consists of nubs projecting above the rim.

Fig. 14.7b — *Omasuyo (?)*
PASTE AND TEMPER: Orange (2.5YR 4/8) color, fully fired, fine grained, well-knit paste. Temper consists of 0.4–1.00 mm gold mica.
SURFACE TREATMENT: Orange (2.5YR 4/8) burnished slip on exterior and interior of rim. Remainder of interior is orange (2.5YR 4/8) smoothed, unslipped.
DECORATION: Black (2.5YR 3/0) and red (10R 3/6) paint.

Fig. 14.6 — PASTE AND TEMPER: Orange (2.5YR 4/8) color, fully fired,
Fig. 14.8b — medium grained, slightly porous. Temper consists of 0.2–0.9 mm white mineral, gold mica.
SURFACE TREATMENT: Orange (2.5YR 6/6) smoothed slip on exterior and interior.
DECORATION: Black (2.5YR 3/0) paint.

References

Abercrombie, Thomas Alan
  1986   The Politics of Sacrifice: An Aymara Cosmology in Action. Unpublished Ph.D.
          thesis. Department of Anthropology, University of Chicago.
Adams, Robert McC., and Hans J. Nissen
  1972   *The Uruk Countryside.* Chicago: University of Chicago Press.
Albarracin-Jordan, Juan
  1992   Prehispanic and Early Colonial Settlement Patterns in the Lower Tiwanaku Val-
          ley, Bolivia. Unpublished Ph.D. thesis. Department of Anthropology, Southern
          Methodist University.
Albarracin-Jordan, Juan, and James E. Mathews
  1990   *Asentamientos Prehispánicos del Valle de Tiwanaku.* Volumen 1. La Paz.
Arellano López, Jorge
  1975a   La ciudad prehispánica de Iskanwaya. *Centro de Investigaciones Arqueológicas*
          6. La Paz.
  1975b   La cerámica de las tumbas de Iskanwaya. *Instituto Nacional de Arqueología* 8.
          La Paz.
  1977a   Reconocimiento arqueológico de la zona de Tarija. *Documento interno INAR*
          29/77. La Paz.
  1977b   Determinación del antiplástico en algunas cerámicas precolombinas de Bolivia
          y Perú. In *Jornadas*, Tomo II, pp. 75–103. La Paz: Franz Tamayo.
  1977c   La cerámica de las tumbas de Iskanwaya. In *Jornadas*, Tomo II, pp. 103–25. La
          Paz: Franz Tamayo.
  1978a   La cultura Mollo y su influencia en el área lacustre. *Documento interno INAR*
          48/78. La Paz.
  1978b   La cultura Mollo: ensayo de síntesis arqueológica. *Pumapunku* 12:87–115.
  1984a   Apuntes para una nueva arqueología boliviana. *Arqueología Boliviana* 1:9–15.
  1984b   La cultura Tarija, aporte al conocimiento de los señoríos regionales del sur Bo-
          liviano. *Arqueología Boliviana* 1:73–83.
  1985   Síntesis cultural prehispánico de la zona circumlacustre norte de Bolivia. *Ar-
          queología Boliviana* 2:6–17.
Arellano López, Jorge, and Eduardo E. Berberián
  1981   Mallku: el señorio post-Tiwanaku del altiplano sur de Bolivia. *Boletín del Insti-
          tuto Frances de Estudios Andinos* X(1–2): 51–84.
Arensberg, Conrad M., and Solon T. Kimball
  1965   *Culture and Community.* New York: Harcourt, Brace and World.
Arnold, Jeanne E.
  1992   Complex hunter-gatherer-fishers of prehistoric California: Chiefs, specialists,
          and maritime adaptations of the Channel Islands. *American Antiquity* 57(1):60–
          84.
Arnold, Philip J., III
  1990   The organization of refuse disposal and ceramic production within contempo-
          rary Mexican houselots. *American Anthropologist* 92(4):924–32.
Ashmore, Wendy, and Richard R. Wilk
  1988   Household and community in the Mesoamerican past. In *Household and Com-*

munity in the Mesoamerican Past, edited by Richard R. Wilk and Wendy Ashmore, pp. 1–27. Albuquerque: University of New Mexico Press.

Bandelier, Adolph
1910   *The Islands of Titicaca and Koati*. New York: The Hispanic Society of America.

Barba, Luis
1986   La quimica en el estudio de areas de actividad. In *Unidades Habitacionales Mesoamericans y sus Areas de Actividad*, Serie Antropológica 76, edited by Linda Manzanilla, pp. 21–39. México D.F.: Universidad Nacional Autónoma de México.

Barreto, Christiana
n.d.   Culture change and built environment in three native communities of central Brazil: Implications for archaeology. Manuscript.

Baudin, Louis
1928   *L'empire socialiste des Inka*. Paris.

Bawden, Garth
1982   The household: A study of pre-Columbian social dynamics. *Journal of Field Archaeology* 9:165–81.
1990   Domestic space and social structure in pre-Columbian northern Peru. In *Domestic Architecture and the Use of Space*, edited by Susan Kent, pp. 153–71. Cambridge: Cambridge University Press.

Bender, Donald R.
1967   A refinement of the concept of household: Families, co-residence, and domestic functions. *American Anthropologist* 69:493–504.

Bennett, Wendell C.
1934   Excavations at Tiahuanaco. *Anthropological Papers of the American Museum of Natural History* 34(3):361–513. New York.
1936   Excavations in Bolivia. *Anthropological Papers of the American Museum of Natural History* 35(4):331–505. New York.
n.d.   Bolivian expedition field notes. December 1933–April 1934. On file at The American Museum of Natural History. New York.

Berberián, Eduardo E.
1977   El problema de la expansión de la cultura Tiwanaku en el noroeste argentino. In *Jornadas*, Tomo II, pp. 171–81. La Paz: Franz Tamayo.
1980   *Bibliografía Antropológica de la Provincia de Tucumán*. Córdoba.

Berberián, Eduardo E., and Jorge Arellano López
1980   Desarrollo cultural prehispánico en el altiplano sur de Bolivia. (Pcias. nor y sud Lípez–Dpto. Potosí). *Revista do Museu Paulista* n.s. XXVII: 259–81.

Berenguer, José
1986   Relaciones iconográficas de larga distancia en los Andes: nuevos ejemplos para un viejo problema. *Boletín del Museo Chileno de Arte Precolombino* 1:55–78.

Berenguer, José, Victoria Castro, and Osvaldo Silva
1980   Reflexiones acerca de la presencia de Tiwanaku en el norte de Chile. *Estudios Arqueológicos* 5:81–94.

Bermann, Marc
1989a   Una visión de las casas del período Tiwanaku en Lukurmata. In *Arqueología de Lukurmata*, Volume 2, edited by Alan Kolata, pp. 113–53. La Paz: Instituto Nacional de Arqueología.
1989b   Una excavación de prueba cerca del templo semisubterráneo de Lukurmata. In *Arqueología de Lukurmata*, Volume 2, edited by Alan Kolata, pp. 93–113. La Paz: Instituto Nacional de Arqueología.

1990   Prehispanic Household and Empire at Lukurmata, Bolivia. Unpublished Ph.D. thesis. Department of Anthropology, University of Michigan.

1993   Continuity and change in household life at Lukurmata. In *Domestic Architecture, Ethnicity, and Complementarity in the South-Central Andes*, edited by Mark S. Aldenderfer, pp. 114–35. Iowa City: University of Iowa Press.

n.d.   Lukurmata: The archaeology of households. Manuscript.

Bermann, Marc, and Gray Graffam

1989   Arquitectura residencial en las terrazas de Lukurmata. In *Arqueología de Lukurmata*, Volume 2, edited by Alan Kolata, pp. 153–73. La Paz: Instituto Nacional de Arqueología.

Binford, Lewis R.

1964   A consideration of archaeological research design. *American Antiquity* 29(4): 425–41.

1978   Dimensional analysis of behavior and site structure: Learning from an Eskimo hunting stand. *American Antiquity* 43(3):330–61.

Binford, Lewis R. (ed.)

1983   *Working at Archaeology*. New York: Academic Press.

Binford, Michael, and Mark Brenner

1989   Resultados de estudios del primer año de la limnología en los ecosistemas de Tiwanaku. In *Arqueología de Lukurmata*, Volume 2, edited by Alan Kolata, pp. 213–37. La Paz: Instituto Nacional de Arqueología.

Blake, Thomas Michael

1984   Canajaste: An Evolving Postclassic Maya Site. Unpublished Ph.D. thesis. Department of Anthropology, University of Michigan.

1991   An emerging Early Formative chiefdom at Paso de la Amada, Chiapas, Mexico. In *The Formation of Complex Society in Southeastern Mesoamerica*, edited by William Fowler, Jr., pp. 27–46. Boca Raton: CRC Press.

Blanton, Richard E., Stephen A. Kowalewski, Gary Feinman, and Jill Appel

1981   *Ancient Mesoamerica: A Comparison of Change in Three Regions*. Cambridge: Cambridge University Press.

Bourdier, Jean-Paul, and Nezar Alsayyad (eds.)

1989   *Dwellings, Settlement and Tradition: Cross-Cultural Perspectives*. Lanham: University Press of America.

Branisa, Leonardo

1957   Un nuevo estilo de cerámica precolombina de Chuquisaya: Mojocoya tricolor. In *Arqueología Boliviana*, edited by Carlos Ponce Sanginés, pp. 289–320. La Paz: Biblioteca Paceña.

Braudel, Ferdinand

1981   *The Structures of Everyday Life: The Limits of the Possible. Civilization and Capitalism 15th–18th Century*, Volume 1. New York: Harper and Row.

Brockington, Donald L., David Pereira Herrera, Ramón Sanzetenea R., and Ricardo Céspedes P.

1985   Informe preliminar de las excavaciones arqueológicas en Sierra Mokho y Chullpa Pampa. *Cuaderno de Investigación, Serie Arqueología* 5. Cochabamba: Universidad Mayor de San Simón.

1986   Excavaciones en Maira Pampa y Conchu Pata, Mizque. *Cuaderno de Investigación, Serie Arqueología* 6. Cochabamba: Universidad Mayor de San Simón.

Browman, David L.

1974   Pastoral nomadism in the Andes. *Current Anthropology* 15(2):188–96.

1978a   Toward the development of the Tiwanaku state. In *Advances in Andean Archaeology*, edited by David L. Browman, pp. 327–49. The Hague: Mouton.

Browman, David L.

1978b   The temple of Chiripa (Lake Titicaca, Bolivia). In *III Congreso Peruano. El Hombre y la Cultura Andina*, edited by Ramiro Matos M., pp. 807–13. Lima.

1980   Tiwanaku expansion and altiplano economic patterns. *Estudios Arqueológicos* 5:107–20.

1981   New light on Andean Tiwanaku. *American Scientist* 69(4):408–19.

1984   Tiwanaku: Development of interzonal trade and economic expansion in the altiplano. Social and economic organization in the prehispanic Andes. *British Archaeological Reports International Series* 194:117–42.

1985   Cultural primacy of Tiwanaku in the development of later Peruvian states. In *Diálogo Andina* 4, edited by Mario Rivera, pp. 59–72. Arica.

Brown, James A.

1976   The Southern Cult reconsidered. *Midcontinental Journal of Archaeology* 1–2:115–35.

Brush, Stephen B.

1977   The myth of the idle peasant: Employment in a subsistence economy. In *Peasant Livelihood: Studies in Economic Anthropology and Cultural Ecology*, edited by Rhoda Halperin and James Dow, pp. 60–78. New York: St. Martin's.

Buechler, Hans, and Judith Marie Buechler

1971   *The Bolivian Aymara*. New York: Holt, Rinehart and Winston.

Burger, Richard L., and Frank Asaro

1977   Análisis de rasgos significativos en la obsidiana de los Andes Centrales. *Revista de Museo Nacional* XLIII:281–326. Lima.

Bustos Santelices, Victor

1978   Una hipótesis de relaciones culturales entre el altiplano y la vertiente oriental de los Andes. *Pumapunku* 12:115–26.

Caballero, Geraldine Byrne de

1984   El Tiwanaku en Cochabamba. *Arqueología Boliviana* 1:67–72.

Carlevato, Denise

1988   Late ceramics from Pucara, Peru. *Expedition* 30(3):39–45.

Casanova, Eduardo

1937   Investigaciones arqueológicas en el altiplano boliviano. *Relaciones de la Socieded Argentina de Antropología*. Tomo 1, pp. 167–73.

1942   Dos yacamientos arqueológicas en la península de Copacabana (Bolivia). *Anales del Museo Argentino de Ciencias Naturales* XL:333–99.

Chang, Kwang-Chih

1958   Study of the Neolithic social grouping: Examples from the New World. *American Anthropologist* 60(2):298–334.

Chávez, Karen L. Mohr

1985   Early Tihuanaco related ceremonial burners from Cuzco, Peru. In *Diálogo Andino* 4, edited by Mario Rivera, pp. 137–78. Arica.

1988   The significance of Chiripa in Lake Titicaca Basin developments. *Expedition* 30(3):17–26.

Chávez, Sergio J.

1976   The Arapa and Thunderbolt stelae: A case of stylistic identity with implications for Pucara influences in the area of Tiahuanaco. *Ñawpa Pacha* 13:3–25.

1985   Ofrendas funerarias dentro do los límites meridionales del territorio Huari en el Depto. del Cuzco. In *Diálogo Andina* 4, edited by Mario Rivera, pp. 39–58. Arica.

Chávez, Sergio J., and Karen L. Mohr Chávez

1975   A carved stela from Taraco, Puno, Peru, and the definition of an early style of stone sculpture from the altiplano of Peru and Bolivia. *Ñawpa Pacha* 13:45–83.

Chayanov, A. V.
1977   On the theory of non-capitalist economic systems. In *Peasant Livelihood: Studies in Economic Anthropology and Cultural Ecology*, edited by Rhoda Halperin and James Dow, pp. 257–68. New York: St. Martin's.

Clark, John E.
1982   Modern Lacandón lithic technology and blade workshops. Paper presented at the Second Conference on the Study of Stone Tools and the Development of Ancient Maya Civilization. San Antonio, Texas.

Collier, George A.
1976   *Fields of the Tzotzil: The Ecological Bases of Tradition in Highland Chiapas.* Austin: University of Texas Press.

Collier, George A., Renato I. Rosaldo, and John D. Wirth (eds.)
1982   *The Inca and Aztec States, 1400–1800.* New York: Academic Press.

Collins, Jane
1983   Translation traditions and the organization of productive activity: The case of Aymara affinal kinship terms. In *Bilingualism: Social Issues and Policy Implications*, edited by A. W. Miracle, Jr., pp. 11–21. Athens: University of Georgia Press.

Columba Salvatierra, Teresa
1978   Análisis de la cerámica de la península de Copacabana. *Documento interno* 47/78. La Paz.

Condarco, Lisandro A.
1959   Archaeological notes on the Oruro region, Bolivia. *Ethnos* 3–4:202–7.

Conklin, William J.
1983   Pucara and Tiahuanaco tapestry: Time and style in a sierra weaving tradition. *Ñawpa Pacha* 21:1–44.

Conrad, Geoffrey W., and Arthur A. Demarest
1984   *Religion and Empire: The Dynamics of Aztec and Inca Expansion.* Cambridge: Cambridge University Press.

Cook, Anita G.
1983   Aspects of state ideology in Huari and Tiwanaku iconography: The Central Deity and the Sacrificer. In *Investigations of the Andean Past*, edited by D. Sandweiss, pp. 161–185. Latin American Studies Program, Cornell University, Ithaca.
1985a   Art and Time in the Evolution of Andean State Expansionism. Unpublished Ph.D. thesis. Department of Anthropology, State University of New York–Binghamton.
1985b   The politico-religious implications of the Huari offering traditions. *Diálogo Andina* 4, edited by Mario Rivera, pp. 203–22. Arica.

Cordero Miranda, Gregorio
1967   Valioso testimonio arqueológico en Niño Korin–Charazani. *Khana* 1(38):139–44.
1971   Reconocimiento arqueológico de Pucarani y sitios adyacentes. *Pumapunku* 3:7–29.
1972   Estudio preliminar en las Islas Intja y Suriki del Lago Titicaca. *Pumapunku* 5:22–40.
1977   Descubrimiento de una estela lítica en Chiripa. In *Jornadas*, Tomo II, pp. 229–32. La Paz: Franz Tamayo.
1984   Reconocimiento arqueológico en los márgenes del río Beni. *Arqueología Boliviana* 1:15–38.

Costin, Cathy L., and Timothy K. Earle
    1989   Status distinction and legitimation of power as reflected in changing patterns of consumption in late prehispanic Peru. *American Antiquity* 54(4):691–714.

Cunningham, Clark E.
    1973   Order in the Atoni house. In *Right and Left: Essays on Dual Symbolic Classification*, edited by Rodney Needham, pp. 204–38. Chicago: University of Chicago Press.

D'Altroy, Terence N.
    1987a   Introduction. *Ethnohistory* 34(1):1–13.
    1987b   Transitions in power: Centralization of Wanka political organization under Inka rule. *Ethnohistory* 34(1):78–102.
    1992   *Provincial Power in the Inka Empire*. Washington, D.C.: Smithsonian Institution Press.

D'Altroy, Terence N., and Timothy K. Earle
    1985   Staple finance, wealth finance, and storage in the Inka political economy. *Current Anthropology* 25(2):187–206.

Dauelsberg, Percy
    1985   Desarrollo regional en los valles costeros del norte de Chile. In *Diálogo Andino* 4, edited by Mario Rivera, pp. 277–86. Arica.

David, N. C.
    1971   The Fulani compound and the archaeologist. *World Archaeology* 3:111–31.

Deetz, James J. F.
    1982   Households: A structural key to archaeological explanation. *American Behavioral Scientist* 25(6):717–24.
    1988   Material culture and worldview in colonial Anglo-America. In *Recovery of Meaning: Historical Archaeology in the Eastern United States*, edited by Mark Leone and Parker Potter, pp. 219–33. Washington, D.C.: Smithsonian Institution Press.

Demarest, Arthur A.
    1981   Viracocha, the nature and antiquity of the Andean High God. *Peabody Museum, Harvard University Monograph* 6. Cambridge.

Denevan, William M.
    1970   Aboriginal drained-field cultivation in the Americas. *Science* 169:619–52.
    1980   Tipología de configuraciones agrícolas prehispánicas. *America Indígena* 40:619–52.

Dillehay, Tom D.
    1976   Competition and Cooperation in a Prehispanic Multi-ethnic System in the Central Andes. Unpublished Ph.D. thesis. Department of Anthropology, University of Texas.
    1979   Prehispanic resource sharing in the central Andes. *Science* 204(6):24–31.

Disselhoff, Hans D.
    1968   Huari und Tiahuanaco: Grabungen und Funde in Sud-Peru. *Zeitschrift für Ethnologie* 93:207–16.

Donley, Linda
    1982   House power: Swahili space and symbolic markers. In *Symbolic and Structural Archaeology*, edited by Ian Hodder, pp. 63–73. Cambridge: Cambridge University Press.
    1987   Life in the Swahili town house reveals the symbolic meaning of spaces and artifact assemblages. *The African Archaeological Review* 5:181–92.

Donnan, Christopher B.
    1973   Moche occupation of the Santa Valley, Peru. *University of California Publications in Anthropology* 8. Los Angeles: University of California Press.

Douglas, Mary
 1972 Symbolic orders in the use of domestic space. In *Man, Settlement, and Urbanism*, edited by Peter J. Ucko, Ruth Tringham, and Geoffrey W. Dimbleby, pp. 505–12. London: Gerald Duckworth.
Doyle, Michael W.
 1986 *Empires*. Ithaca: Cornell University Press.
Drennan, Robert D.
 1976 Fábrica San José and Middle Formative society in the Valley of Oaxaca. *Memoirs of the Museum of Anthropology, University of Michigan* 8. Ann Arbor.
 1987 Regional demography in chiefdoms. In *Chiefdoms in the Americas*, edited by Robert D. Drennan and Carlos A. Uribe, pp. 307–24. Lanham: University Press of America.
Drennan, Robert D., Luis Gonzalo Jaramillo, Elizabeth Ramos, Carlos Augusto Sánchez, María Angela Ramírez, and Carlos A. Uribe
 1991 Regional dynamics of chiefdoms in the Valle de la Plata, Colombia. *Journal of Field Archaeology* 18:297–317.
Drennan, Robert D., and Carlos A. Uribe (eds.)
 1987 *Chiefdoms in the Americas*. Lanham: University Press of America.
Earle, Timothy K.
 1978 Economic and social organization of a complex chiefdom: The Halelea District, Kaua'i, Hawaii. *Museum of Anthropology, University of Michigan Anthropological Paper* 63. Ann Arbor.
 1991 The evolution of chiefdoms. In *Chiefdoms: Power, Economy and Ideology*, edited by Timothy Earle, pp. 1–15. Cambridge: Cambridge University Press.
Eisleb, Dieter, and Renate Strelow
 1980 Tiahuanaco. *Altperuanische Kulturen* III. Museum für Völkerkunde. Berlin.
Ember, Carol, and Melvin Ember
 1985 *Anthropology*. 4th ed. Englewood Cliffs: Prentice-Hall.
Erickson, Clark L.
 1985 Applications of prehistoric Andean technology: Experiments in raised field agriculture, Huatta, Lake Titicaca. *British Archaeological Reports International Series* 232:209–32.
 1987 The dating of raised-field agriculture in the Lake Titicaca Basin, Peru. *British Archaeological Reports International Series* 359:373–84.
 1988 An Archaeological Investigation of Raised Field Agriculture in the Lake Titicaca Basin of Peru. Unpublished Ph.D. thesis. Department of Anthropology, University of Illinois.
Errington, Shelley
 1979 The cosmic house of the Buginese. *Asia* (Jan.–Feb):8–13.
Estévez Castillo, José
 1983 Tiwanaku: de la estructura aldeana al estado. *Documento interno INAR*. La Paz.
 1985 Prospección y catalogación de asentamiento prehispánicos del norte del Departamento de La Paz. *Arqueología Boliviana* 2:89–101.
 1987 Evidencias de asentamientos precolombinas en sud Chicas. *Presencia*; 30 de agosto. La Paz.
 n.d. Excavaciones en Lukurmata: sitio urbano tiwanancota centro de dominoeconomico regional. Manuscript.
Faldín Aranciba, Juan D.
 1978b Prospecciones arqueológicas en el valle de Tiwanaku. *Documento internal INAR* 46/78. La Paz.
 1985 La arqueología de las provincias de Larecaja y Muñecas y sus sistemas precolombino (1ra parte). *Arqueología Boliviana* 2:53–74.

Feinman, Gary, Richard Blanton, and Stephen Kowalewski
    1984   Market system development in the prehispanic Valley of Oaxaca, Mexico. In *Trade and Exchange in Early Mesoamerica*, edited by Kenneth G. Hirth, pp. 157–78. Albuquerque: University of New Mexico Press.

Fiedel, Stuart
    1987   *Prehistory of the Americas*. Cambridge: Cambridge University Press.

Fjeldså, Jon
    1985   Origin, evolution, and status of the avifauna of the Andean wetlands. In *Neotropical Ornithology, Ornithological Monographs* 36, edited by P. A. Buckley et al., pp. 85–112. Washington, D.C.: American Ornithologists' Union.

Flannery, Kent V.
    1972   The cultural evolution of civilizations. *Annual Review of Ecology and Systematics* 3:399–426.
    1976a   The Early Mesoamerican house. In *The Early Mesoamerican Village*, edited by Kent V. Flannery, pp. 16–24. New York: Academic Press.
    1976b   Evolution of complex settlement systems. In *The Early Mesoamerican Village*, edited by Kent V. Flannery, pp. 162–72. New York: Academic Press.
    1983   The Tierras Largas phase and the analytical units of the early Oaxacan village. In *The Cloud People: Divergent Evolution of the Zapotec and Mixtec Civilizations*, edited by Kent V. Flannery and Joyce Marcus, pp. 43–45. New York: Academic Press.

Flannery, Kent V. (ed.)
    1976   *The Early Mesoamerican Village*. New York: Academic Press.
    1986   *Guila Naquitz: Archaic Foraging and Early Agriculture in Oaxaca, Mexico*. Orlando: Academic Press.

Flannery, Kent V., and Joyce Marcus
    1983a   The growth of site hierarchies in the Valley of Oaxaca: Part 1. In *The Cloud People: Divergent Evolution of the Zapotec and Mixtec Civilizations*, edited by Kent V. Flannery and Joyce Marcus, pp. 53–64. New York: Academic Press.
    1983b   San José Mogote in Monte Albán II: A secondary administrative center. In *The Cloud People: Divergent Evolution of the Zapotec and Mixtec Civilizations*, edited by Kent V. Flannery and Joyce Marcus, pp. 111–13. New York: Academic Press.
    1983c   San Jose Mogoté and the *Tay Situndayu*. In *The Cloud People: Divergent Evolution of the Zapotec and Mixtec Civilizations*, edited by Kent V. Flannery and Joyce Marcus, pp. 289–90. New York: Academic Press.

Flannery, Kent V., Joyce Marcus, and Stephen A. Kowalewski
    1981   The Preceramic and Formative of the Valley of Oaxaca. In *Supplement to the Handbook of Middle American Indians*, Volume 1, edited by Jeremy A. Sabloff, pp. 48–93. Austin: University of Texas Press.

Flannery, Kent V., and Marcus Winter
    1976   Analyzing household activities. In *The Early Mesoamerican Village*, edited by Kent V. Flannery, pp. 34–47. New York: Academic Press.

Focacci Aste, Guillermo
    1983   El Tiwanaku clásico en el valle de Azapa. In Asentamientos aldeanos el los Valles Costeros de Arica, edited by Ivan Muñoz Ovalle and Guillermo Focacci Aste, pp. 94–113. *Documento de Trabajo* 3, Universidad de Tarapaca.

Foster, George M.
    1962   *Traditional Cultures and the Impact of Technological Change*. New York: Harper and Row.

Freeman, L. G., Jr.
    1968   A theoretical framework for interpreting archaeological materials. In *Man the*

Hunter, edited by Richard B. Lee and Irven Devore, pp. 262–67. Chicago: Aldine.

Girault, Luis
  1977a   Exploration archeologique dans la region d'Ixiamas. In *Jornadas*, Tomo II, pp. 125–28. La Paz: Franz Tamayo.
  1977b   Las ruinas de Chullpa Pata de la comunidad de Kallamarca. In *Jornadas*, Tomo II, pp. 181–210. La Paz: Franz Tamayo.

Glassie, Henry
  1975   *Folk Housing in Middle Virginia*. Knoxville: The University of Tennessee Press.

Gnivecki, Perry
  1987   On the quantitative derivation of household spatial organization from archaeological residues in ancient Mesopotamia. In *Method and Theory for Activity Area Research: An Ethnoarchaeological Approach*, edited by Susan Kent, pp. 176–235. New York: Columbia University Press.

Goldstein, Paul S.
  1985   Tiwanaku Ceramics of the Moquegua Valley. Unpublished M.A. thesis. Department of Anthropology, University of Chicago.
  1989   Omo, A Tiwanaku Provincial Center in Moquegua, Peru. Unpublished Ph.D. thesis. Department of Anthropology, University of Chicago.
  1993   Tiwanaku temples and state expansion: A Tiwanaku sunken-court temple in Moquegua, Peru. *Latin American Antiquity* 4(1):22–47.

Gordon, Stewart
  1979   Recovery from adversity in Eighteenth-Century India: Re-thinking "villages," "peasants," and politics in pre-modern kingdoms. *Peasant Studies* 8(4):61–79.

Graffam, Gray
  1988   Back across the Great Divide: The Pakaq señorío and raised field agriculture. In Multidisciplinary studies in Andean Anthropology, edited by Virginia J. Vitzhum, pp. 33–50. *Michigan Discussions in Anthropology* 8. Department of Anthropology. University of Michigan, Ann Arbor.
  1989   Una excavación de prueba en la acrópolis de Lukurmata, Bolivia. In *Arqueología de Lukurmata*, Volume 2, edited by Alan Kolata, pp. 89–93. La Paz: Instituto Nacional de Arqueología.
  1990   Raised Fields Without Bureaucracy: An Archaeological Examination of Intensive Wetland Cultivation in the Pampa Koani Zone, Lake Titicaca, Bolivia. Unpublished Ph.D. thesis. Department of Anthropology, University of Toronto.
  1992   Beyond state collapse: Rural history, raised fields, and pastoralism in the south Andes. *American Anthropologist* 94(4):882–904.

Gundermann K., Hans
  1984   Ganadería Aymara, ecología y forrajes: evaluación regional de una actividad productiva andina. *Chungará* 12:99–124.

Hally, David
  1983   The interpretive potential of pottery from domestic contexts. *Midcontinental Journal of Archaeology* 8(2):163–96.
  1984   Vessel assemblages and food habits: A comparison of two aboriginal southeastern vessel assemblages. *Southeastern Archaeology* 3(1) (Summer):46–64.

Hammel E. A., and Peter Laslett
  1974   Comparing household structure over time and between cultures. *Comparative Studies in Society and History* 16:73–109.

Hassig, Ross
  1985   *Trade, Tribute and Transportation: The Sixteenth-Century Political Economy of the Valley of Mexico*. Norman: University of Oklahoma Press.

Hastorf, Christine A.

1990a   The effect of the Inka state on Sausa agricultural production and crop consumption. *American Antiquity* 55(2):262–90.

1990b   One path to the heights: Negotiating political inequality in the Sausa of Peru. In *The Evolution of Political Systems: Sociopolitics in Small-Scale Sedentary Societies*, edited by Steadman Upham, pp.146–76. Cambridge: Cambridge University Press.

Hastorf, Christine A., and Timothy K. Earle

1985   Intensive agriculture and the geography of political change in the Upper Mantaro Region of central Peru. In Prehistoric Intensive Agriculture in the Tropics, edited by Ian Farrington, pp. 569–95. *British Archaeological Reports International Series* 232.

Hayden, Brian, and Aubrey Cannon

1982   The corporate group as an archaeological unit. *Journal of Anthropological Archaeology* 1:132–58.

1984   The structure of material systems: Ethnoarchaeology in the Maya highlands. *Society for American Archaeology Papers* 3.

Helms, Mary

1979   *Ancient Panama: Chiefs in Search of Power*. Austin: University of Texas Press.

1987   Art styles and interaction spheres in Central America and the Caribbean: Polished black wood in the Greater Antilles. In *Chiefdoms in the Americas*, edited by Robert D. Drennan and Carlos A. Uribe, pp. 67–84. Lanham: University Press of America.

Hill, James N.

1970   Broken K Pueblo: Prehistoric social organization in the American Southwest. *Anthropological Papers of the University of Arizona* 18. Tucson: University of Arizona Press.

Hirth, Kenneth G.

1993   The household as an analytical unit: Problems in method and theory. In *Prehispanic Domestic Units in Western Mesoamerica: Studies of the Household, Compound, and Residence*, edited by Robert S. Santley and Kenneth G. Hirth, pp. 21–36. Boca Raton: CRC Press.

Hodder, Ian

1987   The meaning of discard: Ash and domestic space in Baringo. In *Method and Theory for Activity Area Research: An Ethnoarchaeological Approach*, edited by Susan Kent, pp. 424–48. New York: Columbia University Press.

Horn, Darwin D., Jr.

1984   Marsh Resource Utilization and the Ethnoarchaeology of the Uru-Muratos of Highland Bolivia. Unpublished Ph.D. thesis. Department of Anthropology, Washington University.

Huidobro Bellido, José

1980   Expansión de la cultura Mollo hacia los llanos. Estudio arqueológico de la necrópolis de Pallapalla. In *Segundo Reunión Boliviano-Peruano*,Volume 2, pp. 87–102. La Paz: Instituto Nacional de Arqueología.

Ibarra Grasso, Dick Edgar

1944   Las ruinas y las culturas de los Yuras. *Revista Geográfica Americana* XXI(127):208–21.

1956   Esquema de la arqueología Boliviana. *Khana* I(15–16):124–32.

1957a   Un nuevo panorama de la arqueología boliviana. In *Arqueología Boliviana*, edited by Carlos Ponce Sanginés, pp. 235–88. La Paz: Biblioteca Paceña.

1957b   Nuevas culturas arqueológicas de los antiguos indígenas de Chuquisaca, Potosi y Tarija. In *Arqueología Boliviana*, edited by Carlos Ponce Sanginés, pp. 321–42. La Paz: Biblioteca Paceña.

1965   *Prehistoria de Bolivia*. La Paz: Los Amigos del Libro.

Ibarra Grasso, Dick Edgar, and Roy Querejazu Lewis

1986   *30,000 Años de Prehistoria en Bolivia*. La Paz: Los Amigos del Libro.

Ibarra Grasso, Dick Edgar, José de Mesa, and Teresa Gisbert

1955   Reconstrucción de Taypicala (Tiahuanaco). *Khana* V(9–10):99–121.

Iribarren Charlín, Jorge

1957   Dispersión meridional de formas tiwanacoides. In *Arqueología Boliviana*, edited by Carlos Ponce Sanginés, pp. 165–72. La Paz: Biblioteca Paceña.

Isbell, William H.

1983   Shared ideology and parallel political development: Huari and Tiwanaku. In *Investigations of the Andean Past*, edited by D. Sandweiss, pp.186–208. Latin American Studies Program, Cornell University, Ithaca.

1988   City and state in Middle Horizon Huari. In *Peruvian Prehistory*, edited by Richard W. Keatinge, pp. 163–89. Cambridge: Cambridge University Press.

Isbell, William H., and Gordon F. McEwan (eds.)

1991   *Huari Administrative Structure: Prehistoric Monumental Architecture and State Government*. Washington, D.C.: Dumbarton Oaks.

Isbell, William H., and Katharina Schreiber

1978   Was Huari a state? *American Antiquity* 43:372–89.

Janusek, John, and Howard Earnest

1988   Urban residence and land reclamation in Lukurmata: A view from the core area. Unpublished report of the Proyecto Wila-Jawira, University of Chicago.

Johnson, Allen W., and Timothy K. Earle

1987   *The Evolution of Human Societies: From Foraging Group to Agrarian State*. Stanford: Stanford University Press.

Johnson, Gregory A.

1977   Aspects of regional analysis in archaeology. *Annual Review of Archaeology* 6:479–508.

1982   Organizational structure and scalar stress. In *Theory and Explanation in Archaeology*, edited by Colin Renfrew, M. J. Rowlands, and Barbara A. Segraves, pp. 389–421. New York: Academic Press.

Julien, Catherine J.

1982   Inca decimal administration in the Lake Titicaca region. In *The Inca and Aztec States, 1400–1800*, edited by George A. Collier, Renato I. Rosaldo, and John D. Wirth, pp. 119–51. New York: Academic Press.

1988   The Squier Causeway at Lake Umayo. *Expedition* 30(3):46–55.

Kapches, Mima

1990   The spatial dynamics of Ontario Iroquoian longhouses. *American Antiquity* 55(1): 49–67.

Kelm, Heinz

1963   Archäologische Fundstücke aus Ostbolivien. *Baessler-Archiv, Neue Folge* XI:65–92.

Kent, Susan

1984   *Analyzing Activity Areas: An Ethnoarchaeological Study of the Use of Space*. Albuquerque: University of New Mexico Press.

1987   Understanding the use of space: An ethnoarchaeological approach. In *Method and Theory for Activity Area Research: An Ethnoarchaeological Approach*, edited by Susan Kent, pp. 1–62. New York: Columbia University Press.

1990a   Activity areas and architecture: An interdisciplinary view of the relationship between use of space and domestic built environments. In *Domestic Architecture and the Use of Space*, edited by Susan Kent, pp. 1–8. Cambridge: Cambridge University Press.

Kent, Susan
    1990b   A cross-cultural study of segmentation, architecture, and the use of space. In *Domestic Architecture and the Use of Space*, edited by Susan Kent, pp. 127–52. Cambridge: Cambridge University Press.

Kent, Susan (ed.)
    1987   *Method and Theory for Activity Area Research: An Ethnoarchaeological Approach.* New York: Columbia University Press.
    1990   *Domestic Architecture and the Use of Space.* Cambridge: Cambridge University Press.

Kidder, Alfred, II
    1943   Some early sites in the northern Lake Titicaca Basin. *Papers of the Peabody Museum, Harvard University* XXVII (1). Cambridge.
    1948   The position of Pucara in Titicaca Basin archaeology. *Memoirs of the Society for American Archaeology* 4:84–89.
    1956   Digging in the Lake Titicaca Basin. *University Museum Bulletin* 20(3):16–29. Philadelphia.

Knapp, Ronald G.
    1986   *China's Traditional Rural Architecture: A Cultural Geography of the Common House.* Honolulu: University of Hawaii Press.

Kolata, Alan L.
    1982   Tiwanaku: Portrait of an Andean civilization. *Field Museum of Natural History Bulletin* 53(8):13–28.
    1983   The south Andes. In *Ancient South Americans*, edited by Jesse D. Jennings, pp. 241–84. San Francisco: W. H. Freeman.
    1985   El papel de la agricultura intensiva en la economía política del estado Tiwanaku. In *Diálogo Andina* 4, edited by Mario Rivera, pp. 39–58. Arica.
    1986   The agricultural foundations of the Tiwanaku state: A view from the heartland. *American Antiquity* 51(4):748–62.
    1989   Introducción: objetivos y estratégias de la investigación. In *Arqueología de Lukurmata*, Volume 2, edited by Alan Kolata, pp. 13–41. La Paz: Instituto Nacional de Arqueología.
    1991   The technology and organization of agricultural production in the Tiwanaku state. *Latin American Antiquity* 2(2):99–125.
    1992   Economy, ideology, and imperialism in the south-central Andes. In *Ideology and Pre-Columbian Civilizations*, edited by Arthur A. Demarest and Geoffrey W. Conrad, pp. 65–86. Santa Fe: School of American Research Press.

Kolata, Alan L. (ed.)
    1989   *Arqueología de Lukurmata.* Volume 2. La Paz: Instituto Nacional de Arqueología.

Kolata, Alan L., and Gray Graffam
    1989   Los campos elevados de Lukurmata, Bolivia. In *Arqueología de Lukurmata*, Volume 2, edited by Alan Kolata, pp. 173–213. La Paz: Instituto Nacional de Arqueología.

Kolata, Alan L., and Charles Ortloff
    1989   Thermal analysis of Tiwanaku rasied field systems in the Lake Titicaca Basin of Bolivia. *Journal of Archaeological Science* 16:233–63.

Kowalewski, Stephen A.
    1983   Valley-floor settlement patterns during Monte Albán IIIa. In *The Cloud People:*

Divergent Evolution of the Zapotec and Mixtec Civilizations, edited by Kent V. Flannery and Joyce Marcus, pp. 148–50. New York: Academic Press.

Kramer, Carol
    1979   An archaeological view of a contemporary Kurdish village: Domestic architecture, household size, and wealth. In *Ethnoarchaeology: Implications of Ethnography for Archaeology*, edited by Carol Kramer, pp. 139–63. New York: Columbia University Press.
    1982a   *Village Ethnoarchaeology: Rural Iran in Archaeological Perspective.* New York: Academic Press.
    1982b   Ethnographic households and archaeological interpretation. *American Behavioral Scientist* 25:633–74.

Kuljis Meruvia, Danilo, and Victor Bustos Santelices
    1977   Prospección arqueológica en el departamento de Chuquisaca (201101). *Pumapunku* 11:7–43.

La Barre, Weston
    1948   The Aymara Indians of the Lake Titicaca Plateau, Bolivia. *Memoir of the American Anthropological Association* 68.

Lange, F. W., and C. R. Rydberg
    1972   Abandonment and post-abandonment behavior at a rural Central American house-site. *American Antiquity* 37(3):419–32.

Laslett, Peter
    1972   Introduction: The history of the family. In *Household and Family in Past Time*, edited by Peter Laslett and Richard Wall, pp. 1–89. Cambridge: Cambridge University Press.

Lawrence, Roderick
    1982   Domestic space and society: A cross-cultural study. *Comparative Studies in Society and History* 24(1):104–30.
    1987   *Housing, Dwelling, Homes: Design Theory, Research and Practice.* New York: Wiley and Sons.
    1989   Translating anthropological concepts into architectural practice. In *Housing, Culture, and Design: A Comparative Perspective*, edited by S. M. Low and E. Chambers, pp. 89–113. Philadelphia: University of Pennsylvania Press.

Le Paige, R. P. Gustavo
    1961   Cultura de Tiahuanaco en San Pedro de Atacama. *Anales de la Universidad del Norte* 1:19–20. Antofagasta.
    1963   Continuidad o discontinuidad de la Cultura Atacameña. *Anales de la Universidad del Norte* 2:7–28. Antofagasta.

Leeds, Anthony
    1973   Locality power in relation to supralocal power institutions. In *Urban Anthropology: Cross-Cultural Studies of Urbanization*, edited by Aidan Southall, pp. 15–41. Oxford: Oxford University Press.

Lennon, Thomas J.
    1982   Raised Fields of Lake Titicaca, Peru: A Pre-Hispanic Water Management System. Unpublished Ph.D. thesis. Department of Anthropology, University of Colorado–Boulder.
    1983   Pattern analysis of prehispanic raised fields of Lake Titicaca, Peru. *British Archaeological Reports International Series* 189:183–200.

Lévi-Strauss, Claude
    1953   Social structure. In *Anthropology Today*, edited by A. L. Kroeber, pp. 524–53. Chicago: University of Chicago Press.

Lévi-Strauss, Claude
    1960   On manipulated sociological models. *Bijdragen. Tot de Taal-Land en Volkenkunde* 116:45–54.

Liendo Lazarte, Manuel
    1956   Excavaciones en Churijahuira–Cuyahuani. *Khana* IV(21–22):23–56.

Lightfoot, Kent
    1984   *Prehistoric Political Dynamics: A Case Study from the American Southwest.* DeKalb: Northern Illinois University Press.
    1987   A consideration of complex societies in the U.S. Southwest. In *Chiefdoms in the Americas*, edited by Robert D. Drennan and Carlos A. Uribe, pp. 43–57. Lanham: University Press of America.

Linton, Ralph (ed.)
    1940   *Acculturation in Seven American Indian Tribes.* New York: Appleton-Century-Crofts.

Liverani, Mario
    1979   The ideology of the Assyrian empire. In Power and Propaganda, edited by Mogens Trolle Larsen, *Copenhagen Studies in Assyriology* 7, pp. 297–318. Copenhagen: Akademisk Forlag.

Longacre, William
    1970   Archaeology as Anthropology: A Case Study. *Anthropological Paper of the University of Arizona* 17. Tucson: University of Arizona Press.

Lorandi, Ana María
    1986   "Horizons" in Andean archaeology. In *Anthropological History of Andean Polities*, edited by John V. Murra, Nathan Wachtel, and Jacques Revel, pp. 35–45. Cambridge: Cambridge University Press.

Loza Balsa, Gregorio
    1971   La vivienda Aymara. *Pumapunku* 3:68–74.

Lumbreras, Luis G.
    1974   *The Peoples and Cultures of Ancient Peru.* Washington, D.C.: Smithsonian Institute.

Lumbreras, Luis G., and Elias Mujica B.
    1982   50 años de investigaciones en Tiwanaku. *Gaceta Arqueológica Andina* 2:7–8. Lima.

Luttwak, Edward
    1976   *The Grand Strategy of the Roman Empire from the First Century A.D. to the Third.* Baltimore: Johns Hopkins University Press.

Lynch, Owen M.
    1984   Introduction. In *Culture and Community in Europe: Essays in Honor of Conrad M. Arensberg*, edited by Own M. Lynch, pp. 1–10. Delhi: Hindustan Publishing Company.

McBain Chapin, Heath
    1959   The Adolph Bandelier Archaeological Collection from Pelechuco and Charassani, Bolivia. Universidad Nacional del Littoral, *Revista del Instituto de Antropología*, Tomo I, pp. 9–80. Rosario.

Mackey, Carol J.
    1987   Chimu administration in the provinces. In *The Origins and Development of the Andean State*, edited by Jonathan Haas, Shelia Pozorski, and Thomas Pozorski, pp. 121–29. Cambridge: Cambridge University Press.

McGuire, Randall H., and Michael B. Schiffer
    1983   A theory of architectural design. *Journal of Anthropological Archaeology* 2(3):277–303.

Maclachlan, Morgan D. (ed.)
  1987   Household economies and their transformations. *Monographs in Economic Anthropology* 3. Lanham: University Press of America.
Manzanilla, Linda, and Luis Barba
  1990   The study of activities in Classic households, two case studies: Coba and Teotihuacan. *Ancient Mesoamerica* 1:41–47.
Marcus, Joyce
  1983   The Espiridión complex and the origins of the Oaxacan Formative. In *The Cloud People: Divergent Evolution of the Zapotec and Mixtec Civilizations*, edited by Kent V. Flannery and Joyce Marcus, pp. 42–43. New York: Academic Press.
  1987a   Late intermediate occupation at Cerro Azul, Perú. A preliminary report. *University of Michigan Museum of Anthropology Technical Report* 20. Ann Arbor.
  1987b   Prehistoric fishermen in the kingdom of Huarco. *American Scientist* 75(4):393–401.
  1989   From centralized systems to city-states: Possible models for the Epiclassic. In *Mesoamerica after the Decline of Teotihuacan A.D. 700–900*, edited by R. Diehl and J. C. Berlo, pp. 201–8. Washington, D.C.: Dumbarton Oaks.
  1992   Royal families, royal texts: Examples from the Zapotec and Maya. In *Mesoamerican Elites: An Archaeological Assessment*, edited by Diane Z. Chase and Arlen F. Chase, pp. 221–41. Norman: University of Oklahoma Press.
Marcus, Joyce, and Jorge E. Silva
  1988   The Chillón Valley "Coca Lands": Archaeological background and ecological context. In Conflicts over Coca Fields in XVIth-Century Perú. *Memoir of the Museum of Anthropology, University of Michigan* 21. Ann Arbor.
Matos M., Ramiro (ed.)
  1978   *El Hombre y La Cultura Andina.* Tomo II. Lima.
Mesa F., José de, and Teresa Gisbert C.
  1957   Akapana, la pirámide de Tiwanacu. In *Arqueología Boliviana*, edited by Carlos Ponce Sanginés, pp. 141–64. La Paz: Biblioteca Paceña.
Métraux, Alfred
  1969   *The History of the Incas.* New York: Schocken.
Mitchell, William P.
  1991   *Peasants on the Edge: Crop, Cult, and Crisis in the Andes.* Austin: University of Texas Press.
Modjeska, C. N.
  1982   Production and inequality: Perspectives from central New Guinea. In *Inequality in New Guinea Highlands Societies*, edited by Andrew Strathern, pp. 50–108. Cambridge: Cambridge University Press.
Moholoy-Nagy, Hattula
  1990   The misidentification of Mesoamerican lithic workshops. *Latin American Antiquity* 1(3):268–79.
Mohr, Karen L.
  1966   An Analysis of the Pottery of Chiripa, Bolivia: A Problem in Archaeological Classification and Inference. Unpublished M.A. thesis. Department of Anthropology, University of Pennsylvania.
Molinié-Fioravanti, Antoinette
  1986   The Andean community today. In *Anthropological History of Andean Polities*, edited by John V. Murra, Nathan Wachtel, and Jacques Revel, pp. 342–58. Cambridge: Cambridge University Press.

Montané, Julio C.
  1977   Esquema de la prehistoria chilena. *Pumapunku* 11:43–59.
Moore, Henrietta
  1986   *Space, Text and Gender: An Anthropological Study of the Marakwet of Kenya.*
             Cambridge: Cambridge University Press.
Moorehead, E.
  1978   Highland Inca architecture in adobe. *Ñawpa Pacha* 16:65–95.
Morris, Craig
  1988   Progress and prospect in the archaeology of the Inca. In *Peruvian Prehistory*,
             edited by Richard W. Keatinge, pp. 233–56. Cambridge: Cambridge University
             Press.
Moseley, Michael E.
  1978   The evolution of Andean civilization. In *Ancient Native Americans*, edited by
             Jesse D. Jennings, pp. 491–514. San Francisco: W. H. Freeman.
  1983   Central Andean civilization. In *Ancient South Americans*, edited by Jesse D.
             Jennings, pp. 179–239. San Francisco: W. H. Freeman.
  1992   *The Incas and Their Ancestors.* New York: Thames and Hudson.
Moseley, Michael E., and Kent C. Day (eds.)
  1982   *Chan Chan: Andean Desert City.* Albuquerque: University of New Mexico
             Press.
Muelle, Jorge C.
  1978   Tecnología del barro. In *Tecnología Andina*, edited by R. Ravines, pp. 573–80.
             Lima: Instituto de Estudios Peruanos.
Mujica Barreda, Elías
  1978   Nueva hipótesis sobre el desarrollo temprano del altiplano, del Titicaca y de sus
             áreas de interacción. *Arte y Arqueología* 6:285–308.
  1985   Altiplano-coast relationships in the south central Andes: From indirect to direct
             complementarity. In *Andean Ecology and Civilization*, edited by Shozo Masuda,
             Izumi Shimada, and Craig Morris, pp. 103–40. Tokyo: University of Tokyo
             Press.
Muñoz Ovalle, Ivan
  1983   El poblamiento aldeano en el valle de Azapa y su vinculación con Tiwanaku. In
             Asentamientos aldeanos el los valles costeros de Arica, edited by Ivan Muñoz
             Ovalle and Guillermo Focacci Aste, pp. 42–93. *Documento de Trabajo* 3,
             Universidad de Tarapaca.
Murra, John V.
  1968   An Aymara kingdom in 1567. *Ethnohistory* 15:115–51.
  1972   El 'control vertical' de un máximo de pisos ecológicos en la economía de las
             sociedades andinas. In Visita de la Provincia de Léon de Huánuco en 1562, pp.
             427–76. *Documentos por la Historia y Etnología de Huánuco y la Selva Central*
             2.
  1980   The economic organization of the Inca state. *Research in Economic Anthropol-
             ogy*, Supplement 1. Greenwich: JAI.
Murra, John V., and Nathan Wachtel
  1986   Introduction. In *Anthropological History of Andean Polities*, edited by John V.
             Murra, Nathan Wachtel, and Jacques Revel, pp. 1–8. Cambridge: Cambridge
             University Press.
Murra, John V., Nathan Wachtel, and Jacques Revel (eds.)
  1986   *Anthropological History of Andean Polities.* Cambridge: Cambridge University
             Press.

Nash, Manning
  1967   The organization of economic life. In *Tribal & Peasant Economies*, edited by George Dalton, pp. 3–11. Austin: University of Texas Press.
Netherly, Patricia J.
  1984   The management of late Andean irrigation systems on the north coast of Peru. *American Antiquity* 49(2):227–54.
  1990   Out of many, one: The organization of rule in the north coast polities. In *The Northern Dynasties: Kingship and Statecraft in Chimor*, edited by Michael Moseley and Alana Cordy-Collins, pp. 461–88. Washington, D.C.: Dumbarton Oaks.
Netting, Robert McC.
  1979   Household dynamics in a Nineteenth-Century Swiss village. *Journal of Family History* 4:39–58.
Netting, Robert McC., Richard R. Wilk, and Eric. J. Arnould
  1984   Introduction. In *Households: Comparative and Historical Studies of the Domestic Group*, edited by Robert McC. Netting, Richard R. Wilk, and Eric. J. Arnould, pp. xiii–xxxviii. Berkeley: University of California Press.
Netting, Robert McC., Richard R. Wilk, and Eric J. Arnould (eds.)
  1984   *Households: Comparative and Historical Studies of the Domestic Group.* Berkeley: University of California Press.
Nordenskiöld, Erland
  1953   *Investigaciones arqueologícas en la región fronteriza de Perú y Bolivia.* La Paz: Paceña.
Nuñez A., Lautaro, and Tom D. Dillehay
  1978   *Movilidad giratoria, armonía social y desarrollo en los Andes meridionales. Patrones de tráfico e interacción económica.* Antofagasta: Universidad del Norte.
Nuñez, Mario, and Rolando Paredes
  1978   Esteves: un sito de ocupación Tiwanaku. In *III Congreso Peruano del Hombre y la Cultura Andina*, Volume 2, edited by R. Matos, pp. 757–64. Lima.
Oakland Rodman, Amy
  1993   Textiles and ethnicity: Tiwanaku in San Pedro de Atacama, North Chile. *Latin American Antiquity* 3(4):316–40.
Orellana Rodríguez, Mario
  1963   Problemas de la arqueología de San Pedro de Atacama y sus alrededores. *Anales de la Universidad del Norte* 2:29–41.
  1985   Relaciones culturales entre Tiwanaku y San Pedro de Atacama. In *Diálogo Andina* 4, edited by Mario Rivera, pp. 247–58. Arica.
Ortloff, Charles, and Alan Kolata
  1989   Hydraulic analysis of Tiwanaku aqueduct structures at Lukurmata and Pajchiri, Bolivia. *Journal of Archaeological Science* 16:513–35.
Ortloff, Charles R., and Alan Kolata
  1993   Climate and collapse: Agro-ecological perspectives on the decline of the Tiwanaku state. *Journal of Archaeological Science* 20:195–221.
Oswald, Dana
  1987   The organization of space in residential buildings: A cross-cultural perspective. In *Method and Theory for Activity Area Research: An Ethnoarchaeological Approach*, edited by Susan Kent, pp. 295–344. New York: Columbia University Press.
Parenti, Lynne R.
  1984   A taxonomic revision of the Andean killifish genus *Orestias* (Cyprinodonti-

formes, Cyprinodontidae). *Bulletin of the American Museum of Natural History* 178(2). New York.

Parry, William J.
 1987   Chipped stone tools in Formative Oaxaca, Mexico: Their procurement, production and use. *Memoirs of the Museum of Anthropology, University of Michigan* 20. Ann Arbor.

Parsons, Jeffrey R.
 1968   An estimate of size and population for Middle Horizon Tiahuanaco, Bolivia. *American Antiquity* 33(2):243–45.
 1974   The development of a prehistoric complex society: A regional perspective from the Valley of Mexico. *Journal of Field Archaeology* 1:81–108.

Pasternak, Burton, Carol Ember, and Melvin Ember
 1976   On the conditions favoring extended family households. *Journal of Anthropological Research* 32:109–24.

Paynter, Robert
 1982   *Models of Spatial Inequality: Settlement Patterns in Historical Archaeology.* New York: Academic Press.

Peebles, Christopher S.
 1978   Determinants of settlement size and location in the Moundville phase. In *Mississippian Settlement Patterns*, edited by Bruce Smith, pp. 369–416. New York: Academic Press.

Peebles, Christopher S., and Glenn A. Black
 1987   Moundville from 1000–1500 AD as seen from 1840 to 1985 AD. In *Chiefdoms in the Americas*, edited by Robert D. Drennan and Carlos A. Uribe, pp. 21–42. Lanham: University Press of America.

Peebles, Christopher S., and Susan M. Kus
 1977   Some archaeological correlates of ranked societies. *American Antiquity* 42(3):421–48.

Perrin Pando, Alberto
 1957   Las tumbas subterráneas de Wakuyo. In *Arqueología Boliviana*, edited by Carlos Ponce Sanginés, pp. 173–208. La Paz: Biblioteca Paceña.

Pia, Gabriela Erica
 1987   Asentamientos y pinturas rupestres en el oriente Boliviano. La Paz: Instituto Nacional de Arqueología.

Platt, Tristan
 1986   Mirrors and maize: The concept of *yanatin* among the Macha of Bolivia. In *Anthropological History of Andean Polities*, edited by John V. Murra, Nathan Wachtel, and Jacques Revel, pp. 228–59. Cambridge: Cambridge University Press.
 1987   Entre *Ch'axwa* y *muxsa*. Para una historia del pensamiento político aymara. In *Tres Reflexiones Sobre el Pensamiento Andino,* by Thèrése Bouysse-Cassagne, Olivia Harris, Tristan Platt, and Verónica Cereceda, pp. 61–132. La Paz: HISBOL.

Pollard, Gordon C.
 1984   Interregional relations in the southern Andes: Evidence and expectations for understanding the late prehistory of northwest Argentina and north Chile. *British Archaeological Reports International Series* 194:205–47.

Ponce Sanginés, Carlos
 1947   Cerámica Tiwanacota. *Revista Geográfica Americana* 28:204–14.
 1957a   La cerámica de Mollo. In *Arqueología Boliviana*, edited by Carlos Ponce Sanginés, pp. 35–120. La Paz: Biblioteca Paceña.

1957b   Una piedra esculpida de Chiripa. In *Arqueología Boliviana*, edited by Carlos Ponce Sanginés, pp. 119–38. La Paz: Biblioteca Paceña.

1961   Informe de labores. *Centro de Investigaciones Arqueológicas en Tiwanaku* 1. Tiwanaku.

1969a   *Descripción Sumaria del Templete Semisubterraneo de Tiwanaku*. 4th rev. ed. La Paz: Los Amigos de Libro.

1969b   *Tunupa y Ekako*. La Paz: Academia Nacional de Ciencias de Bolivia.

1969c   La ciudad de Tiwanaku. Separata de *Arte y Arqueología* 1.

1970   Las culturas Wankarani y Chiripa y su relación con Tiwanaku. *Academia Nacional de las Ciencias* 25. La Paz: Academia Nacional de las Ciencias.

1971   La cerámica de la Epoca I de Tiwanaku. *Academia Nacional de las Ciencias* 28. La Paz: Academia Nacional de las Ciencias.

1975a   Origen del dualismo cultural en Bolivia. *Pumapumku* 9:9–31.

1975b   Reflexiones sobre la ciudad precolombiana de Iskanwaya. *Pumapumku* 10:63–73.

1980   *Panorama de la Arqueología Boliviana*. La Paz: Juventud.

1981a   *Tiwanaku: Espacio, Tiempo y Cultura. Ensayo de síntesis arqueológica*. 4th ed. La Paz: Los Amigos de Libro.

1981b   Nueva perspectiva para el estudio de la expansión de la cultura Tiwanacu. *Arte y Arqueología* 7:135–48.

1989   *Arqueología de Lukurmata*. Volume 1. La Paz: Instituto Nacional de Arqueología.

Ponce Sanginés, Carlos (ed.)

1957   *Arqueología Boliviana*. La Paz: Biblioteca Paceña.

Ponce Sanginés, Carlos, Arturo Castaños Echazú, Waldo Avila, and Fernando Urquidi Barrau

1971   Procedencia de las areniscas utilizadas en el templo precolombino de Pumapunku (Tiwanaku). *Academia Nacional de Ciencias de Bolivia* 22. La Paz: Academia Nacional de las Ciencias.

Portugal Ortíz, Max

1972a   Apuntes para la arqueología de Yungas y Rurrenabaque. *Pumapunku* 5:17–22.

1972b   La arqueología de las llanuras tropicales en Bolivia. *Pumapunku* 4:49–60.

1980   Testimonios arqueológicos para la historia de la expansión cultural altiplánica sobre los valles y costas del Pacifico. In *Segundo Reunión Boliviano-Peruano*, Volume 2, pp. 9–25. La Paz: Instituto Nacional de Arqueología.

1981   Expansión del estilo escultorico Pa-Ajanu. *Arte y Arqueología* 7:149–59.

1984   Testimonios arqueológicos para la historia de la expansión cultural altiplánica sobre los valles y costas del Pacifíco. *Arqueología Boliviana* 1:115–26.

1985a   Informe de la Departamento de La Paz (1ra & 2da partes). *Arqueología Boliviana* 2:17–41.

1985b   Excavaciones arqueológicas en Titimani (3ra parte). *Arqueología Boliviana* 2:41–53.

1987   Descubrimiento de restos de viviendas tiwanacotas. Paper presented at the Tercera Mesa Redonda de Arqueología de Bolivia. La Paz.

Portugal Ortíz, Max, and Maks Portugal Zamora

1977   Investigaciones arqueológicas en el valle de Tiwanaku. In *Jornadas*, Tomo II, pp. 243–84. La Paz: Franz Tamayo.

Portugal Zamora, Maks

1954   Noticia arqueológica de la provincia Manco Kapac. *Khana* III(5):49–56.

1955   El misterio de las tumbas de Wanqani. *Khana* III(11–12):51–67.

1956   Plano arqueológico de la ciudad de La Paz, la antigua Chuki Apu Marki. *Khana* II(17–18):85–122.

Portugal Zamora, Maks
1957a   Sullkatata. In *Arqueología Boliviana*, edited by Carlos Ponce Sanginés, pp. 225–34. La Paz: Biblioteca Paceña.
1957b   Arqueología de La Paz. In *Arqueología Boliviana*, edited by Carlos Ponce Sanginés, pp. 343–404. La Paz: Biblioteca Paceña.
1961   Nuevos hallazgos arqueológicos en la zona noroeste del Lago Titicaca. *Khana* II(17–18):34–43.
1967   Un ídolo más en "Tambo Kusi." *Khana* I(38):238–41.
1980   Petroglifos en el valle de Tiwanaku. In *Segundo Reunión Boliviano-Peruano*, Volume 2, pp. 78–86. La Paz: Instituto Nacional de Arqueología.

Portugal Zamora, Maks, and Max Portugal Ortíz
1975   Qallamarka, nuevo yacimiento arqueológico descubierto cerca a Tiwanaku. *Arte y Arqueología* 3–4:195–216.

Rapoport, Amos
1969   *House Form and Culture*. Englewood Cliffs: Prentice-Hall.
1990   Systems of activities and systems of settings. In *Domestic Architecture and the Use of Space*, edited by Susan Kent, pp. 9–20. Cambridge: Cambridge University Press.

Rapoport, Amos (ed.)
1976   *The Mutual Interaction of People and Their Built Environment*. The Hague: Mouton.

Rathje, William, and Randall H. McGuire
1982   Rich men . . . Poor men. *American Behavioral Scientist* 25:705–16.

Redfield, Robert
1955   *The Little Community*. Chicago: University of Chicago Press.
1956   Societies and cultures as natural systems. *Journal of the Royal Anthropological Institute* 85:19–32.

Renfrew, Colin
1974   Beyond a subsistence economy: The evolution of social organisation in prehistoric Europe. In Reconstructing complex societies: An archaeological colloquium, edited by C. B. Moore, pp. 69–95. *Supplement to the Bulletin of the American Schools of Oriental Research* 20. Chicago.

Reyna, S.
1976   The extending strategy: Regulation of household dependency ratio. *Journal of Anthropological Research* 32(2):189–99.

Richerson, Peter J., Patrick J. Neale, Wayne Wurtsbaugh, Rene Alfaro T., and Warwick Vincent
1986   Patterns of temporal variation in Lake Titicaca. A high altitude tropical lake. I: Background, physical and chemical processes, and primary production. *Hydrobiologia* 138:205–20.

Ríos Rocha, Jenny
1967   Dos ejemplares de cerámica Tiwanacota. *Khana* 1(38):157–61.

Rivera, Mario A.
1985   Alto Ramirez y Tiwanaku, un caso de interpretación simbólica a través de datos arqueológicos en el área de los valles occidentales, S. del Perú y N. de Chile. In *Diálogo Andino* 4, edited by Mario Rivera, pp. 39–58. Arica.

Rivera, Mario A. (ed.)
1984   *Diálogo Andino* 4: *La Problemática Tiwanaku Huari en el Contexto Panandino del Desarrollo Cultural*. Universidad de Tarapacá. Arica.

Rivera Sundt, Oswaldo
1978a   Arqueología de la Península de Copacabana. *Pumapunku* 12:69–87.

1989   Resultados de la excavación en el centro ceremonial de Lukurmata. In *Arqueología de Lukurmata*, Volume 2, edited by Alan Kolata, pp. 59–89. La Paz: Instituto Nacional de Arqueología.

Rock, Cynthia, Susana Torre, and Gwendolyn Wright

1980   The appropriation of the house: Changes in house design and concepts of domesticity. In *New Space for Women*, edited by G. Wekerle, pp. 83–100. Boulder: Westview Press.

Rock, James T.

1974   The use of social models in archaeological interpretation. *The Kiva* 40(1–2):81–91.

Rodman, Margaret

1985   Contemporary custom: Redefining domestic space in Longana, Vanuatu. *Ethnology* 24(4):269–79.

Rogers, J. Daniel

1990   *Objects of Change: The Archaeology and History of Arikara Contact*. Washington, D.C.: Smithsonian Institution Press.

Roseberry, William

1991   Potatoes, sacks, and enclosures in early modern England. In *Golden Ages, Dark Ages: Imagining the Past in Anthropology and History*, edited by Jay O'Brien and William Roseberry, pp. 19–47. Berkeley: University of California Press.

Rowe, John H.

1963   Urban settlements in ancient Peru. *Ñawpa Pacha* 1:1–27.

1982   Inca policies and institutions relating to cultural unification. In *The Inca and Aztec States, 1400–1800*, edited by George A. Collier, Renato I. Rosaldo, and John D. Wirth, pp. 93–118. New York: Academic Press.

Rowe, John H., and Catherine Terry Brandel

1970   Pucara style pottery designs. *Ñawpa Pacha* 7–8:1–16.

Rowlands, Michael

1979   Local and long distance trade in the formation of the Bemba state. *Paideuma* 9:1–17.

Rydén, Stig

1947   *Archaeological Researches in the Highlands of Bolivia*. Göteborg.

1956   The Erland Nordenskiöld archaeological collection from the Mizque Valley, Bolivia. *Etnologiska Studier* 22. Göteborg.

1957   Andean excavations I. *Statens Etnografiska Museums Monograph Series* 4. Stockholm.

1959   Andean excavations II. *Statens Etnografiska Mueums Monograph Series* 6. Stockholm.

1961   Complementary notes on pre-Tiahuanaco site Chullpa Pampa in Cochabamba area and notes on one Tiahuanaco site in La Paz, Bolivia. *Ethnos* 1–2:40–55.

1964   Tripod ceramics and grater bowls from Mojos, Bolivia. Beiträge zur Völkerkunde Südamerikas. *Völkerkundliche Abhandlungen*. Band 1:261–70.

Sahlins, Marshall

1972   *Stone Age Economics*. Chicago: Aldine.

1976   *Culture and Practical Reason*. Chicago: University of Chicago Press.

Saignes, Thierry

1986   The ethnic groups in the valleys of Larecaja: From descent to residence. In *Anthropological History of Andean Polities*, edited by John V. Murra, Nathan Wachtel, and Jacques Revel, pp. 311–41. Cambridge: Cambridge University Press.

Saile, David G.
    1977a   'Architecture' in prehispanic Pueblo architecture; examples from Chaco Canyon, New Mexico. *World Archaeology* 9(2):157–73.
    1977b   Making a house: Building rituals and spatial concepts in the Pueblo Indian world. *Architectural Association Quarterly* 9(2/3)72:81.

Sanders, William T.
    1974   Chiefdom to state: Political evolution at Kaminaljuyu, Guatemala. In Reconstructing complex societies, edited by C. B. Moore, pp. 97–112. *Supplement to the Bulletin of the American Schools of Oriental Research* 20. Chicago.
    1978   Ethnographic analogy and the Teotihuacan horizon style. In *Middle Classic Mesoamerica*, edited by E. Pasztory, pp. 33–44. New York: Columbia University Press.

Santley, Robert S., and Kenneth G. Hirth (eds.)
    1993   *Prehispanic Domestic Units in Western Mesoamerica: Studies of the Household, Compound, and Residence*. Boca Raton: CRC Press.

Schortman, Edward M., and Patricia A. Urban
    1987   Modeling interregional interaction in prehistory. In *Advances in Archaeological Method and Theory*, Volume 11, edited by Michael B. Schiffer, pp. 37–97. San Diego: Academic Press.

Schreiber, Katharina J.
    1987a   From state to empire: The expansion of Wari outside the Ayacucho basin. In *The Origins and Development of the Andean State*, edited by Jonathan Haas, Shelia Pozorski, and Thomas Pozorski, pp. 91–96. Cambridge: Cambridge University Press.
    1987b   Conquest and consolidation: A comparison of the Wari and Inka occupations of a highland Peruvian valley. *American Antiquity* 52(2):266–84.
    1992   Wari imperialism in Middle Horizon Peru. *Anthropological Paper of the Museum of Anthropology, University of Michigan* 87. Ann Arbor.

Serracino, George
    1980   Tiwanaku desde San Pedro de Atacama. *Estudios Arqueológicos* 5:95–106.

Seymour, Denia, and Michael Schiffer
    1987   A preliminary analysis of pithouse assemblages from Snaketown, Arizona. In *Method and Theory for Activity Area Research: An Ethnoarchaeological Approach*, edited by Susan Kent, pp. 549–603. New York: Columbia University Press.

Sheehy, James J.
    1991   Structure and change in a Late Classic Maya domestic group at Copan, Honduras. *Ancient Mesoamerica* 2:1–19.

Sheets, Payson D.
    1992   *The Ceren Site*. Fort Worth: Harcourt, Brace, Jovanovich.

Silverman, Sydel
    1984   Toward an anthropology of urbanism: The view from the village (Italy). In *Culture and Community in Europe,* edited by Owen M. Lynch, pp. 13–35. Delhi: Hindustan Publishing Corporation.

Smith, Carol A.
    1976   Analyzing regional social systems. In *Regional Analysis*, Volume 2: *Social Systems*, edited by Carol A. Smith, pp. 6–20. New York: Academic Press.

Smith, C. T., William M. Denevan, and P. Hamilton
    1968   Ancient ridged fields in the region of Lake Titicaca. *The Geographical Journal* 134:353–67.

Smith, Michael E.
    1987   Household possessions and wealth in agrarian states: Implications for archaeology. *Journal of Anthropological Archaeology* 6:297–335.

Smyth, Michael P.
    1991   Modern Maya storage behavior: Ethnoarchaeological case examples from the Puuc region of Yucatan. *University of Pittsburgh Memoirs in Latin American Archaeology* 3. Pittsburgh.

Spencer, Charles S.
    1981   Spatial organization of an Early Formative household. Appendix X. Excavations at Santo Domingo Tomaltepec: Evolution of a formative community in the Valley of Oaxaca, Mexico, by Michael E. Whalen. *Memoirs of the Museum of Anthropology, University of Michigan* 12. Ann Arbor.
    1982   *The Cuicatlán Cañada and Monte Albán: A Study of Primary State Formation.* New York: Academic Press.
    1987   Rethinking the chiefdom. In *Chiefdoms in the Americas*, edited by Robert D. Drennan and Carlos A. Uribe, pp. 369–90. Lanham: University Press of America.
    1990   On the tempo and mode of state formation: Neo-evolution reconsidered. *Journal of Anthropological Archaeology* 9:1–30.

Spicer, Edward H.
    1961   Types of contact and processes of change. In *Perspectives in American Indian Culture Change*, edited by Edward H. Spicer, pp. 517–43. Chicago: University of Chicago Press.

Spickard, Lynda
    1985   El análisis formal de la arquitectura de los sitios Huari y Tiwanaku. In *Diálogo Andina* 4, edited by Mario Rivera, pp. 73–88. Arica.

Stahl, Peter W., and James A. Zeidler
    1990   Differential bone-refuse accumulation in food-preparation and traffic areas on an early Ecuadorean house floor. *Latin American Antiquity* 1(2):150–69.

Stanish, Charles
    1985   Post-Tiwanaku Regional Economies in the Otora Valley, Southern Peru. Unpublished Ph.D. thesis. Department of Anthropology, University of Chicago.
    1989a   Household archaeology: Testing models of complementarity in the south central Andes. *American Anthropologist* 91(1):9–24.
    1989b   Tamaño y complejidad de los asentamientos nucleares de Tiwanaku. In *Arqueología de Lukurmata*, Volume 2, edited by Alan Kolata, pp. 41–59. La Paz: Instituto Nacional de Arqueología.
    1992   *Ancient Andean Political Economy.* Austin: University of Texas Press.
    n.d.   Archaeological research at Juli, Peru. Manuscript.

Steponaitis, Vincas
    1978   Location theory and complex chiefdoms: A Mississippian example. In *Mississippian Settlement Patterns*, edited by Bruce Smith, pp. 417–54. New York: Academic Press.
    1981   Settlement hierarchies and political complexity in nonmarket societies: The Formative Period of the Valley of Mexico. *American Anthropologist* 83:320–63.

Stevenson, Marc G.
    1982   Toward an understanding of site abandonment behavior: Evidence from historic mining camps in the southwest Yukon. *Journal of Anthropological Archaeology* 1:237–65.
    1991   Beyond the formation of hearth-associated artifact assemblages. In *The Inter-*

pretation of Archaeological Spatial Patterning, edited by Ellen M. Kroll and T. Douglas Price, pp. 269–300. New York: Plenum Press.

Stocking George W., Jr.
    1974   Introduction: The basic assumptions of Boasian anthropology. In *A Franz Boas Reader*, edited by George W. Stocking, Jr., pp. 1–20. Chicago: University of Chicago Press.

Storey, Rebecca
    1992   *Life and Death in the Ancient City of Teotihuacan*. Tuscaloosa: University of Alabama Press.

Stuiver, Minze, and Gordon W. Pearson
    1986   High-precision calibration of the radiocarbon time scale, AD 1950–500 BC. *Radiocarbon* 28(2B):805–38.

Sutro, Livingston D., and Theodore E. Downing
    1988   A step toward a grammar of space: Domestic space use in Zapotec villages. In *Household and Community in the Mesoamerican Past*, edited by Richard R. Wilk and Wendy Ashmore, pp. 29–50. Albuquerque: University of New Mexico Press.

Tainter, Joseph A.
    1988   *The Collapse of Complex Societies*. Cambridge: Cambridge University Press.

Tapia Pineda, Félix
    1977   Cerámica Tiwanakota en Puno. In *Jornadas*, Tomo II, pp. 339–60. La Paz: Franz Tamayo.
    1978   Investigaciones arqueológicas en Kacsili. *Pumapunku* 12:7–38.
    1984a   Informe preliminar sobre las excavaciones en Camata. Provincia Omasuyos. Departamento de La Paz. *Arqueología Boliviana* 1:39–48.
    1984b   Excavaciones arqueológicas en el sector habitational de "El Fuerte" de Samaipata, Santa Cruz. *Arqueología Boliviana* 1:49–66.
    1984c   La cultura Tiwanaku y su influencia en los valles orientales de Bolivia. Unpublished Ph.D. thesis. Universidad Nacional de San Augustin, Arequipa.

Thomas, Carlos, María Antonieta Benavente, and Claudio Massone
    1985   Algunos efectos de Tiwanaku en la cultura de San Pedro de Atacama. In *Diálogo Andina* 4, edited by Mario Rivera, pp. 259–76. Arica.

Thomas, David Hurst
    1983   The archaeology of Monitor Valley: 2. Gatecliff Shelter. *Anthropological Papers of the American Museum of Natural History* 59(1):1–552.

Thompson, L., E. Moseley-Thompson, J. Bolzan, and B. Koci
    1985   A 1500 year record of tropical precipitation records in ice cores from the Quelccaya ice cap, Peru. *Science* 229:971–73.

Thompson, L., M. Davis, E. Moseley-Thompson, and K.-B. Liu
    1988   Pre-Incan agricultural activity recorded in dust layers in two tropical ice cores. *Nature* 336:763–65.

Torres, Constantino
    1985   Estilo e iconografía Tiwanaku en las tabletas para inhalar substancias psicoactivas. *Diálogo Andina* 4, edited by Mario Rivera, pp. 223–46. Arica.

Tourtellot, Gair
    1988   Developmental cycles of households and houses at Seibal. In *Household and Community in the Mesoamerican Past*, edited by Richard R. Wilk and Wendy Ashmore, pp. 97–120. Albuquerque: University of New Mexico Press.

Trimborn, Hermann von
    1959   Archäologische Studien in den Kordilleren Boliviens. *Baessler-Archiv*. Neue Folge Beiheft 2.

1964   Cerro de las Rueditas. Beiträge zur Vökerkunde Südamerikas. *Völkerkundliche Abhandlungen.* Band 1:292–98.
1967   Archäologische Studien in den Kordilleren Boliviens. *Archäologische Studien in den Kordilleren Boliviens* III. Berlin: Dietrich Reimer.

Tringham, Ruth
1991   Men and women in prehistoric architecture. *Traditional Dwellings and Settlement Review* III(1):9–28.

Tschopik, Harry, Jr.
1946   The Aymara. In *Handbook of South American Indians. Bureau of American Ethnology Bulletin* 143, Volume 2, edited by J. H. Steward, pp. 501–73. Washington, D.C.
1951   The Aymara of Chucuito, Peru. 1. Magic. *Anthropological Papers of the American Museum of Natural History* 44(2). New York.

Uhle, Max
1912   Posnansky—guía general ilustrada. *Revista de la Socieded Chilena de Historia y Geografía* II:467–78.
1967   Un tubo inhalante de Tiahuanaco. *Khana* 1(38):162–75.

Unzueta, Orlando
1975   Mapa ecológico de Bolivia: Memoria Explicativa. Ministerio de Asuntos Campesinos y Agropecuarios, División de Suelos, Riegos e Ingeniería, La Paz, Bolivia.

Urquizo Sossa, Carlos
1980   Hipótesis sobre el desarrollo cultural circumlacustre y sus areas de interacción. In *Segundo Reunión Boliviano-Peruano,* Volume 2, pp. 39–48. La Paz: Instituto Nacional de Arqueología.

van den Berg, Hans
1985   *Diccionario Religioso Aymara.* Iquitos: Ceta-Idea.

Venero Gonzales, J.
1987   La fauna y el hombre Andino. Proyecto FAO *Documento de Trabajo* 8. Cuzco.

Villwock, Wolfgang
1986   Speciation and adaptive radiation in Andean *Orestias* fishes. In *High Altitude Tropical Biogeography*, edited by Francois Vuilleumier and Maximina Monasterio, pp. 387–403. New York: Oxford University Press.

Wallace, Dwight T.
1957   The Tiahuanaco Styles in the Peruvian and Bolivian Highlands. Unpublished Ph.D. thesis. Department of Anthropology, University of California–Berkeley.
1980   Tiwanaku as symbolic empire. *Estudios Arqueológicos* 5:133–44.

Walter, Heinz
1966   Beiträge zur Archäologie Boliviens. *Archäologische Studien in den Kordilleren Boliviens* II. Berlin: Dietrich Reimer.

Wassén, S. Henry
1972   A medicine-man's implements and plants in a Tiahuanacoid tomb in highland Bolivia. *Etnologiska Studier* 32:8–114.
1973   Ethnobotanical follow-up of Bolivian Tiahuanacoid tomb material, and of Peruvian shamanism, psychotropic plant constituents, and Espingo seeds. *Göteborgs Etnografiska Museum. Årstryck 1972*: 35–47.

Wasson, John
1967   Investigaciones preliminares de los "Mounds" en Oruro. *Khana* 1(38):145–56.

Webb, M. C.
1987   Broader perspectives on Andean state origins. In *The Origins and Development*

of the Andean State, edited by Jonathan Haas, Shelia Pozorski, and Thomas Pozorski, pp. 161–67. Cambridge: Cambridge University Press.

Welch, Paul
    1991   *Moundville's Economy*. Tuscaloosa: University of Alabama Press.

Whalen, Michael E.
    1981   Excavations at Santo Domingo Tomaltepec: Evolution of a Formative community in the Valley of Oaxaca, Mexico. *Memoir of the Museum of Anthropology, University of Michigan* 12. Ann Arbor.

    1988   House and household in Formative Oaxaca. In *Household and Community in the Mesoamerican Past*, edited by Richard R. Wilk and Wendy Ashmore, pp. 249–71. Albuquerque: University of New Mexico Press.

White, J. Peter
    1985   Digging out big-men? *Archaeology Oceania* 20:49–57.

Wilk, Richard R.
    1983   Little house in the jungle: The causes of variation in house size among modern Kekchi Maya. *Journal of Anthropological Research* 2(2):99–116.

    1984   Households in process: Agricultural change and domestic transformation among the Kekchi Maya of Belize. In *Households: Comparative and Historical Studies of the Domestic Group*, edited by Robert McC. Netting, Richard R. Wilk, and Eric. J. Arnould, pp. 217–44. Berkeley: University of California Press.

    1988   Maya household organization: Evidence and analogies. In *Household and Community in the Mesoamerican Past*, edited by Richard R. Wilk and Wendy Ashmore, pp. 135–52. Albuquerque: University of New Mexico Press.

    1990   The built environment and consumer decisions. In *Domestic Architecture and the Use of Space*, edited by Susan Kent, pp. 34–42. Cambridge: Cambridge University Press.

    1991   *Household Ecology: Economic Change and Domestic Life among the Kekchi Maya in Belize*. Tucson: University of Arizona Press.

Wilk, Richard R., and Robert McC. Netting
    1984   Households: Changing forms and functions. In *Households: Comparative and Historical Studies of the Domestic Group*, edited by Robert McC. Netting, Richard R. Wilk, and Eric. J. Arnould, pp. 1–28. Berkeley: University of California Press.

Wilk, Richard R., and William L. Rathje
    1982   Household archaeology. *American Behavioral Scientist* 25(6):617–40.

Winter, Marcus C.
    1974   Residential patterns at Monte Alban, Oaxaca, Mexico. *Science* 185:981–87.

    1976a   The archaeological household cluster in the Valley of Oaxaca. In *The Early Mesoamerican Village*, edited by Kent V. Flannery, pp. 25–31. New York: Academic Press.

    1976b   Differential patterns of community growth in Oaxaca. In *The Early Mesoamerican Village*, edited by Kent V. Flannery, pp. 227–33. New York: Academic Press.

Wirrmann, D.
    1987   El Lago Titicaca sedimentología y paleohidrología durante el Holoceno (1000 años b.p.-actual). *ORSTOM en Bolivie informe* 6.

Wise, Karen
    1989   Post-Tiwanaku domestic architecture at Lukurmata: Excavations at North Point. Unpublished report, of the Proyecto Wila- Jawira, University of Chicago.

Wolf, Arthur P.

1984   Family life and the life cycle in rural China. In *Households: Comparative and Historical Studies of the Domestic Group*, edited by Robert McC. Netting, Richard R. Wilk, and Eric. J. Arnould, pp. 279–98. Berkeley: University of California Press.

Wolf, Eric R.

1966   *Peasants*. Englewood Cliffs: Prentice-Hall.

Wright, Henry T.

1977   Recent research on the origin of the state. *Annual Review of Anthropology* 6:379–97.

1982   Prestate political formations. In *On the Evolution of Complex Societies: Essays in Honor of Harry Hoijer*, edited by Timothy K. Earle, pp. 41–77. Malibu: Undena Press.

1986   The evolution of civilizations. In *American Archaeology, Past and Future*, edited by D. Meltzer, D. Fowler, and J. Sabloff, pp. 323–65. Washington, D.C.: Smithsonian Institution Press.

Wright, Henry T., and Gregory A. Johnson

1975   Population, exchange and early state formation in southwestern Iran. *American Anthropologist* 77:267–89.

Wright, Henry T., Richard W. Redding, and Susan M. Pollock

1989   Monitoring interannual variability: An example from the period of early state development in southwestern Iran. In *Bad Year Economics: Cultural Responses to Risk and Uncertainty*, edited by Paul Halstead and John O'Shea, pp. 106–13. Cambridge: Cambridge University Press.

Yanagisako, Sylvia J.

1979   Family and household: The analysis of domestic groups. In *Annual Review of Anthropology*, edited by B. J. Siegel, A. R. Beals, and S. A. Tyler, pp. 161–205. Palo Alto: Annual Reviews.

1984   Explicating residence: A cultural analysis of changing households among Japanese-Americans. In *Households: Comparative and Historical Studies of the Domestic Group*, edited by Robert McC. Netting, Richard R. Wilk, and Eric. J. Arnould, pp. 330–52. Berkeley: University of California Press.

Yellen, John

1977   *Archaeological Approaches to the Present: Models for Reconstructing the Past*. New York: Academic Press.

Index

ZAKJ 2559 1/27/95 hill

Simplified Profile of E 1915 West Baulk Showing Major Features

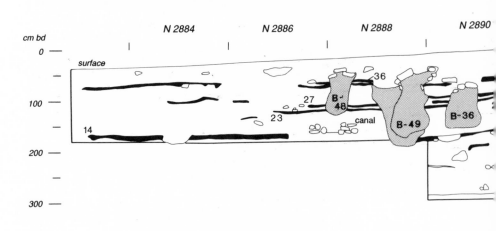

Simplified Profile of N 2892 North Baulk Showing Major Features

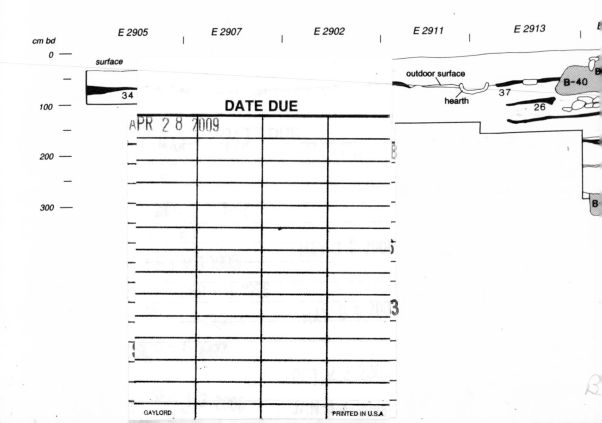